MAN
IN THE PACIFIC
ISLANDS

MAN
IN THE PACIFIC
ISLANDS

Essays on Geographical Change in the
Pacific Islands

EDITED BY
R. GERARD WARD

Professor of Human Geography
Australian National University

OXFORD
AT THE CLARENDON PRESS
1972

Oxford University Press, Ely House, London W. 1

GLASGOW NEW YORK TORONTO MELBOURNE WELLINGTON
CAPE TOWN IBADAN NAIROBI DAR ES SALAAM LUSAKA ADDIS ABABA
DELHI BOMBAY CALCUTTA MADRAS KARACHI LAHORE DACCA
KUALA LUMPUR SINGAPORE HONG KONG TOKYO

330.99
W21m
101161
May 1977

*Printed in Great Britain
at the University Press, Oxford
by Vivian Ridler
Printer to the University*

CONTENTS

LIST OF MAPS AND FIGURES

LIST OF CONTRIBUTORS

R. G. CROCOMBE, PH.D. (A.N.U.), Professor of Pacific Studies, University of the South Pacific, was formerly Field Director of the New Guinea Research Unit, Australian National University. He is author of *Land Tenure in the Cook Islands*, editor of a new volume of essays on land tenure in the Pacific, and has published many papers on the Pacific Islands.

B. H. FARRELL, PH.D. (N.Z.), Professor of Geography, University of Victoria, British Columbia, is the author of *Power in New Zealand*. He has carried out intensive fieldwork in Western Samoa, American Samoa, and Fiji and has published a number of papers dealing with land use in the Pacific Islands.

J. GOLSON, M.A. (Cantab.), Professor of Prehistory, Australian National University, inaugurated the teaching of archaeology at the University of Auckland and since then has played a key role in the development of archaeological field research and publication in the South-west Pacific.

D. A. M. LEA, PH.D. (A.N.U.), Professor of Geography, University of Papua and New Guinea, has specialized in the study of agricultural systems in New Guinea and has contributed several articles on this topic. He is co-author and co-editor of *An Atlas of Papua and New Guinea*.

W. D. McTAGGART, PH.D. (A.N.U.), Associate Professor of Geography, Arizona State University, is the author of *A Social Survey of Nouméa, New Caledonia*, and several papers dealing with urban areas in the Pacific and South-east Asia.

C. W. NEWBURY, PH.D. (A.N.U.), University Lecturer in Commonwealth History, and Fellow of Linacre College, Oxford, is editor of J. Davies, *The History of the Tahitian Mission, 1799–1830*, and author of a number of papers on French Polynesia, as well as a range of works in African history.

O. W. PARNABY, D.PHIL. (Oxon.), Master, Queen's College, University of Melbourne, was formerly Associate Professor of History, University of Auckland. He is the author of *Britain and the Labor Trade in the Southwest Pacific*.

P. N. D. PIRIE, PH.D. (A.N.U.), Associate Professor of Geography, University of Hawaii, and Associate of the Population Institute, East-West Center, Honolulu, has completed several periods of fieldwork in Western Samoa and published a number of papers on the population of this and other Pacific territories.

R. G. ROBBINS, PH.D. (N.Z.), formerly Senior Lecturer in Biology, University of Papua and New Guinea, and a member of the Land Research Division of the Commonwealth Scientific and Industrial Research Organization, Canberra. He has published several articles on the rainforests of the Pacific area and on vegetation change.

R. G. WARD, PH.D. (Lond.), Professor of Human Geography, Australian National University, is the author of *Land Use and Population in Fiji*, editor and co-editor respectively of *American Activities in the Central Pacific, 1790–1870*, and *An Atlas of Papua and New Guinea*, and author of several papers dealing with the Pacific Islands. He was formerly Professor of Geography, University of Papua and New Guinea.

INTRODUCTION

THE Pacific islanders are now regaining the right of self-government taken from them during the nineteenth century. Western Samoa, Tonga, Nauru, and Fiji are independent states; the Cook Islands have full and New Caledonia and French Polynesia some internal self-government; the British Solomon Islands Protectorate, the Territory of Papua and New Guinea, and the Trust Territory of the Pacific are all moving rapidly towards independence. But though the right of self-government may be an old one repossessed, the reality over which it is exercised is new. For nowhere in the Pacific (contrary to the tourist-oriented publicity) are the land and the people untouched. Two centuries or more of contact with the technological world have reshaped the environment of the islands, restructured their population, and re-formed their societies. The essays in this volume are concerned with some aspects of these interrelated processes, both past and present.

In the last two decades the number of research workers in the Pacific Islands has greatly increased, yet there are still wide lacunae in our knowledge, and perhaps even wider in our understanding. No volume of this size could hope to cover the full range of themes related to the modification of the Pacific landscape. Neither is it possible to do more than provide interim reports on some of the themes. Relatively few areas have been examined archaeologically; palynology has only begun to reveal the vegetation changes of the last few thousand years, and then only in New Guinea, in the extreme west of the region; many archives are as yet unordered and unexplored; and many islands have received only fleeting visits from social scientists. Nevertheless, it was felt that for many topics it was now possible to provide general views for the whole region, and authors were asked, wherever possible, to do this, and then focus attention on the particular detail of one area, island, or territory. The majority of the essays, therefore, are organized in this way though lack of data prevents this form of treatment in some cases. Perhaps the most striking example relates to mining, an industry which has physically destroyed island landscapes, removed indigenous populations, introduced alien groups, and impoverished some islanders and enriched others. Yet as Newbury points out, there is no adequate history of any Pacific mining company and very few studies of any aspect of the impact of mining. A general assessment is not possible, and Newbury has therefore limited his aim and provides one of the first detailed studies of the social and administrative stresses which mining has brought to a Pacific island.

The first two essays in the volume provide a general context for the later chapters. Golson summarizes the rapidly changing body of knowledge on the prehistoric settlement of the Pacific Islands and shows that changing relationships between population and available resources are not new to the region. As production systems were elaborated and populations grew, the islanders modified their environment both by intent and accident. As new and varied technologies, organizations, and ideologies were brought into the Pacific by European and Asian traders, settlers, missionaries, and administrators, the pace of change increased. Farrell discusses the forces, means, and results of the alien invasion and provides a wide summary view, against which the later chapters elaborate some of the detail. His paper touches many aspects of change which are not otherwise considered in this volume.

The subsequent chapters all provide variations on the theme of how the operation of the man-environment system has been changed by the alien invasion and how old institutional controls in the system have been modified or replaced. Trades initially developed to fulfil the needs of distant countries brought changes to indigenous life and organization (Ward, Chapter 4, and Parnaby, Chapter 5). New demands were generated within the indigenous societies themselves (Lea, Chapter 10) and these created stresses which could only be partially relieved by changes in the existing social organization (Crocombe, Chapter 9). As European involvement grew and the alien administrations dominated, new forms of control were often imposed (Newbury, Chapter 7), and misunderstanding of the old structures was common (Crocombe, Chapter 9). New economic systems (Newbury, Chapters 6 and 7) demanded new spatial organization, and the distribution of population and the forms of settlement were changed (Crocombe, Chapter 9, and McTaggart, Chapter 11). The processes of adjustment are far from complete and the pressures of population growth alone (Pirie, Chapter 8) will ensure continued change in the ways the islanders use and modify their environment and attempt to control their relationships with it.

The ten contributors to this volume include an archaeologist, a botanist, three historians, and five geographers. But such classifications are imprecise and the essays are problem-oriented and not confined by artificial academic barriers. Inevitably there is some overlapping of material, for the themes discussed cannot be considered in isolation. The systems of agriculture, old and new, described by Lea are an important factor influencing the vegetational changes Robbins discusses and the changing land tenure structures which Crocombe portrays. The nineteenth-century trades which Ward and Parnaby consider influenced the population trends which Pirie assesses. In this situation the authors sometimes interpret events or data in different ways. In part this is because the scale of consideration varies from chapter to chapter, and a problem viewed at different scales may require different explanations. Other differences in interpretation reflect the authors' varied assessments of the evidence. Uniformity of opinion has not been imposed editorially as our knowledge of many of the topics is incomplete and a revealed uncertainty is better than an imposed orthodoxy.

As editor of the volume I would like to thank the authors for their contributions and their patience. I would also like to acknowledge my wife's encouragement and helpful comments during the long period this volume has been in preparation. We all owe thanks to the Cartography Unit, Department of Geography, University College London, and Mrs. Marlous Ploeg, Department of Geography, University of Papua and New Guinea, for drawing the maps and diagrams, and to Mrs. P. Barnes for typing most of the final text.

R. GERARD WARD

1

THE PACIFIC ISLANDS AND THEIR PREHISTORIC INHABITANTS

J. GOLSON[1]

THE biogeographical distinctiveness of islands (Darlington, 1957: 479–87) is a result of their separateness and smaller size, and the smaller the islands and more permanent the separateness, the greater is the distinctiveness. Other factors affecting islands include the nature of the source areas for colonization by plants and animals; the powers of dispersal over water barriers of potential colonists; the pattern of winds and currents; and the mutual response of recipient environments and colonizing elements. The most important principles are distance—small water barriers are more likely to be crossed more often than large ones—and size—island environments are in varying degree closed systems, sealed by their separateness. All these considerations apply to man's settlement of islands and the development of human societies in island environments.

The vast Pacific Ocean has been a permanent feature of world geography since Cretaceous times. In its present form its southern islands exhibit a general pattern of decreasing size and increasing isolation from west to east, with a wide, deep ocean gap devoid of island stepping-stones beyond to the Americas. The western islands are geologically complex, being the upfoldings of ancient continental rocks. To the east basalts are exposed to form high islands or are capped with the carbonate rocks of reef and atoll. Atoll environments, at once specialized and uniform, are harshly selective of colonizing life and markedly less diversified in life forms than the high islands with their larger, more differentiated and more hospitable land surfaces. Of all the climatic elements that lead to further diversification,

---

[1] Professor Golson is Professor of Prehistory, Research School of Pacific Studies, Australian National University.

rainfall is the one of greatest variability and its incidence and amount have important consequences for the variety and vitality of vegetation on both high island and atoll. Gressitt (1963) discusses the biogeographical character of the Pacific Islands that has resulted from the interaction of all these factors and the contribution that each has made to its variability. Fosberg (1963) considers the potential of the resulting environments for human settlement, the effect of man's activities on them, and their role in shaping the character of his societies.

The present essay is an attempt to explore the historical dimension of these questions. This involves consideration not only of the undisturbed environments into which man came as a disruptive factor but of the nature of the colonizing process and of the terrestrial and maritime technologies and economies by which it was accompanied. For this purpose the archaeological evidence that has become increasingly available over the past twenty-five years is especially significant, since archaeology, which aims to discover, date, and interpret the actual relics of past occupancy, bears directly on the developmental questions which are our main concern.

Like other forms of anthropological investigation, however, archaeological research is unevenly distributed in the Pacific. It also suffers from inherent limitations, in that only those aspects of a society's activities which receive material expression in a durable form ever enter the archaeological record. In consequence the record is always incomplete and is frequently an ambiguous and enigmatic statement about past reality. In the South Pacific, however, traditional ways of life only began to be altered by European contact, which occurred in few places more than 200 years ago and in many places much more recently, and has been varied in the degree and extent of its impact. Ethnographic data gathered in the early years of contact and subsequently, including the findings of modern social anthropology, can thus serve to offset normal limitations on archaeological reconstructions. From historical, linguistic, ethnographic, traditional, and other appropriate sources, it is possible to establish a baseline before the onset of appreciable European-induced change, against which archaeological evidence can be measured and in the light of which archaeological insights and interpretations can be improved. Although the baseline will vary in completeness and reliability in different islands and different spheres of culture, it may enable archaeological research to make a richer than normal contribution to South Pacific studies and perhaps in fields normally closed to it.

THE CULTURAL PATTERN

Like Gaul, the South Pacific is traditionally divided into three parts. This tripartite division, as it emerged in the nineteenth century, represented a view of the region as exhibiting the segregated occupation of definable areas by peoples not only physically distinct but, some came to argue, representative of the three major divisions of mankind, the Mongoloid in Micronesia, the Negroid in Melanesia in oceanic guise, the Caucasoid in Polynesia in modified form. Growing involvement with Pacific Islands populations during the nineteenth and early twentieth centuries increased the store of knowledge of their cultures and of the similarities and differences between them. Some of the data could be fitted into the tripartite scheme and seemed therefore to confirm it; other data cut across the proposed divisions and suggested they were too simple.

One valid generalization emerged strongly. The over-all cultural unity of Polynesia, which so impressed the early voyagers, was in general confirmed by subsequent research and could be set against the marked heterogeneity of the Melanesian islands and the diversity found within Micronesia. In this situation lay the germ of the Polynesian problem to whose solution so much effort has been directed, for if the lesser differentiation of Polynesian cultures suggested a relatively recent dispersal of the Polynesians through the scattered islands and archipelagos of the Central Pacific, the greater differentiation particularly of the Melanesian cultures should indicate a long occupation of those particular islands. The question then became, how did the Polynesians get into the Central Pacific after the settlement of Melanesia but without appreciable contact with its inhabitants. A Micronesian route that avoided Melanesia and was only subsequently occupied by Mongoloids from the Asian mainland and its archipelagos and an American source area that cut through all such complications have been variously proposed and argued.

The concept of Micronesia, Melanesia, and Polynesia has persisted in South Pacific studies because it registers some hard facts about the cultural geography of the area at European contact. The import of recent research, however, has been to reject the assumption underlying migration theories advanced to explain these facts. Instead of the terms representing fixed and exclusive cultural categories for whose human representatives some extra-Oceanic homeland needs to be postulated and particular routes of migration traced, it is now suggested that the three-fold division is an artifact of the prehistoric settlement history of the South Pacific, which made its appearance in discoverable and datable circumstances.

Excepting the futuristic tailpiece of Antarctica, the settlement of the Pacific Islands is the final chapter in man's occupancy of the terrestrial quarters of the globe. While the presence of man in continental South-east Asia is of immense antiquity and the outlying landmass of Australia–New Guinea had been settled before 20,000 years ago, the earliest dates for Oceania are as yet no older than the second millennium before Christ, and discovery and colonization proceeded throughout the first millennium A.D. With few exceptions the South Pacific islands are inhabited by people speaking varyingly related languages of Austronesian stock, to which the languages of Indonesia, Malaysia, the Philippines, the Taiwan aborigines, and Malagasy also belong. Languages of non-Austronesian type are found in small numbers scattered through the Solomons as far as Santa Cruz. Since this is an area of little archaeological exploration, it is quite uncertain how long they have been established there, though it is evident that they have a long history on the New Guinea mainland, where Austronesian languages are coastally distributed and obviously intrusive. If they are indicative of the earliest populations to push into the insular Pacific, it is significant that their distribution is virtually restricted to the large and closely spaced islands that trail eastwards from New Guinea.

Settlement beyond this demanded maritime skill and technology of a high order, qualifications that can be predicated from an early date for members of the world's most widely distributed language stock. The achievements of Oceanic seamanship, manifest in the successful colonization of virtually every inhabitable island in the South Pacific and the incorporation of wide areas in systems of regular intercommunication, impressed the early European voyagers and inclined later theorists of Pacific Islands settlement to ignore the possibility of any restriction on its potential. The balance has been redressed by the work of the New Zealand historian Andrew Sharp (1963), who has stressed the essential limitations to any system of navigation without instruments. In brief Sharp argues against the possibility of deliberate two-way voyaging between islands separated by at most 300 or so miles of open water. The settlement of the more isolated of the Pacific Islands and island groups would not result from deliberate voyages of exploration followed by colonization, but from accidental discovery by canoes, either blown off course in areas of regular navigation or manned by voluntary or involuntary exiles. In either case they would be unable, even if anxious, to find their way back home. Whatever the criticisms of his thesis (cf. Finney, 1967), Sharp's arguments make it impossible any longer to accept the free-ranging voyaging implicit in many migration theories and necessary to consider cultural distributions in their light.

Radiocarbon dates are beginning to provide the outlines of the course of island settlement, though they are still few and scattered and at times problematical. They present a picture of a fairly rapid penetration of the Pacific but apparently not by an orderly sequence of island stepping-stones. A date around the mid-second millennium B.C. is on record for the island of Saipan in western Micronesia and though it was derived from shell, a material that raises problems in dating, experience with dating tropical and subtropical shells suggests that an age inflation of no more than about 300 years would be involved. Man was in the south-east Melanesian islands of New Caledonia and Fiji by 1000 B.C. and in the western Polynesian islands of Tonga and Samoa before, possibly well before, the birth of Christ. The earliest dates for eastern Polynesia so far come from its periphery, where the Marquesas group seems to have been settled by A.D. 500, and perhaps by A.D. 300: more centrally located groups either have not been investigated (Cook Is.) or have produced dates half a millennium and more later (Society Is., Austral Is.).

Eastern Melanesia—Western Polynesia

The archaeological materials associated with the earliest dates in Tonga, Fiji, and, it appears, New Caledonia consist of a distinctive kind of pottery known as Lapita ware and a range of stone and shell tools and ornaments, including some of a quite distinctive style. They are evidence of a community of culture in the South-west Pacific straddling the traditional boundary between Melanesia and Polynesia and antedating its appearance. The Tongan evidence has been interpreted to suggest that this is the cultural base from which the Polynesian cultures directly developed: archaeologically, it is claimed, the entire span of Tongan prehistory is characterized by the modification in effective isolation from external contact of the originally introduced cultural materials, and the Lapita colonists may thus be seen as the direct ancestors of the Polynesian population of Tonga at European contact.

Similar conclusions have been reached about the relationship between the pioneer settlers and historic Polynesian inhabitants of Samoa on the basis of the types of stone woodworking adze that characterize Samoan prehistory. This being so and in view of the cultural similarities exhibited by Tonga and Samoa at European contact, a close relationship between the earliest archaeological assemblages in the two island groups should be recognizable. But this relationship is by no means clear, and disagreement exists as to whether the early Tongan and contemporary Samoan assemblages are directly related, indirectly related, or not really related at all.

On the other hand both Polynesian groups are separately seen as substantially deriving their historic cultures from their founder populations and as showing little if any evidence of subsequent alien cultural influence. Over the border, so to speak, in southern Melanesia the situation is quite different. Here archaeology records the arrival and establishment of other cultural traditions. These were subsequent to first settlement, though apparently by no more than a few centuries, and are represented by different pottery and variant fashions in other artifacts, which penetrated no further east. These factors may serve to explain both the genesis of Melanesian cultural complexity and the basis of Polynesian cultural homogeneity.

Eastern Polynesia

The archaeological evidence reveals some basic continuities between the early assemblages of West Polynesia and the earliest so far accepted for East Polynesia. The latter have been excavated in the Marquesas and are interpreted as including marked parallels with Samoa, particularly in adze forms. They also have pottery, the only occurrence in East Polynesia so far. In addition they provide the earliest acceptable settlement dates for East Polynesia, back perhaps as far as A.D. 300. Close cultural relationships in terms of fishhooks, adzes, or ornaments are claimed between the early Marquesan materials and the earliest known assemblages of Easter Island, Mangareva, Hawaii, and the Societies. As a result the Marquesas have now generally come to be regarded as the primary centre of population dispersal throughout East Polynesia, with a claim for a contribution also to New Zealand, a temperate and isolated landmass that falls outside the scope of this review. The Society Islands, hitherto often regarded as the primary centre of dispersal, is relegated to a secondary role with responsibility for the primary settlement of New Zealand and a later contribution to Hawaii.

These conclusions are based not only on the archaeological data but also on the historical implications of the different degrees of relationship exhibited by Polynesian languages, and a close correspondence is claimed between the results of the two lines of inquiry (Green, 1966). The situation is a favourable one for such a correspondence to appear. With the possible exception of Easter Island we are dealing only with Polynesians when we discuss the settlement of eastern Polynesia and the implications of area and distances are such that the first successful settlement of an island should in normal circumstances have set the basic pattern of its subsequent development, even though secondary settlement or contact might have taken place.

Full archaeological sequences to test this proposition are not really available but continuities from first to last can be seen in some aspects of the archaeological materials from the Marquesas, Easter Island, Hawaii, and perhaps New Zealand. The evidence suggests the development and maintenance of regional variants of a general cultural configuration. At the same time certain items like the formalized temple complex (*marae*) and the developed stone food-pounder are not present everywhere in East Polynesia and may be later developments secondarily distributed. Easter Island has been nominated as a special case but reinterpretation of the Heyerdahl expedition's archaeological data allows at most the possibility of limited contact with or from South America after the settlement of the island by Polynesians (Green, 1967a: 221–8).

Eastern and Western Polynesia

While the role currently claimed for the Marquesas in East Polynesian prehistory has been challenged on a number of grounds, the most telling argument against its primacy is to be found in the very real differences that exist, side by side with the admitted similarities, between the early West Polynesian and Marquesan assemblages. These latter and all other early East Polynesian assemblages for which there is evidence possess features of fishing equipment, of woodworking adzes, and apparently of ornaments unknown in or different from western Polynesia. Since at least the more important of these are abiding features incorporated by Burrows (1938) in the assembly of ethnographic evidence he used to demonstrate the cultural differentiation of West and East Polynesia at European contact, it is evident that such differentiation was already well advanced by the time the Marquesas were settled around perhaps A.D. 300.

Where and how this differentiation took place is completely unknown. It may have been generated within the culture itself, as some have claimed for the adzes (Emory, 1968: 157) and as certain functional arguments suggest as a possibility in respect of the proliferation of East Polynesian fishhook forms (cf. Reinman, 1970). On the other hand it is impossible at this stage to rule out influence from Micronesia, where a similar high development of hook fishing gear took place.

An immediate origin for Polynesian culture in general in the islands of southern and eastern Melanesia is more certain (Green, 1967a), for it is here that the nearest relatives of the Polynesian languages are to be found as well as the closest archaeological parallels, despite current disagreement about the nature and significance of these. In addition the evidence of physical type and blood-group genetics does not forbid the suggested relationship.

Melanesia

The evidence now available on the culture history of Melanesia itself is quite insufficient to draw even the general outlines. Archaeological research has been largely restricted to the south-eastern islands, where the prehistoric record for Fiji and New Caledonia is culturally complex in contrast to that for Polynesia. The cultures represented in the first two island groups, defined in terms of their pottery, have much in common, though the end-products of the cultural process are substantially different. In addition both have some relationship with the central New Hebrides, where, with the present exception of one variant Lapita site going back to 350 B.C. or so, the entire sequence is occupied by assemblages with an incised and relief-decorated pottery from the seventh century B.C. to the disappearance of pottery itself shortly after A.D. 1000. Pottery in the same tradition becomes important in New Caledonia from at least the birth of Christ and in Fiji about 1,000 years later. This may account for some of the differences their cultures exhibit.

With the exception of Lapita ware, known from a handful of sites in the northern New Hebrides and the Bismarck Archipelago, the further relationships of the south-eastern Melanesian materials are unknown. Recent work on Buka in the northern Solomons has illuminated the last 2,500 years of what must be a much longer sequence, disclosing the existence of a number of ceramic styles. There seem to be few specific resemblances between these materials and those further south, where the major formative traditions had of course been established before the date at which the present Buka sequence starts. This situation may reflect the importance of geographical location, which renders Buka more liable to external influence from a number of directions than the more remote and isolated islands at the end of the Melanesian chain. Particularly important is the proximity of the huge island of New Guinea, adjacent to Indonesia in the west and with a long northern coastline open to receive and transmit cultural influences at all times during the seagoing era.

At present the complexity of Melanesia is most easily grasped by a consideration of its languages, which have long been recognized as including some of the most diverse and aberrant in the Austronesian group. Various interpretations, none of them entirely satisfactory, have been offered for this situation: on-the-spot diversification as a function of geographical separation and length of settlement; a view of Melanesia as the primary centre of development and dispersal of the Austronesian languages; pidginization with languages of non-Austronesian type already established in the Melanesian islands from the direction of New Guinea. A further hypothesis (Wurm, 1967) proposes the arrival of Austronesian speakers in eastern New Guinea and their association there to varying degrees of intensity with long-established resident populations different in language and physical type. Austronesian-speaking populations differentially effected by this association linguistically, culturally, and physically were available for primary and subsequent settlement of the islands east and south, where they brought and developed the characteristics subsequently thought of as Melanesian.

Archaeological evidence to test any of the historical reconstructions from the linguistic data is deficient and restricted to the terminal Melanesian island groups. The actual or inferred primacy of Lapita ware here would favour the Wurm hypothesis for this particular area, should the notion of Lapita's connection with the genesis of the Polynesian cultures be sustained.

Micronesia

The scattered Micronesian islands are candidates for cultural diversification by varying liability to outside contact and by internal differentiation. In western Micronesia the climatically favoured high islands are advantageously situated for contact with the archipelagos of South-east and East Asia, as the pre-European cultivation of rice in the Marianas shows. Eastwards through the Carolines we are in an increasingly oceanic world to the atolls of the Marshalls and the Gilberts at the threshold of Polynesia. The relationships of the Micronesian languages, all of them Austronesian, seem to reflect this geographical situation and suggest the possibility of appreciably different histories for the islands of the west and east. The languages of the Marianas and Palaus are not closely related either to each other or to the other Micronesian languages and seem to have closer affiliations in island South-east Asia to the west. The eastern languages, Gilbertese, Marshallese, and the languages of the Carolines excluding Yap, are included by linguists in the same subgroup and find their closest relatives, depending on the criteria of comparison, in the New Hebrides or Polynesia.

We are able to bring little archaeological evidence to bear on the evolution of the Micronesian cultural pattern, since the limited work done has virtually been restricted to western Micronesia and the data here are as yet not well integrated from group to group. Interestingly enough, however, the limit of pottery in Micronesia as known approximates to the linguistic boundary between western and eastern Micronesia.

The most informative results for our present purposes have been achieved in the Marianas, where occupation accompanied by pottery seems likely to go back to the second millennium B.C. The persistence of one of the two main pottery types and at least the major adze type throughout the sequence as defined suggests that some basic cultural patterns were established by the original settlers. With the limited archaeological evidence available change is clearly reflected only in the ceramics, particularly in the disappearance of a major pottery type, Marianas Red, which is quite well represented in the early stages of the sequence.

In point of diversification of vessel and rim types Marianas pottery bears a much greater resemblance to Lapita ware than to any other of the ceramic styles known from island Melanesia. Indeed the sharply angled profiles and flat bases present in Marianas Red, and the thin, red slip applied to vessels in this ware, echo features of Lapita pottery in which Lapita differs from subsequent ceramics in its area. In addition some general comparisons can be drawn between the products of the shell industry of the Marianas, and also of Yap, and of Lapita sites in the southern islands, though the forms in question are not restricted to these particular contexts but are present in other associations in the intervening areas. The known occurrence in Oceania of one specific ornament, however, is at present limited to the Marianas and Lapita assemblages in Fiji and Tonga (Spoehr, 1957: fig. 77).

The type also occurs in South-east Asia where it belongs to a loose and poorly dated complex of ornaments and pottery, which bear general similarities to some of the prehistoric materials of the Pacific Islands. Though precise archaeological links cannot as yet be described between the two areas, there is no doubt that future research will establish them. The evidence of the languages, which we have mentioned, and of the food plants, to which we shall shortly turn, are unequivocal as to the important South-east Asian element basic to the cultural traditions of Oceania. At the same time, though archaeological data on the question are deficient, there are linguistic and other indications that the New Guinea area played a formative role in the development of the cultural pattern of the Melanesian islands. Finally, it is not impossible that the fishing technology characteristic of Micronesia and eastern Polynesia, in which (in contrast to that of western Polynesia and Melanesia) the hook was a normal part of the equipment, derived its distinctive features from Japan and the North Pacific (cf. Reinman, 1967: 186–7; 1970). The presence of harpoons for sea mammal hunting in historic and prehistoric contexts in the Marquesas and their discovery archaeologically in New Zealand, though not as yet elsewhere, strengthens the case for a North Pacific contribution to the diversification of Oceanic cultures. The possibility of a minor South American contribution to the culture of Easter Island has been mentioned.

THE SUBSISTENCE PATTERN

The cultural traditions of the South Pacific world as outlined above reproduce a well-known characteristic of its terrestrial plants and animals, namely poor numerical representation of types becoming increasingly poorer from west to east. Pacific Islands flora is a depauperate derivative of the rich Malaysian plant-geographic province (political Malaysia, Indonesia, and New Guinea), with a proportionately small Australian contribution and very limited American influence even in the easternmost islands. The representation of terrestrial vertebrates falls off very sharply eastwards from New Guinea; strictly fresh-water fishes and non-marine turtles are not known east of that island; one marsupial and several rat genera extend to the Solomons; snakes reach Fiji; lizards Fiji and Tonga; fruit and insectivorous bats Samoa; and landbirds the Tuamotus.

The marine fauna in contrast is not only rich but relatively homogeneous throughout the islands. It forms a division of an Indo-West Pacific province, whose marine shore component is the richest in the world, containing, with few exceptions, representatives of every tropical shallow water marine fish family and a very high percentage of all genera occurring in tropical regions.

At European arrival this pattern of indigenous resources was incorporated in a locally varying subsistence system in which the bulk of the vegetable foods was provided by the cultivation of tropical crops of largely South-east Asian and/or Malaysian (including New Guinea) origin (yam, taro, banana, coconut, breadfruit, sugar cane). The flesh foods were provided by three introduced domesticates, pig, chicken, and dog; by the intro-duced rat; by the resources of the sea; and occasionally and locally by man himself. For a variety of reasons there is little detailed evidence about the respective contributions of wild and cultivated plant foods, fish, and domesticated animals in any of the contributory subsystems.

It is often said that horticulture was a prerequisite for man's successful colonization of the Pacific Islands with their limited indigenous land resources, and it is usually taken for granted that the food plants—and animals—were introduced and distributed as a complex. Gaps in the distribution of specific plants and animals, where not due to the inadequacies of the historical record, have been attributed to the hazards of dis-persal or to environmental intolerances of various kinds.

None of these propositions can be taken for granted. From the point of view of subsistence it is not poverty in plant genera that is important but the existence of sufficient populations of utilizable species. Botanically the colonists of the Pacific Islands, whether Austronesian or non-Austronesian speakers, were moving into a familiar world and indigenous plants came to play a not insignificant role in the economies of a number of

Pacific islands, as they or their relatives had in Malaysia. It may well be that the bigger, ecologically diversified islands near New Guinea were able, with the bonus of their coastal resources, to support hunting and gathering groups as New Guinea itself did before the advent of horticulture. Also it is possible that economic plants were introduced at different times into the South Pacific and some of the observed variations in distribution may be due to this. A signal example is provided by the sweet potato which from a South American source spread through most of Polynesia in pre-European times but only very marginally into Melanesia.

Archaeology may make its contribution to the elucidation of questions such as these in a number of ways. Food and other plants may prove amenable to identification from their carbonized remains, as sweet potato and sugar cane have in a fifteenth- to sixteenth-century A.D. context on Easter Island. In exceptional circumstances of permanent dryness or wetness plant remains may be preserved, as in the lower waterlogged levels of Karobo, belonging to the second stage of the Fijian cultural sequence, where edible and other economically useful nuts and indications of the manufacture of coconut oil were found (Palmer, 1968: 22). Even more exceptionally the presence of plants may be attested by impressions on pottery vessels, as on the large flat-bottomed dishes also belonging to the second stage of the Fiji sequence, which bear the marks of the leaves and mats on which they were moulded (Lambert, 1971).

Less direct but potentially more abundant information about food plants may be provided by the presence of food preparation equipment in archaeological deposits, some of which may be specialized enough to be referable, with the aid of ethnographic evidence, to a particular food plant or a particular food plant complex. Examples include coconut graters, reported for the earliest levels in the Marquesas, and, less certainly, vegetable peelers, made by perforating the wall of a shell and abrading the edges of the hole. These implements, whether interpreted as peelers or not, are quite widely distributed in archaeological contexts in the Pacific but nowhere as yet apparently in the earliest sites apart from Tonga. Their presence here with Lapita ware has been used as evidence for the horticultural status of the pioneer settlers of these southern islands, but the interpretation is not as soundly based as could be wished.

There are some structural features associated with horticulture and the use of cultivated plants in the Pacific which may be expected to contribute to the study not only of the age of horticulture there but also of the origin and development of some of its particular techniques. Pacific agricultural systems have generally been viewed as representing a regional expression of South-east Asian shifting cultivation, wherein agricultural variations are largely ecologically controlled and similar ecological situations have evoked similar horticultural responses. Ecological considerations are obviously of great importance, particularly in any discussion of horticultural practices on coral atolls with their severely limiting conditions. However, in a recent review of the development of agriculture in Oceania, using historical and distributional data supported by archaeological evidence where it exists, Yen (1971) has suggested a formative role for the islands of the East Melanesian/West Polynesian border zone, reflected in discontinuities with New Guinea and western Melanesia but providing the complex of agricultural practices and associated traits out of which the East Polynesian subsystems were derived. The distinguishing features are the use for food of Cordyline root, the semi-anaerobic fermentation of breadfruit, and the practice of agricultural terracing mainly for the irrigated cultivation of taro. None of these is necessarily viewed as originating in the area: the analogues of terraced agriculture are well known in mainland and island South-east Asia and fermentation is a feature of food technology in the same areas. The Polynesian method of breadfruit preparation is approximated in parts of Micronesia.

The three practices under discussion have structural connotations. Terracing persists as a feature of the landscape susceptible of study in the field. In Samoa a distinctive type of large oven has been identified ethnographically as for the cooking of Cordyline root and traced back archaeologically as far as about A.D. 1200. Breadfruit fermentation in pits was noted from the earliest days of European contact with eastern Polynesia. Prehistoric pits interpreted as being for fermentation have been found in the Marquesas, the Societies, Samoa, and Tonga.

Some of the Samoan pits at the Vailele site are sealed by a pottery-bearing layer dated to the first century A.D. and belonging on present knowledge to a very early stage of Samoan prehistory. The evidence would point therefore not only to the antiquity of the fermentation technique but to its presence, and with it the presence of horticulture of some sort, at the beginning of the Samoan sequence.

This last conclusion about the nature of the earliest Samoan economy is independently supported by archaeological evidence of a different sort—the character and distribution of early archaeological sites. While the Vailele site is situated on the coast, other sites of similar and greater antiquity have been found inland. At least some of these possess features indicative of stable settlement rather than bush foraging. They testify to an effective land base to the Samoan economy from its very beginning, which additional evidence shows to be characteristic of the entire prehistoric sequence.

A notable and doubtless correlated feature of Samoan field archaeological evidence is the total absence at any stage of concentrated dumps of discarded food shells, such as are recorded for example for the Marquesas, the Societies, Hawaii, and New Zealand. The greatest contrast, however, is with Tongatapu, the major island of the Tongan group, where the mounds and middens which have produced the rich collections of Lapita pottery derive much of their bulk from shellfish remains. It has been noted that both shell middens and pottery are concentrated around the shores of the lagoon and that the occurrences of both are very limited not only elsewhere on Tongatapu but throughout the Tongan group as a whole.

The coastal distribution of all known Lapita sites, scattered widely but thinly through the islands of the South-west Pacific, has also been a matter for comment. Some of them at least have shell-fishing associations, especially those reported for New Caledonia. Coastal middens with shellfish are, however, a prominent feature throughout the entire span of New Caledonian prehistory and may reflect the increased importance of the sea as a protein source with the failure of any man-transported animal, except the chicken and the rat, to reach the island in prehistoric times. This is in itself a surprising circumstance, since two of the cultures contributing to New Caledonia's prehistory seem elsewhere to have had at least pig from the very beginning—Lapita in Tonga and the incised and relief ware populations of the central New Hebrides.

Since the survival of bone on archaeological sites is generally good, it should be much easier to establish the distributions of the introduced animals through Oceania, and their dates, than of the introduced plants. Ritual or other special considerations may prevent the appearance of animal bones in the normal refuse dump, but other types of site or the use of domesticated animal bones for implement manufacture should balance the picture. Thus while dog bones are prominent items of food refuse from the beginning of the sequence in New Zealand, where it is the only domesticate, they do not occur amongst the midden materials in the early Marquesan levels, but only as formal burials. Since the dog was extinct in the Marquesas by European contact, we have here an example of archaeology correcting conclusions from the historical record that it had never existed there. Pig has not yet been confirmed for the earliest Marquesan levels, but both pig and dog are present from the beginnings of the Hawaiian sequence.

The possibility of making detailed statements about the marine orientation of Pacific Islands societies in the past is limited by insufficient quantitative information about the composition of the refuse deposits where the relevant remains of shell and scale fish, turtle, and occasional sea mammal bones are found and sometimes by a lack of information on the kinds of fish that are represented. New Zealand, the best served, falls outside our present scope; in other islands, for example Mo'orea in the Societies, local conditions prevent the separation of man-deposited from sea-deposited shells in investigated coastal middens. For the tropical Pacific, therefore, Reinman's (1967) survey has not been much added to and such additions as there have been, for example with information from Tonga, confirm his general conclusions. On the basis of data from sites in western Micronesia and south-eastern Melanesia, fishing and shellfish collecting are seen to have had a certain importance throughout the investigated sequence; variations in the proportional representation of shells and fishbone in the middens from island to island and over time are interpreted as suggesting changes in their subsistence role. All fish species present are reef and inshore varieties that could be easily taken by trapping, netting, spearing, or poisoning. These are techniques well documented ethnographically for the region but would leave little evidence in the archaeological record beyond the net sinkers recorded for some sites.

It is Reinman's argument that the exploitation of the sub-surface offshore waters is possible only with the fishhook and that the use of the hook as a normal part of the fisherman's equipment means a greater ability to use the resources of the sea. The fishhook is not unknown in the areas under present discussion and may have been of importance in the Marianas where its presence may serve to explain the bones of a deepwater sailfish found in levels of a midden there. In the archaeologically relatively well-known islands of south-eastern Melanesia and western Polynesia, hooks, when found, are of simple form and occur in very small numbers. We may be sure therefore that here bait hook fishing was as unimportant throughout the pre-historic period as it appears to have been in recent times from historical and ethnographic sources.

The situation in the eastern islands of Polynesia is quite different, for here, and from the earliest times, fishhooks are common finds and exhibit a great variety of forms. According to Reinman (1970) the variables are governed by interdependent considerations including the materials used for manufacture, the enticing, penetrating, and holding qualities desired of the hook, the habits of the fish being sought, and the environment they frequent. The very existence of the range of hook types known from East Polynesia, as an addition to the fishing methods practised elsewhere, must, by this argument, be evidence of a greater interest in and knowledge of fishing and a greater efficiency and wider range in its execution. The archaeological evidence is not yet available to test these propositions. Figures from two small Hawaiian sites show a rather greater density of fishbone in the deposits than is recorded for the western Pacific, but the fish species are unidentified. We have such identifications as yet only for one site on Easter Island and with two possible exceptions none of the represented fishes is pelagic.

From the evidence of early contact descriptions and museum specimens it would appear that the trolling hook was extensively employed in both western and eastern Polynesia in the quest for the surface-feeding bonito. It is interesting to note, however, that while both lure shanks and points have been excavated from sites in East Polynesia, including the earliest levels, extensive work has produced only a single and doubtful specimen of shank from an archaeological context in West Polynesia.

The trolling hook apart, the fishing techniques of the western Pacific are very similar to those recorded for Malaysia and South-east Asia. It may be suggested that the island environments stimulated a more intensive application of established practices in response to the scarcity of their land-based animal protein resources other than those provided by the far from ubiquitous domesticated forms, the fellow-travelling rat, and man himself. It is likely that this development proceeded furthest where food plant resources were also subject to environmental limitations as on coral atolls. The evidence is not yet available to measure this either from the Asian or the Oceanic side. The development or adoption, in eastern Polynesia and parts of Micronesia, of a diversified bait hook technology might theoretically represent a qualitatively different stage in the exploitation of marine resources, though this has yet to be demonstrated. As we have seen, the model for this development in the eastern islands may have been supplied from the north-east Asian/Japanese area.

Technology and its Raw Materials

It is impossible, as the foregoing has shown, to separate from any discussion of subsistence the technology by which it was carried out. The important organic element in that technology rarely survives archaeologically, so that the archaeological record in our area consists of pottery and objects in stone, bone, and shell. All these are materials known and extensively worked in the regions from which Pacific Island populations were drawn. The interest of the Oceanic situation lies not in the employment of new materials but in the ways those available were used and the responses made to any limitation of supply.

Workable stone for implement manufacture was present everywhere, except on coral islands where it was totally absent. Useful bone of sufficient size was everywhere in short supply, with the exception of New Zealand before the extinction of the moa. Marine shell was the most generally available raw material to which only inland dwelling groups on the larger islands did not have ready access.

The recent discovery on Palawan in the Philippines of woodworking adzes of giant clam shell older than 2000 B.C., as well as evidence on prehistoric mainland South-east Asian sites of a rich and diversified shell industry, make it certain that the use of shell as an alternative to or substitute for stone antedated the colonization of the South Pacific, where, however, environments existed in which the practice proved a vital asset. On some high islands, such as Yap, New Caledonia, and certain of the New Hebrides, there is evidence of a long and persistent use of shell in this way, side by side with stone. On the other hand, as petrological analysis of their stone implements shows, the inhabitants of coralline Tongatapu were throughout its pre-history tapping the hard rock supplies of neighbouring Eua and more distant islands in the centre of the Tongan group and at some stage receiving oceanic basalts from outside the area, though at all times adzes of presumably local clam shell were in use.

In general in Oceania the bone industry is not particularly well developed. Dog, pig, and man were the major sources of the material for industrial use. Of these the first two were not available everywhere, while all three supplied bones of limited size. The manufacture of bone fishhooks in two pieces in Hawaii, Easter Island, and New Zealand may have been a response to this limitation, when occasion demanded larger hooks. On Easter Island, where the only domesticated animal was the chicken, bait fishhooks were normally made of human bone but some by a technical *tour de force* were fashioned from basalt. Basalt hooks were also made by the vanished populations of Pitcairn Island.

Polynesian hook fishing gear, both baited and trolled, was, however, normally of shell, preferentially pearl shell. Although bone was available, there seems to have been no bone fishing equipment in Polynesia in prehistory outside Hawaii (where pearl shell was also used), Easter Island, and New Zealand, and the use of bone in these islands is perhaps related to the local absence of pearl shell in the first and its total absence from the other two. In the Marquesas a few porpoise-bone hooks have been found in the earliest levels, together with the pearl shell hooks which subsequently totally replaced them. The predominance of bone points on trolling hooks from Tahiti and the Marquesas in early museum collections reflects the importance and scarcity of pearl shell, which could not be spared for articles of gift or sale to Europeans (Green et al., 1967: 184). Archaeological survey and excavation has shown that pearl shell rarely occurs unworked and always in small fragments on prospected islands in the Societies and it is possible that it was brought from as far away as the Tuamotus in prehistory.

Other types of shell were in use, and for a variety of purposes, in fishing, food preparation, ornamentation, and the general work of cutting and scraping. Sea urchin spines for filing bone, and branch or block coral files for use on shell have been recorded. Pumice where available was used for grinding. Flaked obsidian has been found on a number of islands, but only in quantity on Easter Island, where it was commonly employed for spearheads, and in New Zealand, Hawaii, and Samoa (Green and Davidson, 1969: 169). Most of the above information comes from Polynesia, where our data are fullest on the prehistoric employment of resources.

The original use of pottery in Polynesia has now been archaeologically established for Tonga, Samoa, and the Marquesas. Whatever the Tongan experience may have been, pottery manufacture ceased in Samoa and the Marquesas within a relatively short time of initial settlement. No explanation can as yet be offered for this disappearance of a normally useful art: it is not to be found in any deficiencies of local raw materials. Garanger (1971) describes a prehistoric situation in the central New Hebrides where a number of local pottery industries disappeared shortly after A.D. 1000 perhaps as a consequence of social upheavals in the area. There are other less well-known examples in the Bismarck Archipelago.

While, by the evidence of petrography, Samoan and Marquesan pottery was definitely of local manufacture, the source of the temper and indeed the clays used for the Lapita ware of Tongatapu is unknown; certainly the former and possibly the latter are foreign to this coral island with its thick overburden of clayey soil derived from decomposed limestone and wind-transported volcanic ash. This being so, it is possible that what were imported into Tongatapu were the manufactured vessels and not the raw materials.

The application of scientific techniques of analysis to the materials out of which archaeological objects are made gives valuable evidence about the movements of resources and goods in prehistory. In harness with other types of investigation it can afford some indication of the establishment of those inter-island links basic to the systems of resource exploitation and exchange described for parts of the Pacific in the historical and ethnographic literature and involving food and other perishables as well as stone, pottery, and other potentially archaeological materials. Whatever the degree of formalization and elaboration these achieve, as in the western Carolines or the Santa Cruz archipelago (Lessa, 1950; Alkire, 1965; Davenport, 1962; cf. Lewthwaite, 1966: 47–51), they seem to depend at base on regional specialisms determined by local environmental situations that might be susceptible of archaeological recognition.

SETTLEMENT AND POPULATION

Having reviewed the subsistence pattern and technology employed by Oceanic populations in the different Pacific environments and the time depths involved, we are in some position to consider the extent of prehistoric man's impact on the island world and the nature of the limitations it placed on him.

The natural vegetation of the islands shows the marked influence of man, to a degree in certain zones and certain areas that makes difficult the reconstruction of the original environment (see Chapter 3). The strand formation occupying the coasts of the high islands and the entirety of the atolls has been most affected, mangroves being severely reduced and the coastal forest giving way to introduced coconut and breadfruit. Lowland rain forest, which is absent from most Pacific islands owing to their lack of coastal plain, has been altered by agriculture in the islands of north-west Melanesia and replaced over large areas by secondary vegetation of various types (Fig. 3.1). Foothill and mid-altitude rain forests show signs of human interference with breaks in canopy, floristic imbalances and large trees with well-developed canopy growing on old archaeological sites. The higher montane forests seem to have been little affected by man and the mist forests of the highest mountains not at all.

Grasslands and savannahs are fairly widely distributed through the tropical Pacific basin at low and middle altitudes. Though their origin has been the subject of debate, they are generally ascribed, where not obviously the result of volcanic activity, to man's clearance of original forest cover for agriculture. They occur in areas where lower or unevenly distributed precipitation, coupled with fire, prevents the rapid regeneration of forest. Examples include the rain-shadow region of western New Caledonia and the 'dry' north-west of Fiji where, although annual rainfall is rarely less than 70 inches, under 3 inches per month falls between June and October. There are similar areas in south-eastern Polynesia, where we may instance Mangareva and the Australs. The most striking example is perhaps Easter Island, with its low rainfall and rapid runoff, where woody plants are now restricted to cliffs and craters. Analysis of pollen grains from crater bogs has shown the existence at man's arrival of a forest vegetation. His subsequent extinction of this with the aid of fire has some connection presumably with the characteristic use of stone for statues and in house building on Easter Island.

The nature and developing scope and intensity of the human activities that gave rise over time to effects such as these can best be assessed through the particular type of archaeological approach known as field or topographical archaeology. This involves the systematic search for the archaeological field evidence produced by man's past activities, detailed recording in local areas of their characteristics, number, size, location, and distribution, and selective excavation to answer specific questions about their function, age, chronological relationships, and incidence of reuse. In an important article Green (1967b), who has pioneered this method in the Pacific, has emphasized and illustrated the conditions necessary for its greatest success: the existence of a cultural landscape not significantly disturbed within the period since European contact; the ability to interpret the functions of archaeological sites and their role within the society that produced them; the use of historical and ethno-historical sources to provide information of this sort, together with its social organizational, economic, political, and demographic connotations, as a basis for projections into the past on many fronts; and finally the appreciation that some European-induced change may have occurred before the date at which the first documentary sources appear. This last point is a vital one that has often been overlooked in attempts to reconstruct traditional situations in the Pacific from historical and ethnographic materials. The archaeological work of Green and his colleagues in Samoa, for example, seems to demonstrate the existence of appreciable inland settlement on Upolu into the early years of European contact around A.D. 1800 and beyond, whereas when fuller historical documentation becomes available at about A.D. 1840 it describes the population, as today, concentrated in villages round the coast.

How fully extended the resources of any Pacific island were at any period in the prehistoric past we are at present in no position to detail. Reports on archaeological survey work in the Marquesas describe the presence of numerous prehistoric settlement remains in almost every valley. On Nukuhiva, for example, the early populations inhabited the well-watered windward south and east of the island but by about A.D. 1200 settlement had spread into the much less favoured valleys of the arid leeward coast (Suggs, 1961: 181–92). The presence of fortifications during the later phases of Marquesan prehistory is interpreted as reflecting the pressures on available land. Instances of prehistoric fortifications, of settlement in less desirable areas, and of agriculture in marginal conditions could be multiplied, all tending to suggest the build-up of populations in different islands. The widespread occurrence amongst Pacific communities of traditional practices restrictive of birth is some indication that the pressure of population was being felt or feared. For the small island of Tikopia, with maximum dimensions three miles by two miles, Firth reports infanticide, abortion, celibacy, and *coitus interruptus* (Lorimer, 1954: 105–9). Though it is impossible to assess the extent and effects of practices such as these, we may note that they have been recorded for large islands as well as small.

It is possible to argue on general grounds that the pressures of population on exploitable resources would be felt quite quickly after initial settlement. Even though the colonizing groups were probably small, their capacity to increase would be enormous in the untouched and generally benign environments of the Pacific Islands and with the technology and economy at their command. From the demographic histories of Tristan da Cunha, Pitcairn, and the Bass Strait islands, Birdsell (1957) proposes an initial doubling of the population every generation in such conditions. This is a 2·8 per cent annual increase over twenty-five years. A more reasonable over-all increase of 1 per cent per annum would only require about 850 years to bring a founding population of 20 up to the 100,000 level, which is the highest estimate made by any early observer for the Marquesas with its 1,500 years of prehistory and is in excess of the indigenous populations of all but the largest island groups today. Groube (1970) argues for New Zealand that it requires a fairly rapid build-up of population after settlement to explain why its pressures should manifest themselves at all in so large a country and at the date they do.

Quite apart from any cultural restrictions that were practised, some check on population growth was doubtless exerted by widespread endemic diseases for which fevers of the typhoid group, bacillary dysentery, and infantile diarrhoea, all particularly severe on children, are likely candidates. The small populations characteristic of the early stages of settlement everywhere, and of the small islands and atolls at all times, would be particularly susceptible to demographic upset by factors such as these, as well as by famine through drought or severe storms and by losses at sea, all of them occurrences well recorded in the Pacific.

It is likely none the less that the threat of overpopulation arrived early in the small islands and atolls and was of constant recurrence, despite all checks, natural and otherwise. The size and greater ecological diversity of the larger islands would retard the effects of population growth, and would also tend to cushion the consequences of the natural controls upon it. But the very large and malarial islands of western Melanesia may have been the only islands where population pressures were never (or only locally) felt. As yet we lack the evidence of archaeological site distributions by which to make any sort of judgement on this point.

In the context of the South Pacific, population pressures, when first felt, could be relieved by the exploitation of unoccupied islands in the neighbourhood or by the settlement of such as were inhabitable. Where neighbouring islands did not exist or were already occupied, groups might sail into exile voluntarily or under compulsion (Lorimer, 1954: 108), hopeful of discovering another home. Such voyages of exile may have been a major factor in the settlement of the Pacific Islands. If so, we might expect the course and chronology of island colonization not to be entirely random.

We do not know with any accuracy the sizes of the populations with which we are dealing. In a critical review of the early European contact sources McArthur (1967) exposes gross discrepancies and large assumptions in the estimates made for different islands and groups and seems to suggest that the population decline following European arrival was not as great as has been believed. In western Polynesia she argues for a fair demographic stability during the nineteenth century, so that the population of Tonga in A.D. 1826, after twenty-five years of civil war, would have been little more than 20,000 and that of Samoa in A.D. 1800 about 40,000. These figures represent very slow accretions of population over the 2,000 years and more of demonstrated occupation in highly favourable environments and do not accord with the arguments for the onset of population pressures that have already been advanced. Putting these separate indications together Pirie (1968) proposes the operation in the Pacific of long-time cycles of population growth, decline, and recovery, such as demographers have shown to be characteristics of those pre-industrial civilizations for which long-range population data are available (Petersen, 1961: 373). On this reasoning the demographic prehistory of the Pacific islands would be complex with different islands at different stages of the cycle when Europeans first attempted to number their inhabitants.

The complexity is inherent in the ability of the island populations to multiply in excess of the capacity of the island environments to sustain them. This was a permanent situation and continual adjustments were called for to deal with it. Besides restrictive practices like infanticide and competitive ones like warfare, they included the internal spread of settlement to marginal areas, systems of specialized production and exploitation linking districts of the same and different islands, and the hiving off of groups as colonists and exiles, by whose agency we may suppose the settlement of the entire Pacific island world was in part accomplished. These developments were made possible by the possession of a technology and an economy adequate to the particular conditions of island living. The basic elements of both were imported from outside. In the area under review, as we have seen, no innovations were made that allowed fuller use of existing resources. The only possible exceptions are the techniques of agricultural terracing, food fermentation, and bait hook fishing, but these may well have been introduced from outside the area altogether.

POSTSCRIPT

In an important review of the archaeological evidence from Tonga, Groube (1971) has shown that the settlement of that group had taken place by 1000 B.C. and has proposed that the ceramic phase of its prehistory had ended by about the birth of Christ. This reinterpretation fits well with the archaeological evidence from Fiji at the earlier date, removes the discrepancies present in comparisons with Samoa at the later date, and brings the archaeological picture into line with the linguistic one. In Groube's view the first millennium B.C. in Tonga was the time and place that saw the development of the distinctive features of culture, language, and physical type we know as Polynesian.

BIBLIOGRAPHY

References in the text have been restricted to cases of fairly specific citation, especially of opinion and interpretation. Much of the material and most of the issues that go unreferenced are discussed in the many articles in the symposium volumes on Oceanic prehistory edited by Green and Kelly (1970–1). This should be supplemented with Green, 1966 (especially for evaluation of radiocarbon dates), 1967a and 1968. See also Green, 1971.

I wish to thank Dr. J. I. Poulsen for permission to use unpublished information from his work in Tonga and Dr. J. R. Specht for similar permission in respect of Buka (northern Solomons). I have had the benefit of discussions with my colleague Mr. L. M. Groube on many of the issues raised in this review.

Alkire, W. H. 1965. *Lamotrek Atoll and Inter-Island Socioeconomic Ties*, Illinois Studies in Anthropology no. 5, Urbana and London.

Birdsell, J. B. 1957. 'Some Population Problems Involving Pleistocene Man', *Cold Spring Harbor Symposia on Quantitative Biology*, vol. 22, pp. 47–70.

Burrows, E. G. 1938. 'Western Polynesia: a Study in Cultural Differentiation', *Etnologiska Studier*, vol. 7, pp. 1–192.

Darlington, P. J. 1957. *Zoogeography: the Geographical Distribution of Animals*, New York.

Davenport, W. 1962. 'Red-Feather Money', *Scientific American*, vol. 206, no. 3, pp. 94–104.

Emory, K. P. 1968. 'East Polynesian Relationships as Revealed through Adzes', in Yawata and Sinoto (eds.), 1968: 151–69.

Finney, B. R. 1967. 'New Perspectives on Polynesian Voyaging', in Highland *et al.* (eds.), 1967: 141–66.

Fosberg, F. R. (ed.). 1963. *Man's Place in the Island Ecosystem*, Honolulu.

Garanger, J. 1971. 'Incised and Applied Relief Pottery, its Chronology and Development in Southeastern Melanesia and Extra Areal Comparisons', in Green and Kelly (eds.), 1971: 53–66.

Green, R. C. 1966. 'Linguistic Subgrouping within Polynesia: the Implications for Prehistoric Settlement', *Journ. Poly. Soc.*, vol. 75, pp. 6–38.

—— 1967a. 'The Immediate Origins of the Polynesians', in Highland *et al.* (eds.), 1967: 215–40.

—— 1967b. 'Settlement Patterns: Four Case Studies from Polynesia', in W. G. Solheim II (ed.), *Archaeology at the Eleventh Pacific Science Congress*, University of Hawaii, Social Science Research Institute, Asian and Pacific Archaeology Series, no. 1, pp. 101–32, Honolulu.

—— 1968. 'West Polynesian Prehistory', in Yawata and Sinoto (eds.), 1968: 99–109.

—— 1971. 'The Chronology and Age of Sites at South Point, Hawaii', *Archaeology and Physical Anthropology in Oceania*, vol. 6, pp. 170–6.

—— and Davidson, J. M. (eds.). 1969. *Archaeology in Western Samoa*, vol. 1, Auckland Institute and Museum Bulletin no. 6.

—— Green, K., Rappaport, R. A., Rappaport, A., and Davidson, J. M. 1967. *Archaeology on the Island of Mo'orea, French Polynesia*, American Museum of Natural History, Anthropological Papers vol. 51, part 2.

—— and Kelly, M. (eds.). 1970–1. *Studies in Oceanic Culture History*, 2 vols., Bishop Museum, Pacific Anthropological Records, nos. 11–12, Honolulu.

Gressitt, J. L. (ed.) 1963. *Pacific Basin Biogeography*, Honolulu.

Groube, L. M. 1970. 'The Origin and Development of Earthwork Fortifications in the Pacific', in Green and Kelly (eds.), 1970: 133–64.

Groube, L. M. 1971. 'Tonga, Lapita Pottery and Polynesian Origins', *Journal of the Polynesian Society*, vol. 80: in press.

Highland, G. A., Force, R. W., Howard, A., Kelly, M., and Sinoto, Y. H. (eds.). 1967. *Polynesian Culture History: Essays in Honor of K. P. Emory*, Bishop Museum Special Publication 56, Honolulu.

Lessa, W. A. 1950. 'Ulithi and the Outer Native World', *American Anthropologist*, vol. 52, pp. 27–52.

Lewthwaite, G. R. 1966. 'Man and the Sea in Early Tahiti: a Maritime Economy through European Eyes', *Pacific Viewpoint*, vol. 7, pp. 28–53.

Lorimer, F. 1954. *Culture and Human Fertility*, Paris.

McArthur, N. 1967. *Island Populations of the Pacific*, Canberra.

Palmer, J. B. 1968. 'Recent Results from the Sigatoka Archaeological Program', in Yawata and Sinoto (eds.), 1968: 19–27.

Petersen, W. 1961. *Population*, New York.

Pirie, P. N. D. 1968. 'Polynesian Populations: Review', *Australian Geographical Studies*, vol. 6, pp. 175–81.

Reinman, F. M. 1967. *Fishing: an Aspect of Oceanic Economy. An Archaeological Approach*, Fieldiana: Anthropology, vol. 56, no. 2, Chicago.

—— 1970. 'Fishhook Variability: Implications for the History and Distribution of Fishing Gear in Oceania', in Green and Kelly (eds.), 1970: 47–59.

Sharp, A. 1963. *Ancient Voyagers in Polynesia*, Sydney.

Spoehr, A. 1957. *Marianas Prehistory: Archaeological Survey and Excavations on Saipan, Tinian and Rota*, Fieldiana: Anthropology, vol. 48, Chicago.

Suggs, R. C. 1961. *The Archaeology of Nuka Hiva, Marquesas Islands, French Polynesia*, American Museum of Natural History Anthropological Papers, vol. 49, part 1, New York.

Wurm, S. 1967. 'Linguistics and the Prehistory of the South-western Pacific', *Journal of Pacific History*, vol. 2, pp. 25–38.

Yawata, I., and Sinoto, Y. H. (eds.). 1968. *Prehistoric Culture in Oceania*, Honolulu.

Yen, D. E. 1971. 'The Development of Agriculture in Oceania', in Green and Kelly (eds.), 1971: 1–12.

2

THE ALIEN AND THE LAND OF OCEANIA

BRYAN H. FARRELL[1]

SINCE the first European contact with Pacific islanders, in 1521, the geography of the islands has changed markedly. The use of the land, agriculture, population distribution and population structure have all changed significantly and some of these changes are discussed in later chapters of this volume. During the past 400 years islands once isolated have become dependent on world markets for the sale of produce, their inhabitants have contracted European diseases, and most communities have experienced a partial, or even complete, transformation of traditional ways. Substantial areas of land have been lost to the intruding alien and associated injustices created. Labour has become a commodity and farms from which production bears no relationship to the satisfaction of local wants have been created. Standards of living have changed—the outsider would say raised. Beliefs have been modified and lives saved. The horizons of resource perception have been considerably widened as has the economic base (Yanaihara, 1940: 50) and new techniques have been applied to agriculture, sanitation, and public works. Change has taken place everywhere, though its rate and nature has varied. The most effective agents have been economic enterprise, government action, and missionary activity (Nayacakalou, 1963: 175). Referring to the Solomon Islands in 1934 Hogbin noted that

The Administration, sure of the superior merits of British justice is now forcing the natives to accept its benefits; European commercial enterprises desiring cheap labour are employing the people on plantations, and missionaries positive that Christianity is the only

[1] Dr. Farrell is Professor of Geography, University of Victoria, Victoria, B.C. Grateful acknowledgement is made to the University of Victoria who provided aid so that this work might be undertaken.

valid religion are actively engaged in eliminating heathen beliefs and ceremonies. (1939: 141.)

In 1520 Magellan traversed the Pacific and saw only two small uninhabited islands (Maude, 1959: 287) until landfall was made in the Marianas in 1521. This was the beginning of European exploration and the survey voyage for the first regular trans-Pacific shipping route followed by the Acapulco–Manila galleons. Many followed Magellan. Between 1565 and 1606 the Spaniards Mendaña, Quirós, and Torres ranged further south to parts of eastern Polynesia, the Solomons, and the New Hebrides and attempted the establishment of settlements without success. These early navigators affected the land directly by plant and weed introduction, and indirectly by disease and sometimes by slaughtering indigenes. Two hundred people were thought to have been killed by Spaniards in the Marquesas (Oliver, 1958: 67). The seventeenth-century Spaniard was obsessed both with the acquisition of gold and with the conversion of the unbeliever, and his impact was relatively light except in Micronesia and especially the Marianas.

The Dutch, engaged elsewhere, had only marginal interests in the Pacific, but both French and English explorers were active during the second half of the eighteenth century. D'Entrecasteaux, D'Urville, La Pérouse, Bougainville, Drake, Dampier, Wallis, and Carteret all made useful contributions to the knowledge of the Pacific. It was Captain James Cook, however, who, as the result of voyages between 1769 and 1779, reduced the vastness of the ocean to manageable order and cleared the way for subsequent commercial and missionary enterprise. Several notable expeditions, including the United States Exploring Expedition, cruised the Pacific after the death of Cook but such projects filled the gaps rather than made major discoveries. With the way pioneered and clear, increasingly large numbers of missionaries, whalers, and traders began to arrive.

Each group affected the Pacific milieu in its own particular way. The first missionary contact was in Tahiti when the London Missionary Society party from the mission ship *Duff* landed in 1797. British whalers were reported in the Pacific as early as 1776, and Americans in 1792, but the heyday was in the 1850s when hundreds of ships plied the seas and made Hawaii and northern New Zealand centres of operations. Few islands in the eastern Pacific were spared the onslaughts of whalers as ships were refitted and supplied and crews relaxed at the nearest settlement. The traders, like the whalers, were concerned with collecting and foraging but acted mainly as middlemen receiving from local inhabitants *bêche-de-mer*, coconut oil, pearl shell, and aromatic sandal-wood for shipment to Chinese, North American, or European markets (see Ward, Chapter 4).

Between 1850 and the Second World War, economic activity within the Pacific developed and changed. The trader's previous function remained but was supplemented by that of the merchant, and the island economy was sustained by surplus agricultural commodities produced by individual local people, independent planters, or large commercial companies (see Newbury, Chapter 6). The level of development differed in every island group and was dependent partly on the degree of receptivity to change of the indigenes. Yet although local culture could give distinctive complexion to development, as in the Gazelle Peninsula (Irwin, 1963: 42), the main determinant was invariably the prevailing national attitude of the alien.

From 1850 to after 1900, the Pacific powers, including Britain, Germany, France, and the United States, motivated by a variety of interests, jockeyed for position. The indigenes during their major introduction to alien government were influenced by wide-ranging attitudes varying from the permissive paternalism of Americans to the regimented authoritarianism of Germans and, later, Japanese. The final partitioning of the Pacific was disorderly, illogical, and completely unplanned (Grattan, 1963: 453). It has ultimately resulted in Oceania having representatives of every type of government from classic colony to independent nation. This political situation, involving at one time or another ten nations and the United Nations, has been a most potent force in the changing character of Pacific geography.

The effectiveness of alien impact on Pacific geography and the extent of its influence may be understood completely only with reference to politico-economic as well as environmental factors. The immense size of the Pacific Ocean, the great distances between peoples, the size and nature of the islands of

Oceania all played a significant part in determining the place and nature of the impact. The high islands of the Pacific, especially those formed of 'continental' rocks, had more resources than other islands and, if accessible, usually proved attractive to trader, planter, and settler alike. The low atolls on the other hand were unattractive, even to the resourceful Japanese. Frequently they were already heavily populated for their size and thus ill equipped to provide further sustenance or saleable commodities. Consequently they tended to be left strictly alone (Murphy, 1949: 113).

Early visitors approached the favoured high islands from the sea, which remained the avenue of transport as trade was developed and inter-island intercourse increased. Newcomers—planters, traders, and labourers—came to specific anchorages and at these centres alien influence was greatest. The greater the volume of shipping, the more opportunity there was for contact and the friendlier the island people, the more receptive they were likely to be. The impact of a particular group—trader, missionary, administrator, or planter—has varied through time. The pattern of change was not constant, nor did it diffuse uniformly over a wide area. Essentially, a pattern of discrete nuclear dissemination was characteristic in which short radii reached diffidently towards the outsider's unknown, while long radii extended nostalgically and confidently back to London, Hamburg, Boston, and Tokyo. Brookfield has called this 'compartmentalization' (Brookfield, in Nayacakalou, 1963: 186).

Although it is speculative to reconstruct the basic environment and its use, there seems little doubt that the land was clothed from shoreline to ridge top in a relatively dense, broadleaf, evergreen tropical rain forest. The number of species generally diminished with distance away from the original western Pacific source region. It thinned on the periphery and sometimes diminished locally as a result of recent volcanism or other special edaphic factors (see Robbins, Chapter 3).

Early pioneers in the Pacific had to forage for fern roots, berries, or pandanus and depend on seafood until the animal and vegetable food sources they brought with them had developed (Zimmerman, 1963: 57). Like the indigenous vegetation, all cultivated food plants, except probably the sweet potato (*Ipomoea* spp.), were from South-east Asia and included taros and related plants, yams, bananas, and plantains (Merrill, 1954: 195, 243). The beverage plant 'kava' (*Piper methysticum*) originated near the Melanesian-Polynesian boundary and New Guinea was the source of sugar cane *Saccharum officinarum* (St. John, 1953: 152). The few animals, the pig, rat, dog, and fowl, were from South-east Asia and provided food and sometimes ornament. In some places coloured feathers were highly valued.

At the time of first European contact, agriculture was well established but interference with the natural cover was limited. On every inhabited island patches of trees had been cleared for agriculture or village sites. Useful introduced species, coconut, taro, yam, and sweet potatoes were planted with a digging stick (Barrau, 1960: 1), and in places paper-mulberry and pandanus were used for fibre. Indo-Melanesian weeds were in each clearing and the sago palm had spread unevenly over parts of the south-west. Wild plants were gathered for food, ornaments, dyes, and medicines, and timber for construction and the manufacture of artifacts was obtained from the forest interior.

Land was entrusted most frequently to a group or clan and specific parts were allotted for cultivation (see Crocombe, Chapter 9). Land was considered as an essential, often all-pervading, aspect of society and never was it just the means of sustenance. It did not possess a specific monetary value per unit area nor was there any general concept of the European idea of individual ownership and disposal. Few persons were ever denied access to some land. The practice of producing a surplus in excess of immediate food requirements was well developed in response to social and ritual demands. Frequently land gave prestige to its trustees directly and those with rights to it gained a sense of belonging to that place; and as the quality of techniques and soil varied so were there inequalities in wealth between groups and individuals within groups.

Shifting agriculture was largely based on swiddens or bush-fallowed patches which, after the harvest of two or three crops, demanded regeneration for periods from ten to twenty years before recropping. Barrau calls the contemporary counterpart, where the area is limited and cultivators return to the same patches, 'bush-fallowing rotation' (Barrau, 1955: 41). Techniques had not generally been developed to preserve food for protection against famine or shortages, but some barter trade such as the *Kula* rings had been developed especially in Melanesia (Belshaw, 1965: 12–20). Resource perception was necessarily narrow and alternatives limited. Plants, animals, and people played specific, circumscribed roles. It was outside influence which eventually widened perceptual horizons (see Lea, Chapter 10).

Reflecting general community orientation, the settlement pattern of the Pacific islander was generally clustered, though less so in Micronesia (Oliver, 1958: 58) and parts of Polynesia. Settlements were frequently close to the sea which provided a major source of dietary protein and easy communication between islands or between villages separated by rugged forested terrain. Some villages were fortified against enemy attack and occupied elevated prominences from which shore and sea could be under surveillance at all times. The riparian village was more characteristic of Polynesia than Melanesia where numerous settlements on the larger islands were inland. This was the environment into which the alien intruded.

DEMOGRAPHIC DISRUPTION

During the early nineteenth century American and British whaling developed rapidly and reached a peak about 1850. The British whalers were encouraged by a system of bounty payments serving the twofold purpose of increasing national income and the reserve of trained seamen. In addition ship captains often found commercial trading in sandalwood, pearl shells, *bêche-de-mer*, or furs a lucrative venture. Focal points developed where middlemen brought together goods collected by the native peoples and where whaling ships were refitted, food supplies augmented, and crews rested. Numerous Pacific ports and anchorages became well known and it was here that indigenous inhabitants came in contact most frequently with European visitors. But these were not the only parts where contact was made—the traders' activities were wide-ranging and along any convenient coastline landings would be made to replenish supplies or to take on freight. Alien contacts had the multiple effects of diverting indigenes from their usual form of work, forcing the land to provide for more than permanent local inhabitants, causing deforestation in the process of collecting sandalwood or fuel for the *bêche-de-mer* drying houses (see Ward, Chapter 4), creating urbanization (see McTaggart, Chapter 11), and, above all, introducing the inhabitants to new diseases (see Pirie, Chapter 8). Although of negligible effect on the Europeans, many of these diseases proved fatal to vulnerable indigenes.

This continued a trend started long before organized trade; disease and brutality were not new. Magellan had no compunction in shooting down recalcitrant natives while Mendaña and Quirós perpetrated even greater excesses (Kelly, 1966, I: 85–6), frequently in the name of the Lord. Dampier (1697: 300) reported a native uprising in Guam which was dealt with by the Spanish garrison and resulted in a population of 300 to 400 being reduced by something like three-quarters.

The Devastation of Disease

Oliver (1958: 255) estimated that between the time Magellan entered the Pacific and 1939 the population of Oceania declined from about 3,500,000 to 2,000,000 persons, largely as a result of disease introduced by outsiders. Before the European came to the Pacific the area was free of smallpox, measles, typhus, typhoid, leprosy, syphilis, and tuberculosis (Price, 1963: 148, 163). Not only were deaths caused by a general lack of immunity to disease, but the opportunity for infection was increased in the later nineteenth century when the demand for labour within the Pacific resulted in the congregation in ships and on plantations of large numbers of ill-cared-for islanders (see Parnaby, Chapter 5). In strange and congested surroundings, these undernourished people were even more prone to disease than in the home village where yaws, malaria, hookworm, and filariasis had already taken their toll.

The force of disease touched different places at different times and in some areas, after an early start, continued well into the twentieth century. Between 1779 and 1820 Hawaii was visited by 100 ships, and by the later 1840s there were 600 visiting ships a year (Fuchs, 1961: 4, 18). This contact contributed significantly to a reduction in population from about 300,000 in 1779 to about 55,000 in 1875 (Schmitt, 1961: 2). In Melanesia the population of the Solomon Islands was decimated during the period 1870–1900 by chicken pox, whooping cough, measles, influenza, gonorrhoea, tuberculosis, and leprosy (Hogbin, 1939: 125). In the thirty years after 1907 the population of Ontong Java is reported to have declined by nearly 90 per cent (N.I.D., 1944: 630). Low birth-rates in the Marquesas in the nineteenth century were attributable to venereal disease contracted by persons in the 'parent-age category' during youth (Suggs, 1960: 30). Crocombe outlines a horrifying chronology of the Cook Islands between 1827 and 1867, when the population of Rarotonga fell from between 6,000 and 7,000 to 1,856 as a result of whooping cough, mumps, dysentery, fever, and measles (Crocombe, 1964: 68).

In 1875 measles killed a vast number of Fijians, but the greatest over-all loss in Fiji has resulted from tuberculosis. At first contact the estimated population was 250,000; in 1919, after having lost between 20,000 and 30,000 in the measles epidemic (McArthur, n.d.: 263–5) and a large number in the post-First World War influenza pandemic, the population had dropped to 83,000 (McGusty, 1953: 56). An example of accentuated depopulation by infection occurred when a Peruvian recruiter put a boat load of 300 smallpox-infected islanders ashore at Rapa in French Polynesia. All but nine are reported to have either died or drowned (Parnaby, 1964: 13). The pattern of depopulation varied from group to group as did the factors of change and it is only since the Second World War that population problems have appeared less serious. After nearly 450 years of contact the actual physical destruction directly attributable to the alien may have come to an end (see Pirie, Chapter 8).

Disease introduced by outsiders also wrought complicated changes in the indigenous way of life. While disease debilitated the Oceanic peoples new demands were being imposed upon them, especially in the later nineteenth century, when increased agricultural production was expected from the land. During epidemics garden care came to a standstill, forest plantations suffered, and a particularly high infant mortality and declining populations ultimately resulted in fewer persons of working age. In time improved hygiene, medical care, and diet did much to offset the damage caused by old and new diseases. It was commonly alleged, however, that despite improved techniques the traumatic effects of disease resulted in general lethargy which, in turn, was reflected in attitudes to land. The large numbers of deaths which local people attributed to outsiders often engendered bitter resentment and a tendency towards the rejection of techniques and goals which many aliens were attempting to impose.

Labour Demands and Population Movement

After about 1850 alien commercial activity changed in emphasis from collecting and trading to well-organized commercial plantation agriculture and some guano mining. The latter lasted on some central Pacific islands from the late 1850s to the early 1870s. Although European-influenced agriculture and commercial cropping were developing before this time, the American Civil War interrupted British supplies of cotton and encouraged settlers to plant cotton in Fiji, Samoa, and Queensland. Later the crop base was widened and cheap reliable labour was demanded for cotton and sugar cultivation in Queensland, Hawaii, and Fiji; for plantation agriculture and mining in New Caledonia; for phosphate quarrying on Makatea, Nauru, and Ocean Islands; and for general plantation work in the Society Islands and other parts of the Pacific. Local labour was either not available, as in Queensland, or considered unsatisfactory, or inappropriate, as in Samoa and Fiji.

Although labour recruiting in its flagrant form was relatively short-lived, the practice continued in modified form well into the twentieth century (see Parnaby, Chapter 5). It had begun long before the mid-nineteenth century: islanders, like those of Tinian, had been taken by the Spaniards to provide essential labour in Guam during the eighteenth century; in 1847, two shiploads of Pacific islanders were taken to Australia to work as shepherds (Parnaby, 1964: 6). Thereafter momentum and irresponsibility increased and before long some recruiters were behaving like slave traders and taking inhabitants by force as they did on the Loyalty Islands. In 1862, one recruiter, J. C. Bryne, gathered up 3,000 islanders for work in New Caledonia. Two years later the first Melanesian labourers arrived to work in Fiji. In the same decade Peruvian recruiters were busy and according to one missionary's estimate their visit to Penrhyn Island in the Cook Group cost the island 640 out of a population of 700 (McArthur, 1967: 184–6). New Hebridians, Gilbertese, Ellice, Tokelau and Solomon Islanders were brought to Fiji and paid £2 to £3 per annum for a three- to five-year period (Parnaby, 1964: 31).

On the principle that a local man not satisfactory in his own island could work usefully in other places where there were no ties of custom or kin (Lewthwaite, 1962: 142–3), Samoans were transported to the Bismarck Archipelago while after 1867 Micronesians, Niueans, Cook Islanders, and Melanesians were brought to German plantations in Samoa. Dozens of recruiting ships plied the Pacific during the 1890s and in Queensland alone there were about 8,700 islanders. At least 70 per cent were young men between the ages of 15 and 35 (Parnaby, 1964: 138 and 145).

During the second half of the nineteenth century improvements in farming and steel technology created a growing demand for mineral fertilizers and ferro-alloys. Within the Pacific the mineral resources of New Caledonia and the phosphate islands of Makatca, Angaur, Ocean, and Nauru were discovered, and labour was recruited to exploit them. Some of the other consequences of mineral exploitation are discussed by Newbury in Chapter 7.

When indentured labourers returned home after experiencing another social system they sometimes found that absence had limited their ability to progress within their own system. Sometimes, however, working for money provided the means of increasing their perception of their own environment with unexpected results. Goodenough analyses the remarkable changes which took place on Onotoa atoll where modest wages earned at mining on Ocean Island allowed the purchase of North American redwood with which ocean-going fishing canoes were constructed. This in turn resulted in a decline in the importance of competitive activities and of inshore fishing grounds, and a chain reaction throughout the entire structure of social relationships (Goodenough, 1963: 337, 343).

In addition to Pacific islanders, many mining labourers were brought from areas beyond the Pacific Islands. Between 1853 and 1897 40,000 convicts arrived in New Caledonia from

France and markedly changed the population structure. Pardoned convicts worked the deposits of nickel, chrome, manganese, and cobalt being developed on the island and Vietnamese, Javanese, and Japanese were indentured to augment the labour force. The total number of Asians grew steadily until at the Second World War there were over 10,000 in New Caledonia (Dewey, 1964: 18), working in mining, agriculture, and other enterprises. The majority have now returned to their homelands.

Alien groups were also established in the New Hebrides and Tahiti where Vietnamese and Chinese respectively were introduced as plantation labour. Large numbers of Indian agricultural labourers were indentured by the Fiji Government to overcome a possible labour shortage. The first group arrived in 1879 and were the vanguard of 60,500 who provided the labour corps for the Fijian sugar industry. In the Hawaiian Islands, sugar and pineapple interests introduced a very large alien group. Before annexation, in 1898, 46,000 Chinese had arrived to work the plantations. Few, however, remained as agricultural workers for any length of time. After 1886, 180,000 Japanese also arrived while between 1910 and 1932, 160,000 Filipinos entered Hawaii (Fuchs, 1961: 90). The Japanese, Filipinos, Indians, and Vietnamese were the largest alien groups who came into the Pacific as contract labour. Many eventually returned home (the Vietnamese as late as the 1960s), but many others remained, and today Indians constitute the largest group in Fiji and Japanese form the most important single element in the Hawaiian population.

After 1850 an increasing number of permanent European settlers arrived. The French came to the New Hebrides and New Caledonia in the 1850s and by 1900 there were 23,500 Europeans in New Caledonia, the largest European population in any South Pacific group. British settlers arrived in Fiji and New Caledonia in the 1870s and 1880s while Germans and other Europeans settled in Samoa. In the 1890s settlers arrived in the Solomons. Although numerically of little importance, these outsiders exercised immense influence and as a result of their entrepreneurial and economic operations completely upset existing relationships. Their demand for labour wrought spectacular changes in the distribution and structure of population and in the generation of social problems. This reinforced changes introduced by islanders returning to their home group after expiration of labour contracts.

After 1914 the Japanese came in large numbers as individual settlers, as well as indentured labour, to occupy the former German colonies of the Marianas, Caroline Islands, and Marshall Islands. They came to settle, exploit agricultural resources, mine phosphates on Angaur, and provide the homeland with tropical products and chemical raw materials. In 1920 there were 3,700 immigrants, in 1930, 20,000 and in 1940, 85,000 and by this date Japanese outnumbered the indigenes; in Ponape, for example, there were 7,800 Japanese to 5,900 local inhabitants (Murphy, 1949: 165). More than half lived on Saipan, Tinian, and Rota in the Marianas, and in the Caroline Islands over a quarter lived in the Palau Group and about a tenth on Ponape (Gallahue, 1949: 156). In the 1930s about half of the immigrants were Japanese families and the remainder were indentured labour from the Ryukyu Islands.

The initial phase of labour recruiting thus gave way to one in which large numbers of alien peasants, not entrepreneurs, were introduced to Oceania to operate a new agriculture managed by Europeans and staffed by Asians. It involved little contact with the indigenous way of life. The newly introduced group had no traditional rights to land and no means of subsistence except through the sale of their own labour.

While introducing new demographic elements to the population and forcing the importation, and sometimes the cultivation, of new foods to feed the newcomers, the changing labour situation involved an even greater effect. An indigene could now, within this newly imposed economic-cultural system, offer himself as a worker, be paid for his efforts, and as a result buy a number of introduced items. These goods, which were attractive because of their obvious application within the old system, included axes, food, tools, cloth, fish-hooks, and firearms. Labour had become a resource in a way hitherto unknown, and workers could cultivate alienated land which in terms of kinship and tenure was completely unrelated to them. New problems of labour, repatriation, and plural societies developed. Changes, too, could be seen in settlement patterns. Ports and associated facilities and services quickly developed. Small

settlements were built on plantations and, for easy transport to
near-by ports, elementary road patterns emerged and with time
became more complicated and of better quality.

THE MISSIONARIES

In some places missionaries facilitated change by creating some
degree of stability, yet in others their work resulted in discord.
Many missionaries were the first real pioneers (Grattan, 1963:
491–2) and in some places were the first to introduce European
goods to local people. The first organized mission was in Guam
where the Jesuits were active from the latter part of the seventeenth century (Stafford, 1905: 22). At the end of the eighteenth
century the London Missionary Society made contact with
peoples of eastern Polynesia and by 1835 missionary influence
was being felt further west in Fiji (Cargill, 1841: 95). By mid-
century its impact had touched the southern parts of Melanesia
and portions of Micronesia (Murphy, 1949: 164). The influence
of missions varied widely. In Polynesia heathenism was sup-
planted rather than eliminated and almost over-night missionaries had within their control an organized group receptive to
many foreign ideas and to the stimulus of trade and production
(Burton, 1949: 45). Leaders were persuaded to change by the
missionaries and there seems to be little doubt that the well-
organized, hierarchical social systems of Polynesia contributed
to rapid conversion after the leaders had set the initial example
and instructed the people to follow. In Melanesia, with a generally different social structure and small, discrete and less
structured social groupings, the passage towards Christianity
was considerably rougher.

Missions made a major contribution to the cessation of local
warfare. As a consequence, group participation in various
activities increased and greater attention could be paid to the
land. Missionaries by their presence or intervention frequently
helped regulate the operations of labour recruiters, land
speculators, and others who would violently upset the *status quo*.
The provision of a moderating climate helped administrators
extend law and order, and provided an atmosphere for experiments in agricultural extension.

The missions soon became even more directly involved in

THE ALIEN AND THE LAND OF OCEANIA 47

economic activity. Lack of funds from the motherland forced the missionaries to seek support from their converts. In some cases, they were persuaded to donate products such as arrow-root and coconut oil which the missionaries sold. In other cases the missionaries practised agriculture themselves. Most mission-aries using land did so for the sustenance of the church. A few more materialistic members of the group were not averse to land speculation and the 'sugar missionaries' of Hawaii are in this category. One is alleged to have bought and sold no fewer than forty-seven pieces of land. Fuchs reports that in 1852 one-third of the members of the Hawaiian Congregational mission possessed titles to an average of almost 500 acres per man (Fuchs, 1961: 17). Second-generation missionary families actively acquired land and ultimately formed a significant portion of the land and business élite of Hawaii (Fuchs, 1961: 22). But not only the Hawaiian missionaries acquired land; the 1878 native revolt in New Caledonia resulted from the removal of natives from first-class lands taken over by missionaries and settlers (Grattan, 1963: 458).

In general, however, things other than land accumulation concerned the missionaries. In the early eighteenth century the Jesuits of the Marianas ran several flourishing experimental farms (Stafford, 1905: 22) stocked with introduced cattle and horses. Local people were taught to use garden tools, tan bark and cultivate maize, tobacco, cocoa, and other American plants. In 1821, on the other side of the Pacific, the London Missionary Society imported cotton processing machinery and started cotton production in Moorea (Davies, 1961: 233). In many areas missionaries were responsible for the introduc-tion of new crops and agricultural techniques. Bananas were introduced by missions in a number of places. In Samoa the Chinese banana *Musa nana* was imported by the London Missionary Society (Barrau, 1956: 115). At a later period a wide range of vegetable crops were introduced into New Guinea by missionaries (Keleny, 1962: 13).

Missionaries were in the Pacific for the purpose of conversion, and they have been one of the major agencies of alien influence. Individual customs and traditional beliefs were attacked if they contravened Christian principle or impeded the progress of evangelism (Nayacakalou, 1963: 180). Hawaiian missionaries promoted the accumulation of property and conversely in other islands prominent indigenes, such as Pomare in Tahiti and Thakombau in Fiji, gained politically by their conversion to Christianity. Cook Island missionaries rewarded the faithful with land and caused much dissension between local groups (Crocombe, 1964: 67, 77).

Disturbances of social custom occurred in other areas as well. As the result of the work of missionaries the position of headman was considerably weakened in some areas on Guadalcanal. Pagan festivals and feasting which enabled prospective leaders to get to the top were discouraged among Christians (Hogbin, 1939: 214; 1964: 95). In some areas festivals were modified, given another name, and incorporated into the Christian year. The harvest festival, for instance, easily became part of modified local custom (Belshaw, 1949: 179). These changes were reflected in local agriculture. Where the importance of feasting diminished there was a marked decrease in food production.

The influence of the missionaries was immense and their role extremely complex. As much depended on the personality of the individual as on the behaviour of the group as a whole. In general, mission establishment resulted in marked changes in settlement. The church and the mission station drew people to the area for religious services, medical treatment, community activities, and also just because it was a centre of interest. It did not take long before houses were built near missions and enthusiastic converts were moving closer to the scene of activity. In the Cook Islands, for instance, converts previously living in hamlets were persuaded to build villages near mission headquarters on each of the islands. Settlement pattern changed in some areas by the addition of ribbon development along roads to the original nucleated clusters (Crocombe, 1964: 64–6).

MERCANTILE COMPANIES AND PLANTERS

With the growing attraction of the Pacific's resources, companies as well as individuals arrived to trade, to mine, and to exploit land. The most active were German, but British, Australian, French, and Japanese companies played an important part and in Hawaii corporate ownership of land for plantation purposes quickly became established. Many of the companies were financially powerful while some, advancing their own country's imperialistic ambitions, had quasi-government functions. The distribution of individual planters was more widespread than the companies, and together they brought plants, animals, techniques, employment opportunities, social changes, landscape modifications, and different settlement patterns to most parts of Oceania, especially to the high islands.

An early powerful company with a network of international interests was Godeffroy & Son of Hamburg which established itself in Hawaii in 1845 and Samoa in 1857. Later it extended its influence throughout Polynesia, in Fiji, New Guinea, and in parts of Micronesia (Grattan, 1963: 483; Yanaihara, 1940: 13). The company was interested in exporting coconut oil, then copra, and progressively changed its function to include plantation operation as well as trading and shipping.

Several attempts by the company to grow coffee, cocoa, rubber, and cotton were unsuccessful because of disease or unsatisfactory markets. The company itself failed in 1879 but was absorbed by another firm, D.H. & P.G.—Der Deutsche Handels-und-Plantagen-Gesellschaft der Südsee Inseln zu Hamburg. In the 1870s Hernsheim & Company were active in the Marshalls. In 1884 the New Guinea Kompagnie was granted sovereignty over the Bismarcks (Epstein, 1963: 292; Valentine, 1958: 97). This company, one of several working in New Guinea, was given authority to regulate land alienation, recruitment of native labour, and trade of foreign vessels (Valentine, 1958: 97). In 1887 the Jaluit Company was established and after monopolizing copra trade in the Marshalls extended activities to the Caroline Islands.

The German companies in Micronesia and Melanesia set the pattern for Japanese companies which followed and also for the Australian administration of New Guinea. In 1890 Ukichi Taguchi organized the South Seas Company which lasted in Ponape until 1895. Two companies, Kaitsūsha and Kōshinsha, were started in 1891 to trade with Truk. The latter was active in Palaus until 1914 (Kanehira, 1958: 4–5); the former failed. The Nanyō Kaihatsu Kabushiki Kaisha (South Seas Development Company), was active in the early 1920s in Saipan, Tinian, Rota, Palau, Ponape, and Dutch New Guinea and was predominantly interested in sugar production

(Yanaihara, 1940: 54–5). This company, which employed 15,000 Japanese in 1933, had 1,100 acres in sugar in 1920 and 30,000 acres by 1940 (Gallahue, 1949: 156). The South Seas Trading Company, Nanyō Boeki Kaisha, participated in the trade, commerce, and agriculture of Micronesia from Spanish times and operated in the Marianas; the Caroline Islands, especially Palau; Guam; the Gilbert Islands; and New Ireland.

In 1883 Burns Philp, an Australian company with head-quarters in Sydney, and the first real competitor to D.H. & P.G., arrived in the Pacific. During the last sixty years numerous organizations, such as Lever's Pacific Plantations in the Solo-mons, W. R. Carpenter, Morris Hedstrom, and A. B. Donald have been active in a number of fields but with much of their activity being concerned with copra production. In some areas cattle have been run by companies for meat and milk produc-tion and on Easter Island sheep grazing has been a company venture since 1871 (Wright, 1962: 46). Commercial agricultural companies are still active. Some provide the functions of experimentation and plant introduction, and Guadalcanal Plains Limited, concerned with growing rice and soya beans, is one of these (Holsheimer, 1966: 39). Hawaii's original 'big five' sugar factors are now companies of great economic power.

Mining organizations still offer employment. On Nauru and Ocean Islands for example, royalties on phosphate mined are paid to land owners. The German South Seas Phosphate Company developed mining at Angau, La Société Le Nickel in New Caledonia, and the Anglo-German Pacific Phosphate Company was established to develop Nauru and Ocean Islands. Exploitation eventually meant removal of the resource, destruction of the habitat, and finally the relocation of islanders (see Newbury, Chapter 7).

The Introduction of Plants

Although companies and planters focused attention on farming and did introduce plants and animals, such introduc-tions started when the first outsiders entered the Pacific and have continued ever since. Probably every tropical fruit and fibre has been grown at some time in the Pacific. Unsuccessful attempts were made to grow maize in the Marquesas in 1595 but since that time planting has met with success in a number of islands (Barrau, 1956: 104). Minor introductions have included crops such as rubber in Samoa and New Guinea, oranges in the Cook Islands, vanilla in the Society Islands, groundnuts in New Guinea, and macadamia nuts in Hawaii.

The coconut was a pre-contact food plant, but became a major plantation crop. Planters introduced techniques for converting coconut flesh into coconut oil (and later copra) to be shipped to Europe and the United States. Labourers took back to their communities knowledge of the new techniques and coconuts became a source of income to the commercially ambitious indigene who could gather them from family or group land and sell them to the local trader.

This fostered the development of a new and complex situation where aliens and local people were brought closer together. Local inhabitants sold coconuts for processing or made copra with sun-drying techniques and exchanged it for seed-nuts, tools, food, and cash (Yanaihara, 1940: 53). The selling of copra to German trading vessels in Micronesia started in the 1860s (Bascom, 1949: 121). The ease with which the coconut could be adapted to commercial use while still being produced within a subsistence system allowed experimental participation in the new venture by the local farmer with minimal effort or change.

No other commercial crop has challenged the importance of the coconut to indigenes in Oceania. Of much less significance in general, if not in specific areas, are introduced crops used essentially for food: sweet potato, cassava, and rice. The history of sweet potato is obscure but it is possible that Spanish vessels introduced it to the western Pacific in the sixteenth century from the Pacific coast of Mexico (Yen, 1963: 133; Barrau, 1955: 63; Merrill, 1954: 195; Keleny, 1962: 10). Cassava was introduced to places like Ponape by the Micronesians and the Spaniards about 1830 (Murphy, 1949: 165); to New Guinea from Samoa or Tonga in 1852 (Keleny, 1962: 12); and later to other Micronesian islands such as Kusaie by the Japanese. Barrau (1955: 61) states that two species of cassava, *Manihot esculenta* and *Manihot dulcis*, were introduced into Melanesia during last century and in all areas where there was contact with Europeans, its hardiness and yield made it one of the essential subsistence crops. It occasionally ousted established crops, especially where agriculturists were becoming increasingly concerned with cash cropping. Lea discusses the possibility of cassava today replacing the hard-to-grow and time-consuming yam in areas of New Guinea in Chapter 10 below. This substitution of one root crop for another was not uncommon (Watson, 1965: 443) but although rice is an extremely popular food in the Pacific, there is a general apathy towards cultivating this cereal. Islanders would rather buy than grow it (Barrau, 1955: 65; Keleny, 1962: 13).

Of the other plantation crops, sugar is the most important. Sugar production demanded a high degree of organization and was consequently most alien to the local scene. It was introduced to Fiji in 1857 and became a predominantly European and Indian enterprise unrelated to indigenous agriculture. In Hawaii it was introduced a few years earlier and in both territories it was the concern of large companies. After the First World War sugar temporarily became highly significant in the development of Saipan and Tinian. Here it was the monopoly of Nanyō Kohatsu Kabushiki Kaisha (Yanaihira, 1940: 61).

Coffee and cocoa were planted in limited areas and were found to be amenable to both plantation and indigenous production. Pineapples and oranges originally came in as food sources but quickly developed as plantation crops. The Fijian pineapple canning industry started in 1936 but was unable to stand international competition. The Hawaiian industry had the assistance of an assured American market. Banana growers in Fiji, Tonga, and Western Samoa, and producers of pineapples and oranges in the Cook Islands have depended on traditional links with the near-by New Zealand market and the lack of competition from elsewhere. Introduced varieties of bananas grown commercially in Fiji and Samoa were formerly a European enterprise supplying a flourishing market in Australia. The imposition of high tariffs in 1920 to protect Australian producers drove many island growers out of business and since then the New Zealand market has been supplied mainly by indigenous growers.

Plant introductions to Micronesia have played a particularly important part in altering the landscape and widening food and cash-producing resources. The introductions to Ponape (Bascom, 1949: 115–21; Murphy, 1949: 164–7; Sasuke, 1953: 159–70), to Palau (Barnett, 1965: 26–7; Vessell and Simonson,

1958: 296), and to Micronesia as a whole (Kanehira, 1933: 65–84) have been well documented. On Ponape sweet potatoes were introduced during the Spanish regime; pumpkin and squash and different varieties of bananas during the German period; during the Japanese period cassava, coffee, rice, pineapples, and a variety of fresh vegetables were introduced. The Japanese also initiated commercial sugar growing and copra making. According to Kanehira there are 156 species of cultivated introduced plants on Guam and out of a total of 550 species, 113 are of the South American origin and 112 Asian (Kanehira, 1933: 65). Before 1800 large numbers of plants came in on ships which had visited South America and the Philippines. After 1899 U.S. military vessels brought plants from Honolulu. Other introductions were from New Guinea while some arrived on ships of the Norddeutsche Lloyd Line which travelled between Micronesia and Sydney by way of Rabaul.

In general, the introduction of new plant varieties had a marked effect on indigenous agriculture. Improved varieties and new introductions were often found less time-consuming to cultivate and easier to grow than traditional crops and frequently these improved the quality of traditional crops. Cassava, for example, raised by the Japanese for export had a much improved and higher starch content than was normal (Vessell, 1958: 296). In some areas formerly dependent on swamp taro, the entire complexion of agriculture has changed following the introduction of two varieties not requiring irrigation.

Animals and Weeds

Polynesians received gifts of livestock from Cook and other early explorers. Vancouver, for example, presented Hawaiian chiefs with goats, cattle, and sheep, but these were not the earliest livestock introductions to the Pacific. Observers of Tinian under Spanish influence saw an estimated 10,000 livestock and cattle running wild (Midshipman, 1767: 129, 132) and in other Spanish islands cattle had been introduced as beasts of burden. In 1780 the King of Koror in the Palau Islands was presented with cattle by the East India Company and more than sixty years later they were reported to be wild and thriving (Tetens, 1958: 34). Europeans later introduced cattle to many other groups where they grazed clearings, foraged beneath coconut palms, or subsisted on indigenous feed. In most places a wide range of domesticated animals was unknown until introduced by aliens. In Ponape cows, carabao, horses, goats, rabbits, cats, ducks, turkeys, and geese were all introduced after first contact (Bascom, 1949: 115) and a similar situation existed in Palau (Barnett, 1965: 29). In Easter Island sheep were introduced in 1871 (Wright, 1962: 16).

Although livestock introductions provided a widened diet, beasts of burden, extension of existing land use, and improvements to local strains (Oakley, 1944: 222), other results were unfortunate. During the Japanese period in Micronesia, Okinawans brought in the giant African snail, *Achatina fulica*, for food (Murphy, 1949: 168). It was not appreciated by the local people and subsequently spread uncontrollably in parts of Micronesia and Melanesia (Spate, 1953: 155; Coolidge, 1951; 30).

In some places the introduction of livestock has done immeasurable damage to vegetation cover and soil stability. Livestock have damaged soils and vegetation on Easter Island; goats have caused havoc to vegetation in parts of Maui; and the placing of *kapu*[1] upon cattle on the island of Hawaii allowed them to multiply without enemies. In all cases, vegetation was eaten out and was replaced by undesirable weeds, shrubs, and grasses (Bryan, 1954: 20).

Unpalatable weed seeds were often introduced by accident in hay or straw to bed animals on ships and either carried on to the island attached to the animals or with the discarded bedding material. Many weeds were introduced in this way and became well established in areas already weakened by over-grazing or constant cropping (Merrill, 1954: 234, 270; Bryan, 1954: 21).

Weeds came first to island groups from the west with Melanesian, Polynesian, and Micronesian migrants. Between 1565 and 1815 they came in great numbers with the Spanish galleons, this time from the east, and Merrill cites 115 tropical American species established in Guam (Merrill, 1954: 191). On remote and isolated Christmas Island four species of weed were established within two years of alien settlement in 1888;

[1] A prohibition on unauthorized killing.

twelve species by 1897; and a total of thirty species by 1904 (Price, 1963: 188). Among the more undesirable weeds are elephantopus, lantana, and Indian lotus in the Society Islands; mikania and lantana in Samoa and Fiji; *Leucaena glauca* in the Marianas (Barrau, 1956: 6); prickly pear (Mune and Parham, 1956: 12) and *Psidium guajava* (guava) in Fiji (Ward, 1965: 75). Weeds such as these pose a major problem, a threat to land resources and an impediment to both subsistence and commercial agriculture.

Changed Techniques

The introduction of new tools such as the Spanish plough in Guam, the Japanese pick in the Palau, the spade and the hoe in the Cook Islands, the copra knife and the steel axe throughout the Pacific wrought unprecedented and at times staggering changes in the landscape, the application of labour to land, and the close-knit web of man-land and social relationships. The introduction of the axe alone in New Guinea brought 'revolutionary changes in quantitative and qualitative relations between people and land, and as well, significant shifts in the ecological balance' (Spate, 1953: 170).

New crops were planted in rows and new tools were used for clearing, weeding, and sometimes cultivation. In some areas burning and over-grazing were introduced for the first time (Wright, 1962: 16). In the New Guinea highlands, Spate notes increased run-off, unstable surfaces, slides, slips, man-made swamps, ridges stripped of forest—a combination of events which, if allowed to deteriorate, 'may result in the creation of a really distressed area' (Spate, 1953: 170-1). McAuley, too, highlights the relatively recent and complicated changes which have taken place in New Guinea (McAuley, 1948, 1952a, 1952b).

Under Japanese influence on Ponape, continuous use of land was substituted for traditional fallowing (Bascom, 1949: 127); in Tahiti a new type of shifting agriculture developed by Chinese immigrants resulted in serious soil erosion in formerly stable areas (Barrau, 1956: 27). The same type of problem developed on Truk in both deforested areas and sweet-potato-growing areas (Pelzer, 1947: 76), while in the Cook Islands, as elsewhere, emphasis on new cash crops and new eating patterns resulted in the neglect of traditional crops (Barrau, 1956: 108).

Everything was not on the debit side and 'useful' techniques were adopted sometimes for short periods, sometimes permanently. In terms of a European ethnocentric outlook, new tools and techniques widened the cash-cropping potential, increased the production of cash and subsistence crops, introduced an ingredient of efficiency, and also brought hidden unemployment (see Lea, Chapter 10).

Changes in tradition were introduced and encouraged in a number of ways. Frequently the seeds of change were sown by individual planters or plantation companies. The speed and certainty of change was often a matter administrations attempted to control. Success was varied. During the late nineteenth and early twentieth centuries cash cropping was established in a number of areas by a combination of persuasion and force. In Papua the early colonial government encouraged commercial agriculture. This was not considered sufficient. In 1894, coercive ordinances forced indigenes to plant a minimum number of seedling coconuts (Cheetham, 1962: 367). Ordinances of 1918–19 required every male villager to spend sixty days a year tending cash crops, and as an incentive the government supplied seeds, tools, and remitted taxes.

In 1887 German planting ordinances in New Guinea insisted that villagers grow food crops as well as coconuts for sale (Cheetham, 1962: 368); more recently in New Britain in order to regulate planting, cacao plots have had to be registered and planted with a minimum of 500 trees (Irwin, 1963: 38; McAuley, 1952b: 276). In Micronesia both the Germans and later the Japanese ordered forest clearing and planting by indigenes (Pelzer, 1947: 76; Mahony, 1960: 73). A totally different approach took place in Fiji where Sir Arthur Gordon instituted a system of district taxations to be paid in copra, cotton, candlenuts, tobacco, maize, coffee, or other produce (Grattan, 1963: 479).

As cash cropping became established, observation of the power of its monetary rewards to modify standards of living proved, in some groups at least, to be a major stimulus towards further change. And this, like all other stimuli of change, was a more potent factor in places where contact was frequent (Epstein, 1965: 191).

Land Tenure: A Sensitive Area

Probably without exception, the alien intruders had a well-developed sense of individual ownership and the concept of property having monetary value. Broek (1966: 72) states 'each society . . . perceives and interprets its physical surroundings and its relations to other lands through the prism of its own way of life'. The intruder, through his 'prism', perceived the new land as a particular type of resource. It had monetary value and cash production capability. It could be subdivided, individually owned, and bought and sold as a commodity. The outsider had a number of ready-made interlocking notions and patterns of behaviour concerned with land. These were alien to those developed locally where the people had quite different perceptions of the function of the environment. Yet every effort was made to impose them on native peoples.

Then (as now) most visitors to Oceania were critical of indigenous systems of land tenure. The modern-day investigator (Brantjes, 1955: 26; Fox and Cumberland, 1962: 321), the early administrator, and the planter of the later nineteenth century have all been highly critical of systems which, to them, were unfamiliar. Outside observers have frequently blamed land tenure for numerous economic ills affecting an area. But, frequently ignorant of local culture, alien reformers have rarely realized that forced change may very well 'destroy the economic basis of . . . [the] clan system' and thereby destroy essential 'ceremonial activities in which they [the indigenes] find much of their pleasure and excitement' (Geddes, 1960: 54–6).

Changes in land tenure have been of two types. First as a result of alienation, indigenes have through sales, leases, manipulation, or plain chicanery lost rights to large areas of land. Such changes occurred in many places, including Hawaii, New Caledonia, New Britain, the Solomons, Fiji, Samoa, and the phosphate islands of Nauru, Ocean, and Makatea (see Newbury, Chapter 7). The native peoples usually had limited understanding of what was involved in land transfers or what commitments were being undertaken by a few for the group as a whole. Frequently indigenes thought that negotiations transferred only 'usufruct' rather than ownership of the land.

Yet hundreds and thousands of acres of native lands were claimed by aliens before stable governments had been established. Later, court investigations in territories like Fiji and Samoa upheld claims to smaller but still significant areas. These were frequently the best lands (West, 1961: 17) and their disposition together with the treatment of indigenous peoples over land matters almost invariably sowed the seeds of future discontent. The bitterness generated can still be seen in ambivalent attitudes towards Europeans today (Epstein, 1963: 295). The re-location of peoples after land 'sales' and the taking of unused land by governments created overpopulation in areas allotted for settlement or on greatly diminished traditional lands. For example this type of situation, together with government confiscation of land for institutional and military use, led to the development of a landless class in Ponape (Bascom, 1949: 127).

The second type of change involved modifications of tenure systems of indigenous-held land (see Crocombe, Chapter 9). No place remained unaffected by such changes. Hawaiian land tenure was almost completely transformed from quasi-feudal ownership to individualism. A modified form of individual holding was introduced in Tonga. Interference by the government of Western Samoa in the 1920s in an attempt to 'reform' land tenure brought violent reactions. And on Pentecost, the possibility of individual ownership, out of keeping with other customs, introduced dilemmas concerned with inheritance and claims to the fruits of harvest (Lane, 1961: 1). Incompatible notions of land tenure and the imposition of modified systems have been the source of conflict in many areas (Mason, 1953b: 98; Barrau, 1956: 39; Geddes, 1960: 54; Keesing, 1945: 112; France, 1969).

Moves towards individual tenure have affected custom beyond direct relations with land. There are a number of cases in which groups have tried to change to a patrilineal system in order to secure inheritance rights for their children in areas where land tenure systems have been modified. Initial adjustments may involve just one element of the total fabric of activities and relationships, but having taken place, a change in that one element may necessitate compensating changes throughout the entire matrix.

THE EFFECT OF WAR

Wars of all kinds have profoundly changed the geography of Oceania. Invasions of one group by another are recorded in the present racial composition. The expectation of attack in the past was reflected in settlement, land-use patterns, and the siting of villages. More recent wartime activities are reflected directly in the relics of mess-halls and airstrips, wrecked ships, concrete fortifications, and, less directly but more significantly, in the social and economic changes that came during and after the Second World War.

In pre-contact days in many parts of Oceania, inter-clan or inter-island warfare ranging from mild skirmishes to well-planned battles were expectable interruptions to the equilibrium of life and economy. The cessation of 'local' warfare, frequently the result of the work of missionaries as in Fiji (Nayacakalou, 1963: 180) or of administrations or occasionally as the result of sheer exhaustion by warring parties—a request for government conciliation was made in the New Hebrides in 1908 (Baker, 1929: 19)—has been of major consequence in modifying the Pacific *genre de vie*, the look of the land, and relations with it.

The Second World War

Although there have been alien-generated military campaigns for 400 years starting with the burning of houses by Magellan or the war of extermination against Guam indigenes between 1672 and 1695 (Stafford, 1905: 13–15), nothing has so drastically affected life in Oceania as the Second World War. The greatest changes took place in Melanesia and Micronesia. With reference to the war's effect, for example, in New Guinea, Spate says, 'four years of war probably did more to alter the concepts and desires of the people of New Guinea than the preceding fifty-five years of European and Australian control' (Spate, 1953: 151). In times of war there are two main changes affecting geographical relations. Short-term changes included the entry of foreign troops, the drafting of native peoples, and the feeding and accommodating of these groups; long-term changes included permanently altered relationships with land, resources, and traditional institutions.

The war in the Pacific lasted from 1941 to 1945 and one of the first major upheavals was the influx of thousands of American servicemen into bases in Polynesia and Melanesia. Large numbers of Japanese soldiers occupied major strategic points in Micronesia, New Guinea, New Britain, and the Solomon Islands. Australian troops entered New Guinea.

In every area, plantations or native gardens were destroyed to make way for airstrips, encampments, tank farms, and fortifications. On some of the Marshall Islands, for instance, 50 to 75 per cent of the coconut palms were felled by Japanese clearing land for defence installations (MacMillan, 1946: 9). Cash production in places like the Solomon Islands came to a standstill (Belshaw, 1949: 183) and the former flourishing Japanese sugar-growing industry in Micronesia ended (Gallahue, 1949: 157). In some areas a new, more intensified type of subsistence agriculture arose to supplement military supplies and in some cases to support troops entirely from the lands they occupied. In New Guinea, the Solomon Islands, Fiji, and New Caledonia experimental food-farms were pioneered (Bowman, 1948: 40; Holsheimer, 1966: 35), while in Truk, with their outside sources of supply cut, Japanese troops became farmers, drained swamps, and planted quick-growing food crops (Pelzer, 1947: 77). At the same time, in a sporadic unorganized manner, food crops were grown for sale in a few areas by local people living close to military bases. To support the alien war effort, large numbers of indigenes were drafted into labour forces in the Solomon Islands (Belshaw, 1949: 184; Shephard, 1945: 182), in New Guinea (Spate, 1953: 151), and in Japanese-held territory in Micronesia (Beardsley, 1964: 214).

As the result of bombing and strafing many areas of both garden and commercial plantation were destroyed, and villages were demolished. At Rabaul allied bombing destroyed most of the substantial buildings and houses, port facilities, and roads (Epstein, 1963: 300). Hogbin tells of the aerial devastation of the village of Busama in north-east New Guinea, the deaths of many of the villagers, and the fleeing into the forest, with what they could carry, of those who were spared (Hogbin, 1951: 1, 10). The village was not rehabilitated until 1950.

In the Marshall Islands thousands of soldiers foraged the countryside, destroyed livestock, and even used the heart of the coconut palm as food (Mason, 1953a: 161). Each heart taken meant the death of a tree. Parts of Likiep, Wotje, and Eniwetok atolls were completely devastated while Palau Island suffered extensively (MacMillan, 1946: 2, 23). On Puluwat atoll, in the Carolines, 6,000 soldiers were living off the land in 1946 and had already eaten all the pigs and the taro (Wright, 1946: 128).

After the war all activity came to a standstill in many areas. Former plantations were overgrown with vines. Native peoples had been displaced and traditional garden areas were uncultivated. Employment opportunities with the military were no longer available and pre-war Japanese plantations and associated processing plants were no longer working. The 70,000 to 80,000 or more Japanese who had occupied the islands for two decades had left. In Micronesia native workers gradually returned to their own islands. Indigenous agriculture was at its lowest ebb and remained that way until population redistribution was completed. Some areas were so badly bombed they remained practically useless for years (Murphy, 1949: 163). The local reaction against Japan and Japanese institutions was so strong that in a number of places plantations formerly cultivated by Japanese remained untouched. These areas frequently reverted to forest or became smothered by lantana or other introduced weeds. This state of affairs continued during the second half of the 1940s.

The long-term changes are more difficult to define and identify. They are concerned with the more permanent relations between man and land and between man and his own community and institutions. In many parts of wartime Polynesia and Melanesia indigenes had worked for wages, often at a relatively high level (Hogbin, 1951: 19), had been members of military forces (Spate, 1953: 151), or had been entrepreneurs operating on the fringes of large troop concentrations. Wage employment, military training, and in some instances profiteering had given economic and political training of a sort which could not be shed at war's end. A significant group had been separated from traditional ways and after the war this group had little incentive to return to traditional subsistence agriculture. This situation was strengthened in areas where war damage compensation was awarded in cash (Epstein, 1963: 301; Spate, 1953: 154). These funds were available for investment in a number of competing economic enterprises, most of which had not previously been known.

NATIONAL ADMINISTRATION AS A FACTOR IN GEOGRAPHIC CHANGE

In the early years of Pacific contact adventurers and traders came, stayed, and went, and in doing so contributed to change. These persons acted as individuals. At a later period more homogeneous groups occupied territories in a more permanent manner. These groups, frequently dominated by a particular nationality, tended to share similar attitudes to people, and perceptions of resources. Groups of German traders, French planters, Spanish missionaries, and American sailors each had their own particular outlook derived from the culture of the homeland. When these values were strengthened and modified by the addition of further settlers and an administration of the same nationality, the impact on the indigene was strong, decisive, and relatively uniform.

Each national group has had a distinctive impact on the land and the lives of the indigenous people. The relative effectiveness of these impacts depends first on a dynamic aspect of quality: the ability of an outside group to cause change. A second element is duration: the length of the period of alien government. A third is frequency: the number of interchanges that take place between the aliens and the indigenes. The actual force of impact is essentially governed by quality, duration, and frequency together with the inherent resistance of the indigenous peoples.

The time at which contact took place is important but is related directly to quality. There was, for example, a vast difference between the very early governing of the Marianas by the Spaniards, and the administration of Micronesia by the United States as a United Nations Trust Territory. More recently there has been a difference between the governing of Western Samoa before the Second World War by New Zealand and after the war by the same country when more sensitive and sympathetic administration characterized the governing of most Trust Territories. The degree to which national impact can contribute to change is uncertain but deserves considerably more attention than it has previously been given (Spate in Fosberg, 1963: 253, 263). Its contribution to changed techniques and land tenure have been noted elsewhere.

Britain, France, and Germany

By far the greatest impact was made by the three major colonial powers, Germany, France, and Great Britain. During the nineteenth century Britain dominated most of Oceania through the Royal Navy (Oliver, 1958: 87); missions in Tonga, Fiji, the Cook Islands, Samoa, New Hebrides, the Solomons, and New Guinea; and the activities of her planters and traders. Her influence was felt first when Drake entered the Pacific in 1578 and almost continuously after Wallis discovered Tahiti in 1767. Grattan (1963: 453) describes British Pacific policy as one of 'minimum intervention' characterized by inaction and punctuated during crises by expedient solutions imposed 'under the threat of impending chaos'. Although the British were sporadically interested in Spanish gold and harassment for a century and a half after Drake, they were, during the nineteenth century, reluctant colonizers forced to take part in the Pacific intrigues but more interested in less isolated territories closer to home. Britain finally lost her indifference under the prodding of Australia and New Zealand (Oliver, 1958: 87), and ultimately extended authority over Fiji in 1874, Papua in 1884, the New Hebrides (with France) in 1887, the Solomon Islands in 1900, and in the same year, Tonga.

Britain practised a fumbling type of paternalism oriented towards protecting native interests. Colonial policy in practice produced direct administration of the larger group by outsiders but self-government at the local or village level. This tended to insulate the indigene from the outsider and segregate and protect each local community from excessive alien influence (West, 1961: 171). Planters did extend and modify the character of agriculture but protection against alienation or interference with the traditional ways tended to preserve the *status quo* and inhibit the minor changes necessary to accommodate new circumstances. Because the rural dweller was largely separated from the alien and from interference with land tenure, geographic change in rural areas was very much less than in comparable areas administered by Germany, Japan, or France.

Britain's influence was broad and political; contact at the local level was minimal.

German colonialism was initiated by competent, aggressive traders and planters well supported by German financial interests. Trading companies prepared the way for eventual German administration. They even drafted detailed guidelines for trade, land alienation, and administration. There were never large numbers of Germans in the Pacific but dynamic and potent administrative policies tended to offset this fact. In the 1880s, the German government became aggressively imperialistic, annexing and purchasing territory. Activities were concentrated in the western Pacific from the Marianas to New Guinea with Samoa as an eastern outlier.

Rule was direct and authoritarian, and was concerned with supporting commercial plantation agriculture and trade (Oliver, 1958: 96–9). Local legislation aided the importation and transfer of labour about the Pacific, and initiated a system of private titles to land (Murphy, 1949: 165). Wherever they were, Germans emphasized advanced technology in farming, processing, and mining (Yanaihara, 1940: 22). They staffed experimental farms and plant introduction stations; imposed planting and clearing ordinances (Pelzer, 1947: 77); in many areas built good roads and valuable public works; and established land surveys. When they officially relinquished their claim to a number of territories they left a substantial inheritance: a commercial veneer imposed on local subsistence agriculture, thriving plantation areas, and, as a concomitant, alienated land and dispossessed indigenes (Irwin, 1963: 36). It has been estimated that in New Guinea, most of the approximately 500 plantations operating in 1940 had been started by German planters (Spate, 1953: 155).

French policy was guided by the belief that French principles, institutions, and culture were superior to those of Oceania. There was no attempt to preserve or protect traditional ways and assimilation was the policy (see Newbury, Chapters 6 and 7). In order to speed the process, cash cropping was encouraged, land holdings were individualized, and land was taken up without difficulty by Europeans (West, 1961: 72, 83). French colonies were run as a convenience to the mother country. Trade ties were strong and direct with France.

Development priorities always tended to be in the interests first of France, second the alien settlers, and lastly the indigenes. Initial policies of settlement and ease of land-holding led to greater alien settlement than anywhere except Hawaii. This group identified with the area in a very different way from British settlers in British-held islands. Politically, economically, and socially French settlers lived in France overseas. Because of the efficacy of the assimilation process in French Polynesia and New Caledonia, traditional ways quickly succumbed. Obvious problems of a plural society such as beset Fiji were dodged by consciously gallicizing every aspect of living (Beaglehole, 1953: 78).

Less Important Influences

Micronesia is in many ways a laboratory of change, most of it having been influenced by Spain, Germany, Japan, and the United States (Mead, 1955: 128–9) while the Gilbert Islands have been dominated by Britain for three-quarters of a century. The effects have been uneven as every group has had a different experience with the outsider. Although Germany assumed authority over the Marianas and the Caroline Islands after the Spanish–American war, its influence was felt much more in the western Carolines than in the more northerly group (Gallahue, 1949: 156) and despite German, Japanese, and United States influence the Spanish atmosphere still pervades the Marianas in language, food preference, recreation, family life, and church (Mason, 1953b: 96).

Japanese colonial policy resulted in spectacular changes in Pacific geography over a very short period of time—twenty-seven years—from 1919 to 1946. Japanese trade influence had been active for several decades before. Policy was one of intensive economic exploitation in the interests of the home-country and of Japanese settlers. Such activities were most effective in creating in the local people an awareness of world commerce and a taste for foreign material goods. The greatest influence was found in certain islands of the Marianas and in Palau.

Like German rule, the Japanese administration was direct and authoritarian. It encouraged distinct segregation of the two groups and actively engendered a feeling of inferiority among the people (Barnett, 1965: 16). Agriculture, which included the commercial growing of sugar-cane, coconut, cassava, Japanese vegetables, and experimental rice, frequently involved forced labour for cultivation (MacMillan, 1946: 16). It did, however, by means of subsidies and incentive payment, greatly extend areas of commercial land, improve the quality of produce, and increase the numbers of local pigs. Community and agricultural development went hand in hand but it was forcibly imposed development with the long-run objective of trade with Japan. Changes were spectacular. Price, enthusiastic about the 'South Seas agricultural revolution', observed that 'the Spaniards surveying barren Saipan could hardly visualize rich fields of sugar cane twenty feet high . . . producing in Japanese times six million dollars worth of sugar every year' (Price, 1944: 230).

The United States has had a narrower role as a Pacific colonial power except in Hawaii. Like Britain a reluctant colonizer, her interests were usually of a military nature. Initally her prime interest was the possession of strategic bases within the vast area of the Pacific. Outside Hawaii, where active economic exploitation was practised, the Department of the Navy administered American Samoa, Guam, and for a short period the Trust Territory of the Pacific Islands. It was concerned largely with the operation and maintenance of bases which it eventually secured. There was little active economic development. Some attempts were made to introduce plants at experimental farms but the greatest changes involved the extension of medical and social services and the development of a corps of indigenous workers attracted to centres where the Navy, or later the civil administration, offered employment.

Little conscious effort was made to cushion the effect of contact on traditional ways and it was generally understood that in time the outsiders' way of life would be accepted. Policy was never as effective as it could have been because the constantly changing staff allowed little continuity or time for the outsider to learn local ways. Rule was permissive rather than authoritarian and as long as adequate social and medical care was being dispensed, the administration cared little whether traditional ways were maintained or not. The end result of the policy, although it was not stated in so many words, tended to de-emphasize rural economic pursuits and emphasize wage employment and concomitant urbanism. These, together with ease of entry to the mainland, seemed to be the steps necessary to lead to a migration away from the homeland towards the United States.

Australian and New Zealand interests in the Pacific go back a long way. They exerted pressure on Great Britain to become colonially active, and their resolution in this direction stemmed as much from fear of Germany as from colonial enthusiasm. Australia has been by far the more active of the two. In both cases some degree of authoritarianism was maintained through the retention of aspects of German legislation. In New Guinea after the First World War the policy was to encourage a settler-type economy which although strengthening the financial situation did little for the inhabitants as a whole. On the other hand, some attempts were made in Papua and Western Samoa to govern on behalf of the indigenous inhabitants. This has been so especially since the Second World War when, for example, Australia as trustee for the United Nations committed herself to laying 'the foundations in New Guinea of a permanent, willing partnership between the natives and the Australian people' (McAuley, 1952a: 153). In order to achieve this goal it has been policy to bring the entire territory under control (Rose, 1966: 97). This implies the preparation of previously inaccessible areas for a modified type of 'alien' influence repeating, in some respects, the history of contact which the remainder of the territory experienced at an earlier date.

Western Samoa, Nauru, and Fiji already have independence; Hawaii has statehood, and the Cook Islands have gained internal self-government. It will only be a matter of time before most territories throw off the bonds of alien control. Some of the influences associated with earlier administration will remain and may be accepted with a firmness unknown in the past. Changes in relations with the environment will most certainly take place, possibly at a faster rate than previously as the result of self-generation rather than alien imposition. Future adoptions and adaptations will bear little relationship with the former administering country. Those which do may last only so long as first-generation settlers and 'alien traditional' ties remain. Sources of innovation will be wider as the result of improvements in transport and in all types of communication, and through the influence of agents of international foundations and organizations. The most potent force is likely to lie with the dominant trading partner or the country providing the greatest number of tourists. The principles of quality, duration, and frequency will remain in effect but the emphases and the participants will change as will the indigenous attitude towards change.

CONCLUSION

In many parts of Oceania there have been examples of marked resistance to change and everywhere there has been some degree of resistance. Why groups such as the Samoans in Polynesia or the people of Yap in Micronesia have retained so much of their old ways is largely unknown and makes for interesting debate. Much depends on the frequency and intensity of contacts but this does not explain all. For example in Micronesia, the Marshallese and the Palauans were not averse to sampling Western culture but the '. . . people of Yap in the Western Carolines stand almost alone against the foreigner, rejecting his advances and maintaining their old culture with surprising conservatism' (Mason, 1953*b*: 97). The nature of the social structure is an important factor determining the potential of a culture to adapt. There is no agreement whatever as to what part of culture takes the lead in change (Sahlins, 1964: 136).

Probably no area has been free from some type of hostility towards the intruder, and change has been resisted, if only temporarily. The Samoans strongly resisted an attempt on the part of the administration to interfere with traditional land tenure practice (Keesing, 1945: 112); the New Caledonians revolted and killed a large number of settlers as the result of land disputes; the Solomon Islanders and people from various other groups spurned the use of European implements in favour of their traditional digging stick (Hogbin, 1939: 166); while in parts of Papua subsistence farmers were completely indifferent to cash cropping (Cheetham, 1962–3: 69).

In summarizing the degree of acceptance of the outsider by the indigene, Gladwin says that the Micronesians with few exceptions retained their core culture—their social organization, values, and economy—while adopting a wide array of superficial technological changes. In Polynesia, he says, the changes were more sweeping and often devastating, while in Melanesia frequent hostility, suspicion, and bloodshed brought about minimal acceptance of foreign leadership except when imposed by force (Gladwin, 1961: 136).

Geographic change in the Pacific, the theme of this paper, is ultimately a function of missionary, economic, and national impacts; the adaptability of the indigenous culture, and resistance of the environment. Certain environments are inherently easier to modify than others. There are of course other variables not accounted for. Adaptability and resistance must change with time as does virtually every other factor involved. Adaptability certainly changes with increased momentum as more members of the indigenous group accept elements of the alien culture. It may be foolish to look at the inevitable as a process of disintegration as is so common. A more positive approach is taken by Sahlins who states: 'Advanced societies in displacing backward peoples or harnessing them to their own progress become agents of a disruption that frees the backward region from the dead hand of its own past. . . . Hinterlands are not merely disorganized by dominant cultures, they become committed to mainstreams of progress as tributaries of it' (Sahlins, 1964: 143).

BIBLIOGRAPHY

Baker, J. R. 1929. *Man and Animals in the New Hebrides*, London.

Barnett, H. G. 1965. *Being a Palauan*, New York.

Barrau, J. 1955. *Subsistence Agriculture in Melanesia*, Noumea.

—— 1956. *Polynesian and Micronesian Subsistence Agriculture*, Noumea.

—— 1960. 'Plant Introduction in the Tropical Pacific', *Pacific Viewpoint*, vol. 1, pp. 1–9.

—— (ed.). 1963. *Plants and the Migrations of Pacific Peoples*, Honolulu.

—— 1965. 'L'Humide et le sec', *Journ. Poly. Soc.*, vol. 74, pp. 329–46.

Bascom, W. 1949. 'Subsistence Farming on Ponape', *New Zealand Geographer*, vol. 5, pp. 115–29.

Beaglehole, E. 1953. 'Good Administration and Self-Government in the South Pacific', *Proceedings of the 7th Pacific Science Congress*, vol. 7, pp. 77–83.

Beardsley, C. 1964. *Guam Past and Present*, Tokyo and Rutland.

Belshaw, C. S. 1949. 'Trends in Motives and Organization in Solomon Island Agriculture', *Proceedings of the 7th Pacific Science Congress*, vol. 7, pp. 171–89.

—— 1965. *Traditional Exchange and Modern Markets*, Englewood Cliffs.

Bowman, R. G. 1948. 'Land Settlement in New Guinea', *New Zealand Geographer*, vol. 4, pp. 29–68.

Brantjes, J. M. J. 1955. 'Agricultural Development of Netherlands New Guinea', *South Pacific Commission Quarterly Bulletin*, vol. 5, pp. 25–7.

Broek, J. O. M. 1965. *Geography, its Scope and Spirit*, Columbus, Ohio.

Bryan, E. H., Jr. 1954. *The Hawaiian Chain*, Honolulu.

Burton, J. W. 1949. *Modern Missions in the South Pacific*, London.

Cargill, D. 1841. *The Memoirs of Mrs. Margaret Cargill*, London.

Cheetham, R. J. 1962–3. 'The Development of Indigenous Agriculture, Land Settlement, and Rural Credit Facilities in Papua and New Guinea', *The Papua and New Guinea Agricultural Journal*, vol. 15, pp. 67–78.

Coolidge, H. J. 1951. 'Science Lends a Hand', *Paradise of Pacific*, vol. 63, pp. 30–1.

Crocombe, R. G. 1964. *Land Tenure in the Cook Islands*, Melbourne.

Dampier, W. 1697. *A New Voyage Around the World*, London.

Davies, J. 1961. *The History of the Tahitian Mission 1799–1830*, Cambridge.

Dewey, A. G. 1964. 'The Noumea Javanese—An Urban Community in the South Pacific', *South Pacific Bulletin*, vol. 14, pp. 18–26.

Epstein, T. S. 1963. 'European Contact and Tolai Economic Development: A Schema of Economic Growth', *Economic Development and Cultural Change*, vol. 11, pp. 289–307.

—— 1965. 'Economic Change and Differentiation in New Britain', *The Economic Record*, vol. 41, pp. 173–92.

Fosberg, F. R. (ed.). 1963. *Man's Place in the Island Ecosystem*, Honolulu.

Fox, J. W. and Cumberland, K. B. (eds.). 1962. *Western Samoa: Land, Life and Agriculture in Tropical Polynesia*, Christchurch.

France, P. 1969. *The Charter of the Land*, London.

Fuchs, L. A. 1961. *Hawaii Pono: A Social History*, New York.

Gallahue, E. E. 1949. 'The Changing Agricultural Economy of Micronesia', *Proceedings of the 7th Pacific Science Congress*, vol. 7, pp. 155–8.

Geddes, W. R. 1960. 'The Human Background', in U.N.E.S.C.O., *Symposium on the Impact of Man on Humid Tropics Vegetation*, Goroka, pp. 42–56.

Gladwin, T. 1961. 'Oceania', in Hsu, F. L. K. (ed.), 1961, *Psychological Anthropology*, Homewood, Illinois, pp. 135–71.

Goodenough, W. H. 1963. *Cooperation in Change*, New York.

Grattan, C. H. 1963. *The Southwest Pacific to 1900*, Ann Arbor.

Hogbin, H. I. 1939. *Experiments in Civilization: The Effects of European Culture on a Native Community of the Solomon Islands*, London.

Hogbin, H. I. 1951. *Transformation Scene: The Changing Culture of a New Guinea Village*, London.

—— 1964. *A Guadalcanal Society: The Kaoka Speakers*, New York.

Holscheimer, J. G. H. 1966. 'Investigations for Mechanized Rice Production on the Guadalcanal Plains', *South Pacific Bulletin*, vol. 16, pp. 35–9.

Irwin, P. G. 1963. 'European Influence in the Blanche Bay District of New Britain', *Australian Geographer*, vol. 9, pp. 34–42.

Kanehira, R. 1933. *Flora Micronesia*, translated 1958, Tokyo.

Keesing, F. M. 1945. *The South Seas in the Modern World*, New York.

Keleny, G. P. 1962. 'The Origin and Introduction of Basic Food Crops of the New Guinea People', *Papua and New Guinea Agricultural Journal*, vol. 15, pp. 7–13.

Kelly, C. (ed.) 1966. *La Austrialia del Espíritu Santo*, 2 vols., Cambridge.

Lane, R. B. 1961. *Land Tenure and Residence Rules of North Pentecost, New Hebrides*, mimeo, paper read at 10th Pacific Science Congress, Honolulu.

Lewthwaite, G. R. 1962. 'Land Life and Agriculture to Mid-Century', in Fox and Cumberland, 1962: 130–76.

McArthur, N. n.d. *The Population of the Pacific Islands*, part 6, mimeo, Canberra.

—— 1967. *Island Populations of the Pacific*, Canberra.

McAuley, J. 1948. 'Agricultural Production in New Guinea', *South Pacific*, vol. 3, pp. 73–81.

—— 1952a. 'White Settlement in Papua and New Guinea', *South Pacific*, vol. 5, pp. 250–5.

—— 1952b. 'Mechanization and Collectives and Native Agriculture', *South Pacific*, vol. 6, pp. 276–81.

McGusty, V. W. T. 1953. 'The Decline and Recovery of the Fijian Race', *Proceedings of the 7th Pacific Science Congress*, vol. 7, pp. 51–62.

MacMillan, H. G. 1946. *Report on Agricultural Conditions in Micronesia*, U.S. Commercial Co. Economic Survey, Honolulu.

Mahony, F. 1960. *Taro Cultivation in Truk: Taro Culture and Beliefs*, Anthropological Working Paper no. 6, Guam.

Mason, L. 1953a. 'Re-establishment of a Copra Industry in the Marshall Islands', *Proceedings of the 7th Pacific Science Congress*, vol. 7, pp. 159–62.

—— 1953b. 'An Interpretation of "Native Custom" in a Changing Oceania Society', *Proceedings of the 7th Pacific Science Congress*, vol. 7, pp. 95–102.

Maude, H. E. 1959. 'Spanish Discoveries in the Central Pacific', *Journ. Poly. Soc.*, vol. 68, pp. 285–322.

Mead, M. (ed.) 1955. *Cultural Patterns and Technical Change*, New York.

Merrill, E. D. 1954. 'The Botany of Cook's Voyages and its Unexpected Significance in Relation to Anthropology, Biogeography and History', *Chronica Botanica*, vol. 14, pp. 161–383.

'A Midshipman'. 1767. *The History of Commodore Anson's Voyage Round the World . . . Sept. 1740 to June 1744*, London.

Mune, T. L. and Parham, J. W. 1956. *The Declared Noxious Weeds of Fiji and Their Control*, Fiji Department of Agriculture Bulletin, no. 31, Suva.

Murphy, R. E. 1949. 'Changing Patterns of Agriculture in the Easternmost Caroline Islands', *Proceedings of the 7th Pacific Science Congress*, vol. 7, pp. 163–70.

Nayacakalou, R. R. 1963. 'Nature of Change in Living Patterns of Pacific Island Man', in Fosberg, 1963: 175–86.

N.I.D. 1943–4. Naval Intelligence Division, *The Pacific Islands*, vols. 2 and 3, London.

Oakley, R. G. 1944. 'Agriculture in Guam', *Foreign Agriculture*, vol. 8, pp. 215–24.

Oliver, D. L. 1958. *The Pacific Islands*, Cambridge, Mass.

Parnaby, O. W. 1964. *Britain and the Labor Trade in the Southwest Pacific*, Durham, North Carolina.

Pelzer, K. J. 1947. 'Agriculture in the Truk Islands', *Foreign Agriculture*, vol. 11, pp. 74–81.

Pospisil, L. J. 1964. *The Kapauku Papuans of West New Guinea*, New York.

Price, A. G. 1963. *The Western Invasions of the Pacific and its Continents . . . 1513–1958*, London.

Price, W. 1944. *Japan's Islands of Mystery*, New York.

Rose, A. 1966. *Dilemmas Down Under*, Princeton.

Safford, W. E. 1905. 'Useful Plants of the Island of Guam', *The United States National Herbarium*, vol. 9.

Sahlins, M. D. 1964. 'Culture and Environment', in S. Tax (ed.), *Horizons of Anthropology*, Chicago, pp. 132–47.

St. John, H. 1953. 'Origin of the Sustenance Plants of the Polynesians', *Proceedings of the 7th International Botanical Congress at Stockholm, 1950*, pp. 152–4.

Sasuke, N. 1953. 'Bread-Fruit, Yams and Taros of Ponape Island', *Proceedings of the 7th Pacific Science Congress*, vol. 6, pp. 159–70.

Schmitt, R. C. 1961. *Population Trends in Hawaii and French Polynesia*, report no. 29, Romanzo Adams Social Research Laboratory, Honolulu.

Shephard, C. I. 1945. 'Solomon Islands', *Journal of the Imperial College of Tropical Agriculture*, vol. 22, pp. 179–83.

Spate, O. H. K. 1953. 'Changing Native Agriculture in New Guinea', *Geographical Review*, vol. 43, pp. 152–72.

—— 1963. 'Islands and Men', in Fosberg, 1963: 253–64.

Suggs, R. C. 1960. *The Island Civilizations of Polynesia*, New York.

Tetens, A. 1958. *Among the Savages of the South Seas: Memoirs of Micronesia 1862–1868*, Stanford.

Valentine, C. A. 1958. 'Introduction to the Changing Ways of Life on the Island of New Britain', unpublished Ph.D. thesis, University of Pennsylvania.

Vessell, A. J. and Simonson, R. W. 1958. 'Soils and Agriculture of the Palau Islands', *Pacific Science*, vol. 12, pp. 281–98.

Ward, R. G. 1965. *Land Use and Population in Fiji*, London.

Watson, J. B. 1965. 'The Significance of a Recent Ecological Change in the Central Highlands of New Guinea', *Journ. Poly. Soc.*, vol. 74, pp. 438–50.

West, F. J. 1961. *Political Advancement in the South Pacific*, Melbourne.

Wright, C. H. 1946. *U.S. Navy—U.S. Pacific Fleet and Pacific Ocean Areas Inspection of Caroline Islands . . .*, mimeo.

Wright, C. S. 1962. *Soils and Agricultural Development of Easter Island (Hotu-Matua)*, Ministry of Agriculture, mimeo, San Diego, Chile.

Yanaihara, T. 1940. *Pacific Islands Under Japanese Mandate*, London.

Yen, D. E. 1963. 'Sweet Potato Variation and its Relation to Human Migration in the Pacific', in Barrau, 1963: 93–133.

Zimmerman, E. C. 1963. 'Nature of the Land Biota', in Fosberg, 1963: 57–64.

3

VEGETATION AND MAN IN THE SOUTH-WEST PACIFIC AND NEW GUINEA

R. G. ROBBINS[1]

THE great diversity of habitat found throughout the Pacific region is reflected in the pattern of the vegetation. Tall evergreen rain forest is the dominant natural vegetation climax throughout the region, but each island, by virtue of its size and form, its geographical location, and the varying ecological niches offered, presents its own particular range of plant communities. Furthermore, the present vegetation of large areas has been profoundly modified by man.

On a phytoclimatic basis, the South-west Pacific may be divided into three major zones. The tropical zone includes New Guinea, New Hebrides, Fiji, and other islands lying within 20° of the Equator. Along the southern margin of this zone subtle changes occur in the natural and cultural vegetation and a subtropical zone extends southwards from about 20° S. to about 34° S. This includes islands such as New Caledonia, Norfolk, and Pitcairn. South of 34° S. is the temperate zone, which lies outside the scope of this paper.

In the tropical and subtropical zones, tiny coral atolls, a few feet above sea level, may carry only a low growth of sand grasses and salt-tolerant herbs and shrubs. The total flora may amount to less than twenty plant species and frequently the sole economic plant is the ubiquitous coconut palm. In spite of its buoyant nuts, which appear so well adapted for long distance transportation by water, coconuts have a short viability in sea water. Their presence on isolated islets can only be explained by sporadic occupation by early travellers.

On higher islands the pioneer plants of trailing convolvulus,

---

[1] Dr. Robbins was formerly Senior Lecturer in Botany, University of Papua and New Guinea.

swordbean, and other sand binders, together with fleshy sesuviums and portulacas, are backed by a littoral hedge of tough maritime shrubs such as *Scaevola*, *Tournefortia*, *Morinda*, *Gardenia*, and *Dodonea* which can withstand the salt-laden winds. This hedge protects the taller trees of the strand forest which on a thousand Pacific beaches is composed of species of *Barringtonia*, *Calophyllum*, *Terminalia*, *Hibiscus*, *Thespesia*, *Cerbera*, *Inocarpus*, *Hernandia*, *Pisonia*, *Premna*, and *Pandanus*. The seeds of these pan-Pacific trees may drift for thousands of miles in sea currents to be cast up on the shores of isolated islands, and they often appear in the driftline debris as far south as New Zealand (Mason, 1961).

The coral atolls and smaller isolated islands of the Pacific stand apart as a severely limited habitat for man, owing mainly to their erratic rainfall and porous calcareous soils. Frequently the only indigenous food plant is the pandanus which provides an edible nut as well as leaves for thatching and clothing. If strand forest is present, then *Inocarpus*, known as the Pacific chestnut, and *Terminalia catappa*, the sea almond, also provide edible nuts. *Cordia* bark provides rope while the inner bark of *Broussonetia*, or paper mulberry, is beaten out into tapa cloth. The largest tree used for house and canoe building is *Calophyllum*. Some islanders had canoes made from redwood logs which must have drifted across from the Californian coast, and there was certainly a pre-European trade in canoe logs from Fiji to Tonga and the smaller atolls.

Mangrove forests are present only on the larger islands and as far eastwards as Tonga and Samoa. They are absent from the central Pacific. Forming a dense forest which may reach a height of up to 100 feet, the most common association is a *Rhizophora–Bruguiera* woodland. Seaward species are anchored against waves and the two- to three-foot rise and fall of the tide by stout, over-arching strut roots. At low tide the pneumatophores or breathing roots are revealed standing erect in the mud like a fakir's bed of nails. Mangrove timber is not generally durable but serves for house poles and fuel, while the bark, rich in tannin, is used to preserve fishing nets. Mangrove forest is often important both as a protection against coastal erosion and as an aid to accretion of the shoreline. The brackish upper reaches of the mangrove estuaries are lined with the tall feathery fronds of the nipa palm which are used for thatching and basket weaving. In swampy hollows a tropical salt marsh of stiff ferns and sedges may develop while sandy spits support groves of the coastal she-oak, *Casuarina equisetifolia*. Islands possessing interior lowlands may offer a range of herbaceous and palm swamps as well as tall rain forest and savanna, with scrub and open grassland in seasonally dry areas.

There is some relationship between island size and elevation and the range of plant communities found. Only the larger Pacific islands show a full complement of lowland plant communities. For example, the tiny Kermadecs are entirely covered with coastal forest, but in addition to coastal communities Samoa has mixed lowland rain forests with a possible distinction between alluvium and hill forest. In terms of forest composition, the first critical altitude in the tropical Pacific is about 3,000 feet above sea level, but few Pacific islands east of New Guinea reach this elevation. The peaks of Viti Levu, Fiji, just exceed this height, and subtropical New Caledonia has a few mountain ranges reaching 5,000 feet. Above about 3,000 feet a broad mid-mountain belt (embracing the lower montane forest of New Guinea) begins and continues to as high as 10,000 feet. In this belt the trees are shorter and the growth less luxuriant than in the humid lowlands. Canopy trees reach 80 to 100 feet, below which there is only one sub-canopy layer, so that forest structure is reduced from three to two tree layers. Plank buttresses and woody lianes are less evident and palms are largely replaced by treeferns. Many of the lowland species fall out and their place is taken by montane trees including conifers. In New Guinea there is little doubt that the mid-mountain slopes have become a refugium for many migrant plants which arrived under different climatic conditions. The many distinct forest associations found here still reflect their geographical affinities. The oak-laurel lower montane forests of *Castanopsis* and *Cryptocarya* (occupying the lower aspects) have direct affinity with South-east Asia while the relationships of New Guinea's beech forests (*Nothofagus* spp.) lie as far afield as New Zealand and Patagonia.

In places where mists are prevalent lower montane forest is reduced to a stunted, mossed aspect resembling the true montane forest of higher levels. This has led to much confusion in defining the montane forest formation and terms such as 'mossy forest' and 'montane forest' are so loosely applied as to include several formations (Robbins, 1968b: 531). However, somewhere between 9,000 and 10,000 feet altitude the optimum tiers of the forest are reduced to a single layer and true montane forest commences. Misting is common in this belt and the trees are often gnarled and much branched. Beneath the low, close canopy at some 35 feet, the trunks and floor are mantled with a thick layer of liverworts and mosses. Conifers and myrtles may predominate.

At about 11,000 feet is the sunnier subalpine forest characterized by emergent conifers, and this gives way to subalpine scrub and grasslands. In New Guinea the treeline is at about 13,400 feet and above this is a true alpine belt with tussock grassland, fern and sedge bogs, and a moss-lichen tundra vegetation which continues to the snow-line at about 15,000 feet. In the subtropics the altitudinal belts are lower, and in New Caledonia the lower montane habitat commences at approximately 2,500 feet.

A common feature of Pacific islands is a dry leeward region where vegetation ranges from semi-deciduous forest to savanna and scrub. The dry southern Papuan shelf with its seasonally deciduous forests and savannas of scattered eucalypts and paperbark trees is a good example as is the low scrubby *talasiga* or 'sun-burnt land' of western Fiji. Rainfall is often low or has an uneven distribution resulting in marked wet and dry seasons with soils being alternately waterlogged or dried out. Fluctuating swamps may be present in low-lying parts. Tracts of short grassland are common and these are usually the results of man's interference, for here the fine balance of climate, soils, and vegetation is easily deflected. For example, there is accumulating evidence that much of the savanna of southern Papua, in the vicinity of Port Moresby, has replaced an original mixed semi-deciduous forest as a result of pre-European garden clearing and subsequent fires. Pockets of mixed forest still remain, surrounded by open eucalypts and grassland. Similarly, the *talasiga* of Fiji is much modified and extended and now includes many introduced species. No doubt such interference covers a long period of occupation in the pre-European era, and subsequent acceleration of vegetation change followed European contact. Sandalwood is a common small tree of these drier communities throughout the Pacific and its wholesale removal in the early nineteenth century must have had an effect, while Ward (see Chapter 4 below) notes that the drying of *bêche-de-mer* along the coast of Fiji required some nine tons of fuel-wood for each ton of the dried sea-slug.

The small patches of open grassland along the drier west coast of Espiritu Santo in the New Hebrides are coincident with villages, while a map of grasslands in New Guinea is also a map of the settled, or formerly settled, valleys (Fig. 3.1). Like those of Fiji, most of the grasslands of New Caledonia give strong indications of being induced as today they are made up almost entirely of introduced species. Here, too, there is little doubt that the natural areas of *Melaleuca* paperbark savanna, called *niouli*, have been much extended as a result of man's activities within the adjacent mixed forest. In these areas it would appear that man's impact on the vegetation may have been greater than hitherto suspected. Such interference in existing vegetation boundaries is not as obvious as the replacement of forests by grasslands, for in the former situation man has merely upset the equilibrium within the original mixed seasonal forest leading to the invasion of the site by the local savanna. The area is then abandoned by man, except for the annual firing of the ground cover. This is sufficient to maintain the savanna.

In areas with a well-distributed rainfall, ideally in excess of fifty inches annually, the natural vegetation is a tall evergreen rain forest. This occurs on alluvial valley floors and undulating hills and lowland slopes to an altitude of about 3,000 feet. In most Pacific islands the alluvial terrace forests have already been cleared, mostly for farms and plantations, and only New Guinea still has large tracts of lowland alluvium forest. Most of the tropical lowland rain forest covers hilly topography and differs in species composition, structure, and seasonal aspects from terrace forest. The lowland rain forest generally has a canopy of upper trees 100 to 150 feet in height with occasional emergents above. The trunks of these tall trees may have relatively small girths but invariably possess wide flanging buttresses which makes felling difficult as a platform must be built to cut the trunk above them. Subcanopy trees reach to 80 feet while a third layer of small to medium trees is found between 30 and 45 feet. Below 20 feet is the shrub layer and the fifth and final forest stratum is represented by the ground vegetation of seedlings, herbs, ferns, and mosses. Palms are often a feature while both lianes and epiphytes abound. Woody vines loop down for perhaps 100 feet from host trees and some, together with rattans, are used for ropes and bindings. Perching and climbing plants include many orchids and a variety of ferns and aroids. Pandanus, screw pines, and the huge fig trees are notable for their girderwork of stout strut roots. These, and a few species of large trees, are usually left or cut back when making a garden as they may be too difficult to fell. As a result, over-mature individuals within an apparently primary forest may indicate a well-advanced secondary forest on that site. This is true of such sparsely populated areas as the Lower Ramu in New Guinea where a nomadic shifting cultivation is practised and much of the present continuous forest is a mosaic of primary and secondary forest which has been allowed to regain maturity.

Lowland rain forest in the Pacific is of mixed floristic composition and seldom does any one or more species dominate, although the forest type is often named after the timber species it contains. Nor are the Pacific rain forests notable for timber volume per acre in comparison with South-east Asian forests. However, as timber scientists have proved the commercial value of more species, this ratio has increased. With the exception of local stands of conifers, softwoods are rare and the majority of the trees are to be classed as tropical hardwoods.

The gymnosperm element within the tropical Pacific is today a relict distribution which reflects past climates and plant migration patterns. Conifers only occur west of the andesite line and hence are not found east of Fiji or Tonga. They are represented by two groups: the podocarps, or Southern Hemisphere pines, derive from the temperate zone and still dominate the forests of New Zealand and also remain as an important element in the montane forests of New Guinea. The second group is represented by araucarian forests and includes both the kauri pine, *Agathis*, and the various species of *Araucaria*, commonly known as klinkii, hoop, and Norfolk pines. In the past both these groups, moving from the south, extended into the present-day tropics, but the araucarian group is predominantly subtropical and remains only as large outliers within the present tropics. Kauri stands, now largely depleted, were once a feature of the southern islands of the New Hebrides and the Solomons, and stands are still to be found in parts of New Guinea and Fiji although, because of the easily worked and even-grained wood, such forests, where accessible, have been the first to be exploited. The subtropical kauri forests of northern New Zealand had virtually disappeared by the end of the last century while those of New Caledonia soon followed. The tall *Araucaria* forests, if they ever existed there, are not now found in Fiji but have persisted in certain valleys of New Guinea and are currently being exploited for plywood manufacture at Bulolo.

The present scattered occurrence of *Araucaria* in New Guinea points to its once widespread cover and to the present pattern being a retraction one, with denser pockets on the last sites remaining favourable to the species. In Fiji the more inaccessible kauri stands are currently being exploited as, under the impetus of market demand, they have come within reach of modern extraction methods. In general, New Guinea is the only Pacific Territory with any large export potential from natural forests. Elsewhere the natural forests can provide only part of the local timber requirements with the main function of the remaining forests being a protective role on higher watersheds. The comparatively recent establishment of Forest Services in the Pacific has done much to mitigate the early wasteful destruction and exploitation of the forest by indigenes and European settlers alike, while in Fiji and in the Bulolo area of New Guinea large-scale reafforestation has begun. In all territories, timber exploitation continues to be ruled by contemporary and local factors. Profits are finely balanced between difficulties of extraction, market demand, and the price of the finished material. It is regrettable to an extreme that a resource which has its very basis in perpetuity should be at the mercy of the vicissitudes of the moment. Thus, 'trash' species such as water gums (*Eugenia* and *Syzygium spp.*) are being milled from the coastal forest of tiny Efate while many valuable species, such as Australian cedar, are cleared unutilized from the mixed pine forest association at Bulolo, where only the lower portion of the spar-like klinkii trunks is suitable for peeling.

There is no doubt that later generations, albeit in vastly different circumstances, will lament the vanished cabinet woods of New Guinea.

Much of the vegetation of the Pacific can be classed as successional, that is in a state of flux. Successions begun by natural means such as volcanic eruptions, landslides, hurricanes, and fires due to lightning are comparatively rare in the Pacific and most stem from the activities of man and animals. Pre-eminent here is the felling, clearing, and burning of the forest for garden cultivation and farming. This is an example of man the innovator but, as elsewhere in the world, the Pacific also has man the destroyer, either exploiting forests without any follow-up of land settlement or reafforestation, or, as in New Caledonia, modifying the vegetation as a result of nickel prospecting and mining. Once converted into secondary vegetation by whatever means, the area is open to invasion by weed species and further degradation usually follows, and, aided by fire, continues until open grassland results. Many of the weeds are introduced exotic species which prove particularly aggressive in their new habitat. They include the shrubby guajava and lantana and the prickly pear cactus. Trailing *Clidemia* vine is a common wasteland plant in Fiji while 'mile-a-minute', *Mikania*, lives up to its name in many territories. A great number of these weeds are of American origin and have been introduced since the turn of the century. In recent years Pacific territories have tightened up on plant introduction and quarantine while biological control of some weeds by natural insect predators has had encouraging results.

It has been said that for most tropical countries a forest cover of 30 per cent should be a minimum requirement for timber, watershed protection, and other conservation needs. While the figure for Malaya is still about 70 per cent, that for the Philippines has now approached 25 per cent. Fiji has about 35 per cent of its area under forest while the New Guinea figure is nearer to 80 per cent. On most of the smaller Pacific islands today the forest, which was often limited to the coastal fringe, has long since been cleared and replaced by low, shrubby regrowth in which many species are foreign invaders.

Many changes to vegetation have been brought about by the introduction of animals to Pacific islands. On some, domestic animals such as dogs, cats, and cattle have become feral and greatly modified both the local flora and fauna. Thousands of wild sheep on the slopes of Mt. Mauna Loa on the island of Hawaii have drastically altered the landscape. Elsewhere there are examples of rats, pigs, deer, rabbits, and birds which, introduced inadvertently or deliberately, have become serious pests. Today areas in the Pacific where the vegetation has not been modified in some way by man, directly or indirectly, are extremely small. Many smaller islands have suffered complete destruction or a vast modification of their original ecosystem. Changes have been more noticeable where resources are limited and the protection of isolation has suddenly been broken down. Man's impact upon the vegetation of the Pacific has been as diverse as the pattern of island environment. Those changes first initiated by the Melanesians and Polynesians have accelerated greatly since the arrival of Europeans and have grown apace with more intensive settlement and the advances of modern technology.

MAN AND VEGETATION IN NEW GUINEA

Of all the Pacific islands settled by man, New Guinea is unique. It is the largest island, has the greatest population, is the nearest to Asia and, above all, has the widest range of habitat. New Guinea, an island continent of some 310,000 square miles, has littoral habitats embracing offshore islands and coral reefs and an extended coastline made up of sandy beaches, rocky headlands, muddy estuaries, and brackish lagoons. The lowlands include both perennially and seasonally humid areas with alluvial terrace forests and extensive swamps. The tropical rain forests of the undulating lowlands and foothills give way on mid-mountain slopes to a lower montane zone rising to montane valleys above which are mountain peaks reaching into subalpine and alpine altitudes.

Forest and natural vegetation still covers some three-quarters of New Guinea. Villages are frequently located in small ridgetop clearings and near-by slopes are chequered with garden plots both old and new. Abandoned gardens are given over to secondary regrowth and here and there an open hillslope or a whole valley of grassland attests to the continued and long-standing presence of man, and his industry in converting the original forest into grassland. The landscape has been shaped by the shifting agriculture and subsistence economy which is still practised by the majority of the inhabitants.

Over the centuries, and continuing to this day, the forest has played an important part in the lives of the New Guinean people. The early hunters and gatherers depended primarily on products of the forest and in isolated areas these are still more important than garden produce in the village economy. Forest trees are exploited to fill a wide range of needs including timber for buildings, fences, weapons, shields, canoes, drums, and fuel for cooking and warmth. Bark is used for roofing, walls, or when beaten out, for clothing. Vines and rattans provide lashings and, together with palm fronds and bamboo strips, the materials for fish traps.

Of the forest foods, sago (*sak sak*) is the most important and Lea estimates (see below, Chapter 10) that there are some 90,000 people who are primarily sago-eaters in the Sepik, Fly, and Purari river areas. The fruits of several forest trees are collected, including the galip nut from *Canarium* and the okari nut from *Terminalia*. The kernel of the pandanus is used in the highlands and is collected from both wild plants and cultivated groves. Numerous other seeds, leaves, or roots are gathered for food, medicinal materials, dyes, or decoration.

The collection of the many products contributes to the degradation of the forest but man's greatest impact on the New Guinea landscape has been through the piecemeal destruction of this very forest by felling and burning. Slowly the rain forest has been encroached upon for new garden plots until at last under the process of shifting agriculture whole areas of forest have been transformed to a disclimax of open grassland. In clearing the forest, a task which not so long ago was accomplished with stone tools, the undergrowth is first cleared and the smaller trees felled. A few of the larger trees may be laboriously cut down using a platform built above the plank buttresses but usually such trees are merely ringbarked and left to die standing. The tangled debris of those felled is left to dry out and then fired at the first opportunity. Planting takes place among the still-smouldering logs and stumps. In the lowlands tillage is rarely attempted and yams, taro, cassava, sugar-cane, and banana shoots are merely planted in a hole made between the logs with a pointed digging stick. Between the tuber and stem crops, seed crops, such as corn, pumpkin, and peanuts are interplanted. A little weeding is done towards the end of the cropping period. As the gardener harvests the last of the pawpaws, bananas, and pineapples, the pioneer woody regrowth is fairly advanced with quick-growing trees such as *Ficus, Sterculia, Pipturis, Alphitonia, Trema,* and *Macaranga.* These will dominate the site for the next fifteen to twenty years by which time seedlings of the forest trees will be established. However, the clearing cycle may now be repeated. The length of tree fallow depends upon a number of factors, predominant among which are population pressures and site conditions favouring rapid regeneration. It has been found that the initial forest fertility of the upper soil profile, upon which the whole process of shifting cultivation depends, is largely restored at the late pioneer stage of regeneration. Little further advantage is to be gained for garden cropping by allowing the regrowth to proceed into advanced secondary forest stages.

With every successive clearing and gardening on the same site, the following regrowth phases are deflected further away from the original forest vegetation. Woody regeneration becomes less vigorous and more confined to hardy weed species. The community becomes open and scrubby, includes grass tussocks, and is increasingly liable to firing. Once fire occurs it effectively scorches out young tree seedlings but the grasses shoot again from basal root stocks as soon as the next rains come. Small initial patches of grassland soon coalesce to form larger, more continuous tracts where annual fires, deliberately lit to hunt out small game, sweep through the area. Thus grassland becomes a disclimax, initiated and then maintained and stabilized by man (Robbins, 1963a). Anthropogenic grasslands are common throughout the Pacific in Fiji, New Hebrides, New Caledonia, and, most extensively, in New Guinea. In New Guinea their pattern follows the settled coastline, the Markham, Upper Ramu, and Sepik river valleys, and numerous small settled inland valleys throughout the highlands and the lowlands (Fig. 3.1).

Many of the present vegetation patterns suggest that in New Guinea population migration has proceeded along a front

■ Grasslands, Regrowth, and Agricultural land

Fig. 3.1. Areas within the Territory of Papua and New Guinea showing the impact of man on vegetation. Anthropogenic grasslands, forest regrowth, and major areas of current horticulture and plantations are included. Large areas of savanna in Papua have been omitted.

which follows the retreating forest. The current front exhibits areas of virgin forest and a patchwork of cleared garden plots and those reverting to regrowth. In the rear extend the open tracts of established grassland. Grazing animals did not enter the native economy and these grasslands now lie largely uninhabited and are unused, except for hunting. Cattle grazing and afforestation are two possibilities for future utilization of these induced grasslands but both may face problems of inherently poor soils and markedly seasonal rainfall.

The New Guinea grasslands vary in ecological status and in species composition. The short grassland types are the most entrenched, which suggests a long history of interference. Grasses here are of mixed tropical species but often dominated by the 2–3-foot-high Australian kangaroo grass, *Themeda australis*. The short grasslands are frequently burnt and may include scattered cycads and small fire-tolerant trees although many are treeless.

The Sepik grasslands cover some 600 square miles and may well constitute natural grassland (Reiner and Robbins, 1964). The extremely infertile clays are alternately waterlogged in the wet season and drought-cracked in the dry season, and although total rainfall is adequate for forest cover, the extreme seasonal variations restrict tree growth to the incised streams which flow across the plains to the Sepik River. Smaller pockets of natural grasslands must, of course, have been present throughout New Guinea to act as reservoirs to stock other cleared areas.

The tall grasslands appear chronologically more recent and indeed are still successional and dynamic in status. In the lowlands, such grasslands are rare and are composed of several species of cane grasses growing 10 feet high or more. The wild sugars, *Saccharum* spp., and the grass *Imperata cylindrica* are found here although the latter is often a weed of disturbed ground. The extensive tall grasslands of the central highlands are dominated by swordgrass, *Miscanthus floridulus*, which in New Guinea is not found in lowland areas. Swordgrass is a true canegrass reaching 15 to 20 feet high, and, according to its history, is frequently associated with woody regrowth of small trees and shrubs.

It has been suggested (Robbins, 1963b) that the different status of the grasslands may reflect past migrations and that the short grasslands of the Markham Valley mark the passage of a forest clearing population into the interior. Within the highlands there is similar evidence of an east to west migration movement. The extensive short grasslands of the Eastern Highlands which include immigrant species from the adjacent Ramu lowlands are far older in establishment than the tall indigenous swordgrass areas which dominate in the Western Highlands. There are other vegetation gradients such as the progressive clearing of the forest cover indicating an east–west settlement gradient.

In the seasonally dry regions of New Guinea, such as the dry belt of southern Papua, a semi-deciduous mixed forest alternates with savannas composed of scattered *Eucalyptus* spp. and *Melaleuca* spp. over a cover of kangaroo and other short grasses. The equilibrium between the mixed forest and the savanna is finely balanced and in settled areas along the coast gardening activities have certainly much extended the savanna vegetation.

The areas where man has thus far made the least impact upon the natural vegetation are undoubtedly in the vast swamps of the Fly, Ramu, and Sepik Rivers (Robbins, 1968*a*). Life here is adapted to the seasonal inundations covering thousands of square miles of lush floating water grasses and lakes filled with water-lilies and a variety of aquatic growth. Where the water table drops to ground level or just below in the dry season, there are tall 'pit-pit' swamps of *Phragmites* and *Saccharum* cane grasses or tracts of sago palm groves. In the brackish estuaries are mangrove forests and nipa palms. Most of the villages of stilted houses are located on the higher river levees where clearings are made for a few quick-growing garden crops to be harvested during the dry season. Local diet includes fish, crocodile, duck, waterlily stems, seeds, and insects, but above all the swamp-dwellers are sago eaters.

At about 3,000 feet above sea level the humid tropics are left and the cooler lower montane zone commences. Ecologically this continues up to 9,000 feet although settlements are rarely permanent above about 8,000 feet in New Guinea (Robbins, 1964). Within this lower montane zone some half a million Stone Age people were discovered by European explorers in the early 1930s. It is now known that their occupation of the highlands could date back 10,000 years. The first migrants were probably hunters and gatherers, and the mortars and pestles which are frequently found throughout the highlands, and which now have no economic use, may have once been used to grind acorns and other products (R. N. H. Bulmer, 1964). Certainly in his occupation of the lower montane habitat in New Guinea man has followed the oak-laurel forests (Brass, 1941). This zone coincides with an optimum temperature belt most favourable to upland horticulture. It is not known when agriculture was introduced to the highlands, but pigs had been introduced as early as 4,000–3,000 B.C., and as they have to be fed, it is assumed that some garden culture was then present (S. Bulmer, 1966). Pigs have continued to play an important role in horticulture in the highlands and their free scavenging during the day in the abandoned garden and regrowth areas has helped to slow regeneration.

The present reliance of the highlanders on a single root crop, *Ipomea batatas*, the sweet potato, is remarkable (Brookfield, 1964) especially as this is a relatively recent introduction to the New Guinea highlands. The apparent late arrival of the sweet potato has led to much discussion apropos the settlement of the New Guinea highlands, and Watson (1965) postulated a population explosion in the highlands coinciding with the introduction of the sweet potato some 200 years ago. However, garden culture has already been dated back to 350±120 B.C. from a wooden digging stick found in an old ditch in peat swamps near Mount Hagen (Lampert, 1967: 308) and it would appear that intensive horticulture, perhaps based on taro growing, was practised in pre-ipomean times. Barrau (1965) has also suggested that indigenous root crops could have been involved although here the only likely precursor is a wild vine, *Pueraria*. This is no longer cultivated in the New Guinea highlands although the small tubers are used in time of need as food while the long stem is still useful as twine.

The settlement of the highlands meant an adaption to many aspects of the environment for the migrants from the coastal lowlands. Available building materials and other forest resources were different while climatic changes, especially in temperatures, were reflected in vegetation regrowth phases, in the growing seasons, and in the leaching and fertility of the soils. Horticultural methods had to be adapted and there was a trend towards more intensive cultivation and more permanent land use. In many areas cultivation is succeeded by a plantation tree fallow using *Casuarina* trees.

At elevations above 8,000 feet killing frosts can be quite frequent and occasional extreme frosts inhibit practical and sustained gardening and forest clearance. However, the Karam people of the upper Kaironk valley associate extensive clearing at altitudes up to 8,000 feet with the introduction of new varieties of sweet potato over the last three generations (R. N. H. Bulmer, pers. comm.). The mid-mountain slopes up to 10,000 feet, together with the montane, subalpine, and perhaps alpine regions, are exploited for small game and forest products, and there is little doubt that many of the so-called subalpine grasslands in New Guinea have been fire-induced.

The introduction of cash cropping had a radical effect in both lowlands and highlands and has altered both the original vegetation and the landscape. Copra plantations had been established in the coastal areas by the 1880s and were followed by rubber, cocoa, and coffee estates. Oil palm and tea have recently been introduced as smallholder and plantation crops. Many of the highland tea plantations and small holdings are being established on drained phragmites swampland only a short time ago considered marginal land. Indigenous small-holders are playing an increasingly important part in spreading cash crops and today about half of the coffee grown in the highlands is from native growers (see Lea, Chapter 10 and Fig. 10.3).

Although the commercial sector of the agricultural economy depends heavily on these introduced plants, less than one per cent of the country is used for their production. Despite the acceleration of vegetation change through increased cash cropping, timber milling, and mining activities, the over-whelming proportion of the anthropogenic vegetation of Papua and New Guinea is the work of shifting cultivators, hunters, and gatherers through several thousand years of occupation.

BIBLIOGRAPHY

Barrau, J. 1965. 'Witnesses of the Past: Notes on Some Food Plants of Oceania', *Ethnology*, vol. 4, pp. 282–94.

Brass, L. J. 1941. 'Stone Age Agriculture in New Guinea', *Geographical Review*, vol. 31, pp. 555–69.

Brookfield, H. C. 1964. 'The Ecology of Highland Settlement: Some Suggestions', *American Anthropologist*, vol. 66, no. 4, part 2, pp. 20–38.

Bulmer, R. N. H. 1964. 'Edible Seeds and Prehistoric Mortars in the Highlands of New Guinea', *Man*, no. 183, pp. 147–50.

Bulmer, S. 1966. 'Pig Bone from Two Archaeological Sites in the New Guinea Highlands', *Journ. Poly. Soc.*, vol. 75, pp. 504–5.

Lampert, R. J. 1967. 'Horticulture in the New Guinea Highlands—C14 Dating', *Antiquity*, vol. 41, pp. 307–9.

Mason, R. 1961. 'Dispersal of Tropical Seed by Ocean Currents', *Nature*, vol. 191, pp. 408–9.

Reiner, E. J. and Robbins, R. G. 1964. 'The Middle Sepik Plains, New Guinea. A Physiographic Study', *Geographical Review*, vol. 54, pp. 20–44.

Robbins, R. G. 1963a. 'The Anthropogenic Grasslands of Papua and New Guinea', *Proceedings of the UNESCO Humid Tropic Vegetation Symposium, Goroka, New Guinea*, Canberra, pp. 313–29.

—— 1963b. 'Correlations of Plant Patterns and Population Migrations into the Australian New Guinea Highlands', in Barrau, J. (ed.), *Plants and the Migrations of Pacific Peoples—A Symposium*, Honolulu, pp. 45–59.

—— 1964. 'The Montane Habitat in the Tropics', *Proceedings and Papers of the IUCN 9th Technical Meeting (Nairobi 1963)*, IUCN Publications New Series no. 4, pp. 163–71.

—— 1968a. 'Vegetation of the Wewak-Lower Sepik Area', in Haantjens, H. A. *et al.*, *Lands of the Wewak-Lower Sepik Area Papua and New Guinea*, C.S.I.R.O. Land Research Series no. 22, pp. 109–24.

—— 1968b. 'The Biogeography of Tropical Rainforest in South East Asia', *Proceedings of the Symposium on Recent Advances in Tropical Ecology, Part II*, International Society for Tropical Ecology, Varanasi, India, pp. 521–35.

Watson, J. B. 1965. 'The Significance of a Recent Ecological Change in the Highlands of New Guinea', *Journ. Poly. Soc.*, vol. 74, pp. 438–50.

4

THE PACIFIC *BÊCHE-DE-MER* TRADE WITH SPECIAL REFERENCE TO FIJI

R. GERARD WARD[1]

THE impact of the Pacific Islands on the rest of the world has been slight. Yet the impact of that outside, distant, but technically more advanced world on the islands and islanders has been rapid, widespread, and profound. This difference is a function of relative size, technology, and distance. As a result, incidents of little significance to the European intruder and observer were often of great importance to the islander. Furthermore, until relatively recent years, studies of the contact period have tended to reflect the European view and have completely underestimated the change in island societies and ecosystems which followed the first contacts.[2] Recent studies of several of the trades which developed in the late eighteenth and early nineteenth centuries, and of the early European residents, have helped to redress this imbalance.[3] The present paper seeks to examine the development, character, and consequences of another of these commercial activities and to show how a few ships, engaged in minor trade, had a major impact on the islands.

[1] Dr. Ward is Professor of Human Geography, Australian National University. The author wishes to acknowledge the financial assistance of the University of London Central Research Fund.

A shorter version of this paper was read at the 11th Pacific Science Congress, Tokyo, Aug. 1966.

[2] There have been exceptions, notably the widespread recognition that new diseases were introduced by Europeans and that indigenous populations often declined as a result. Ironically, this is one field in which recent research suggests that many earlier accounts exaggerated the effects (McArthur, n.d. and 1966; Pool, 1964).

[3] Notably the papers by Maude (1959 and 1964), Maude and Crocombe (1962), Maude and Leeson (1965), Hainsworth (1965), and Shineberg (1965 and 1966). I am grateful to Mr. H. E. Maude for bringing a number of references to my notice, and to Dr. Shineberg and the Baillie Library, University of Melbourne, for permission to use a microfilm copy of her thesis.

Bêche-de-mer,[1] the dried flesh of the several edible species of the class *Holothurioidea*, the 'sea-cucumbers', has been exported from the Indo-Pacific region to China for several centuries. Apparently it was not imported into China from South-east Asia in the Sung period (Wheatley, 1959) but at a later date Chinese, Malay, and Spanish traders collected and cured holothurians in the Indonesian and Philippine archipelagos. The *bêche-de-mer* was then shipped to China for use as an ingredient in a number of dishes, being valued partly because of its supposed aphrodisiac qualities. It was also an important export to China from Japan, particularly from Nagasaki, before the Meiji era began in 1868. In the last years of the eighteenth and early decades of the nineteenth centuries, European, Australian, and New England traders[2] were increasingly active in the Pacific Islands seeking products to ship to Canton or Manila, to be exchanged there for goods such as tea, sugar, coffee, and silk which were in turn marketed in the traders' home countries. *Bêche-de-mer* was only one of the island products sought, others being sandalwood, tortoiseshell, pearls, pearl shell, edible birds' nests, and coral moss (Fanning, 1833: 456–65).

As agents of cultural and ecological change, the traders had been preceded in the eighteenth century by explorers and other navigators who visited the islands to obtain wood, water, and victuals, and to 'refresh' their crews (see Farrell, Chapter 2). Axes, nails, fish hooks, cloth, and other goods[3] were sought by

---

[1] The name, and other versions of it used by the early traders (e.g. 'beach la mar'), are corruptions of the Portuguese *bicho do mar*. Other common names for the animal or the product include *trepang* (Malay), sea-slug, and sea-cucumber. The islanders use a wide variety of names. The Fijians, for example, distinguish between at least seven types, each with its own name (Turbet, 1942: 150) and the Caroline Islanders use the collective name *menika* and have particular names for at least sixteen types (Christian, 1899: 374–5).

[2] The journals and log books of New England *bêche-de-mer* traders form the basis for much of this paper, and I am particularly indebted to Mr. Ernest S. Dodge, Director, and the staff of the Peabody Museum, Salem, for their help, advice, and kindness when I was searching for material in New England in 1964.

[3] Goods which Europeans had obtained at other islands were often in great demand. In 1769 Cook found that the Maoris of Tolaga Bay 'Valued more than any thing' the bark cloth Cook and his crew had obtained in Tahiti and Ulietia (Beaglehole, 1955: 186) while in 1774 the Tahitians were eager to get red feathers obtained in Tonga (Beaglehole, 1961: 382–3). In the 1850s sandalwood traders had to provide pigs, shell, tortoiseshell and whales' teeth, all traditional trade items, in order to obtain sandalwood at Espiritu Santo and Eromanga. Indeed they

the islanders in exchange for yams and other root crops, pigs, and poultry. This type of commerce was usually easy to establish as inter-island and intra-island trade in these similar commodities was practised by most of the indigenous communities and the concept of barter was familiar. The rapid replacement of stone tools by iron tools brought considerable savings in the labour of implement manufacture, agriculture, and construction tasks (Salisbury, 1962: 109) but the impact of the visitors on island societies and ecosystems was greatly increased after they began to seek goods like sandalwood, pearls, pearl shell, and *bêche-de-mer*.

Several of the new trade items had previously had little or no value to the islanders so that new concepts of value were soon introduced. Whereas the victualling of ships required no new techniques of production or exchange, supplying some of the new trade items did. The collecting and preparation of *bêche-de-mer* in particular demanded that the islander learn new tasks and sometimes undertake labour under European direction, albeit initially through the intermediate authority of their own chiefs. The markets of Asia, Europe, or America could absorb much more produce than could ships seeking only their own immediate requirements. Therefore the new trades allowed the islanders to accumulate many more foreign goods, while the completion of a full cargo often meant the transfer of labour from traditional tasks for considerable periods. The modification of indigenous socio-economic systems was therefore accelerated, while the felling of sandalwood trees, the cutting of firewood, and the gathering of *bêche-de-mer* initiated changes in the island ecosystems which have often proved irreversible.

The first non-indigenous export trade in Polynesia or Melanesia was the shipment of salt pork and live pigs from Tahiti to the convict colony in New South Wales. One shipment was made in 1793 but the Tahitian pork trade really began in 1801. It continued for nearly three decades, by which time it had provided the means for the establishment of political unity throughout the island and 'revolutionized the whole Tahitian way of life, placing the islanders in the stream of progress a decade or more ahead of all the other peoples of the South

had 'to trade with the Solomon Islands for tortoiseshell to trade at Tana for pigs to trade at Santo for sandalwood' (Shineberg, 1966: 140–1).

Seas' (Maude, 1959: 82). During the same period pearls and pearl shell attracted traders to the Tuamotu archipelago.

In 1804 the existence of sandalwood (*Santalum yasi* Seem.) in Fiji was revealed to prospective shippers in Port Jackson (Im Thurn and Wharton, 1925: xlvii) and from then until the end of the decade American, colonial, and 'country' ships from India were active, seeking wood in Mbua Bay and along the Mathuata coast of Vanua Levu. By the end of 1809 reserves had been seriously depleted (Lockerby, unpub.) and soon afterwards Sydney vessels had ceased to call, in part because of the restrictions imposed on colonial merchants wishing to trade with China (Hainsworth, 1965). Occasional American or 'country' ships sought wood during the second decade of the century (Ward, 1965: 19) but the main centres of the trade had moved to the Hawaiian and Marquesas Islands. Nevertheless, by this time the political structure of Fiji had been influenced by the trade, with Mbua temporarily occupying an exalted position. Europeans were living permanently in the islands (Maude, 1964: 261) and with their help Mbau later became the dominant power. How widely the other results of the trade extended through the group is difficult to determine.

Sandalwood had been discovered in the Hawaiian Islands before 1791 but the earliest attempts at shipment to Canton were not followed up (Dodge, 1963: 102) and an active trade did not develop until 1811. The economic, political, and ecological effects were far-reaching; the royal family and lesser chiefs accumulated great wealth, the common people were exploited as labour, agriculture was neglected, and American merchants gained considerable influence. But by 1830 the accessible stands had been felled and the trade ceased (Kuykendall and Day, 1961: 41–3). The Marquesan trade began in about 1814 but lasted for little more than three years (Maude, 1959: 68). Thereafter little wood was shipped from the South Pacific until the later 1820s when Australian vessels obtained cargoes in the New Hebrides (Shineberg, 1965: 22–9). Low prices in Canton and profitable alternative employment in whaling and sealing in Australian waters resulted in a lull until 1841, but from then until the mid-1860s, Australian vessels were very active in the New Hebrides, New Caledonia, and near-by islands (Shineberg, 1965: 41–5). Here, as earlier in

Fiji and the Marquesas, the sandalwood trade enabled the indigenous people to obtain new tools, weapons, cloth, tobacco, and other goods. Sandalwood grew on many of the islands of Melanesia and these were affected directly while others were influenced indirectly. By the time the more accessible stands had been cut out other products, such as *bêche-de-mer* and coconut oil, helped to support the traders (several of whom were now resident in the islands) and to maintain the flow of trade goods into the islands. The process of technological change continued almost unchecked. The old social structures were progressively undermined and the distribution of settlement began to change under the influence of new economics, religion, and government.

The rise of the *bêche-de-mer* trade in Polynesia and Melanesia was closely linked with that of sandalwood, often providing an alternative income to traders faced with the depletion of the sandalwood resource. Therefore, it is often difficult to distinguish the consequences of one trade from that of the other. But in a few areas *bêche-de-mer* was of particular importance, because it preceded other trades, provided the only significant export over a considerable period, or was the product whose collection and processing required the most prolonged contact between the indigenous people and the seamen. That the trade did not attain equal importance as an agent of change in all parts of the Pacific was due to the uneven distribution of the edible holothurians, the relative availability of other trade items, and in some cases the overriding importance of other forms of contact.

At least twelve edible species of holothurians are found in the Pacific Islands but although several have a wide distribution throughout the Indo-Pacific region, the number of species declines to the east of Fiji (Clark, 1946). For example, the 'grey' kind, which Cooper (1888: 264) says was the most valuable,[1]

---

[1] The names given to different kinds of *bêche-de-mer* by Pacific traders varied both over the century of exploitation and from area to area. Because of this, and the fact that no thorough scientific collecting in the islands has been done and therefore, 'knowledge of the echinoderm fauna of the southwestern Pacific is fragmentary and incomplete' (Clark, 1946: 488), it is not always possible to identify species from the names given by the traders. Several species may receive the same trade name and a single species may fall into two commercial categories, according to the individuals' size or colour (Clark, 1921: 156). The characteristics of most

was rare to the east of 180° and it appears that paucity of edible species is one reason why the trade was never important in Hawaii or in the main island groups east of Fiji. 'Ironbound' coasts, as in Savai'i, provide a restricted habitat for the holothurians on some islands and this limited the trade opportunities in groups such as Samoa. Most of the edible species live in shallow water on the fringing reefs and sandy bottomed lagoons of high islands, or in similar habitats within atoll lagoons. Some species ingest sand and extract organic remains or small organisms from it as it passes through their digestive tubes while others 'collect and feed on small sea creatures' (Dakin, 1952: 334).

Before the holothurians became an article of commercial trade, many of the islanders used them for food. Wilkes (1852, i. 164, and ii. 219) reported their use on Tutuila and by the Gilbertese. The Caroline Islanders ate some varieties in times of scarcity (Christian, 1899: 375). The Fijians ate at least one type (Osborn, 1833–6: 250) and both they and the Yapese, who 'would not touch the Holothurians in either their raw or cooked state' (Tetens, 1958: 21), used at least one variety in fishing. When rubbed vigorously between the hands or against the sand or coral, they emitted a red liquid which drugged small fish in the vicinity (Salesius, c. 1906: 146; Hocart, 1929: 115; Thompson, 1940: 135). It seems that none of the islanders dried or cured *bêche-de-mer* until taught the techniques by Europeans or Chinese.

The Rise and Fall of the Trade

Until the early years of the nineteenth century the trade was restricted to the extreme western margins of the tropical Pacific. During the eighteenth century[1] Malays from Celebes visited the northern coast of Australia to collect and cure *bêche-de-mer*, and Flinders encountered part of a fleet of sixty vessels in 1803 (1814: ii. 230). The Sulu Sea was an important supply area but the Spanish monopoly kept out English and

value for classification into species, such as the calcareous particles in the body wall, are not necessarily attributes of commercial importance (Clark, 1946: 383).

[1] Flinders believed that the Malays had been visiting for little more than 20 years (1814: ii. 231) and although R. M. and C. H. Berndt (1953: 15) suggest that the visits may have begun in the early sixteenth century, archaeological evidence should soon provide more reliable dates (Mulvaney, 1966).

American vessels. At the beginning of the nineteenth century, Spanish traders also appear to have operated from Guam, presumably in the Marianas (Admiralty, 1811: 2), while Malay (from Celebes) and Chinese vessels may have obtained *bêche-de-mer* when visiting the north-west coasts of New Guinea for edible birds' nests and other products (Crawford, 1820: iii, 151, 441). Delano listed it as a possible trade item from New Guinea in 1791 (1817: 100).

The eastward expansion of the trade began tentatively in the first years of the nineteenth century. In 1803 the loss of the *Porpoise* and *Cato* on Wreck Reef led to the discovery of *bêche-de-mer* on the Great Barrier Reef and James Aitkin in a Sydney vessel obtained a partial cargo while attempting to recover material from the wrecks (King, 1804: 424; Aitkin, 1805: 620). In the following year Aitkin left Sydney in the *Marcia*, supposedly for 'the reefs and west side of New Caledonia, in quest of Trepang or Beche de Mer' (*Sydney Gazette*, 30 Sept. 1804) but actually went to Fiji for a sandalwood cargo. It must have been about this time also that a ship's officer (and presumably a ship) was 'a considerable time on the Pellew Islands [Palau] for the Purpose of Curing Beach lamar' (Lockerby, unpub.) and there may well have been other vessels working in the western Pacific. For example an English brig, the *Thomas*, was lost in the New Britain area in about 1810–15 while seeking *bêche-de-mer* and other products (Coulter, 1847: ii. 71–2). The earliest sandalwood traders apparently noted the existence of holothurians in Fiji (Kelly, 1820: 463–4) but it appears that no *bêche-de-mer* was actually collected and cured in Fiji until 1813. Small quantities were brought to Sydney by William Campbell in the *Hibernia* in 1810 and from Tahiti or the Tuamotus by Captain Folger in the *Trial* in 1811 (Maude, 1959: 87–8, and Cumpston, 1964: 71) but other commodities offered better prospects and there was little interest in South Pacific *bêche-de-mer* until the 1820s.

Interest then revived and in 1822 Benjamin Vanderford in the *Roscoe* obtained a small amount at Mbua Bay, Fiji ('Roscoe', unpub.) while in the same year a party of thirty-four from Hawaii were 'collecting Beach Lamar' on Fanning Island (*New Bedford Mercury*, 21 May 1824). Two years later a Spanish brig was seeking a cargo in Fiji (Driver, unpub.: 26 Oct. 1827) and in 1825 Morrell found *bêche-de-mer* on Pearl and Hermes Reef, at the western end of the Hawaiian chain (Morrell, 1832: 217). Whether there were similar prospecting voyages in the Carolines and elsewhere at this time is not known, but in 1827 Vanderford returned to Fiji and inaugurated eight years of relatively intense activity by Salem vessels. Sandalwood prices in China were low during the 1830s (Shineberg, 1965: 42) and New England, Hawaiian, and other vessels looked to *bêche-de-mer* as an alternative. Morrell cruised through the western Carolines in 1830 noting the presence of holothurians on several atolls before attempting to set up a shore establishment on Kilinailau.[1] The loss of twelve men forced its abandonment (1832: 376–410) but he later prospected along the coasts of New Britain, New Ireland, and New Guinea. Although he discovered one group where the reef was '*literally covered with* BÊCHE-DE-MER, *of a very superior quality*' (1832: 463) he apparently did not succeed in securing a cargo, nor did he disclose the location of this group. Shortly afterwards Captain Trainer, in the brigantine *Hound*, visited several of the Gilberts collecting *bêche-de-mer* and turtle shell (Coulter, 1847: i. 194–235) before gathering some *bêche-de-mer* at New Hanover and coasting westward along Northern New Guinea (Coulter, 1847: ii. 47, 100–74).

The late 1830s apparently saw a lull although Spanish vessels from Manila did attempt to obtain cargoes at Yap in 1836 (Cheyne, 1852: 154) and 'one or two small Manila vessels' obtained cargoes at Palau during the decade (Cheyne, unpub.: 326). A second peak of American activity in Fiji occurred in the early 1840s while Australian vessels began exploiting the reefs around New Caledonia and adjacent islands (Cheyne, 1852: 43; unpub.[2]). In 1843 Cheyne visited Palau and Yap (Cheyne, 1852: 146) and in 1844 he traded for *bêche-de-mer* at New Georgia. He then cruised northwards for a second visit to the Carolines later in the same year (1852: 94) before returning southwards to continue the trade in the atolls of the Solomons (Cheyne, 1852: 52). Other vessels, both American and Spanish,

---

[1] I am grateful to Dr. Dorothy Shineberg for suggesting that Morrell's establishment was on Kilinailau rather than Tauu.

[2] I am grateful to the Mitchell Library, Sydney, for permission to use a microfilm copy of this manuscript.

were also working in the Carolines in the 1840s and Australian traders operated in the Solomons and adjacent groups.

In the following decades the trade declined in relative importance in several groups, including Fiji, as coconut oil and other goods replaced it as the major export. The organization also changed, with permanent or semi-permanent shore stations buying from the islanders and storing the product until a ship called. Subsequently the main centre for the trade was in Torres Straits, on the Great Barrier Reef (Saville-Kent, 1893), along the south coast of Papua, and in the Louisiade Archipelago (Bevan, 1890; Finsch, 1887) and here the trade was still an important agent of cultural and ecological change in the last years of the century. Cooktown, in northern Queensland, was the base for the trade in this area and it is probable that exports from Queensland, Torres Straits, and Papua in the years 1880 to 1890 were greater than from any other area in the Pacific (excluding the Philippines) for any decade in the previous century. Elsewhere traders operating from Honolulu, Guam, Tahiti, or Manila continued to buy or cure small quantities of *bêche-de-mer* on almost every island where holothurians could be found in sufficient numbers (Cooper, 1888: 270). *Bêche-de-mer* remained a minor export of several territories in the twentieth century, generally being gathered and cured by the islanders and then sold to Chinese buyers. But in the late 1930s the Chinese and Japanese markets were closed and since then trade has not regained its pre-war importance.

It is impossible to trace the consequences of the trade in all the island groups—in some it was little more than a fleeting episode; for others there are virtually no records. But of all the territories which experienced the trade, the intensity and impact were probably greatest in Fiji and therefore the remainder of this paper will examine Fiji in some detail.

THE FIJIAN TRADE—1822–50

The sandalwood traders who reached Fiji in late 1804 included at least one, Aitkin,[1] who had had experience with *bêche-de-mer*, and Lockerby notes that when the *Jenny* left Port

---

[1] His name is spelled in various ways (Hainsworth, 1965: 4). I follow that used in *H.R.N.S.W.* (Aitkin, 1805).

Jackson in March 1808 William Dorr planned to obtain *bêche-de-mer* as well as sandalwood (Im Thurn and Wharton, 1925: 9, 81). But there is no firm evidence that any *bêche-de-mer* was actually collected and cured in Fiji before 1813.[1] In that year Captain Robson, in the East India Company ship *Hunter*, had difficulty obtaining a full cargo of sandalwood and therefore established a *bêche-de-mer* camp on Kamba Point, southeast Viti Levu (Dillon, 1813). The Jeffersonian embargo of 1807–9 and the British blockade of New England ports during the war of 1812 (1812–15) reduced the number of American ships visiting Fiji until the later 1810s (Morison, 1961: 187–212), while the depleted stands of sandalwood attracted few other vessels after 1811.

The re-entry of American interests into the Fiji area was marked by the visit in 1819 of the ship *Indus*, of Salem. The captain, Benjamin Vanderford, had been in Fiji in the *Active* in 1811 (Putnam, 1930: 158–9) and he returned in the *Roscoe* in 1822 to inaugurate the first main period of *bêche-de-mer* trading. The primary aim of the *Roscoe*'s visit was to obtain sandalwood and at least 74 tons were collected at Mbua Bay between 6 April and 21 July.[2] But in addition one of the crew, Benjamin Thomson, was sent ashore on 21 May 'to inform the natives in cureing [*sic*] Beach-le-mer' and a week later he returned on board with six barrels of it. More was obtained in the following month and in all '8 casks and one pipe of Beach-lee-mar' were discharged in Manila (Roscoe, unpub.: 18 Oct. 1822). We can assume from the evidence in the journal of Vanderford's next

---

[1] The *Jenny* had 2 tons (17 bags) of *bêche-de-mer* on board when taken as a prize by H.M.S. *Dover* off Canton in Dec. 1808 (Im Thurn and Wharton, 1825: 202–5) but this was loaded at Guam (Admiralty, 1811: 2). William Campbell landed 4 hogsheads of *bêche-de-mer* at Sydney in February 1810 after a voyage to Tahiti and Fiji (Cumpston, 1964: 71) but it is not certain where he obtained it. James Kelly, who had visited Fiji about 1807, stated in evidence to Commissioner Bigge in 1820 that *bêche-de-mer* 'is' procured there but there are no further details (Kelly, 1820: 464).

[2] The journal ('Roscoe', unpub.) records the amount of wood brought on board each day but the pages for 10–30 Apr. 1822 are missing. The total of 74 tons excludes any wood obtained during these three weeks. The brig reached Manila on 4 Oct. and discharged her *bêche-de-mer* on the 18th. The journal records discharging 2,849 'arrobes', 8 lb. of sandalwood (*c.* 32 tons) between 12 and 19 Nov. but wood discharged on other days is not recorded in the journal. Elsewhere I have ascribed this journal to Vanderford himself (Ward, 1965: 19, 299) but it was apparently kept by another officer.

voyage (Driver, unpub.) that this first consignment was cured by sun drying, a process which was slow and unreliable in Fiji's climate.

The next vessel to seek *bêche-de-mer* was a Spanish brig from Manila.[1] After spending three months at Viwa curing *bêche-de-mer*, the crew mutinied in January 1824 and killed the captain, mate, and boatswain. The Fijians then broke up the vessel for iron and the remainder of the crew, who included at least three Yapese (Cary, 1922: 43), stayed ashore in Fiji (Driver, unpub.: 16 Sept.; 6 Oct. 1827). This visit was to prove important despite its inauspicious ending. In September 1827 Vanderford returned in command of the ship *Clay*, with William Driver as second officer. At Mbua Bay two hundredweight of *bêche-de-mer* were brought on board but 'most was found to spoil . . . the sun not having power enough to dry it' (Driver, unpub.: 1 Oct. 1827). Driver, having learnt of the fate of the Spanish brig, visited Viwa and assisted by 'one of the Crew of the Brig whoo say'd he understood curing Beach le Marr' established a smoke-drying house 'where the Brig had cur'd before' (Driver, unpub.: 22 Oct.; 6 Nov. 1827). In this way the Americans learnt from the 'Manillamen' the smoke-drying technique which made large-scale processing feasible in Fiji.[2] At Viwa, the 'Natives being very eager for trade' (Driver, unpub.: 28 Nov. 1827), more holothurians were brought in than could be handled, there being a shortage of boilers. Within three months of starting curing, the *Clay* had expended her trade goods, obtained a cargo, and sailed for Manila, taking with her some of the crew of the *Laurice*, who were imprisoned

---

[1] Driver (unpub.: 16 Sept. 1827) gives the vessel as the *Laurice*, Captain Josep Belethana. Putnam (1930: 133) gives *Conception*, Captain Beges.

[2] In the *Salem Register*, 25 June 1883 it was claimed that Driver had 'cured' the 'first four cargoes of Beche-de-Mer ever cured by white men' but Vanderford's nephew John Franklin Brooks of Salem (then owner of the *Roscoe* journal) pointed out in the *Register* of 10 July that Vanderford had got *bêche-de-mer* in 1822 (Putnam, 1930: 97). Driver's reaction was to inscribe in red ink (dated 'Nashville, Oct. 27th 1883') across the page in his *Clay* journal for 16–18 Nov. 1827, the following: 'Here at Viwa I stayed and cured 480 Piculs of Beach Le Mar the first ever cured by white man. Ben Vanderford had Read Kotzbues Russian Voyage and dreamed of . . . [word illegible] a fortune by Boiling snails in a Dinner Pot after punching their Enterels out with a Stick etc. See my journal Mark 4 but he knew no more of Curing Beach Le Marr than my Dog does of the "Nicean Creed" and But for the Manilla Pirate our Voyage would have been a Failure. . . .' In view of Robson's venture neither Vanderford nor Driver can claim this honour.

on arrival. Having sold the cargo Vanderford returned to Fiji and Driver again set up a shore establishment on Viwa and cured a further 600 piculs of *bêche-de-mer*.[1]

After selling his second cargo, Vanderford sailed for Salem in the *Clay* but Driver returned to Fiji in the brig *Quill*, Captain Kinsman. The *Quill*, like the *Clay*, was owned by N. L. Rogers Brothers of Salem and she was soon joined in Fiji by the ship *Glide*, Captain Henry Archer, also of Salem, and the brig *Morliana*, Captain Maurice, of Oahu (Endicott, 1923; 23). The first two of these vessels, at least, got cargoes quickly[2] and by the time the *Glide* sailed for Manila in April 1830 the *Clay* was back in Fiji under Captain Millet. The rush was on. From then until 1835 three or four cargoes, each of between 35 and 70 tons of dried *bêche-de-mer*, were collected annually. Salem vessels continued to dominate the trade although at least three schooners from the Hawaiian Islands visited in 1831–2.[3]

By 1834 the holothurian population of the reefs of western and northern Vanua Levu and south-east Viti Levu had become depleted, though five vessels were still at work. Osborn noted that once the reef was cleared of holothurians, 'it is a long time before it is again covered, perhaps never' (Osborn, unpub.: 251), and Joseph Winn of the *Eliza* thought that only two more cargoes could be obtained on the Mathuata coast.[4] Whereas Eagleston had been able to complete cargoes for the *Peru* from only two shore establishments on each of his two visits in 1831–2, he had to build four to fill the *Emerald* in 1834 (Fig. 4.1) and it took him over 12 months to get a cargo for the *Mermaid* in 1837–8 (Eagleston, unpub.: A, B, and C). In order to reduce the time spent on the coast, traders began to employ tenders— vessels built in Fiji or brought from Salem.[5] These enabled a

---

[1] A picul is 133⅓ pounds.

[2] The *Quill* obtained a cargo of *c*. 800 piculs according to Endicott (unpub. B) and 580 piculs according to Putnam (1930: 134); the *Glide* got 'upwards of 1,000 piculs Bêch-le-Mar, 350 pounds T. shell and Some Sandall Wood' (Endicott, unpub. B).

[3] Schooners *Harriet* (Capt. Meak), *Hope* (Capt. Lolly), and *Minerva* (Capt. Peek). Eagleston (unpub. D: 287, 381) says the last two were seeking 'shell' rather than *bêche-de-mer*, and he differs from Endicott (unpub. B) who gives Captain Young as commander of the *Harriet*.

[4] Joseph Winn to John Winn, Aug. 1834 (in Winn, Joseph, unpub.).

[5] For example the *Eliza* brought materials for the schooner *Coral* from Salem and she was built in New Zealand and sailed to Fiji (John Winn to Joseph Winn, in Winn, Joseph, unpub.; S. C. Phillips to Joseph Winn, 23 May 1833, in Winn, Joseph, unpub.).

ship to have a number of shore drying-stations operating at once. Resident Europeans or 'Manillamen' were often employed in these small vessels or as interpreters and drying-house supervisors, thus beginning the change from an essentially ship-based trade to one organized from ashore.

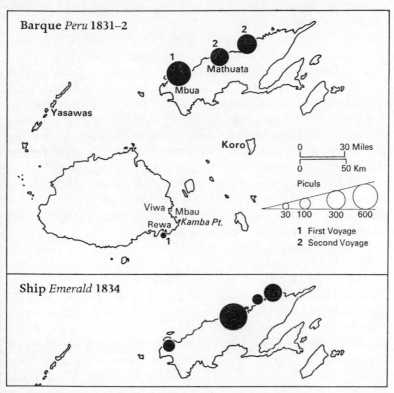

FIG. 4.1. Location and production of shore stations established by Captain Eagleston. Source: Eagleston, unpub. A and B.

The growing difficulties in getting a cargo and the greater number of ships increased the competition and worsened relations between the traders. Whenever possible captains tried to persuade Fijians to trade only with themselves or their agents. In November 1834 a dispute over fishing territories almost ended in fighting as Vanderford and Chapman in the *Consul* threatened to fire on the *Emerald*, and Eagleston in turn threatened to sink the *Consul* (Chapman, unpub.: 14 Nov. 1834;

Eagleston, unpub. B, and unpub. D: 46). The Fijians also became more willing to take offensive action against ships. After they were wrecked, the *Laurice* (1824), *Faun* (1830), *Glide*, and *Niagara* (1831) were all stripped by Fijians seeking iron but the crews were not attacked. However, in late 1833 nine of the crew of the *Charles Doggett* were killed at Kandavu (Eagleston, unpub. D: 9–10) and in July 1834 the French brig, *Amiable Josephine* was captured at Viwa (Osborn, unpub.). In September a chief from Mbau unsuccessfully encouraged Vanua Levu Fijians to seize the *Consul* as taking the French brig had been 'very easy' (Chapman, unpub.: 4 Sept. 1834). The motives for these actions are not always clear from the New Englanders' accounts, but the fact that this might be an easier means of obtaining trade goods now that 'fishing' was harder, plus an accumulation of resentment against some of the traders may have been important.[1] In any case, the greater difficulties within the group combined with falling prices in Manila[2] to bring a lull in the trade. Between 1836 and 1841, it seems that only three vessels came seeking *bêche-de-mer*,[3] though others visited the group for different reasons.

In 1842 the brig *Gambia* of Salem[4] came to Fiji (Putnam, 1930: 46) and was followed in late 1843 by the schooner *Warwick*, Captain Cheever, also of Salem (Cheever, unpub. A). This marked the start of a second period in intensive *bêche-de-mer* trading and in 1844 five, and two years later at least seven, vessels (excluding local cutters) were working along the Fijian coasts. Salem vessels were again prominent and this port accounted for five of the seven vessels known to have been trading in 1846. By this time the internal situation in Fiji was

[1] 'About all the fish at Rewa in July 1831 had been cleared from the reefs, which put a stop to their obtaining any amount of trade. This they much wanted, and as it could not be reached by fair means, they were on the lookout, and ready to do so by foul, if an opening offered' (Eagleston, unpub. D: 296).

[2] The *Clay*'s second cargo had sold for $32.30 per picul in 1829 (Driver, unpub.) but Eagleston received $14 per picul for the *Emerald*'s cargo in 1835. The Chinese were then unwilling to buy 'owing to the ship Augustus, ship Eliza, and Brig Consul having arrived some time before with cargoes and the Chinese fearing there would be another ship arrive after me' (Eagleston, unpub. B: Aug. 1835).

[3] Brig *Mermaid* of Salem, Captain Eagleston, in 1837–8; *Sir David Ogilby* of Sydney, Captain Hutchins, in 1838; *Leonidas* of Salem, Captain Eagleston, in 1840.

[4] Mrs. Wallis states that her husband commanded the *Gambia* on this voyage (1851: 94) but Putnam—not the most reliable of sources—gives Edward A. King as captain.

rather different. The permanent European population was larger; missionaries were quite well established; and British, American, and French naval vessels had visited the group, and on occasion effected reprisals for earlier attacks on *bêche-de-mer* ships. Fiji was a safer place in which to live ashore and to trade than it had been in the mid-1830s.[1]

The main changes in the trade since the previous period arose from the fact that the holothurian population had still not recovered completely. Even the schooner *Warwick*, a relatively small vessel, took 14 months to obtain a full cargo, and had to build seven shore stations to do so. Eagleston had cured an average of 300 piculs at each of the shore stations built on his first three visits (Fig. 4.1) whereas Cheever (unpub. A) averaged only 100 piculs at the five stations for which he records production (Fig. 4.2). Higher prices in Manila helped compensate for the longer time spent in Fijian waters[2] and operations were extended to exploit most of the sizeable reefs in the group. Shore stations were established for the first time in northern and western Viti Levu and apparently in the Yasawas and some of the smaller eastern islands. European residents chartered their small boats to the visiting traders on a bigger scale than previously, and some apparently established curing stations on their own account and sold the dried *bêche-de-mer* to the visiting ships. In this period too, the Fijians began curing small quantities without European direction.

After 1850 the number of ships coming for *bêche-de-mer* again dropped. This was due in part to declining returns, but the disturbed political state in Fiji also contributed. In the early 1850s the power of Mbau was weakened and there was increased internal warfare. Thakombau, who wielded the effective power in Mbau for some years before he became the chief in 1852, had attempted to make a levy, to be paid in *bêche-de-mer*, on the coastal people under Mbau's nominal control. But even supported by several thousand fighting men he was unable to collect sufficient to pay for the vessels he had obtained

---

[1] Although Mrs. Wallis (1851) and William Diaper (1853; 1928) show that safety was only relative. Legge (1966: 76–90) has shown that Diaper was the author of 'Jackson's Narrative' (Diaper, 1853).

[2] Wallis spent a total of 37 months in Fiji waters getting his three cargoes in the *Zotoff* (Wallis, 1851). In 1849 reports reaching Fiji gave the latest price in Manila as $30 per picul (Williams to H. Williams, 26 Sept. 1849, in Williams, unpub.).

from Australia and New England. The latter had been obtained by Captain Wallis in return for a promise of 1,000 piculs of *bêche-de-mer*, but when this was not forthcoming Wallis took a party of Fijians to New Caledonia to get a cargo. This was only partly successful and he gave up waiting for a cargo in Fiji (Derrick, 1957: 105–6). A few vessels continued to call for *bêche-de-mer* but other items were now being exported and *bêche-de-mer* never again dominated Fiji's export trade.[1] In the latter half of the nineteenth century Fijians continued to prepare some for sale to resident or visiting traders. The quantity fluctuated considerably, falling when internal affairs in Fiji were unsettled (Jones, 1865: 26) or when there were 'disturbances' in China (Owen, 1864: 28), and rising when the demand in Manila or elsewhere increased.[2] Production continued in the twentieth century and in 1931 143 tons (valued at £16,045 were exported (Turbet, 1942: 153) but since the middle 1930s exports have been insignificant owing to the closing of the Chinese market. For the last century other products, especially coconut oil and copra, have been much more attractive means of obtaining trade goods or cash, and since 1850 the *bêche-de-mer* trade has not been an important agent of change.

The Trading and Curing Processes and Establishments

For almost 30 years *bêche-de-mer* was the principal export from Fiji. Although the effects of the trade may have been less dramatic than those of the sandalwood trade (and have certainly received less attention from scholars) they were in some respects more far-reaching. For many parts of Fiji, the *bêche-de-mer* traders were the first white people to establish contact. The trade provided the first industrial process to be taught to the Fijians by Europeans. Very large labour forces were required for fishing and curing, and the workers were often employed under European direction for months on end.[3] It appears that

---

[1] In 1865 *bêche-de-mer* accounted for 6 per cent of exports by value (coconut oil, 47 per cent) and in 1869 for only 0·13 per cent (cotton 79 per cent) (*Consular Report*, 1871: 226).

[2] In 1865 it was in 'great demand' in Australia for the use of Chinese immigrants (Jones, 1866: 166).

[3] In the sandalwood trade the wood was usually cut by the ships' crews or bought from the Fijians at the shore, having been cut by them under the supervision of their chiefs (Lockerby, unpub.).

conflicts of interest between indigenous and European labour demands were greater in the *bêche-de-mer* trade than previously. The greater time which vessels spent on the coast, and their greater numbers, increased the impact on indigenous society, and on agriculture and vegetation as food and firewood were required in large quantities. Finally, it seems that the quantity of tools, arms, and other trade goods entering the islands was much greater than was the case with the sandalwood trade, which lasted for a much shorter period and was directly concerned with a relatively small part of the island group.

The effects of the trade in Fiji were closely related to the requirements of collecting and curing. On arrival at a promising stretch of coast the trader endeavoured to negotiate with a local chief for the building of a shore establishment, for the provision of firewood, and for Fijians to collect the *bêche-de-mer* and provide labour on shore. Agreement would be reached on a scale of payment for 'fish', wood, and labour in terms of muskets, pistols, axes, and other trade goods. The drying-houses built by the Americans were usually 100–120 feet long and 20 feet wide and constructed of thatch over a coconut log frame. A trench two feet deep and six feet wide, in which the fire was built, ran the length of the house and above this a frame of coconut logs and battens provided a double rack on which the holothurians were laid for drying. Barrels of water stood alongside the trench for use in controlling the fire or preventing the accidental destruction of the house. A second building contained the trade goods and served as a residence for the trading master. Near by a pit lined with coconut logs and filled with sea water held the holothurians before they were cleaned and boiled in the iron pots standing alongside. Around this complex, which was often sited at some distance from any village, the Fijians usually built a collection of houses to be occupied for the fishing period (Osborn, unpub.: 252–3; Eagleston, unpub. A; Wilkes, 1844: iii. 231–4).

Collection of the holothurians by diving from canoes or by wading along the reef at low water often continued day and night as some species were most easily taken by moonlight (Osborn, unpub.: 251). From 20 to 80 canoes might be working at once (Hartwell, unpub.: 30 June 1845; Endicott, 1923: 25) and Endicott states that there would be an average of ten men for each canoe (1923: 15). On shore the holothurians, generally ranging in length from 6 to 18 inches, were measured into 160-gallon casks to assess payment, and then kept in the sea-water pit. Cleaning and boiling the 'fish' occupied fifteen to twenty men and a similar number were employed in the drying house where the 'fish' were laid on the racks for about 4 days, being turned periodically. More youths and boys assisted in loading the ship with the dried *bêche-de-mer*. Altogether, an average-size establishment employed at least thirty men, and an equal number of boys, on shore, perhaps 200 in collecting, and another 100 or so in cutting firewood. These, plus their dependants, made up what Eagleston called 'our little city' (unpub. D: 328).

With fishing in full swing on an undepleted reef, 3 tons or more of dried *bêche-de-mer* might be obtained in a week (Driver, unpub.: 12 Sept. 1828) but towards the end of operations the quantity usually dropped to one or two piculs per day. In 1847 the *Sir John Franklin* got only 30 piculs in 4 months (Cheever, unpub. B: 21 Nov. 1847). At first a vessel might obtain a full cargo from one or two drying-houses (Fig. 4.1) but later, as the reefs were depleted ten or twelve might be required to gather a cargo of up to 70 tons of dried *bêche-de-mer*. Such a cargo represented 600–700 tons of 'green' holothurians (Finsch, 1887: 17; Cary, 1922: 48). It appears that in the period from 1828 to 1835 some 600 tons of dried *bêche-de-mer* were cured and exported in at least fifteen cargoes. The second main period saw the export of a similar quantity.

Trade Goods and Muskets

As suggested above, the impact of the trade on the indigenous communities was both direct and widespread. Perhaps the most obvious effect was the acquisition by the Fijians of large quantities of new tools, ornaments, and weapons. The trade goods offered by the sandalwood traders included axes, adzes, knives, cloth, mirrors, beads, whales' teeth, and other ivory (Lockerby, unpub.). The *bêche-de-mer* traders continued to supply these goods (see Tables 4.1 and 4.2) which were in considerable demand. The influx of iron tools, begun by the sandalwooders, ended the stone and shell tool-making industries, as it did elsewhere in the Pacific (Shineberg, 1965: 204–11; 1966: 142–6), and greatly lightened many subsistence tasks (Salisbury, 1962: 109). Similarly, imported cloth and ornaments were widely adopted in place of equivalent articles of indigenous manufacture. It is impossible to assess the extent to which these substitutions modified the labour requirements of different sectors of the economy—but elsewhere the effect has been shown to be very considerable and we may assume that the same was true in Fiji in the first 40 years of the nineteenth century.[1] Tables 4.1 and 4.2 show the types of trade goods imported.

TABLE 4.1. *Merchandise Shipped in Brig* Spy *of Salem, Capt. J. B. Knight, 1832*

Fish hooks		1,864	Looking glasses	473
Rings, gilt and brass		852	Earrings (boxes)	12
Razors		300	Scissors	3,621
Files		142	Iron Jews Harps	72
Plane irons		600	Knives	156
Chisels		41	Axes and Hatchets	111
Tobacco (lb.)		2,315+	Shirtings (yards)	5,691
Muskets and guns		241	Pistols	12
Flints	15 lb.+	250	Bullet moulds	44
Iron (lb.)		4,877	Lead (lb.)	719
Whales' teeth (lb.)		571		

In addition to the above, the merchandise included small quantities of beads, bells, caricatures, lace, medallions, prints, and vermilion, together with equipment and clothing obviously for the use of the crew. The total value of the merchandise was apparently $3,614.90 (Phillips, unpub.).

The sandalwood traders do not appear to have used firearms as trade goods and the relatively few muskets which reached Fiji before 1820 came mainly from wrecked ships and were generally used by resident Europeans acting as mercenaries (Derrick, 1957: 42–7). The introduction of large numbers of firearms seems to have been the distinctive contribution of the *bêche-de-mer* traders. In 1827 Driver gave one musket for sixteen hogsheads of fresh holothurians (Cary, 1922: 47) and thereafter firearms were probably the most important single

---

[1] Salisbury (1962: 108) has estimated that amongst the Siane of New Guinea, provision of subsistence requirements absorbed 80 per cent of all labour when stone tools were used, but only 50 per cent after they had adopted steel tools. Shineberg (1966: 143–6) discusses these changes in western Melanesia.

trade item. Almost all the journals which state the amount of trade given in return for *bêche-de-mer*, firewood, or agricultural produce, do so primarily in terms of muskets.[1] It is impossible to calculate accurately the number of weapons imported but the quantities brought in the *Spy*, *Emerald*, and *Eliza* (and schooner *Coral*) together with the prices paid by their captains and other traders for holothurians and firewood,[2] suggest that well over 5,000 firearms were introduced between 1828 and 1835. As many were probably imported between 1842 and 1850.

TABLE 4.2. *Merchandise Shipped in Ship* Emerald *of Salem, Capt. J. H. Eagleston, 1833*

Fish hooks	102,880	Looking glasses	744
Rings, brass, and pewter	288	Scissors	9,238
Beads (doz.)	c. 1,760	Bells, Polish	36
Razors	120	Jews harps	676
Plane irons	1,200	Knives	5,650
Spike Gimlets	24	Adzes	39
Tobacco (lb.)	4,039	Axes and hatchets	300
Cigars	22,825	Pistols	78
Muskets, guns, and rifles	598	Percussion caps	6,000
Bullet moulds	60	Lead (lb.)	2,337

In addition to the above, the merchandise included small quantities of vermilion, brass wire, and garden seeds, together with clothing, sawn timber, tools, casks, and other equipment obviously for use of the crew. Apparently, gunpowder and iron were also shipped but not listed in this invoice. The total value of the goods invoiced was $15,249.87 (invoice given in Eagleston, unpub. D).

The freeing of labour from other tasks, brought about by the introduction of metal tools, and the new firepower provided by muskets, gave a means and incentive for increased warfare

[1] In 1831 Eagleston gave one musket or one keg of powder for twelve 160-gallon casks of holothurians, one pistol for five casks, one axe for two casks (unpub. D: 292). In return for *c.* 438 lb. tortoiseshell, 110 pigs, 3,100 yams, building materials, and several other small items, John Winn in the schooner *Coral* gave sixty firearms, over eight kegs of powder, over 630 balls, 25 lb. lead, thirteen whales' teeth, plus cloth and other items between 23 Jan. and 6 Apr. 1834. By 11 July he had bartered 209 muskets (Winn, Joseph, unpub.).

[2] Eagleston noted that the firewood cost more to obtain than the fresh holothurians. Fifty cords of firewood were needed to cure 100 piculs of *bêche-de-mer* and a musket was given for a heap of wood apparently measuring about eight cords (Eagleston, unpub. B: Jan. 1835).

during the first half of the century. Both tools and weapons were unevenly distributed through the islands, and as the trade moved from one area to another the local balance of power was frequently upset. Those who obtained weapons were often eager to break off 'fishing' to take advantage of their new firepower. Those who did not were often 'Jealous that the tribe fishing is getting too much property & so burn' the drying-houses to stop the trade (Osborn, unpub.: 257). On other occasions preventive wars were waged (Eagleston, unpub. D: 339–40). In the wider political scene, the forces of Mbau greatly increased their firepower during the *bêche-de-mer* period as Mbau had close relations with many of the coastal groups in the main production areas. This was to be an important factor enabling Thakombau to establish Mbau as the dominant political unit in the 1850s.[1] What pork did for Tahiti, *bêche-de-mer* did for Fiji.

The Changing Population

The acquisition of muskets in large numbers led to changes in the techniques of war, in the mode of fortifying villages, and to an increased death toll from local warfare. There is in-sufficient evidence to assess the increase in deaths with any accuracy and there must have been considerable regional variation in death rates. Wallis, for example, quotes a Fijian observer to the effect that the decline of population due to the use of firearms had been particularly marked along the Mbua coast (1851: 383–4). Furthermore, the increased number of deaths did not follow solely from the greater effectiveness of the musket as a relatively long-range weapon. The general increase in warfare meant more destruction of villages and gardens and the consequent hardship suffered by whole communities had a serious effect on the demographic situation (*Report* . . ., 1896: 81–2).

The indirect effects of war and disruption were accompanied by the direct effects of the introduction of new diseases. Epidemics had followed the wreck of the *Argo* in 1800 and the visit

---

[1] In the late 1820s Mbau had about 100 muskets when a party of 4,000 warriors attacked villages on the island of Koro (Cary, 1922: 29) but in June 1846 a force under Thakombau had at least 484 muskets (Wallis, 1851: 213–15).

of the *El Plumier* in 1801 (Im Thurn and Wharton, 1925: xli–xlvi) and the tradition of these afflictions was retained in songs recorded in the 1890s (*Report*, 1896: Appendix, 1–2). There is little firm evidence to connect specific illnesses with visits by *bêche-de-mer* ships. A skin disease introduced in the early 1820s (*Report*, 1896: 36) may have resulted from the visit of the *Roscoe* in 1822 or the *Indus* in 1819, but the traders themselves rarely made any mention of the health of the Fijians. Nevertheless there can be little doubt, in view of the notes of illness among the crews, that the illnesses thereby introduced had a deleterious effect on the Fijian population.[1]

The *bêche-de-mer* trade and traders also influenced the population in other ways. McArthur (1966) has shown the extent to which miscegenation in the late eighteenth and early nineteenth centuries must have modified the island populations of later generations and Fiji was certainly no exception. Paddy Connel and Diaper, both of whom worked for *bêche-de-mer* traders though neither came to Fiji as a direct result of the trade, are reported to have had forty-eight (Derrick, 1957: 67) and thirty-eight (Diaper, 1928: 6) children respectively. Other Europeans may have had fewer children but, quite apart from those who didn't stay, the number of sailors from *bêche-de-mer* ships who deserted, were paid off, or wrecked in Fiji during the period 1827 to 1850 was considerable and their total demographic effect must have been quite significant. The visiting vessels provided employment on board and ashore for the European residents and were thus instrumental both in bringing and maintaining many of those who founded Fiji's part-European population. It is also fair to say that certain of the special occupational roles of this component of Fiji's population were established at this time. The European residents built the first small vessels, began internal commercial trading, provided skilled labour, and acted as intermediaries between Europeans and Fijians.

[1] There is, however, no Fijian equivalent of the case of the Anchorite islanders of the western Bismarck archipelago who were virtually eliminated by disease brought home by some of the islanders who had gone to the Carolines to work as *bêche-de-mer* divers (N.I.D., 1945: iv. 145). It might also be noted that on occasion the crews were infected by 'Fijian diseases'. Two men of the bark *Pallas*, Captain H. Archer Jr., of Salem, contracted 'a Disorder Called the thauk perculiar to the Fegee Islands Coming in Large Ulcers or Sores' (Archer, unpub. B: 11 Oct. 1835).

The number of non-Europeans who came to Fiji with the *bêche-de-mer* ships was also considerable, and Larsson (1961) has pointed out that they may have been important and largely unrecognized agents of inter-island cultural diffusion. A few Chinese and 'Lascars' had been in Fiji on sandalwood vessels, but the *bêche-de-mer* traders with their larger labour requirements brought many more people from a much wider range of places. For example in 1828 on her second visit to Fiji the crew of the *Clay* (excluding officers) consisted of eleven Salem men, four 'Manillamen', seven Tahitians, two Caroline Islanders, and one 'Bengalla' (Driver, unpub.: 28 May 1828). In the following year the *Glide* brought six Maoris from New Zealand (Endicott, unpub. A: 23 May 1829), and this became a recommended practice.[1] At least two of the *Glide*'s Maoris attempted to desert to live with the Fijians within a month of their arrival (Endicott, unpub. B) and after the wreck of the vessel in March 1831 they all may have stayed. Other Polynesians certainly stayed in Fiji, as did the three Rotumans and two Tahitians discharged at Rewa from the bark *Pallas* (Archer, unpub. A: 8 Sept. 1833). At the same time Fijians were carried to other islands, to Manila, and even to New England.[2] At first the numbers were small but late in the *bêche-de-mer* period considerable numbers were involved, and in 1853 seventy to eighty men were recruited to go to New Caledonia in the *J. H. Millay*.[3] Although these population movements have had some demographic effects their main significance lies in the rapid widening of communications between Fijians and other communities. The traders not only established contact with Australasia, New England, and Manila, but also with neighbouring island groups. It is important to stress that those who brought 'western' ways to Fiji were often 'Manillamen', Tahitians, or other

---

[1] For example Captain Kinsman recommended shipping four 'Manila men' (he paid them $4.00 per month) or six Maoris as 'most of them have been brought up in English Whale ships' (Kinsman, letter of 18 Sept. 1830, in Winn, Joseph, unpub.).

[2] Eagleston took a Fijian to New England and in 1836 he was being 'exhibited at the Baltimore Museum' (*Lynn Record*, 5 May 1836). A Fijian girl also made two visits to the United States with Captain Wallis (Wallis, 1851: 413). Eagleston also took Brown, one of Paddy Connel's sons, to Manila in 1831. While there he contracted smallpox but recovered and when discharged at Rewa in July 1832 was 'in as good order, as when he left' (Eagleston, unpub. D: 344, 392).

[3] J. B. Williams to Henry Williams, 24 Jan. 1853 (Williams, unpub.).

Polynesians who had had longer and more intense contact with Europeans or Americans. Furthermore, the communication links established in this way also provided opportunities for the interchange of ideas and artefacts between island groups which hitherto had been relatively isolated.

Contact with other Pacific islanders who had adopted some foreign ways, together with the experience of working under the direction of persons other than traditional leaders helped institute the processes of change in socio-economic organization which have continued until the present. It was not uncommon for the labour demands of the *bêche-de-mer* trade to conflict with traditional labour requirements. Labour was withdrawn from fishing or drying for many reasons—to attend a feast (Eagleston, unpub. D: 339), to take part in a local war (Archer, unpub. C: 6 Sept. 1846), or 'to take care of . . . the harvest' (Hartwell, unpub.: 1 Jan. 1845). The traders did what they could to prevent such interruptions, to the extent of putting two leading chiefs in irons to prevent their followers from holding a *solevu*[1] (Wallis, 1851: 117). This attempt proved unsuccessful, but more subtle forms of persuasion sometimes worked. The conflicting requirements and new choices in labour allocation and systems of authority which were thus introduced accelerated the processes of social change.

Food and Agriculture

Even if on specific occasions the Fijians were unwilling to engage in the trade, in general they were very anxious to do so until such time as the depletion of the holothurian population reduced the returns in proportion to the labour required. That the Fijians were willing partners in the trade process is indicated by the fact that they were prepared to cut down valuable coconut palms to provide building materials for the drying-houses, sea-water ponds, and other structures. The construction

---

[1] A large feast and presentation. This was in 1835 and the vessel was probably the *Pallas*, Captain Henry Archer. Archer's own journal (unpub. B) has no entries between 13 March and 4 Oct. 1835 and therefore does not mention the incident. The entry for 4 Oct. 1835 states that 'After a Long Stay at the Fejees we are about leaving it after Trying Every way to please the Native Chief by giving presents and etc. they would not fish any More'. Mrs. Wallis (1851: 124) states that the story of the chiefs in irons preceded them around the group and the Fijians feared to have anything to do with them.

of a drying-house of average dimensions required the trunks of about 35 palms,[1] equivalent to nearly half an acre of palms at average planting density. This makes no allowance for the coconut logs used to line the sea-water ponds or to build the trade house, and it suggests that at a time when coconut stands were apparently smaller than they are today the trade made considerable inroads into village groves, particularly along parts of the north and west coasts of Vanua Levu.

A more positive consequence for agriculture was the market for foodstuffs provided by the visiting vessels, their crews, and local employees. Earlier visitors had also traded for foodstuffs but the *bêche-de-mer* captains had bigger crews to feed for longer periods and therefore extended the business to many other parts of the group. While fishing and drying proceeded on shore the vessel sometimes cruised along the coast and to other islands seeking yams, pigs, and tortoiseshell while in the 1840s local cutters were often employed trading for foodstuffs throughout the group. They also bought *yanggona* (*Piper methysticum*) 'among the Lee Ids. where it is plenty and . . . took it to windward for presents to the chiefs' (Osborn, unpub.: 249). That the total quantities bought were considerable is indicated by the fact that even the small schooner *Warwick* (Fig. 4.2) collected at least 32 tons of yams and 128 pigs during 13 months (Cheever, unpub. A). The search for foodstuffs and shell extended the direct influence of the *bêche-de-mer* vessels beyond those areas where the 'fishing' actually took place and enabled coastal people in almost every island to obtain firearms and other trade goods straight from the visitors.[2] From this time onwards the supplying of foodstuffs to visiting vessels and to European residents increased steadily and a commercial element was firmly established in the agriculture of some coastal villages.

The supply of garden produce was not restricted to indigenous crops. As early as 1809 Fijians in Mathuata were cultivating pineapples and pumpkins 'with some care' and offered them

---

[1] Estimate based mainly on description of houses in Eagleston (unpub. B: Jan. 1835) and Osborn (unpub.: 252–3).

[2] Representative of the prices paid were one musket per 1,000 yams (but one for 700–800 of the large yams from Taveuni) in 1832 (Eagleston, unpub. D: 395) and one musket for six pigs and 700 yams and another for seven pigs and 300 yams in 1834 (Winn, John, unpub.: 22 May 1834).

for sale to a group of missionaries waiting there for the repair of the vessel in which they were *en route* to Sydney from Tahiti (Davies, 1925: 145). These crops had been introduced from sandalwood vessels, and the *bêche-de-mer* traders continued the practice. Eagleston brought boxes of seeds with him on his

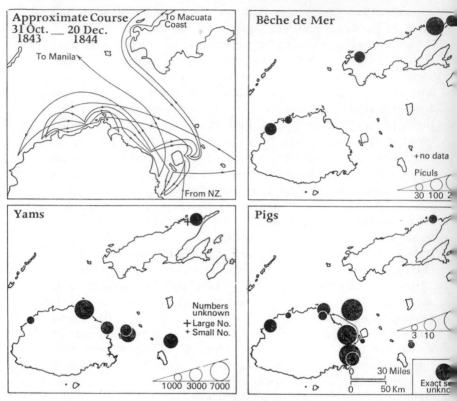

FIG. 4.2. *Bêche-de-mer* stations and purchase of supplies, schooner *Warwick*.
Source: Cheever, unpub. A.

visits to Fiji (Table 4.2), and other traders apparently did the same.[1] Potatoes may have been introduced in this way as Chapman (unpub.: 30 Oct. 1834) records how Vanderford

---

[1] During his ill-fated visit to Kilinailau in May 1830, Morrell planted 'potatoes, yams, pumpkins, oranges, apples, pears, peaches, plums, onions, cabbages, beets, carrots, parsnips, artichokes, beans, pease, watermelons, and musk-melons' and endeavoured to instruct the islanders in the care of the garden (Morrell, 1832: 404).

returned on board the *Consul* off Mathuata with 'the boat loaded with potatoes'.[1] In addition to introducing seeds, Eagleston also brought six two-year-old calves to Fiji in 1834 and he claimed that these were the first cattle introduced to the group. They were 'the great attraction and wonder of all' at Rewa and he gave two to the chief Phillips (Thokanauto) who had accompanied him on the voyage to Tahiti (Eagleston, unpub. D: 29).[2] By this time goats had been introduced and Captain Knight was able to purchase one at Moala in 1833 (Knight, unpub.: 19 May 1833) while two years previously Eagleston had been offered some at Rotuma (Eagleston, unpub. D: 346).

Firewood and Vegetation

In addition to bringing changes to agriculture, the *bêche-de-mer* trade had a profound effect on the vegetation of some coastal areas. In some parts of the Pacific sun-drying was an effective means of curing the holothurians, but in Fiji's climate it was unreliable and the boiling and drying process required half a cord of firewood for every picul of *bêche-de-mer* produced.[3] Such was the demand for wood that on occasions the absence of sufficient quantities prevented the building of drying-houses in what otherwise would have been suitable places. There is no evidence to suggest that any particular species was preferred and it seems that anything that would burn was cut. Several of the small islands, such as Mali, off the north shore of Vanua Levu, lost most of their timber at this time. On Ngaloa Island, the wood available for building and firewood was soon exhausted and Eagleston had to have further supplies brought from the mainland of Vanua Levu (Eagleston, unpub. D: 307–8). Eagleston once measured 110 cords of logs (*c.* 13,000 cubic feet

---

[1] The journal also records trading for 'hogs and potatoes' at Rotuma (Chapman, unpub.: 12 Jan. 1835). It is possible that Chapman is using the word 'potatoes' to refer to yams, sweet potatoes, or other root vegetables.

[2] Derrick (1957: 57), following Wall (1919), says that 'Cokanauto styled himself Phillips on the strength of a voyage to the United States in a whaler'. But in July 1831, when about 16 years old, Thokanauto was sent on board Eagleston's bark *Peru*, as a hostage by his brother Mbanuve (Kania) of Rewa. He became 'quite attached to the ship, and a great favourite with all hands, and so much so with me that I gave him the name of S. C. Phillips, after my owner, and by the last he was ever after called' (Eagleston, unpub. D: 292).

[3] Finsch (1887: 17) writing about the trade in New Guinea, states that nine tons of firewood were needed to produce one ton of *bêche-de-mer*.

stacked) piled up around one of his Mathuata drying-houses (unpub. A: 20 Sept. 1832) and it is not surprising therefore that all the burnable timber in the vicinity of the larger houses was removed or that the need to bring wood from ever-increasing distances led to the Fijians demanding higher prices for fire-wood (Eagleston, unpub. A: 11–12 Sept. 1832). Indeed the 'fish [holothurians] costs much less than the wood' (Osborn, unpub.: 255).

In the period 1827–35 well over 500,000 cubic feet of stacked firewood must have been burnt by the traders. All this came from areas close to the coast and most was cut in the drier western parts of the main islands where the vegetation was lighter than in the more humid east. The second boom in the 1840s consumed a similar quantity and these two periods therefore saw a dramatic start to the increasing pressure on the vegetation of the group which has continued to the present time.

Although we shall never know the full details of the impact of the nineteenth-century trading activities on the political, social, and ecological situation in Fiji, or any other island group, the evidence that is now becoming available shows that the consequences in the early decades of the century were more varied and far-reaching than has generally been believed. The *bêche-de-mer* traders, by widening the areas in contact with the outside world, providing a market for foodstuffs produced by Fijians, and bringing agents of demographic change, were continuing the processes begun by their predecessors, the sandalwood traders. But by employing large numbers of indigenous workers and teaching them new jobs, depleting the holothurian fauna and the vegetation around the shore stations, selling large numbers of weapons and bringing Tahitians, Maoris, and other islanders to Fiji, the *bêche-de-mer* traders proved to be much more effective as agents of socio-economic and landscape change than were their predecessors. It is clear that the missionaries and the observers of the middle of the nineteenth century, and the administrators of the last quarter of the century, were viewing a people whose life and land had already been profoundly changed by the 'invasion' of visiting European and New England mariners.

BIBLIOGRAPHY

Admiralty. 1811. *Proceedings of Admiralty Appeal Court, London, in case of ship Jenny, William Dorr the younger, Master 1811*, London.

Aitkin, J. 1805. James Aitkin to Governor King, 13 May 1805, in *Historical Records of New South Wales*, (*H.R.N.S.W.*), vol. 5, Sydney, 1897, pp. 620–2.

Archer, H., unpub. A. 'Journal of Voyage from Salem to Fegees and Manila in Bark Pallas commanded by Captn. Henry Archer . . . 1832, 1833–1834,' Essex Institute, Salem.

—— unpub. B. 'Journal of a Voyage from Salem to New Zealand in the Bark Pallas, Salem, commanded by Captn. Henry Archer, Jr. . . . 1834–36', Essex Institute, Salem.

—— unpub. C. 'Journal of Bark Samos on a Voyage to New Zealand and the South Pacific, Henry Archer, Master, 1845–7', Essex Institute, Salem.

Beaglehole, J. C. (ed.). 1955. *The Journals of Captain James Cook on his Voyages of Discovery*, I, *The Voyage of the Endeavour*, Cambridge.

—— (ed.). 1961. *The Journals of Captain James Cook on his Voyages of Discovery*, II, *The Voyage of the Resolution and Adventure 1772–1775*, Cambridge.

Berndt, R. M. and C. H. 1953. *Arnhem Land*, Melbourne.

Bevan, T. F. 1890. *Toil, Travel and Discovery in British New Guinea*, London.

Cary, W. S. 1922. *Wrecked on the Feejees*, Nantucket, Mass.

Chapman, I. N., unpub. 'Journal of a Voyage from New York to the Pacific in the Brig Consul 1834', Essex Institute, Salem.

Cheever, G. W., unpub. A. 'Journal of Schooner Warwick from Boston to New Zealand, 1843–1845', Essex Institute, Salem.

—— unpub. B. 'Journal Kept on Board the Sch. Warwick Cruising Among the Fee Gee Islands Begun Augst the Thirteene 1845, G. W. Cheever, Master,' Essex Institute, Salem. Journal kept by Capt. Saunders after 23 Jan. 1847.

Cheyne, A. 1852. *A Description of Islands in the Western Pacific Ocean*, London.

—— unpub. 'Account of Trading Voyages in the Western Pacific, 17 July 1841–12 Sept. 1844', Mitchell Library, Sydney.

Christian, F. W. 1899. *The Caroline Islands*, London.

Clarke, H. L. 1921. *The Echinoderm Fauna of Torres Strait: Its Composition and Its Origin*, vol. 10, Carnegie Inst. of Washington, Washington, D.C.

—— 1946. *The Echinoderm Fauna of Australia*, Carnegie Inst. of Washington, publ. 566, Washington, D.C.

Consular Report. 1871. *Consular Report for 1869*, in [C 343], *P.P.*, 1871, lxv, pp. 225–8.

Cooper, H. S. 1888. *The Islands of the Pacific*, London.

Coulter, J. 1847. *Adventures on the western coast of South America, and the interior of California: including a narrative of incidents at the Kingsmill Islands, New*

Ireland, New Britain, New Guinea, and other islands in the Pacific Ocean . . ., 2 vols., London.

Crawfurd, J. 1820. *History of the Indian Archipelago*, 3 vols., Edinburgh.

Cumpston, J. S. 1964. *Shipping Arrivals and Departures Sydney, 1788–1825*, parts 1, 2, and 3, Canberra.

Dakin, W. J. 1952. *Australian Seashores*, Sydney.

Davies, J. 1925. 'Journal of the Missionaries put ashore from the "Hibernia" on an islet in the Fiji Group in 1809', in Im Thurn and Wharton, 1925: 117–60.

Derrick, R. A. 1957. *A History of Fiji*, 3rd edition, Suva.

Diaper, W. 1853. 'Jackson's Narrative', in Erskine, 1853.

—— 1928. *Cannibal Jack*, London, Author's name given as 'Diapea' in this volume.

Dillon, P. 1813. 'Deposition of Peter Dillon', 6 Nov. 1813. Enclosure No. 4, Governor Macquarie to Earl Bathurst, 17 Jan. 1814. In *Historical Records of Australia*, series I, 8, Sydney, 1916, pp. 103–7.

Dodge, E. S. 1963. 'Early American Contacts in Polynesia and Fiji', *Proceedings of the American Philosophical Society*, vol. 107, pp. 102–6.

Driver, W. R., unpub. 'Journal of Ship "Clay" on Voyages from Salem, Mass to Fiji Islands and Manila, 1827–1829. Benjamin Vanderford, Master', Peabody Museum, Salem.

Eagleston, J. H., unpub. A. 'Journal of two Voyages to the Islands in the Pacific Ocean in the Barque Peru of Salem . . . during the years 1830, 1, 2, and 3', Essex Institute, Salem.

—— unpub. B. 'Journal of ship Emerald of Salem, 1833–1836, J. H. Eagleston, Master', Essex Institute, Salem (typescript in Peabody Museum, Salem).

—— unpub. C. 'Journal of a Voyage from Salem to New Zealand = the Society Fegee = Friendly & other Islands in the Pacific . . . in the Brig. Mermaid, J. H. Eagleston, Master, Octr. 1836–April 1839', Essex Institute, Salem.

—— unpub. D. Journal, 'Ups and Downs'. Typescript in Peabody Museum, Salem. Original written in last part of Eagleston, unpub. C.

Earl, G. W. 1846. *Enterprise in Tropical Australia*, London.

Endicott, W., unpub. A. 'Journal of a Voyage from Salem to the South Seas in the Ship Glide. Commanded by Henry Archer Jr. Began May 20th 1829', Peabody Museum, Salem.

—— unpub. B. 'Narrative of a Voyage to the South Seas, Shipwreck etc. In the Years 1829, 1830 and 1831', Peabody Museum, Salem.

—— 1846. *Wreck of the Glide: with an account of Life and Manners at the Fijii Islands*, Boston.

Erskine, J. E. 1853. *Journal of a Cruise Among the Islands of the Western Pacific*, London.

Fanning, E. 1833. *Voyages Round the World . . .*, New York.

Finsch, O. 1887. *Über Naturprodukte der westlichen Sudsee, besonders der deutschen Schutzgebiete*, Berlin.

Flinders, M. 1814. *A Voyage to Terra Australis . . . in the Years 1801, 1802 and 1803*, 2 vols., London.

Hainsworth, D. R. 1965. 'In Search of a Staple: the Sydney Sandalwood Trade 1804–09', *Business Archives and History*, vol. 5, pp. 1–20.

Hartwell, J., unpub. 'Log of Brig Gambia, on voyage from Salem to New Zealand and Fiji from 26 June 1844 to 26 Feb. 1846, under Joseph Hartwell', Peabody Museum, Salem.

Hocart, A. M. 1929. *Lau Islands, Fiji*, Bishop Museum Bull. no. 62, Honolulu.

Im Thurn, E. and Wharton, L. C. (eds.). 1925. *The Journal of William Lockerby*, London.

Jones, H. M. 1865. *Report on the Trade of Feejee for the Year 1864*, in [3518], *P.P.*, 1865, LIV, pp. 25–8.

—— 1866. *Report for the Year 1865*, in [3654], *P.P.*, 1866, LXX, pp. 165–7.

Kelly, James. 1820. Evidence of James Kelly before Commission of Inquiry, Hobart 1820, in *Historical Records of Australia*, series III, vol. 3, Sydney, 1921, pp. 458–64.

Kuykendall, R. S. and Day, A. G. 1961. *Hawaii: A History*, Englewood Cliffs, N.J.

King, Governor P. G. 1804. Governor King to Lord Hobart, 14 Aug. 1804, *H.R.N.S.W.*, vol. 5, Sydney, 1897, pp. 418–46.

Knight, J. B., unpub. 'Journal of Brig Spy of Salem, 1832–4', Peabody Museum, Salem.

Larssen, K. E. 1961. 'Early Channels of Communication in the Pacific', Paper read at 10th Pacific Science Congress, Honolulu.

Legge, C. 1966. 'William Diaper, a Biographical Sketch', *Journal of Pacific History*, vol. 1, pp. 79–90.

Lockerby, W., unpub. 'Directions for the Fegee Islands', n.d., Peabody Museum, Salem.

Lynn Record. 1836. Extract published as article 'FIJI 16' in Ward, 1967.

Maude, H. E. 1959. 'The Tahitian Pork Trade: 1800–1830', *Journal de la Société des Océanistes*, vol. 15, pp. 55–95.

—— 1964. 'Beachcombers and Castaways', *Journ. Poly. Soc.*, vol. 73, pp. 254–93.

—— and Crocombe, M. T. 1962. 'Rarotongan Sandalwood. An Ethnohistorical Reconstruction', *Journ. Poly. Soc.*, vol. 71, pp. 32–56.

—— and Leeson, I. 1965. 'The Coconut Oil Trade in the Gilbert Islands', *Journ. Poly. Soc.*, vol. 74, pp. 396–437.

McArthur, N. n.d. (1957?). *The Population of the Pacific Islands*, Canberra.

—— 1966. 'Essays in Multiplication: European seafarers in Polynesia', *Journal of Pacific History*, vol. 1, pp. 91–106.

Morison, S. E. 1961. *The Maritime History of Massachusetts, 1783–1860*, Riverside Press edition, Cambridge, Mass.

Morrell, B. 1832. *A Narrative of Four Voyages* . . . New York.

Mulvaney, D. J. 1966. 'Bêche-de-mer, Aborigines and Australian History', *Proceedings of the Royal Society of Victoria*, vol. 79, pt. 2, pp. 449–57.

N.I.D., 1945. Naval Intelligence Division, *Pacific Islands*, vol. iv, Cambridge.

New Bedford Mercury. 1824. Extract published as article 'FANNING 8' in Ward, 1967.

Osborn, J. W., unpub. 'Journal of a Voyage in the Ship Emerald of Salem. . . commanded by John H. Eagleston . . . 1833, 4, 5 & 6', Essex Institute, Salem.

Owen, Consul. 1864. *Report for the Half Year ending June 30 1863*, in [3393], P.P., 1864, lxi, pp. 28–9.

Phillips, S. C., unpub. 'Account Book, 1831–33', Peabody Museum, Salem.

Pool, I. D. 1964. 'The Maori Population of New Zealand', Ph.D. thesis, Australian National University, Canberra.

Putnam, G. G. 1922–30. *Salem Vessels and Their Voyages*, Salem, Mass. vol. 1, 1922; vol. 2, 1924; vol. 3, 1925; vol. 4, 1930.

Report . . . 1896. *Report of the Commission appointed to inquire into the Decrease of the Native Population*, Suva.

Roscoe, unpub. 'Journal of a Passage from Salem towards the Pacific Ocean on board the Brig Roscoe of Salem, Benjamin Vanderford, Master 1821–3.' This journal was not kept by Vanderford but author is not given. Peabody Museum, Salem.

Salesius, Father. *c.* 1906. *Die Karolinen—Insel Jap*, Berlin. Translated by Human Relations Area Files, New Haven, 1963.

Salisbury, R. F. 1962. *From Stone to Steel*, Melbourne.

Saville-Kent, W. 1893. *The Great Barrier Reef of Australia*, London.

Shineberg, D. 1965. *Sandalwood Trade in the South-west Pacific, 1830–65*, Ph.D. thesis, University of Melbourne.

—— 1966. 'The Sandalwood trade in Melanesian economics, 1841–65', *Journal of Pacific History*, vol. 1, pp. 129–46.

Sunter, G. H. 1937. *Adventures of a Trepang Fisher*, London.

Sydney Gazette. Quoted in Im Thurn and Wharton (1925: 181).

Tetens, A. 1958. *Among the Savages of the South Seas*, ed. F. M. Spoehr, Stanford, Cal.

Thompson, L. 1940. *Southern Lau, Fiji: An Ethnography*, Bishop Museum Bull. no. 162, Honolulu.

Turbet, C. R. 1942. 'Bêche-de-mer—Trepang', *Transactions & Proceedings of the Fiji Society*, vol. 2, pp. 147–54.

Wall, C. 1919. 'Sketches in Fijian History (Part 2)', *Transactions of the Fijian Society for* . . . *1919*, not paginated.

Wallis, M. D. 1851. *Life in Feejee*, Boston.

Ward, R. G. 1965. *Land Use and Population in Fiji*, London.

—— (ed.). 1967. *American Activities in the Central Pacific 1790–1870*, 7 vols., Ridgewood, N.J.

Wheatley, P. 1959. 'Geographical Notes on some Commodities involved in Sung Maritime Trade', *Journal of the Malayan Branch, Royal Asiatic Society*, vol. 32.

Wilkes, C. 1844. *Narrative of the United States Exploring Expedition, During the Years 1838, 1839, 1840, 1841, 1842*, vol. iii, Philadelphia. Also 2 volume edition, London, 1852.

Williams, J. B., unpub. Papers of John B. Williams, Peabody Museum, Salem.

Winn, Joseph, unpub. 'Journal of a Voyage from Salem to the Pacific Ocean in the Ship Eliza commanded by Joseph Winn Jr. begun May 28th 1833 and terminated May 5th 1835', Essex Institute, Salem.

5

THE LABOUR TRADE

OWEN W. PARNABY[1]

No aspect of European contact wrought more change in the lives of the Pacific islanders than that occasioned by the labour recruiter. The explorer had made them aware of a world beyond their horizons, and of some of the material advantages to be gained from it. With the missionary came a new ideology which undermined old views and won acceptance, in part at least, because it ensured European support in local disputes. In this respect the *mana* of the missionary was little different from that of a beachcomber like Savage in Fiji, who received royal treatment because of the inestimable advantages his firearms gave in intertribal warfare. There were, of course, other European products which islanders sought—axes and tools to aid them in their own productive occupations, and consumer items to be enjoyed for their own sake—tobacco, cloth, and alcohol. These were their incentive for trade, items which they wanted as much as Europeans wanted their *bêche-de-mer*, sandalwood, and their labour.

It is probably impossible to estimate the separate effect of each agency of change in the contact of European and islander (see Farrell, Chapter 2). With the settlement of Europeans in the islands, administrations were bound to follow, and to restrict and modify local authority. The sum of all these changes as they accelerated throughout the nineteenth and twentieth centuries has produced the present pattern of life in the islands, and the purpose here is to estimate the part of the labour trade in this process. It was very considerable, because it was both a form of island trade bringing into play bargaining power on both sides, and also a two-way migration between island and European cultures with the consequent assimilation of values and customs.

[1] Dr. Parnaby is the Master, Queen's College, University of Melbourne.

In the broad sense it is hardly possible to say when the labour trade began. Was it in 1769 when Cook took aboard Tupaea, the Tahitian chief, and sailed with him to New Zealand and beyond, or in the early 1800s when Maoris engaged as crews of ships sailing to Port Jackson? They were selling their labour for what they considered a fair advantage, spending some time in a European setting, and returning more experienced and with new ideas and techniques to their native environment. This is essentially what happened on a mass scale when the labour trade was at its height. With increasing frequency through the early part of the nineteenth century islanders engaged as ship's crew, and with *bêche-de-mer* and sandalwood traders. Recent work has shown direct links between the sandalwood trade and the labour trade. For example, Robert Towns, a Sydney merchant, entered the sandalwood trade with the vessel *Elizabeth* which he acquired cheaply in the depression of 1844. He employed Melanesians as ship's crew, sandalwood cutters, and general labourers. Almost twenty years later he invested capital in land in Queensland with a view to producing cotton to take advantage of the booming prices for that commodity. As a long-standing employer of Melanesians he naturally sought them as plantation labourers. His ship, the *Don Juan*, which sailed to the islands in 1863 recruited the first labourers for Queensland, and began a trade which lasted until 1906 (Shineberg, 1967: 110, 118, 193).

Towns was not the first to recruit Pacific islanders for plantation or pastoral work in Australia. Benjamin Boyd arrived in New South Wales in 1842, and took up whaling and pastoral interests. In 1847, after conversations with sandalwood traders, he sent two vessels to recruit labour for his pastoral runs in southern New South Wales. But financial disaster overtook Boyd and the project failed.

The most extensive early recruiting was done by J. C. Byrne, an Irishman with French citizenship. He recruited for New Caledonia in the 1850s, and in 1862 he received a licence from the government of Peru to recruit 'natives of the South Western islands of the Pacific' for agricultural work and as domestic servants in Peru. During the following twelve months about 1,200 islanders were recruited from the Marquesas, the Gambiers, the Australs, the Tuamotus, the Tokelaus, the Gilbert

and Ellice Islands, and the Cook Islands. Rumours of kidnapping led to protests to the Peruvian Government, and the
trade was stopped, but almost all the recruits died either in
Peru or on the voyages to and from the islands (Parnaby, 1964:
12–14).

Not all the recruiting was for plantations on the continental
periphery. Many workers were sought for plantations within
the island groups themselves. The largest island recruiter was
Fiji, where Berthold Seemann, botanist to the British Government's mission of 1860 to inquire into Fiji's offer of cession,
reported favourable conditions for the cultivation of cotton.
With cotton prices booming because of the interruption of
Britain's supply by the American Civil War, prospective planters
flocked to Fiji to take up land. The number of Europeans
increased from 200 in 1860 to 862 in 1868, and by 1867 3,200
acres were planted with cotton and another 1,500 cleared for
planting (Ward, 1965: 23). Cotton required at least one
labourer for each two to two and a quarter acres, but planters
were not able to persuade Fijian chiefs to provide the numbers
required. They therefore sought them from other islands, and
in 1864 the first labourers were brought from the New Hebrides.
Recruitment continued, mainly from the New Hebrides, the
Solomons, the Gilbert and Ellice Islands, and New Guinea,
until 1911. Other areas within Oceania employing immigrant
island labourers were New Caledonia and Samoa, while there
was a small recruiting trade in the New Hebrides and the
Solomons for service on the plantations in those groups.

Throughout the period of the labour trade the main employment area was Queensland to which over 60,000 islanders were
taken between 1863 and 1904 (Parnaby, 1964: 203). Probably
about 20,000 went to Fiji between 1864 and 1911 (Fig. 5.1).
New Caledonia, which began recruiting earlier and continued
longer than any other area, was the third in terms of numbers
introduced, followed by Samoa which ceased recruiting in the
1890s (Scarr, 1967a: 138).

The most frequent recruiting areas were the New Hebrides
and the Solomons. The Gilbert and Ellice Islands and the
islands to the north and east of New Guinea were secondary
areas. Recruiting was probably at its peak in the early 1880s.
In 1880 Fiji had thirteen vessels (Wilson, 1882: 606), and there

were twenty-eight vessels recruiting for Queensland in 1884
(C.O. 234/45). In addition the settlers of New Caledonia,
Samoa, the New Hebrides, and the Solomons each had two or
three boats recruiting on their behalf (Scarr, 1968: 53).

The Source Area

The islands of Melanesia, the main recruiting area for the
labour trade, lie in an arc roughly parallel with the coast of
Queensland and about 1,200 miles from it. They stretch from
New Caledonia just north of the Tropic of Capricorn to the
Bismarck Archipelago 5° south of the Equator. Between these
extremities lie the Loyalties, the New Hebrides, Banks, Torres,
Santa Cruz, and Solomon Islands. The interiors of most of
these islands consist of well-wooded mountains while the area
of coastal plains is restricted. Not all the islands are blessed
with good harbours, but most have safe anchorages.

The prehistory of these islands is still imperfectly known.
There were probably a series of arrivals from mainland and
insular Asia and later additions in some of the eastern islands
of Melanesia of lighter skinned people who probably drifted
back westwards from Polynesia. Among most of the people the
unit of social organization was small. It did not extend much
beyond the family group gathered in villages and ruled by an
informal council of its senior members. There were few chiefs,
especially in the southern New Hebrides, with any extensive
authority. Social influence was achieved in these communities
through the accumulation of wealth and the giving of feasts in
which the much-prized spiral-tusked pigs were ceremonially
killed, a prelude to the admission of their owners to a higher
level of the graded societies.

The main economic occupation of the islanders was fishing
and the cultivation of small garden plots. Ownership was not
a simple institution, but a combination of individual and
communal rights. Land was held by the largest social unit, the
tribe or clan, which alone had the right of alienation. Land was
allocated to smaller groups or even individuals who enjoyed
the right of usufruct, but who had no right to assign this to
anyone else except perhaps by inheritance. Large objects
produced by communal labour, such as canoes, were usually
held in common. Where this was not so, those who contributed

labour retained a right of use. Smaller objects, individually produced, were individually owned, but even here the concept of outright ownership, prohibiting use by others without permission, did not apply. Living objects such as plants or trees

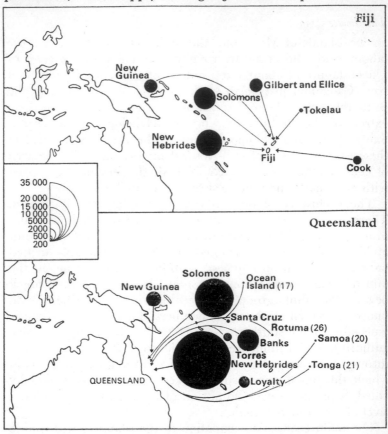

Fig. 5.1. Origins of Pacific Island labourers in Fiji, 1864–1911, and Queensland, 1863–1904. Source: Parnaby, 1964.

were considered the property of those who planted them. Communal rights were invested in the council of elders or chiefs where they existed, and they could command both labour and property.

There was some trade between these village communities, especially between those of the sea coast who traded fish for the yams of the inland villages. But the area controlled by another village was usually hostile territory, and warfare between villages was frequent. This separateness was accentuated by the remarkable number of languages and dialects that existed even on a relatively small island. Because of these characteristics, European traders generally had to make direct contact with each group and could not use depots and native middlemen serving a wider area.

Conditions and Control of Recruiting

Labour recruiting, particularly in the southern New Hebrides, had been preceded by sandalwood trading in which some islanders had served as cutters and boat's crew and gained experience as contract labourers. This knowledge of what was to be gained, and willingness to bargain for it, was their protection against exploitation by the first labour recruiters. Until Queensland passed its Polynesian Labourers Act in 1868, recruiting was unregulated and was only as responsible as those engaged in it.

Captain Towns, the first Queensland employer, was a member of the New South Wales Legislative Council. He had as his business partner Robert Brooks, M.P. for Weymouth in the House of Commons, and was later in business with Charles Cowper who had been Premier of New South Wales. In a form given to the master of his recruiting vessel, he set out clearly and in detail terms of employment which seemed fair and reasonable. The period of employment was to be six or twelve months after which he promised to return the labourer. Wages were to be paid in kind to the value of 10 shillings a month, and food and housing would be provided (*P.P.*, 1867/8*a*). However, Towns's recruiting agent was Ross Lewin who had been cashiered from the Royal Navy and who appeared subsequently in Queensland courts on charges of kidnapping and rape, and was later murdered in the islands by natives.

Recruiting for Fiji was supervised unofficially by the Consul who examined the labourers on arrival to try to satisfy himself that they had been engaged voluntarily. The agreement between the labourer and his employer was ratified in his presence. The usual payment was £2 to £3 per annum, and the term of service three to five years. Food, clothing, and shelter were provided (*P.P.*, 1871).

In these early years, the Presbyterian missionaries in the southern New Hebrides, particularly James McNair in Eromanga, watched the interests of the islanders carefully. In September 1867 they reported that eighteen recruiting vessels had called at the one island of Efate and taken off 250 islanders in the previous eighteen months (*P.P.*, 1867/8*c*). The non-return of some of these islanders was thought to have provoked attacks on Europeans (*P.P.*, 1867/8*b*), and led the Queensland Government to pass the Polynesian Labourers Act of 1868 (31 Vict., No. 47).

Henceforth all ships recruiting for Queensland were to be licensed and the master was to give a bond of £500 against kidnapping. Employers were to take out a licence to import labourers, and a bond of £10 for the cost of the return passage of each labourer. On the vessel's return to port, the recruiting agent was required to produce the licence, the bonds, and a form of agreement between himself and the labourer signed by a missionary or European resident on the islands that the islander had understood the contract and engaged voluntarily.

In Fiji the Consul withdrew his supervision of recruiting after Captain Hovell and a native member of the crew of the *Young Australian* had been charged with the murder of three islanders from Epi in the New Hebrides. The accused were found guilty, but the sentences of death were remitted on the grounds that the evidence of natives had not been properly sworn. This was one of the deficiencies in the law which the imperial government sought to remedy in the Pacific Islanders Protection Act passed in 1872 (35 and 36 Vict., c. 19).

Up to this time it had been assumed that any offences by British subjects engaged in recruiting could be dealt with under 4 Geo. IV, c. 96, and 9 Geo. IV, c. 83, which gave the Supreme Courts of New South Wales and Van Diemen's Land power to 'enquire of, hear, and determine all treasons, piracies, felonies, robberies, murders, conspiracies, and other offences' committed within Admiralty jurisdiction or in the islands of the Indian or Pacific Oceans not subject to Her Majesty or any European states. It was also thought that the Slave Trade Acts could be invoked, but this was proved to be an illusion by a judgement of Sir Alfred Stephen, the New South Wales Chief Justice, in the *Daphne* case in 1869. The *Daphne* was licensed under the

Queensland Act of 1868 to recruit fifty-eight labourers for Queensland. Instead, she took 100 islanders to Fiji where she was seized by Commander Palmer of H.M.S. *Rosario* who charged the master and crew with slave dealing under 5 Geo. IV, c. 113. The charges were dismissed on the grounds that there was no offence under the Act if there was any agreement limiting the time of service or providing for payment for the labour.

The 1872 Pacific Islanders Protection Act was passed by the imperial government in order to make kidnapping an offence by British subjects and to provide for the seizure of British ships engaged in it. All British ships engaged in recruiting were to be licensed, and their masters were required to give a bond of £500 against kidnapping. The Act also empowered courts to bring witnesses from outside British territory to assist hearings, and allowed the courts to exercise discretion in accepting native evidence.

It was not always practical to issue licences to all British ships that wanted to recruit. After Fiji was annexed, the unofficial authority of the Consul, and the *de facto* supervision of the Thakombau government over recruiting and employment of immigrant labourers was replaced by the Queensland Act whose clauses, with a few minor exceptions, were proclaimed in Fiji in December 1874. But British settlers in the New Hebrides and Solomons who wished to recruit for their plantations in those islands found difficulty in getting licences.

The Governors of the Australian Colonies were empowered to issue licences by the 1872 Act, and the amending Act of 1875 included the Governor of Fiji. But at such a distance from the New Hebrides it was difficult to assess applications and to see that the terms of the licence were observed. For this reason, Commodore Goodenough had banned recruiting by New Hebridean planters in 1874. When Sir Arthur Gordon was appointed High Commissioner he had hoped to be given powers by the Western Pacific Order in Council of 1877 to supervise both recruiting and employment, but he found he had no power to make regulations for the latter, and he could not agree on an arrangement for the issue of licences that would assure reasonable supervision.

There were, therefore, in the recruiting grounds, British vessels licensed to recruit for Queensland and Fiji, vessels owned

by British subjects in the New Hebrides and either recruiting
without a licence or sailing under French colours, and German
and French vessels recruiting respectively for Samoa and New
Caledonia.

Before a British vessel could receive a licence to recruit for
Fiji or Queensland, it had to comply with the terms of the
legislation for those two colonies. Fiji prescribed a minimum
tonnage of twenty-five, and allowed three adult passengers for
each two tons (Ordinance XXIV, 1876). Queensland vessels
could carry one adult for every 12 superficial feet. All passengers
were to be berthed between decks, the minimum height of
which was to be 6 feet 6 inches. Not more than two tiers of berths
were permitted with a minimum of 2 feet 6 inches between them
(31 Vict., No. 47, s. 16). When a vessel was too old and leaky
to continue as a cargo carrier, these modifications to the hold
were sufficient for it to enter the labour trade, and the human
cargo could be usefully employed manning the pumps to keep
her afloat (Scarr, 1967a: 146). To ensure the prescribed rations
to each passenger, the legislation fixed the maximum length of
the voyage, which, in the case of Queensland licensed ships, was
thirty days for sail. This seems rather meaningless, for the
typical recruiter might spend up to three months cruising
among the islands before it had a full complement of labourers.
In 1877 the *Bobtail Nag* left Rockhampton on 17 April and
arrived off the Isle of Pines on 4 May. She remained in the
islands until 17 July, arriving back at Rockhampton on 29 July.
The voyage home was a race against the ravages of dysentery
and dwindling rations (Scarr, 1968, 115–17).

Recruiting vessels were checked at their departure and on
their return to port, but little was known of what went on in the
islands. This was the point at which the labour trade was most
criticized by missionaries, humanitarians, and, to a lesser extent,
colonial officials and naval officers who were responsible for
law and order in the area. The Navy had commissioned five
schooners to patrol the islands and seize any vessel contra-
vening the 1872 Act, but they could do little more than check
the number of recruits on board against the licence. In November 1871 Captain Markham of H.M.S. *Rosario* boarded the
Carl off Eromanga in the New Hebrides. He found twenty
islanders on board, and the ship in good condition, and left

after an exchange of greetings with Dr. James Murray, the owner. Two months earlier off Buka Island in the Solomons, the crew of the *Carl* had dropped cannon shot, iron spars, and lengths of heavy chain into the boats of islanders who had come alongside. About eighty of the islanders had then been taken on board and imprisoned in the hold. That night, and the following night, the natives' efforts to break out so frightened the crew that they raked the hold with gunfire until the islanders were silent. About forty were found to be dead and, with thirty badly wounded, were thrown overboard. Murray then set about removing all trace of the massacre, and was successful enough to pass inspection by Captain Markham. The atrocity became known only when Murray turned Queen's witness after a quarrel with the mate, Armstrong. This happened shortly after the murder of Bishop Patteson at Nukupu in the Santa Cruz group in September 1871 which was thought to be in retaliation for depredations of labour recruiters. As a result of these events popular feeling in Australian colonies ran very strongly against the labour trade. At the Christmas pantomime of the Theatre Royal in Melbourne in 1872 a replica of a labour vessel appeared on stage, and thunderous applause greeted the capture of the vessel by a girl dressed as an ensign and carrying a Union Jack (*P.P.*, 1873).

Although some missionaries and humanitarians were outright opponents of the labour trade, and careful not to do anything which even implied acquiescence, others acknowledged that it could serve the interests of all parties if based on a free contract. An obvious parallel was drawn with Indian indentured labour which was often quoted as an example of the harmony of interests. Colonial capital needed labour, and the worker from the overcrowded labour market of India had something to gain by engaging for service overseas. The evidence and proof of this was the free contract which would not otherwise have been entered into. Similarly, if the labour agreement were explained to the islander and he accepted it freely, there could be no fundamental objection to the labour trade. Various suggestions were made of ways by which the making of the agreement might be supervised. Some wanted depots in the islands similar to those in India for the engagement of Indian indentured labour, but this raised problems of jurisdiction in territories not under any European power, and in any case was not practical when recruiting was spread over such a wide area. A more practical suggestion, adopted by Queensland in December 1870, and in Fiji somewhat later, was the appointment of government agents to all recruiting ships.

The Queensland government agents were responsible to the government to see that the provisions of the Act concerning recruiting were observed. They were required to inspect the accommodation, food, and clothing provided for the islanders, to see that any returning islanders were landed at their own islands, together with their property, and to return a certificate to this effect to the immigration agent on return to port. They were to see that islanders engaging for service understood the contract, and they were responsible for the islanders' fitness (*Qd. Govt. Gazette*, 1871: 202).

To carry out his task effectively the government agent needed an independence and authority which even a man of character and skill, well supported by the administration, would find hard to achieve in relation to the master of a recruiting vessel. The Queensland appointments were for one voyage only until the first permanent appointments were made in 1875 in the hope of attracting a better type of man. The earlier casual appointments were made on the recommendation of a local person and often went to a friend of the owner or captain. William Matson, a government agent giving evidence to a select committee in 1876, said he was told by the master of a vessel to which he was appointed that other government agents had given him a free hand, and he would be expected to do the same (Qd. V. and P., 1876: iii. 117–22). When Commodore Goodenough of H.M.S. *Pearl* boarded the *May Queen* off Eromanga in April 1875 he found that the government agent was a lad of 21 who looked several years younger, and who had neither the experience nor the authority to carry out his responsibilities (C.O. 83/7). If a government agent refused to comply, the master could make his life a hell. There is some grounds for believing that some 'accidents' which befell government agents were deliberately contrived (Scarr, 1967*b*: 12).

It was for these reasons that many people doubted the efficacy of government agents. Lorimer Fison, an enlightened missionary in Fiji, had suggested them in 1869 as a means of preventing recruiting abuses and stated that if this could be done he would find nothing objectionable in the labour trade (F.O. 58/128). But by 1875 he doubted if the trade could be free from abuses. Layard, the British Consul in Fiji at the time of annexation, did not appoint government agents to Fiji recruiting vessels because he believed they had been proved ineffective on Queensland vessels, and Des Voeux, the Governor of Fiji from 1880 to 1887, doubted whether the function of government agents was 'to be other than make believe' (Des Voeux, 1903: ii. 92).

Even if the relations of the government agent and the master and crew were good, it was no simple task to see that the islanders engaged voluntarily. When a vessel arrived in the islands, it usually picked up a crew of island boatmen who had served in this way before, and who would be useful for their local knowledge and as interpreters. They might direct the vessel to places where recruits could be had, or it might put in where islanders had lit fires on shore to attract their attention. The recruiting boat was rowed inshore, turned to face seawards, with the native boatmen remaining at their oars to make a quick departure if trouble occurred. Islanders were not supposed to pass beyond the stroke oar of the boat, to avoid it being surrounded. The Europeans were armed with revolvers and sniders, and carbines were kept in the boat for use by native oarsmen in an emergency. A second boat frequently stood off shore to cover the recruiting boat. By the Queensland regulations only the boat with the government agent was allowed to engage in recruiting, but by regulations issued under the Fiji Ordinance XXIV, 1879, recruiting was allowed by both boats. These safety regulations, though enjoined upon the crew, were often neglected to their own detriment (Scarr, 1968: 40).

After some preliminary trading of yams, coconuts, and bananas for tobacco, the trade box would come out and cloth, tomahawks, and muskets would be offered to the friends and relatives of those who were willing to recruit. Opponents of the labour trade often quoted this practice as evidence of slave dealing, but it was consistent with the Melanesian custom of reciprocity, and trouble invariably followed if attempts were made to recruit without acknowledging the action with a gift.

It was open to abuse by the islanders themselves as some islanders accepted to gain trade goods but with the intention of escaping from the vessel subsequently. There is also some evidence that bushmen of the islands were sold to recruiters by salt-water people (Scarr, 1968: 17). The same charge was levelled against certain powerful chiefs in the Solomons who acted as intermediaries to gain supplies of trade goods (Scarr, 1967b: 18). The practice of exchanging gifts for recruits was described by Nixon, the government agent on the *Bobtail Nag*, in a newspaper article in December 1877. As a result the Colonial Secretary issued an instruction that masters, crew, and government agents must be cautioned against making any such transactions in future (Qd. V. and P., 1878: ii. 51).

The giving of gifts was the equivalent of asking community consent to recruiting. There were occasions on which runaways were recruited—men threatened with punishment for something they had done, or women wishing to escape from an unacceptable marriage alliance or to elope with a lover. It would be easy to justify these on the grounds of individual consent, but community consent was just as essential. Many of the crimes associated with the labour trade were in retaliation for recruiting without community consent.

In areas where recruiting vessels were familiar sights, islanders knew enough about the trade to understand what was involved. There were usually among them returned labourers, some of whom re-engaged, and they came to express preferences for the various employment areas (Scarr, 1967a: 141). Queensland was generally most popular because the wages there were £6 a year, whereas in Fiji they were only £3. Some said they preferred the wages of Queensland, but the food rations of yams in Fiji to the rice that was offered in Queensland (C.O. No. 40, 1870). Their system of preferences, not only where they wanted to go, but what they wanted for themselves or relatives in return, were clearly known. Firearms were the most sought-after item, and thus there was much reluctance to accede to the British Government's request to ban the sale or gift of firearms to Pacific islanders. This was finally agreed upon by Fiji and Queensland in 1884, but it then put their recruiting vessels at a disadvantage in competition with German and French recruiters.

In new recruiting areas there was little possibility of the islanders understanding where they were being invited to go, and for how long they would be away. It was common for a recruiting agent to hold up three fingers to indicate three years, but an islander who had little or no previous contact with Europeans would almost certainly take this to mean three months. The evidence given to the Royal Commission which inquired into the circumstances under which labourers were recruited from New Guinea in 1883 and 1884 made it clear how little they understood.

When inquiries were held it often transpired that the government agent had not followed his instructions. One of the most frequent lapses was his absence from the recruiting boat. Sometimes he thought he knew the mind of the labourer better than the labourer himself. In 1874 Pelham Obbard, for instance, refused to accept an interpreter's statement that an Ureparapara islander did not wish to recruit, saying that this was a whim of the moment and that he would be landed on the ship's return from the Torres Islands if he still felt like that. The ship, of course, did not return that way (Codrington, 1 Mar. 1875).

The government agents were not given much support by officialdom in Queensland. In 1871 Captain Coath of the *Jason* was found guilty of kidnapping, but no action was taken to forfeit his bond of £500 against kidnapping. The government agent of the *Fanny* stated in his log that he believed an attack on that ship by the Mann islanders in the New Ireland area in 1883 was in retaliation for an earlier attack made on them by the *Hopeful*. Yet the *Hopeful* had twice returned to port, and its government agent had resigned and left the colony before an inquiry was begun.

There was not only a reluctance of officials to take action, but also of Queensland courts to convict. In 1883 the master, four members of the crew, and the government agent of the *Alfred Vittery* were charged with the murder of two islanders who caused trouble on board when the ship was off the coast of Malaita. Although the evidence was clear that the islanders were shot without it being shown that their behaviour was a threat to life or the safety of the ship, the jury found all but one not guilty. Grimes, the crew member who had delivered the death-blow to one of the natives who was still alive as he was being thrown overboard, was found guilty of manslaughter, but discharged on giving a bond to appear for judgement if required (C.O. 234/44).

Areas and Conditions of Employment

There was no simple means of assuring a fair contract between the recruiting agent and the islander. In the early stages the main objection to recruiting appeared to be that it took place where no European administration existed to supervise it. However, the frequent ineffectiveness of government agents, and absence of diligence and impartiality on the part of administrations and courts in countries where recruiting ships were registered, made it clear that the problem would still have been considerable even if the recruiting grounds were administratively controlled. Most of the plantations where islanders worked were in territories with some form of European administration, yet the chances that the terms of the labour contract would be fulfilled were not much greater than that the original agreement was freely and fairly made.

The largest number of labourers at work at any one time was between 10,000 and 11,000 in Queensland in the mid-1880s (Parnaby, 1964: 204). Fiji reached a peak employment of between 5,000 and 6,000 in the early 1880s. While the number employed in Queensland remained fairly steady until the last labourers were returned in 1906, the number employed in Fiji declined considerably after 1890 when Indians were increasingly in favour as plantation workers. Pacific islanders continued to be employed in a wide range of occupations by a variety of employers. They were engaged by copra planters whose needs might be met by employing no more than half a dozen islanders at any one time. Throughout the period there were many employers of one or two islanders only, and these included the Anglican vicar, the Revd. Mr. Floyd, the Levuka Hospital, the Suva Club, and the aide-de-camp to the Governor (Dept. of Labour, Fiji). This was more like indentured service than plantation labour.

In Queensland the trend was the reverse. In the early years there was no restriction on the type of employment available to Pacific islanders, and of the 1,539 in Queensland on 4 March

1868, 771 were employed in agriculture, 697 on pastoral
properties, and 71 in urban occupations (Parnaby, 1964: 126).
However, from the beginning working-class interests wanted
to restrict island labour to occupations that were not competitive
with white labour. This meant tropical agriculture, as it was
assumed that white men were incapable of undertaking manual
work in the tropics. A clause to this effect was included, but
withdrawn, from the 1868 Bill. It reappeared briefly in regulations gazetted by the Douglas Ministry in 1877, and was part of
the 1880 Act. It applied only to the first contract entered into
by an islander, but after 1884 it covered all Pacific islanders in
Queensland, except those who had resided there continuously
for more than five years (47 Vict. No. 12, ss. 2, 11).

As a consequence of this legislation Pacific islanders were
concentrated in the sugar-growing areas of Queensland after
1880. The largest of these in 1881 was the Mackay district,
where about one-third of the Pacific islanders in the colony
worked. They constituted more than one-third of the population of the district; Bundaberg and Maryborough were the next
most extensive sugar-growing areas, and therefore centres for
Pacific islanders (Parnaby, 1964: 125, 129).

In both Fiji and Queensland the conditions of employment—
living conditions, clothing, rations, and wages—were all prescribed by the legislation of the colonies. These looked adequate
on paper, but, as with recruiting, the problem was to see that
they were observed, and to amend and extend where experience
showed inadequacies.

There was a difference in the wages prescribed, which
worked to the disadvantage of Fiji, as Queensland offered £6
per annum against £3 by Fiji. However, it was not uncommon
for a Fijian employer to offer a labourer more than the minimum, even for the initial engagement, if he thought he was
worth it. An experienced labourer on engaging for a second or
later contract could be paid up to £12 per annum (Dept. of
Labour, Fiji). In Queensland, wages were not paid until the
end of the three-year contract. As there was no provision for
the payment of a deceased labourer's wages to his next of kin, the
death of a labourer relieved the employer of any payment.
There were other circumstances in which a labourer might lose
wages owing over a long period. For example, if a mortgage on

an estate was resumed, the mortgagee was not liable for unpaid wages. By Ordinance XI of 1877 the Fijian employer was required to pay wages every six months to the Immigration Fund, including those owing to deceased labourers. The Immigration agent then paid the labourers at the end of their contract, and he had discretion to pay the wages owing to a deceased labourer to his next of kin. The Queensland Act of 1880 required wages to be paid by the employer every six months in the presence of an inspector who was also to receive wages owing to deceased labourers.

There is some evidence of appalling treatment by employers. On Kandavu, in Fiji, a planter, Achilles Underwood, was murdered by a labourer from Tana. Underwood had kept some of his labourers confined in a small hut with no food and little water, and with broken sticks so arranged as to prevent them lying down. When other labourers had protested and asked for their release they had been threatened with similar treatment. This provoked the attack on Underwood (C.O. 83/76; *Fiji Times*, 29 Mar. 1871). In 1875 a planter named Evans and his agent Brodziah were charged with causing the death of 24 of 31 labourers engaged by them. They had failed to provide them with shelter, food, or clothing (C.O. 83/6).

In Queensland the very high mortality rate among island labourers caused concern and led to inquiries into their treatment on the plantations. On five occasions in the 1870s and 1880s, the mortality rate for Pacific islanders rose above 80 per 1,000, reaching a peak of 147 per 1,000 in 1884. This was among an almost entirely male population in the prime of life, as over 70 per cent of the islanders were in the age group from 15 to 35. It compared most unfavourably with the death rate for the whole of the white population which never at any time rose above 25 per 1,000 (Parnaby, 1964: 145–6).

It was natural to associate unregulated hours of work and inadequate medical care as possible causes of the high mortality rate. In Fiji, Ordinance XI of 1877 prescribed a nine-hour work day from Monday to Friday, five hours on Saturday, and no work on Sunday. Although the Queensland Government were urged by the Colonial Office to limit the hours of work, this got no further than an amending clause in the 1880 Bill which was later dropped. The usual length of the working day for the labourer was from 7 a.m. to 6 p.m. with a one-hour break at midday.

Until 1876 medical care for labourers depended on the willingness of employers to accept responsibility for it. Where employers were willing to pay, labourers were admitted to public hospitals at a charge of 1s. 6d. per day. The 1880 Act empowered inspectors to order hospital treatment at the employer's expense where they thought it necessary. Under this Act employers could also be levied for the support of a hospital for Pacific islanders in any district where the Governor considered one necessary. Extensive provisions were made in Ordinance XI 1877 for the medical care of labourers in Fiji.

It is significant that the highest mortality rate in Queensland was in the year that large numbers of labourers were introduced from New Guinea. They had had very little previous contact with Europeans, and were unaccustomed to plantation work. In varying degrees the basic cause of high mortality among the Pacific islanders was the different environment, food, and strenuous and continuous work to which they were unaccustomed.

It is estimated that about 25 per cent of the Pacific islanders who came to Queensland died in the colony (Parnaby, 1964: 201). With the exception of several hundred who were allowed to remain permanently in Queensland, the rest returned to the islands. The return voyage could be as perilous as service in Queensland. The government agent was obliged to see that they were safely landed at their own island with their belongings. Unless they were landed in the territory of their own people they could perish at the hands of a hostile tribe. The products bought with three years' wages—firearms, tools, and clothes—were eagerly sought booty. For this reason the instructions to government agents in 1878 required them to land returnees at the exact spot where they were recruited, but their papers often did not contain this information, and they had to rely on the labourers recognizing their landing. Captains and recruiters were unlikely to spend time looking for landings not immediately recognized (Scarr, 1967b: 10; 1968: 15).

Conclusion

It is quite obvious just from the number involved that the labour trade must have had profound repercussions on the island communities. At its height in the early 1880s, there were approximately 15,000 labourers in Queensland and Fiji, about half of these from the New Hebrides. The population of the New Hebrides was estimated at about 60,000 in 1910, but was considerably more in earlier years (Belshaw, 1954: Appendix II). If it were 100,000, then approximately 7 per cent of the population was overseas under labour contract. As most of these were males in the age group 15 to 30, the islands were deprived of a fairly high percentage of their most vigorous male members.

On the other hand, the absence of these people was compensated for to some extent by the stimulus to trade and the provision of tools and firearms brought back by returning labourers or provided as 'trade' by recruiters. Returned labourers had the experience to bargain better with traders and recruiters. Their attitudes depended on their experience. Sometimes recruiters found them helpful in encouraging others to recruit, while in some instances they incited hostility to recruiters. The comments of missionaries on the role of returned labourers reveal the same diversity. Some missionaries hoped that labourers would bring back to the islands the best of Western civilization, but found instead that they were often an embarrassment to their work. However, those who had come under the influence of Florence Young and her Kanaka Mission in Queensland returned to continue missionary work in the Solomons as the South Seas Evangelical Mission (Scarr, 1967a: 159).

Judgements on the labour trade and attitudes to it were much influenced in the early years by the way in which recruiting was conducted. As the years passed, attention turned more and more to the effect it had on the island communities, and whether their needs might not be better served by using their labour with imported capital for the development of their own resources. Federation and the White Australia policy meant the end of the Queensland labour trade. The labour trade to Fiji ended in 1911 when the Colonial Office decided that the Solomon Islands Protectorate could no longer afford to export its labour.

BIBLIOGRAPHY

COLONIAL OFFICE RECORDS

C.O. 83/6. Gordon to C.O., 22 July 1875.

C.O. 83/7. Ad. 9253. Commodore Goodenough's Report of H.M.S. *Pearl's* visit to the New Hebrides.

C.O. 83/76. Jackson to C.O., 2 Feb. 1903.

C.O. 234/44. Musgrave to Derby, 10 Apr. 1884.

C.O. 234/45. Enclosure in Musgrave to Derby, 13 Aug. 1884.

C.O. C.P. No. 40. Colonial Office Confidential Print No. 40, 1870. Evidence of Leonard Bolkin to Cakobau Government Committee on Polynesian Labour.

FOREIGN OFFICE RECORDS

F.O. 58/128. Enclosure in Foreign Office to Colonial Office, 28 July 1870.

STATUTES OF THE UNITED KINGDOM OF GREAT BRITAIN AND IRELAND

4 Geo. IV, c. 96. An Act to Provide . . . for the better Administration of Justice in New South Wales and Van Dieman's Land . . . 1823.

5 Geo. IV, c. 113. The Slave Trade Consolidation Act.

9 Geo. IV, c. 83. An Act to Provide for the Administration of Justice in New South Wales and Van Diemen's Land . . . 1828.

35 and 36 Victoria, c. 19. An Act for the Prevention and Punishment of Criminal Outrages upon Natives of the Islands in the Pacific Ocean, 1872.

BRITISH PARLIAMENTARY PAPERS

P.P. 1867–8. Correspondence relating to the importation of South Sea Islanders into Queensland, 1867–1868, xlviii. 391; (*a*) enclosure in Bowen to Newcastle, 16 Sept. 1863, (*b*) Bowen to Buckingham, 13 July 1867, (*c*) enclosure 2 in Belmore to Buckingham, 29 Feb. 1868.

P.P. 1871. Further correspondence respecting the Deportation of South Sea Islanders, 1871, xlviii. 245, March to Clarendon, 17 Dec. 1869.

P.P. 1873. Communications respecting outrages committed upon natives of the South Sea Islands, 1873, l. 244.

GOVERNMENT OF FIJI

Department of Labour. Unpub. Polynesian Plantation Register 1875–1914.

Ordinance XXIV. 1876. To Regulate and Control the Conveyance and Recruiting of Polynesian Immigrants.

Ordinance XI. 1877. The Immigration Ordinance.

Ordinance XXIV. 1879. The Polynesian Immigration Recruiting Ordinance.

GOVERNMENT OF QUEENSLAND

Qd. V. and P. 1876. Report of the Select Committee on the General Question of Polynesian Labour, *Votes and Proceedings of the Legislative Assembly*, 1876, vol. iii, pp. 51–150.

Qd. V. and P. 1878. Recruiting Agents and Introduction of Polynesians, *Votes and Proceedings of the Legislative Assembly*, 1878, vol. ii, pp. 47 ff.

Wilson, Commodore. 1882. 'Labour Trade in the Western Pacific', *Votes and Proceedings of the Legislative Assembly*, 1882, vol. ii, p. 606.

Qd. Govt. Gazette. 1871. 'Polynesian Immigration. Appointment of Government Agents to Accompany Recruiting Vessels. Instructions to Government Agents', *Queensland Government Gazette*, 1871, p. 202.

STATUTES

31 Vict., No. 47. 1868. An Act to Regulate and Control the Introduction and Treatment of Polynesian Labourers, 1868.

44 Vict., No. 17. 1880. An Act to make provision for Regulating and Controlling the Introduction and Treatment of Labourers from the Pacific Islands, 1880.

47 Vict., No. 12. 1884. An Act to Amend the Pacific Islands Labourers Act of 1880, 1884.

OTHER WORKS

Belshaw, C. S. 1954. *Changing Melanesia*, Melbourne.

Codrington, R. H. 1875. Letter in *Anti-Slavery Reporter*, London, 1 Mar. 1875.

Des Voeux, G. W. 1903. *My Colonial Service*, 2 vols., London.

Parnaby, O. W. 1964. *Britain and the Labor Trade in the Southwest Pacific*, Durham, N.C.

Scarr, D. 1967a. *Fragments of Empire*, Canberra.

—— 1967b. 'Recruits and Recruiters', *Journal of Pacific History*, vol. 2, pp. 5–24.

—— (ed.). 1968. *A Cruise in a Queensland Labour Vessel to the South Seas*, Canberra.

Shineberg, D. 1967. *They Came for Sandalwood*, Melbourne.

Ward, R. G. 1965. *Land Use and Population in Fiji*, London.

6

TRADE AND PLANTATIONS IN EASTERN POLYNESIA
The Emergence of a Dependent Economy

COLIN NEWBURY[1]

FROM the late eighteenth century, the inhabitants of Tahiti and neighbouring islands[2] have been progressively drawn into contact with European, American, and other Pacific markets. At the same time as their economic isolation was broken down, the islanders' religious beliefs and political structure have undergone varying degrees of destruction and adaptation. Moreover, the population of Eastern Polynesia went through a long phase of demographic decline from initial European contact till about the middle of the nineteenth century. In a few cases, such as the Marquesas Group and Mangareva, the decline continued disastrously (Fig. 8.1); elsewhere, notably in Tahiti, Moorea, and the Leeward Islands, population figures levelled off and with some immigration from other groups began to increase slowly to the total of about 30,000 inhabitants of French Polynesia in 1907[3] (McArthur, 1967: 319). Thus, as the commercial exploitation of the islands' natural resources began, the indigenous *Ma'ohi* suffered severe political and social set-backs from which they had hardly recovered when further demands

---

[1] Dr. Newbury is University Lecturer in Commonwealth History, and Fellow of Linacre College, Oxford.

[2] The main islands of French Polynesia are Tahiti, Moorea, Huahine, Borabora, Raiatea, Tahaa, the Marquesas Islands, the Tuamotu Archipelago, the Gambier (Mangareva) Islands, the Austral Islands, and Rapa. Their superficial area is 366,379 ha. (Bureau des Terres, 1950) with a population of 84,000 (1962 census), including 8,000 Chinese. First occupied by France in 1842, Tahiti, Moorea, the Marquesas, and the Tuamotu were ruled for nearly forty years before annexation of the rest of the Leeward and Austral groups. As an Overseas Territory, the colony is administered by an official executive with advice from an Assembly elected by universal suffrage.

[3] For an analysis of the 1951 census see McArthur, 1961.

were made on their labour and their land. For, from the date of French occupation in 1842, a determined effort was made by their European protectors to stimulate agriculture for export. This essay is concerned with the results of this policy in the nineteenth century and some of its long-term effects on the economy today.

Looked at in broad perspective the history of French Polynesia offers two striking developments during the last 100 years. The first is the total collapse of traditional authorities—the paramount and lineage district chiefs—under European rule; and the second is the natural increase in the population of the area after 1907 to slightly more than twice its size by the 1950s. The decline of the chiefs and in particular the royal house of the Pomares contrasts strongly with the tenacity of traditional political structure elsewhere in the Pacific. A full discussion of the reasons for this political change cannot be undertaken here, but they lie in the length of European administration (compared with Samoa, Fiji, the Cook Islands) and in deliberate interference with title successions and the substitution of other functionaries, such as the *gendarme*, at district level. The Leeward Islands (Raiatea, Huahine, Borabora) which escaped annexation till 1888 were noticeably less politically depressed than their neighbours. But by and large political representation and organization at the capital of Papeete have remained in the hands of European settlers and literate Euro-Polynesians, or *demis*, who are closely associated with foreign administration and commerce. The expansion of the capital's population from 3,600 in 1907 to 15,000 (or half the inhabitants of Tahiti) by 1951, reflects this concentration of business and authority at the principal port (Dauvergne, 1959: 113–45; Auzelle, 1951: 81–128).

Compared with the striking political and demographic changes in French Polynesia, the development of the economy has been fitful and unspectacular. Until recently, there has been a feeling in much of the official and popular literature describing the group that the bulk of the *Ma'ohi* population is hardly advanced beyond subsistence agriculture and that cash crops are something of a sideline, easily forgone in times of bad prices. A few detailed studies, however, have begun to demonstrate how quickly in Tahitian districts a rural population can become dependent on imported foodstuffs obtained by sale of staples or by wage labour (Finney, 1965: 62).[1] A closer interpretation of nineteenth-century records would throw more light on this transition process, though it is doubtful whether a very hard line can be drawn between 'subsistence' farmers and cash-cropping peasants at any stage of French Polynesia's history after 1842. Moreover, as long as the place of fishing and sea-food consumption in the local economy remains unexamined, generalizations about how the bulk of the population live and derive income at any period should be approached with caution.

The sources for the study of the economic history of Eastern Polynesia are rich in official data but hindered by the super-ficial nature of much of this material.[2] There were several agricultural surveys in the nineteenth century, but any report on land utilization was (and still is) hampered by the lack of cadastral maps or aerial photographs. As late as the 1950s only one-third of the territory's 366,379 hectares had been surveyed.[3] The local Department of Agriculture dates from the late 1940s, though there were various *ad hoc* commissions at earlier periods. Consequently, information on the development of cash crops comes mainly by way of trade statistics; and these, whether from official French or consular returns, must be used with care, since Tahiti was an entrepôt for neighbouring groups, and Papeete exports do not accurately reflect the state of production in the main island alone.

Development of the Export Trade

Using trade returns as a guide, one can discern three phases in the production of agricultural exports in French Polynesia.

[1] There is evidence of such a dependence developing in the Tuamotu in the early 1870s (*Messager de Tahiti*, No. 42, 17 Oct., 1872). By then agents of the mer-chant trader John Brander had established a monopoly of credit sales of cloth and foodstuffs at Anaa and Fakarava (A.C.O., série Océanie, E. 26, c. 57, Correy to de la Roncière, 23 June 1868). A similar situation developed at Mangareva in the 1860s, when agricultural labour was diverted to shell diving (Laval, n.d.: chaps. xxviii–xxxi).

[2] Most of the sources examined here were used for a thesis: 'The Administration of French Oceania, 1842–1905', Australian National University, 1956, part of which is published in Newbury, 1959: 97–154. Two field trips were made to Tahiti in 1955 and 1964 to examine the records of the Bureau des Terres, Papeete.

[3] Roucaute, 1951; Bureau des Terres, 1950. See, too, F. Ravault, 1970, for an assessment of the recent decline in 'communal' land-holding.

The first dates from the beginning of the nineteenth century when a profitable pork and provisions trade with visiting ships had already been developed by Tahitian and Leeward Islands chiefs (Maude, 1959: 55–95). It was expanded by traders from New South Wales and Valparaiso in search of pearls and pearl shell, sandalwood, arrowroot, and coconut oil in the 1820s, and was supplemented during the next decade by the whaling traffic which reached its zenith at eighty arrivals at Papeete in 1840 (Vandor, 1866; A.C.O., J. 3, c. 55). By then, exports from Tahiti were valued at 53,000 *piastres* a year (£10,600) and were made up of 180 tons of coconut oil, 150 tons of raw sugar, 50 tons of arrowroot and unknown quantities of pearl shell. This phase, which was marked by freedom from all forms of commercial restriction, port duties, or taxes, lasted through the early years of the French protectorate till about 1864, when duties on enumerated articles were levied.

From the early 1860s until the discovery and exploitation of Makatea phosphates, the staples of Tahiti's export trade were pearl shell (from the Tuamotu and Gambier Islands), oranges (Tahiti, Moorea, and the Leewards), cotton, copra, and vanilla. Their relative importance can be seen from the following table.

TABLE 6.1. *French Polynesia: Export Staples by Value and as a Percentage of Export Values*

Selected years	Coconut oil		Pearl shell		Oranges		Copra		Vanilla		Cotton	
	Fr.*	%	Fr.	%	Fr.	%	Fr.	%	Fr.	%	Fr.	%
1850	97	35	31	11	15	5						
1855	92	26	93	26	150	42						
1860	285	50	201	35	46	8						
1864	357	47	60	8	173	22			9	1	1	0·1
1875	76	3	358	15	124	5	400	17	16	0·3	958	40
1880			422	16	494	17	505	18	17	0·6	1,490	54
1884			661	13	76	2	799	22	40	1·1	1,551	42
1889			865	25	42	1	1,043	30	?	?	503	14
1898			909	36	21	0·8	1,214	48	517	20	27	1
1906			650	18	28	0·8	2,044	55	542	15	26	0·7

SOURCES: A.C.O., J. 3, c. 55; British Consulate, 1838–83; *Rapport d'ensemble*, 1908: 12, 23–6.

* Thousands; 25 fr. = £1.

Pearl shell is the oldest staple in the territory and enjoyed a steady rise in price from 200 fr. per ton to 700 fr. between 1845 and 1860. It is still exported in much the same quantities (400–500 tons a year) as it was in the nineteenth century. The

Tahitian orange trade to San Francisco flourished in the third quarter of the century, until the market was lost to California and local trees were ruined by blight. Coconut oil accounted for about half the total value of exports in the early 1860s, but was replaced in the same decade by copra, vanilla, and cotton. Of these, cotton maintained a high export value during the American civil war and declined slowly in value and quantity over the next half-century. Copra, on the other hand, advanced to become the principal staple from the 1890s, when 400–500 tons began to be exported annually in roughly equal proportions from Tahiti, the Tuamotu, the Marquesas, and the Leewards.

The third phase in Tahiti's export economy includes the exploitation of phosphates after 1907. This mineral grew in volume to 368,000 tons by 1961 and accounted for 42 per cent of the territory's export values for the year (I.N.S.E.E., 1962: 23–5). Other current exports are mainly the traditional staples —copra which had quadrupled in quantity exported and accounted for 25 per cent of export values by the late 1950s, and vanilla which made up 17 per cent of values by that date.

TABLE 6.2. *Principal Exports*

Annual Average in tons

Period	Phosphate	Copra	Vanilla	Coffee
1899–1901		5,592·0	76·06	0·33
1909–11	4,008·9	8,557·8	225·20	0·73
1920–2	54,510·9	10,303·8	123·86	1·20
1924–31	178,468·9	16,022·8	73·60	3·96
1936–8	133,221·4	21,064·1	108·43	53·8
1951–3	228,786·0	22,640·0	174·1	68·6
1954	228,894·0	22,889·7	130·2	34·3
1961	368,784·0	21,692·0	223·0	49·0

SOURCES: *Rapport d'ensemble*, 1908: 12, 23–6; Guillaume, 1958: 295; I.N.S.E.E., 1962

The basis for the export economy of the territory has always been a narrow one. With the exhaustion of phosphate deposits at Makatea in 1966, about half the foreign exchange earnings (other than from tourism) of French Polynesia disappeared, as the main purchasers of the mineral were Japan, the U.S.A., and New Zealand. The remaining staples, moreover, have always been subject to severe fluctuations in price—particularly vanilla, the production of which tends to lag behind any improvement in the overseas market by a period of eighteen months. Added to these drawbacks is the small scale of total production for exports which in the nineteenth century hardly exceeded £300,000 annually and included a fair percentage of European goods for re-export. In 1961, import values accounted for 60 per cent of total external trade (£1,324,000) which is typical of the unfavourable balance the colony has known for most of its economic history, the difference being made up in the nineteenth century by the export of specie paid out by the administration for imported goods and local wages.

Indeed, the administration, whose services have steadily multiplied since 1947, has become a major factor in the territory's economy, a liberal provider of public works programmes, port development, defence, and social security, while the output of the agricultural sector has lagged behind (I.N.S.E.E., 1965: 3).[1] Yet, for most of the period of French rule, and especially in the nineteenth century, the express policy of the colonial government has been to stimulate primary production.

Agricultural Developments

The groundwork of agricultural and commercial policy was laid down by six governors who followed each other in quick succession in the 1850s and 1860s. Each added something to the work of his predecessor; and the whole was intended, in the phrase of Governor Bonard, to: 'galvaniser les indigènes' (A.C.O., A. 68, c. 13, Bonard to Ministry of Marine, 16 July 1850). The main elements of their legislation were enclosure of agricultural land against damage by livestock, compulsory registration of land titles by Tahitians (law of the Tahitian Assembly, 1852, and decree of 1862), the organization of a lands and survey department, a system of subsidies for plantations, and an agricultural bank to facilitate the purchase of land. The crowning achievement of their work under Governors de la Richerie and de la Roncière (1860–9) was their patronage of the largest single agricultural enterprise ever attempted in the colony—the Atimaono plantation founded by William Stewart

---

[1] The estimate of productivity in the agricultural sector for 1963 was 990 m.F. (CFP), compared with 1,150 m.F. for building construction, 1,080 m.F. for services, 2,013 m.F. for commerce.

for the Soarès Company on some 10,000 acres of land purchased with official backing and worked by 1,000 Chinese coolies imported with official permission.

With variations, these developments were accepted by the administration till the 1880s, when a new decree of 1887 reintroduced compulsory land registration. The Agricultural Bank was reformed several times with a view to making loans easier. Committees of settlers for agriculture, commerce, and indentured labour were set up; agricultural shows were held; the official gazette devoted numerous issues to articles on tropical produce. Within the limited resources of the budget, a considerable effort was made to turn Polynesians into peasant proprietors, or, at least, into wage labour for European planters.

The details of this development policy have been examined elsewhere (Newbury, 1959: 123–43). It had a certain initial success among the district co-owners (*ra'atira*) of Teahupoo, Hitiaa, Faaa, Mahaena, Pueu, and Mataiea in Tahiti, where enclosures were kept in repair, cotton and sugarcane plantations were begun, and orange groves were weeded and harvested under the authority of the *ari'i* titleholders. Governor Saisset observed in 1859 that Tahitian cash crops were best produced in those districts where the chief was accepted as the lineal descendant of senior families and enjoyed rights over land set aside by the district population for the *ari'i's* personal wealth (A.C.O., A. 75, c. 14, Saisset to Ministry for Algeria and Colonies, 15 Feb. 1859). Such lands (*fari'i-hau*) were worked by district labour, and the returns from the sale of produce were distributed according to rank. Where the representatives of the district lineages had been replaced by a nominee of the administration, the chief's real authority and ability to organize large-scale agriculture were diminished. The most important leader in district affairs might well be the district pastor or district judge; but these would not have rights over *fari'i-hau* lands. Control of plantation agriculture on a limited scale passed to household heads (*ra'atira*), and many of these after the 1887 land decree were beset by problems of divided inheritance which made large-scale co-ownership impossible to organize.

On the other hand, as the power of traditional authorities to administer agricultural production weakened, Europeans did

not flood into Tahiti to purchase large blocks of land. Apart from
the Stewart enterprise, alienation was officially discouraged;
Polynesians were not eager to part with their inheritance; and
it was difficult to obtain a valid title, once litigation between
Tahitians had begun. A partial survey of plantations was made
in 1866 and yielded the results given in Table 6.3.

TABLE 6.3. *Tahiti Plantations and Gardens, 1866 (excluding
Atimaono)*

Areas in acres

Under customary tenure (chiefs and *ra'atira*)	European titles (84)		
	Area owned	Area cultivated	Total area cultivated
713	943·7	509·7	1,222·7

SOURCES: *Rapport* . . ., 1866; Consul Miller, Reports for 1860s, in
British Consulate, 1838–83.

Coconut plantations were not included in the survey. The
main products were cotton, coffee, sugar, oranges, maize, and
livestock. The European 'planters', however, cannot be regarded
as full-time primary producers. If the biographies of those
named in the survey are examined, it is seen that fifteen of them
were also traders, three owned schooners, three were doctors,
and three were officials. Some ten others were retired soldiers
and marines. One was a Catholic missionary. In other words,
over half of the European title-holders were deriving income
from other occupations.

The 1,222 acres listed as under cultivation in Tahiti in 1866
were hardly as much as the area brought into production by
Stewart in 1870. He had some 2,000 acres under cotton and
maize, out of 9,875 acres auctioned in 1875, after the bank-
ruptcy of the company. Altogether, in Tahiti, about 2,500
acres (excluding coconuts) were producing just over £100,000
of plantation produce in 1868—the highest figure reached before
the 1880s (Candelot, 1870: 25).

After the collapse of the price of cotton in 1866, no one
imitated Stewart's investment in a single crop so dependent
on the supply of labour. The Plantation Company was liqui-
dated in 1874 and the land at Atimaono was auctioned off to a

number of private speculators, few of whom were planters. Official encouragement through the Agricultural Bank continued to draw more European small-holders into part-time cultivation of cash crops, using some of the Chinese and Polynesian labour thrown on to the market after Stewart's fall. From a survey of sixteen districts of Tahiti and Moorea in 1877, it appears there were at least 196 Europeans employing 224 Pacific islanders and Chinese in this way.

Although incomplete, the agricultural survey of 1877 raises some points of interest, when different districts are compared (Fig. 6.1). The amount of land occupied by coconut and orange plantations is not given in the areas under 'cultivation'; and this term is somewhat notional when it is remembered that grassland supporting cattle is also included. The districts listed had some 2,000 ha. in cotton, vegetables (including taro, breadfruit, and sweet potatoes), grassland, maize, and small amounts of vanilla and sugar cane. The annual production of cultivated areas, orange trees, and coconut plantations was valued at only £27,000 (667,000 fr.).[1] Copra, oranges, and cotton were the most valuable cash crops in the districts surveyed. Districts which earned an estimated income above the average *per capita* 144 fr. (£6) were Vairao, Afaahiti, Teahupoo, Mahaena, and Tiarei. The small European population in each of these might have been expected to raise the local level of income.[2] But their presence was not a decisive factor. For example, Punaauia, with the largest number of European settlers, was well below the general average. It is noticeable, too, that European-style plantations such as cotton, coffee, or sugar-cane were not sufficient to account for the relative agricultural prosperity of the districts mentioned; and this is confirmed by their small amount of plantation labour, while Punaauia and other below-average districts have as many as seventy labourers listed.

The factors which made a difference in the case of the districts with a high estimated return on produce were, first, a large proportion of cultivated land per head of population (one

---

[1] A probable figure when compared with a later estimate which evaluated total agricultural production in Tahiti and Moorea in 1884 at £42,800 (*Annuaire des É.F.O.*, 1885: 150–1).

[2] Europeans in each of these districts respectively numbered 15, 32, 17, 0, 13. Plantation labour for the five districts consisted of 48 Chinese and 'Polynesians'.

TABLE 6.4. *Estimated Agricultural Production and Value of Crops, 1877. Tahiti and Moorea (sixteen districts)*

Districts	Population	Land cultivated including grasslands (hectares)	Cotton (ha.)	Cotton (kg.)	Vanilla (ha.)	Vanilla (kg.)	Grass (ha.)	Maize (ha.)	Cane (ha.)	Vegetables (ha.)	Coconut trees	Copra (tons)	Orange trees	Labour	Total value (fr.)
Tahiti															
PUNAAUIA (1)	589	194	89	44,500	4	160	53	1	2	45	19,500	125	160,000	70	70,700
Value (Fr.)				26,700		4,800	5,000	300	1,200	4,500		25,000	3,200		
ARUE (2)	245	96	23	11,500	2	80	24	6	4	35	12,900	99	240,000	18	42,700
Value (Fr.)				6,900		2,400	2,000	1,800	?	3,100		19,800	4,800		
MAHINA (3)	260	114	..	..	0·5	20	80	1	0·5	32	(25,000)*	159	400,000	23	50,600
Value (Fr.)						600	7,500	300	?	3,000		31,800	8,000		
PAPENOO (4)	277	202	..	..	0·5	20	170	0·5	0·5	30·5	2,350	23·5	45,000	5	24,750
Value (Fr.)						600	15,800	150	?	2,600		4,700	900		
TIAREI (5)	201	104	..	..	..	..	57	0·5	0·5	46	2,740	27	850,000	8	31,630
Value (Fr.)							5,000	150	?	4,000		5,480	17,000		
MAHAENA (6)	143	95	..	..	0·25	10	64·25	..	0·5	30	1,260	12·6	1,000,000	8	31,020
Value (Fr.)						300	5,500		?	2,700		2,520	20,000		
HITIAA (7)	443	99	12	6,000	1	40	48	2·5	0·5	35	6,500	65	700,000	10	38,540
Value (Fr.)				3,600		1,200	3,800	840	?	3,100		13,000	14,000		

AFAAHITI (8)	160	113	26	13,000	2	80	49·5	..	0·5	35	9,910	99	850,000	21	51,400
Value (Fr.)				7,800		2,400	4,000	..	?	2,000		18,200	17,000		
PUEU (9)	313	89	1·75	800	..	..	18	..	0·25	69	9,263	90	1,500,000	17	53,480
Value (Fr.)				480		..	1,000	..	?	4,000		18,000	30,000		
TAUTIRA (10)	461	190·5	..	..	1	40	24	..	0·5	165	(9,000?)	90	1,500,000	21	66,800
Value (Fr.)				..		1,200	2,000	..	?	15,600		18,000	30,000		
TEAHUPOO (11)	279	186	8·5	1,750	1	40	85	2	2·5	92	(8,500?)	82	1,200,000	20	57,850
Value (Fr.)				930		1,200	6,900	600	?	8,200		16,000	24,000		
VAIRAO (12)	415	209	1·5	750	2	80	71	..	0·5	134	11,800	118	1,200,000	..	66,850
Value (Fr.)				450		3,400	6,000	..	?	11,000		22,000	24,000		
PAPEARI (13)	260	165	0·5	25	2	80	82	1	1	78·5	(4,000?)	37	1,200,000	18	48,780
Value (Fr.)				180		2,400	7,500	300	?	7,200		7,200	24,000		
Moorea															
PAPETOAI (14)	300	61	3	1,500	1	40	35·5	1	0·5	20	(2,000?)	19	40,600	2	11,860
Value (Fr.)				900		1,200	3,000	300	?	1,800		3,960	800		
TEAHAROA-TEAVARO (15)	?	100	47	23,500	0·25	20	22·5	0·25	1	29	(8,000?)	78	50,000	19	36,570
Value (Fr.)				14,100		600	2,000	70	?	2,600		15,600	1,600		
AFAREAITU (16)	279	42	5·5	3,000	1	40	12·5	0·5	2·5	20	(6,000?)	63	50,000	3	20,050
Value (Fr.)				1,800		1,200	1,200	150	?	2,000		12,700	1,000		

* Estimate based on production.
SOURCE: A.C.O., J. 20, c. 64. MS. dated 1 July 1877. Small areas of maize, rice, and coffee have been excluded from the table. Coconut stands and orange groves are not included in totals of cultivated land.

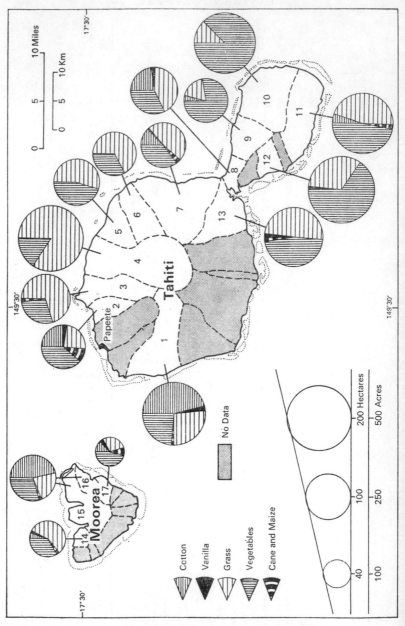

FIG. 6.1. Land use by districts, 1877. Source: A.C.O., J. 20, c. 64.
MS. dated 1 July 1877.

acre or more) used for tobacco, coffee, maize, vegetables, cotton, grass, vanilla, in variable amounts;[1] and second a high proportion of coconut and orange trees. Districts with the lowest estimated revenue—Papetoai, Afareaitu, Papenoo, Hitiaa, and Tautira—were further removed from the Papeete market and had a low yield of copra and oranges both absolutely and in proportion to population. The Papenoo valley is something of a special case with a large grass acreage and livestock (including 132 head of cattle) valued at £1,230—much more than any other district.

The general picture, then, of plantation production in Tahiti and Moorea is one of limited investment in land and labour in the 1850s and 1860s for the sale and export of cotton, sugar, coffee, vanilla, and tobacco. The acreage given over to these crops remained fairly constant for the rest of the century.

TABLE 6.5. *Land under Cultivation*

(Acres)

	Tahiti		Tahiti and Moorea	
	1864	1884	1891	1899
Cotton	1,375	1,167	745	?
Sugar cane	375	189	332	665
Coffee	85	67	137	295
Vanilla	14	202	477	870
Tobacco	7	12	?	?
Total	1,856	1,607	1,691	2,530

SOURCES: Vandor, 1864; *Annuaire des É.F.O.*, 1885: 150–1; Lemasson, 1900: 41–4.

The area under cotton in both islands rapidly decreased after 1880, while vanilla and, to a lesser extent, coffee and sugar expanded. The only recorded estimate of the area of land occupied by coconut plantations was made in 1884, when 5,697 acres were ascribed to this crop. The acreage under orange trees is unknown, but it seems fairly certain that they were replaced by coconut stands between the end of the nineteenth century and the present day.

The predominance of small plantation agriculture for cash

[1] The ratio of cultivated land to population was: Vairao, 1 acre per head; Afaahiti, 2:1; Teahupoo, 1·5:1; Mahaena, 1:1; Tiarei, 1:1.

crops, practised in the main by Polynesians, was largely confirmed before the First World War. With the single exception
of phosphates, no European enterprise has sought to challenge
the place left to indigenous production, *faute de mieux*, since the
days of William Stewart.

Some of the reasons for this state of affairs have already been
touched on. The general run of nineteenth-century settlers in
French Polynesia were traders, not planters.[1] Those who
handled the bulk of Tahiti's exports in the 1860s—for example
John Brander, Alfred Hort, Andrew Gibson, or Étienne Amiot
—made their money out of the schooner traffic and invested
relatively little of it in land. Many of them, like Brander,
married into Polynesian families and founded dynasties of small
business men, junior officials, school teachers, and artisans who
became the core of the *demis* literate class in the next two
generations.[2] Their interest in land has been speculative at
periods of rising values—in the 1920s and from the 1940s
onwards. But they were not planters, in the normal sense of the
term, preferring to lease harvesting rights to the vanilla and
copra staples, rather than experiment in coffee, cocoa, or sugar
cane, for which local labour was not readily available.

Apart from Stewart, very few with small land-holdings could
afford to import labour from Asia or the Pacific Islands.
Altogether, between 1862 and 1892, some 2,600 Chinese,
Melanesians, and Polynesians were recruited from Hong Kong,
the New Hebrides, the Gilbert Islands, the Cook Islands, and
Tongareva (Newbury, 1958:49). Some of these were repatriated;
many, like the Chinese, spread throughout the colony; a few
ran small plantations of their own; hardly any were willing
to continue as wage labour once their contracts ended. Under-
standably nervous about recruiting foreign immigrants, the
administration and the Papeete settlers refused to contemplate
the kind of decision made to remedy the shortage of labour

---

[1] They numbered 660 in 1860 (69 married to Polynesians); by 1865 they had
increased to 785—excluding 400 officials and troops. *Annuaire des É.F.O.*, 1863:
335–6; *Messager de Tahiti*, 2 Dec. 1865. In 1907 the European population of the
territory numbered 2,108 French and 858 other nationalities.

[2] For example, the children and grandchildren of John Brander (1814–77) by
Tataua Salmon (an Anglo-Tahitian) were married to foreign consuls, naval
officers, or became traders, officials, and in a few cases a consul, a merchant, and
a sugar planter.

in Fiji (see Parnaby, Chapter 9). It was cheaper to leave the production of staples in Polynesian hands.

There were similar diseconomies of scale in the financing of agriculture. The Agricultural Bank never had sufficient capital to purchase more than small scattered lots of land, as they became available; and these were sold at once to settlers who could contract loans under £440 for ten years at a rate of interest which rose from 6 per cent to 8 per cent in the 1870s. By 1883, 180 small loans had been made. The Bank's capital, raised from savings, amounted to only £7,268 by 1896; and for some years it paid no interest at all, before being superseded by a branch of the Bank of Indo-China which assisted trading operations, but provided no credits for agriculture.

The only security for the advance of money to settlers by the administration would have been land; and it was clear, even in the 1860s, that local conditions of tenure precluded large mortgages on doubtful titles. The preliminary inscription made after 1852 in Tahiti and Moorea and the effort made to secure compulsory registration in the 1860s did not result in the issue of deeds to ra'atira co-heirs, but merely in lists of land blocks in the name of one adult in each household.[1] Counter-claims, which grew in volume and complexity, gradually emphasized the judicial, rather than the productive aspects of land tenure, as district councils and the Tahitian Court of Appeal tried to reduce usufructuary rights to freehold. Claimants established as kin were accorded fractions; and as bilateral inheritance was admitted, these fractions were scattered among the ancestral lands of both parents. By the end of the Protectorate period in 1880, there were three classes of land in Tahiti and Moorea: those lands for which a title deed had been issued on the basis of an undisputed or successfully contested inscription—mostly in the western and north-western districts; lands still in a chaos of litigation; and the majority of usehold areas which were uninscribed. After annexation, further attempts were made in 1887 and in the 1920s to speed up registration of titles throughout the territory, but with little success. The publication of a

---

[1] As listed in the committee register (*Puta tomite*), the inheritance register (*Puta monoraa*), and the register of chiefs' lands (*Puta fari'i-hau*). There were others in the care of the district councils—registers of sales, donations, and judgements. Few of these have survived.

claim or delivery of a certificate, without proper survey, despite popular belief to the contrary, has never constituted a title valid in French law. The case of Makatea threw the whole system into disrepute, so far as the outer islands were concerned (see Chapter 7), and gave an unheeded warning of possibilities of land speculation by Tahitians themselves, when values rose in and around the capital after 1947 (Panoff, 1964: 5–19). By then, some sixty years after the 1887 decree, only 30 per cent of all land in French Polynesia was held under private title and four per cent by the Colony. Records were confused by destruction and deterioration of the district registers, by inadequate census, frequent changes of name, and lack of survey.

In a sense the confusion of land tenure in French Polynesia has been the *Ma'ohi*'s best defence against dispossession. It is also a product of genuine inability to understand alien regulations and to recall, after several generations, the genealogies, land-names, donations, and inheritances necessary to prove usehold rights. Oral tradition was not the least important victim of the social and political changes of the early nineteenth century and the levelling out of the hierarchy of claimants of both sexes. Moreover, since land even along the fertile littoral of Tahiti has not been subject to population pressure outside Papeete, there has been a tendency among the peasant co-heirs to indulge in acrimonious quarrels about usehold rights to vanilla and copra, while leaving family lots for intensive cultivation uncontested (Panoff, 1964: 115). This differentiation in the way land is regarded—as a speculative gamble, or as indivisible family patrimony—has its roots in *Ma'ohi* attitudes to cash crops which are not a source of regular income, but a periodic windfall. If the debate between families or individuals concerning such usehold becomes too difficult, the collection and sale of the crop may be sacrificed.

Conversely, as in the Tuamotu, excessive reliance on the sale of a single crop—copra—sometimes leads to neglect of traditional horticulture in favour of imported foodstuffs. This tendency is increased whenever wage labour replaces farming as a livelihood, and fertile land, uncontested or not, may go out of production (Finney, 1965: 19; see also Lea, Chapter 10).

From inadequate surveys of agricultural production made in

the 1950s, it would appear that French Polynesia's economy is approaching a dangerous climax, when century-old methods of cash-cropping on insecure tenure will no longer provide more than a fraction of exchange-earning exports.[1] From tables prepared in the early years of the decade, there are some 50,000–60,000 hectares, or some three-quarters of agricultural land, in use, producing the bulk of the group's copra, vanilla, and coffee for export. A further 20,000 hectares are devoted to pastures and gardens.

TABLE 6.6. *Agricultural Land Use*

(In hectares)

	Total area	Land in use	Coconuts	Vanilla	Coffee	Total	Pastures and gardens
Tahiti and dependencies (1951)	122,385	21,260	9,600	500	500	10,600	10,600
Leeward Islands	41,455	16,150	8,900	1,858	270	11,028	5,122
Austral Islands	15,068	4,000	1,500	12	690	2,202	1,798
Tuamotu and Gambier	89,931	29,000	28,200	..	40	28,240	760
Marquesas	97,540	7,700	5,570	..	200	5,570	1,930
Total	366,379	78,110	53,770	2,370	1,700	57,850	20,260

SOURCES: Bureau des Terres, 1950; Guillaume, 1958: 210.

The highest percentage of land in agricultural use in the early 1950s was in the Leeward Islands, the lowest in the Marquesas group. Tahiti and Moorea had some 17·3 per cent of their total area in use, against a general percentage of 21·3 per cent. It is apparent, too, in the case of the main islands that the area given over to coconut plantations must have quadrupled since the 1890s, while vanilla and coffee plantations have doubled in the last half-century (cf. Table 6.5). It is not possible to make a valid comparison in the case of pasture and vegetables, without more detailed data. It is clear, however, that the 15,830 head of cattle in Tahiti and Moorea in 1951 represented a considerable increase over the 2,328 counted in a survey of 1884. Cattle production has probably kept pace with the expansion of coconut plantations. The present stocking ratio in the two main islands is 0·75 ha. per head (with an overall average of 0·9 ha.). Herds are generally small (less than

[1] See F. Ravault, 1970, pp. 26–9. The critical date in the decline of copra and vanilla would appear to be 1964, after acceleration of the local *C.E.P.* programme.

ten), only six owners in the group possessing more than 100 head of stock.

On the other hand, while total plantation agriculture has expanded, it is probable that the area per head under intensive cultivation of gardens and fruit has declined. Again the statistics are slender, but a survey of two districts of Tahiti in 1955 produced the following returns:

TABLE 6.7. *Land Use in Papeari and Faaone Districts, Tahiti, 1955*

Population	Land cultivated per head	Land in cash crops per head	Garden area per head	Cultivated land and pasture per head
848	1 ha.	0·495 ha.	0·015 ha.	1·68 ha.

The average area of garden cultivated per head in Papeari in the 1877 survey was 0·3 hectare, while the average for fifteen districts was 0·16 hectare—which is considerably more than the fraction at Papeari and Faaone in 1955 (0·015 hectare). Attempts have been made to approach the problem of domestic production another way, by noting the increase in calories consumed in imported foodstuffs per head of population between the 1920s and 1950s (Jacquier, 1949). But with the exception of the Tuamotu, where the daily diet of the inhabitants has been more carefully measured, the results are not very conclusive, unless other variables, such as calorie content of certain items and European consumption patterns, are excluded. In the final analysis, one may say that certain sections of the Tahitian population, especially those living in and around Papeete, and wage-earners in other areas, are almost wholly dependent on imported foodstuffs and on food grown and marketed by other districts. What is certain is that rising imports, whether for Polynesians or Europeans, have to be paid for from a narrow range of cash crops which are being seriously depleted by the rising level of domestic consumption.

By the early 1950s, out of a total copra production of 30,000 tons for the territory, some 7,400 tons were being consumed locally, thus keeping the level of exported copra down to 1940 tonnages. Almost the total of coffee production in 1950 was consumed locally.

The general conclusion is that French Polynesia has become an economic dependency which is rapidly outrunning its agricultural resources in terms of production and land utilization. At a conservative estimate perhaps 2,000–2,500 hectares might be opened up around the coast and in the interior of the two main islands, though the expense of building valley roads and driving market gardens further up eroded slopes is a deterrent to this policy. Pepper and rice might be added to the short list of staples for export and local consumption. Butter and

TABLE 6.8. *Evolution of Domestic Consumption*

	Leeward and Windward groups			Tuamotu, Austral Islands, Mangareva, Marquesas		
	Coconuts consumed (tons)	Oil	Soap	Coconuts consumed (tons)	Oil/Soap	Total
1897	1,211			3,519	747	5,277
1911	1,395			2,202	544	4,141
1926	1,696			2,270	394	4,360
1931	1,902		246	2,666	399	5,213
1941	2,559	124	312	2,801	471	6,267
1951	3,195	138	383	3,207	568	7,491

SOURCE: Guillaume, 1958: 574–5.

milk production could be improved. But even the most generous suggestions for raising productivity[1] must allow for factors which have always been present in French Polynesia's market and plantation structure since the 1860s.

The first of these is the almost total absence of a planter class in the territory. Production since the middle of the nineteenth century has been left to the *ra'atira* and a few amateur Europeans and *demis* who have cultivated a narrow range of crops for quick returns. Even today, most copra and nearly all vanilla production is harvested by small co-owners and peasants renting harvesting rights as *métayers*. Where the plantation has been established by the useholder, his share of the harvest may be as large as 50 per cent or more. But the

[1] The bulk of Inspector Guillaume's report, for example, is devoted to recommendations for increasing agricultural productivity. For a comparison with other parts of the Pacific see Pitt, 1962: 110–17; and for a special study of the decline of agriculture production on Moorea, Cl. Robineau, 1970.

general practice of *métayage* on lands acquired or inherited by owners in employment other than agriculture is widespread in Tahiti and the Leeward group. The interest of co-users in improving such plantations is small; and the professional 'landlord' may rest content with his 'rents' in kind, without investing in replacing declining coconut stands.

Land held under customary tenure (generally less than two hectares per family) has become so divided by multiple inheritance that it may pass out of production, but not pass on to the market for sale or lease. It is not easy to see how suggestions for regrouping fractioned inheritance by compensating some of the claimants could be put into practice without a better system of agricultural credit and a new generation of educated peasants. Fundamentally, changes in land legislation in the territory are a political problem. It may now be too late to carry through the radical reforms necessary in the late 1940s, before the attractions of wage labour in and around Papeete began to turn peasants into an urban proletariat.

Whatever improvements are made in crop production, communications, and agricultural extension services, there is no guarantee that the present rate of demographic mobility from the outer islands to the commercial centre of Tahiti, or from the rural districts to the town, will decrease. Indeed, with continued French investment in public works and defence there is every likelihood that more wage labour will be required than the territory can provide. If this is so, and the high level of government spending continues, cash crop production will drop absolutely and in proportion to population growth, and dependence on French subsidies to maintain the expensive administrative structure will increase still further.

BIBLIOGRAPHY

A.C.O.[1] Archives des Colonies (Rue Oudinot, Paris), série Océanie.

Annuaire des É.F.O. 1863. *Annuaire des Établissements Français de l'Océanie,* Papeete.

Annuaire des É.F.O. 1865. *Annuaire des Établissements Français de l'Océanie,* Papeete.

[1] Now ANSOM, Archives Nationales Section Outre-mer.

Auzelle, R. 1951. 'Plan directeur de Papeete', *La Vie urbaine*, no. 60, pp. 81–128.

British Consulate. 1838–83. Tahiti, British Consulate Papers, Annual Reports, Mitchell Library, Sydney.

Bureaux des Terres. 1950. Tahiti et dépendances. Tableaux comparatifs, Papeete.

Candelot, E. 1870. *Plantation de coton de Tahiti. Compagnie 'Tahiti Coffee and Cotton Plantation'*, Océanie orientale, Paris.

Dauvergne, R. 1959. 'Les débuts du Papeete français: 1843–1863', *Journal de la Société des Océanistes*, vol. 15, pp. 113–45.

Finney, B. R. 1965. *Polynesian Peasants and Proletarians*, Polynesian Society Reprint Series, 9, Wellington.

Guillaume, M. 1958. 'Économie rurale de l'Océanie française. Esquisse de développement agricole', *Agronomie tropicale*, vol. 13, pp. 279–99, 448–57, 558–629.

I.N.S.E.E. 1962. Institut National de la Statistique et des Études Économiques, *Statistiques du commerce extérieur des Territoires d'Outre-mer en 1961*, Paris.

—— 1965. Institut National de la Statistique et des Études Économiques, *Comptes économiques de la Polynésie française 1963–1964*, Paris.

Jacquier, H. 1949. 'Contribution à l'Étude de l'Alimentation et de l'Hygiène Alimentaire en Océanie Française', *Bulletin de la Société des Études Océaniennes*, Mar.

Laval, H. n.d. *Histoire de Mangareva: Tome II, Ère chrétienne*, Picpus Congregational Archives, Rome.

Lemasson, H. 1900. *Les Établissements français de l'Océanie*, Paris.

Maude, H. E. 1959. 'The Tahitian Pork Trade: 1800–1830', *Journal de la Société des Océanistes*, vol. 15, pp. 55–95.

McArthur, N. 1961. 'Population and Social Change: the Prospect for Polynesia', *Jour. Poly. Soc.*, vol. 70, pp. 393–400.

—— 1967. *Island Populations of the Pacific*, Canberra.

Messager de Tahiti . . . *Messager de Tahiti, Journal officiel des Établissements français de l'Océanie*, Papeete.

Newbury, C. W. 1956. 'The Administration of French Oceania, 1842–1905', unpublished Ph.D. thesis, Australian National University, Canberra.

—— 1958. 'Aspects of French Policy in the Pacific, 1853–1906', *Pacific Historical Review*, vol. 27, pp. 45–56.

—— 1959. 'L'Administration de l'Océanie française de 1849 à 1866', *Revue française d'Histoire d'Outre-mer*, vol. 46, pp. 97–154.

Panoff, M. 1964. *Les Structures agraires en Polynésie française*, Paris.

Parnaby, O. W., 1964. *Britain and the Labor Trade in the Southwest Pacific*.

Pitt, D. 1962. 'Some obstacles to Economic Development in Fiji and Island Polynesia', *Jour. Poly. Soc.*, vol. 71, pp. 110–17.

Rapport d'ensemble . . . 1908. *Rapport d'ensemble, année 1907*, Papeete.

Rapport . . . 1866. *Rapport fait à M. le Commissaire Impérial par la Commission d'inspection des Cultures*, Papeete.

Ravault, F. 1970. 'Le problème foncier' in *Tahiti et Moorea. Études sur la Société, l'Économie et l'Utilisation de l'Espace*. Travaux et Documents de l'O.R.S.T.O.M., Paris.

Robineau, Cl., 1970. 'Moorea' in *Tahiti et Moorea*. . . .

Roucaute, J. 1951. 'Réglementation foncière', manuscript, 30 Nov. 1951, Bureau des Terres, Papeete.

Vandor, J. 1866. 'Report of Consul J. Vandor', Despatches from U.S. Consuls in Tahiti, microfilm in National Library, Canberra, vol. 5, 1861–8.

7

THE MAKATEA PHOSPHATE
CONCESSION

COLIN NEWBURY

ONE of the cruder ways of changing the landscape of a South
Sea island is to dig it up. Few places in the Pacific contain
minerals in quantities sufficient to attract this rigorous form
of economic development. But where mining does take place,
as in New Caledonia and the phosphate islands, the social
and economic consequences of industrialization have received
relatively little study, compared with the production of agricultural staples. 'Mining' does not figure in the index of C. R. H.
Taylor's *Pacific Bibliography*. There is a surprisingly small
amount of printed literature devoted to the origins and operations of the nickel, chromite, and iron companies in New
Caledonia, considering that the establishment and financing of
these enterprises formed the essential basis of French, German,
and Japanese interest in the South-west Pacific from the last
decades of the nineteenth century. If it is hard to document
the links between Noumea, Rothschild, Krupp, and Nippon
Soda, it is no less difficult to find an adequate history of the
Pacific Phosphate Company, to explain its relations with
German concessionnaires on Ocean Island and its eventual
transfer of rights to the British Phosphate Commissioners. We
are left, on the whole, with some very general accounts by
servants of the companies concerned, export statistics, and
congratulatory assurances that the effects of half a century of
experiments in wage labour have been for the general good.[1]

---

[1] See Belshaw (1950) for New Caledonia; and Danks (1956). Economic questions
are treated in the general literature on New Caledonia, but there is no detailed
study of the history of mining and land tenure. For the Pacific Phosphate Company,
see brief references in Pope (1921) and Ellis (1935). There is a short account of the

This essay makes no claim to comprehensive treatment of industrial mining in Melanesia and Polynesia. It deals with the particular case of the Compagnie Française des Phosphates de l'Océanie (C.F.P.O.). Here, too, there are limitations. The substantial contributions made by the Company to the balance of payments in French Polynesia or its assistance to the local budget cannot be examined in detail. The sources are essentially official colonial records, for the Company archives are not open to research workers. On the other hand, if no long-term evaluation of the economic results of the phosphate concession can be made, the immediate impact of industrial enterprise on an agricultural economy is sufficient to suggest parallels with similar enterprises elsewhere. The discovery of phosphates at Makatea, in particular, raised fundamental questions about the transfer of land rights, thus exposing weaknesses in French policy towards this aspect of local Polynesian economic and social structure. In addition, the establishment of the C.F.P.O. entailed a revision of legislation concerning indentured labour and mineral exploitation. Above all, the new enterprise tested the ability of the local administration to enforce its own regulations over an area of wide responsibilities and to stimulate economic development for the benefit of the population of the group.

Much of the difficulty encountered by officials in their double role of 'trustee' and 'developer' stemmed from the isolation of Makatea some 135 miles north-east of Papeete. Until 1911 it was included for administrative purposes in the Tuamotu division. It had a chief, a district council, and a small population of about 250 Polynesians grouped in two villages on the west and east shores of the island. It was rarely visited. The seat of government in the Tuamotu was at Fakarava—160 miles away; and only in 1909 was the Administrator provided with a schooner to enable him to reach the outliers in his group. Even then, instructions concerning Makatea were slow in coming from Papeete; reports, in turn, were spasmodic. Placing the island directly under the Governor at Papeete in 1911 did not really improve communications with the Special Agent posted there. Moreover, between 1907 and 1918, Tahiti and its

recruitment of labour by the Compagnie Française des Phosphates de l'Océanie in 'Makatéa: Bilan social-économique d'un demi-siècle d'expérience', *Journal de la Société des Océanistes*, vol. 15, 1959, p. 202.

dependencies were administered by no less than six governors and acting-governors. Two of these—Governors François and Bonhoure—were capable enough and well informed about the phosphate question, but there was a tendency for vested interests to catch the ear of new officials and keep alive issues which ought to have been settled at once. In the background, too, was the Ministry of Colonies—open to commercial pressures in Paris and anxious for a minimum of complications in an unimportant possession.

Despite the factors of distance and indecision which served to aggravate tensions between Polynesians, the Company, and the Administration, one fairly clear line of policy can be seen in official attitudes and actions. Once the Company had established itself on Makatea in 1909 support for its continued existence was never in doubt. All governors were agreed that the hitherto unsuspected phosphate riches were to be mined; and it was taken for granted that export duties and wage labour would bring a certain prosperity to French Polynesia. What was in doubt was how to make the enterprise legal.

It is not known with certainty who discovered Makatea phosphates. The most likely candidate for the honour would be an American geologist, Alexander Agassiz, who led a scientific expedition to the Tuamotu and other parts of the Pacific in 1899 (Agassiz, 1903: 56–64). Phosphates are not specifically discussed in the published account of the voyage. It may well be, as suggested by a German traveller and scientist who followed up Agassiz's work, that the American either ignored the commercial significance of the deposits or deliberately omitted to refer to them (Friederici, 1911: 8). But there was plenty in the description of Makatea geology to arouse the interest of a prospector. The similarity between Makatea, Nauru, and Ocean Island was too striking to be passed over when John T. Arundel, Vice-President of the Pacific Islands Company, compared samples with those shown to him by Agassiz (Agassiz, 1903: xxii, xxvi, 8, 19, 171–4, 180–7, 241).[1] As from 1902 his newly founded Pacific Phosphate Company occupied all his attention. Not till three years later is there evidence that Arundel, though keeping well in the background,

[1] For John Arundel's early career as a copra planter and guano inspector, see Morrell (1960: 264) and Ellis (1935: 137).

made any use of his knowledge that Makatea contained phosphates.

In 1905 a Marseille ship-broker, Eugène Salles (who claimed backing from 'Australian engineers') applied to the Colonial Ministry for a concession to exploit mineral deposits in Makatea and paid for an urgent cable to the governor of Tahiti to make inquiries on his behalf.[1] The local administration delayed nearly five months before Governor Jullien replied. He had ordered the administrator of the Tuamotu to investigate; otherwise he remained vague and discouraging (A.C.O., E. 56, c. 123. Jullien to Ministry of Colonies, 8 Dec. 1905). Another year elapsed before Jullien wrote again on the subject, forwarding a report by Administrator Marcadé who claimed he could find no phosphates and sent a small bag of earth for analysis to support his contention they did not exist.[2] On this basis the Colonial Ministry informed Salles at the beginning of 1907 that he was wasting his time: there were no phosphates in Makatea; and even if there were, exploitation was impossible, because (according to Marcadé) all the plateau of the island was under some form of cultivation (A.C.O., E. 56, c. 123. Ministry of Colonies to Salles, 17 Jan. 1907).

Administrator Marcadé may have been genuinely mistaken about the deposits (he was no geologist), but he deliberately exaggerated the extent of cultivated land on the island. It was not the last occasion on which this official, who was in the Tuamotu from 1904 till 1914, did his best to protect the small society in his charge with all the jealous devotion of a missionary keeping whalers and traders at bay.[3]

For his part, Eugène Salles did not press the matter further. His name, however, appears among the first directors of the Société Française des Îles du Pacifique (S.F.I.P.) created early in 1907 with a small capital of 125,000 fr. and backed and advised by Arundel's Pacific Phosphate Company.[4] Delaying

---

[1] A.C.O., E. 56, c. 123. Ministry of Colonies to Jullien, 28 Aug. 1905. This was followed by a second dispatch and a cable in Sept. 1905.

[2] A.C.O., E. 56, c. 123. Marcadé to Jullien, 9 Oct. 1906, encl. in Jullien to Ministry of Colonies, 8 Dec. 1906.

[3] Charles Marcadé (1877–1919?) was a naval ensign appointed as administrator to the Tuamotu in 1904. He was praised by visiting officials for his linguistic abilities and his encouragement of copra production. In 1914 he went on active service and later served as an administrator in Dakar.

[4] The other directors were: Jules Mesnier (director of the Société du Port de

tactics were in vain. In any case rumour was already at work. In the close-knit society of Papeete, a request of the kind made by Salles was interesting enough to become common gossip in the space of two years. In July 1907 (a few months after Governor Jullien had officially refused to believe in phosphates) two leading citizens, Albert Goupil and his brother-in-law Étienne Touze, went to Makatea to see for themselves. It is possible that Albert's father, Auguste Goupil—lawyer, politician, editor, and *grand seigneur*—was already in correspondence with the Pacific Phosphate Company.[1] A month after the Goupil– Touze mission, John T. Arundel together with a geologist and two of his employees, G. C. and J. M. Ellis, arrived at Tahiti on a chartered steamer, the *Tyrian*. To the public at large they were described as 'tourists'. But with the permission of Governor Charlier, who had only just been informed of their real intentions by the Colonial Ministry, Arundel and his experts proceeded to Makatea.[2] There they joined forces with Goupil and Touze. The geologist, L. Rozan, commenced a report for the S.F.I.P.; and the 'tourists', who stayed only two weeks in French territory, needed little convincing about the extent or quality of the deposits. After a preliminary inspection they settled down to the serious business of arranging contracts with Polynesian proprietors. Before the last of the expedition left in February 1908, Rozan had completed his survey, the S.F.I.P. (backed by the Pacific Phosphate Company) was formally registered in Papeete, and the first of hundreds of paper contracts were obtained by Goupil.

In his survey, Rozan estimated that the phosphate deposits covered about 400 hectares of the plateau, or one-fifth of the surface of the island.[3] Their cubic content he set at the slightly low figure of 8,000,000 tons. In his budget of working costs, proprietors of phosphate lands were to receive up to 4 fr. 50 for

Rosario), president; Albert Taraud and Félix Gorchs-Chacou from the Société commerciale d'affrètement et de commission; Voss (a director of the Pacific Phosphate Company); and two English financiers, Balding and Caryford. J. T. Arundel was listed as a 'consultant'.

[1] There is no satisfactory evidence so far on this point. See O'Reilly, 1952: 277–81.

[2] A.C.O., J. 28, c. 123. Milliès-Lacroix to Charlier, 3 Aug. 1907. The minister warned Charlier not to commit the administration in any way.

[3] A.C.O., J. 28, c. 123. L. Rozan, 'Gisements de phosphates de l'archipel Paumotu', MS., 8 Mar. 1908.

every ton of phosphate exported. Annual export, he estimated, would be in the region of 100,000 tons. But this figure would not be reached without considerable investment in heavy equipment, docking facilities, the construction of a small railway, and housing for labour—all of which would take three or four years to complete. On the example of Ocean Island, for every 180,000 tons exported, at least 1,200 labourers would be needed—900 to dig phosphate and 300 for auxiliary services. Rozan was optimistic about obtaining these in neighbouring islands and, if necessary, supplementing them with Japanese labour, which was first used at Ocean Island and Nauru in 1908.

The geologist was over-generous in the compensation he allowed local proprietors for the right to export phosphate from their lands. Already before Arundel and his party arrived, the indispensable Albert Goupil had begun to make contracts with the inhabitants of Makatea—or indeed with anyone who had a claim to land on Makatea. The sum offered for mining rights was 1 fr. per ton of phosphates exported. Additional compensation was to be paid for the destruction of crops and trees.[1] The first of these contracts was registered at Papeete, 4 October 1907. Three days later Madame Marau Taaroa Salmon, widow of Pomare V, registered her own series of contracts, obtained by the influence of her family name and by the offer of a higher price of 2 fr. 25 per ton. Both Queen Marau and Albert Goupil then sold their mining rights to the S.F.I.P.,—the Queen for a profit of 70,000 fr. and Goupil for equally substantial rewards. Albert Goupil became manager of the Company at Makatea; his father, Auguste, became its legal counsellor; and Étienne Touze resigned from the Public Works to begin his career as Director for the Company 'in Oceania'. Altogether the S.F.I.P. bought up 956 contracts made with proprietors on Makatea and on Niau Island and registered between 1907 and 1909. The Company accepted the obligation to pay proprietors 1 fr. per ton and Goupil's rates for damage to plantations.[2]

Nevertheless, a doubt persisted concerning the validity of the 'proprietors'' claims to phosphate lands. The blocks mentioned in the contracts were by no means co-extensive with the area

---

[1] At the rate of 25 fr. (£1) for a coconut tree, 40 fr. for a breadfruit tree, 20 fr. for a mango, and 10 fr. for an orange tree.

[2] A.C.O., J. 28, c. 123. Charlier to Ministry of Colonies, 15 Feb. 1908; E. 62, c. 122, Fillon to Ministry of Colonies, 31 Aug. 1909.

of deposits examined by Rozan. So as a special safeguard the Company bought from Goupil two additional contracts made with the district councils of Makatea and Niau.[1] These documents stated that all phosphates on district domain were sold outright to the S.F.I.P. for the usual price of 1 fr. per ton. Such lands (and therefore the phosphates on them) had been transferred to the control of the councils under the terms of a Decree of 1887, as unclaimed estate.[2] The Niau contract mentioned the same legislation, but was vaguer: the district council sold its right to phosphates on lands 'dont le vendeur est propriétaire seul ou avec d'autres personnes' [sic].

On this basis of sub-contracts from legal 'proprietors'—whether individuals or the district councils—the Société Française des Îles du Pacifique began its operations. That there were no valid title deeds in existence or any way in which district councils could transfer property to Europeans mattered little as yet. The ineffectual Governor Charlier merely informed the Colonial Ministry that he had been 'completely neutral', according to instructions, during Arundel's visit (A.C.O., J. 28, c. 123. Charlier to Ministry of Colonies, 30 Apr. 1908). The Registrar of Lands, Émile Vermeersch, did not report on the contracts to the governor (though he later claimed he had advised Goupil against them). The Administrator of the Tuamotu received no instructions about the speculation going on in his division; nor was he informed by Chief Teare a Tematuanui about the council's transaction, when he met him by chance in Papeete.[3] The Administration had been hoodwinked by skilful profiteers.

Unfortunately for the Company it had no sooner begun to consolidate its position than it was placed on the defensive by a rival organization which used similar methods and, thereby,

[1] A.C.O., J. 30, c. 134. Copies of contracts between Chief Teare a Tematuanui and Albert Goupil, 21 Mar. 1908 (registered Papeete, 2 Apr. 1908); between Pia a Tema Tuku (for the Niau district council) and Goupil, 11 Apr. 1908 (registered Papeete, 16 Apr. 1908); between Albert Goupil and the S.F.I.P., 9 Dec. 1908 (two copies, registered Papeete, 1 Feb. 1909). See Marcadé, 'Note sur la cession des gisements de phosphates de Niau et de Makatea', MS., 28 Apr. 1909.

[2] By para. 2, Article 11 of the Decree of 24 Aug. 1887 on land registration in French Polynesia, all lands not claimed after a year became 'district domain' (faufa-'a mata 'eina 'a).

[3] Marcadé first learned of the sale of mining rights on district land when he visited Makatea in July 1908 and examined the district council minute-book. 'Note sur la cession . . .' 28 Apr. 1909.

raised doubts about all the phosphate contracts. In Europe, news of the Makatea discoveries was broken by the British Consul R. T. Simons in a number of the *Mining Journal* for May 1908. A month later two French financiers and one French adventurer—Bonnel de Mézières—hastily formed the Compagnie de l'Océanie Française (C.O.F.) in Paris and requested a concession from the Colonial Ministry.[1] The new company was told to do business directly with the inhabitants of Makatea, because there was no mining legislation in French Polynesia under which a concession could be made. Bonnel de Mézières arrived in Tahiti with a sharp lawyer, Jean Delpit, in July 1908 and openly announced to Charlier that his purpose was to 'break' in the local courts all contracts claimed by the S.F.I.P. (A.C.O., J. 28, c. 123. Charlier to Ministry of Colonies, 17 Aug. 1908). Backed by German money, he joined up with an expedition sent by the Hanseatisches Südsee-Syndikat and set out for Makatea. When Administrator Marcadé called at the island in July, he found Mézières systematically testing Goupil's contracts by offering 1 fr. 50 per ton and a special price of 3,000 fr. per hectare for the outright sale of phosphate lands.[2] But Albert Goupil was also present to look after the interests of the S.F.I.P.; and despite his wild promises, Mézières won away only forty-six contracts on Makatea and Niau from proprietors who had promised phosphates to Goupil.

With so little in hand the C.O.F. was bold enough to petition once more in October 1908 for a concession, making a patriotic issue out of a rumour of British and American designs on French Polynesia (A.C.O., J. 28, c. 123. C.O.F. to Ministry of Colonies, 5 Oct. 1908). The Ministry was asked for special legislation leaving the field clear for 'French' societies. Patriotic or not, the C.O.F. was enlarged and transformed into the Compagnie Française des Phosphates du Pacifique (C.F.P.P.) in March 1909 by a financial group headed by the German National Bank and with a Franco-German Board of Directors.[3]

---

[1] A.C.O., J. 28, c. 123. C.O.F. to Ministry of Colonies, 28 Aug. 1908. The new company had only £2,000 capital in 100 shares.

[2] A.C.O., J. 28, c. 123. Charlier to Ministry of Colonies, 17 Aug. 1908 (encl. copies of contracts).

[3] The C.F.P.P. had a capital of £24,000 in 1,200 shares, a quarter of which were held by the founder, Gaston Séguin. The other directors were two Frenchmen—Baron Jean ed Bethmann, William Le Cesne—and four Germans—Dr. Sandheimer,

At Tahiti, Mézières left his forty-six proprietors to fend for themselves in the local courts where they were sued by the S.F.I.P. for damages and costs amounting to 65,000 fr. In the meantime, the S.F.I.P. was making demands of its own. In September 1908 the Company requested the Ministry for land legislation to guarantee titles to the proprietors who had signed the Goupil contracts (A.C.O., J. 28, c. 123. S.F.I.P. to Milliès-Lacroix, 1 Sept. 1908). Special protection was claimed against unscrupulous competitors. With this patronage, the Company promised to expand its capital to 6,000,000 francs and change its name to the Compagnie Française des Phosphates de l'Océanie. There is no evidence that the Minister, Milliès-Lacroix, made any promise to guarantee titles. Indeed, a few days after this petition he telegraphed the Governor of Tahiti that no special privileges were to be granted: the exploitation of phosphates was open to all, and the interference of the administration was to be limited to the enforcement of health and labour regulations and the levy of an export duty (A.C.O., J. 28, c. 123. Milliès-Lacroix to Charlier, 5 Sept. 1908). But whether officially encouraged or not, the new C.F.P.O. was founded on 15 October 1908 with a third of its 12,000 shares held by the Pacific Phosphate Company and with an Anglo-French Board of Directors which included Arundel (Compagnie . . ., 1908).[1]

However much the Ministry may have attempted to be equitable in its dealings with the rival companies, their chances were far from equal in Polynesia. In April 1909 the C.F.P.O. was authorized by Governor François to occupy large sections of the beach on Makatea, which gave them a monopoly of harbour facilities. When François visited Makatea in August 1909 (the only governor to do so) he found that the Company had rapidly consolidated its position. A wooden jetty with a

Dr. Strube, Dr. Naumann, A. Kröller (*Statuts* . . ., 1909; E. 62, c. 122, Fillon to Ministry of Colonies, 31 Aug. 1909).

[1] The new board of directors included Mesnier as president, Taraud and Gorchs-Chacou from the S.F.I.P., Georges Hersent (President of the Société du Port de Rosario), J. B. Hersent (engineer), Raoul Johnston (engineer and vice-president of the Société des Mines d'Albi), Léon Bertrand (engineer), and the British directors, Sir John Pilter (former president of the Paris Chamber of Commerce), John Ervart (director of the South Metropolitan Gas Company), Arundel, Voss, and Balding of the S.F.I.P. Rozan was one of the consulting engineers.

tram-line had been constructed, and a force of 250 men, including 180 Polynesians from Tahiti and the Leeward Islands, was engaged in building a camp and other installations about a mile inland on the plateau above the harbour (A.C.O., J. 28, c. 123. François to Ministry of Colonies, 27 Sept. 1909). By the end of 1909 it was clear that the Franco-German company would not be able to dislodge the C.F.P.O. In February the following year a merger was effected, the holders of C.F.P.P. shares retaining 2,000,000 francs of C.F.P.O. subscribed capital which was raised shortly after from 6,000,000 to 11,000,000 francs.

A difficulty had been removed. There were others arising from the unsettled conditions of land tenure on Makatea. The second challenge to the position won by the C.F.P.O. came from Colonial Inspector Fillon who had visited Makatea some five months before Governor François and whose reports in July 1909 criticized the failure of the local administration to control the activities of Goupil (A.C.O., J. 30, c. 134. Fillon to Ministry of Colonies, 21 July 1909). With a wealth of supporting material Fillon exposed the worthlessness of contracts made with proprietors who held no valid titles. The 1887 Decree, claimed Fillon, had been applied in the Tuamotu 'avec la plus grande fantaisie'; such blocks as were registered had never been surveyed; claims printed in the *Journal officiel* had appeared long after the date allowed by law; counter-claims had not been settled in court. The Inspector also criticized the Registrar, Vermeersch, for allowing the contracts to be officially accepted. He concluded that the transfer of rights to the C.F.P.O. was illegal and that the contracts made with the district councils should be officially repudiated. In a final thrust he accused Governor François of 'partiality' because of his disinclination to look too closely into C.F.P.O. claims.

Fillon's evidence carried considerable weight in the Colonial Ministry where the wide gap between paper contracts and rights enforceable in law was clearly perceived. The problem, as seen by officials there, was to determine the extent of phosphate lands held by co-owners and by district councils. Then somehow the Company had to be given title to each of these categories. Secondly, a new decree was needed to replace the outdated legislation in force in Tahiti concerning lease of rights to quarries. In March 1910 the Colonial Minister, Georges Trouillot, after rereading Fillon's analysis and fresh complaints from the C.F.P.O., ordered Governor François to cut through all difficulties with a decree containing 'le principe de la concession applicable en matière minière' (A.C.O., E. 62, c. 122. Trouillot to François, 25 Mar. 1910).

François set up a small commission of officials to work out a draft to cover the case of Makatea. At the end of the year the commission (which included Marcadé) was still arguing whether a concession would amount to expropriation. The Minister ordered the new governor, Bonhoure, to end the deadlock by annulling the Goupil contract with Makatea district council and making a concession of domain on behalf of the colony. In December 1910 Bonhoure attempted to do this. A new contract was approved between the governor and Étienne Touze, for the C.F.P.O., by which the Company was granted the right to mine phosphates on all lands 'dont le district est propriétaire en vertu de l'article 11 s 2 décret du 24 août 1887'. The royalty of 1 fr. per ton was still levied and was to be paid to the administration. The Company was given permission to make roads and erect buildings wherever necessary (A.C.O., E. 62, c. 122. Contract, 29 Dec. 1910; J. 30 c. 134, Bonhoure to Ministry of Colonies, 13 Jan. 1911).

Thus, for lack of adequate mining legislation the Papeete administration was obliged to fall back on the provisions of the land law of 1887 which made over unclaimed areas to Tuamotu district councils. The least of the objections to the new contract with the company was that it begged the question: what was the extent of 'district' land on Makatea; and how much of it contained phosphate?

One of the serious features of the phosphate controversy was that evidence of the conditions of land tenure at Makatea did not accumulate until relatively late in the day, after the Company was well established. The first attempt to register claims on the basis of individual ownership had been carried out three or four years after the promulgation of the 1887 decree. These claims arising from the survey of 1890–1 were not published in the *Journal Officiel* until 1902—a fair indication of the mountainous backlog of paper work in the Lands Office by the end of the century (*Journal* . . . 24 Apr.; 1, 8, 15, and 29 May;

24 and 31 July; 7 and 13 Aug. 1902). No property titles were requested or issued. A copy of the original claims register for the Makatea district was sent to the Colonial Ministry in November 1913—the first indication in Paris that such a thing existed.[1] The register may be usefully compared with materials collected by the lawyer, Jean Delpit, who made a thorough investigation of Makatea claims in 1911.[2] From these two sources and from a cadastral map made for the Company by L. Lippert in 1911, it appears the position with regard to land blocks was as follows:

TABLE 7.1. *Makatea Land Blocks*

1890–1 Survey (published *J.O.*)	Listed by Delpit inside or touching the phosphate area		
Total	Claimed	Unclaimed	Total
190*	111	54	165

* Including seventeen claims published in the *Journal Officiel*, but omitted from the 1913 copy of the register.

In Lippert's map (Fig. 7.1), it is noticeable that many of the blocks claimed by Polynesians had only a fraction of their area in the phosphate zone. Some named blocks were not claimed at all. Many lay outside the plateau—about eighty-nine in all—along the shore where the villages stood. Nevertheless, a considerable proportion of claims was inland; and these had been made before the presence of phosphates was suspected.

As elsewhere when registration was attempted in French Polynesia, small patches of cultivable land and stands of trees became the object of multiple claims from co-owners, whether living on the island or not. After 1907, the promise of easy income from phosphate royalties exaggerated the tendency to inscribe all claims as having equal validity, whatever the genealogical relationship of the Polynesians concerned. Furthermore, the 1890–1 survey had not paid much attention to the size of the claims. Groups of adjacent blocks are named and

[1] A.C.O., J. 32, c. 124. 'Île et district de Makatea. Relevé des déclarations de propriétés faites après le délai prévu au décret du 24 août 1887, soit postérieurement au 3 janvier 1889', encl. in Fawtier to Ministry of Colonies, 15 Nov. 1913.

[2] A.C.O., J. 30, c. 124. 'Liste des terres phosphatifères', encl. in Delpit to Ministry of Colonies, 6 June 1911, together with a copy of the map by L. Lippert.

listed together and their superficial area roughly estimated.
Next to these blocks a number of co-owners are listed. If the

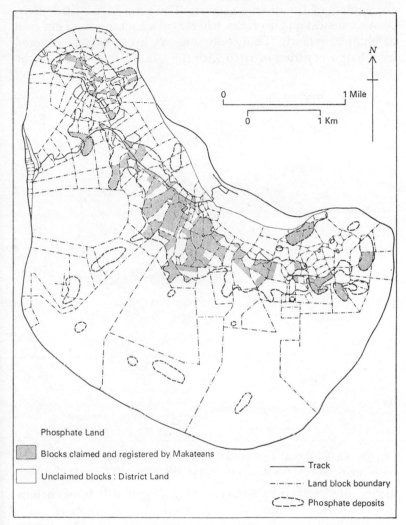

FIG. 7.1. Land blocks, phosphate deposits, and land claims on Makatea,
1911. After L. Lippert.

areas in the register are worked out and added together, their
total amounts to about 4,770 hectares—or twice the superficial
area of Makatea!

According to the survey made by Lippert, claims which fell within the phosphate zone did not leave much land over for the control of the district council. The total area of the phosphate zone was 394 hectares, whereas 319 hectares were claimed as phosphate lands. Thus, only some 75 hectares were covered by the new contract of 1910 with the administration. From the

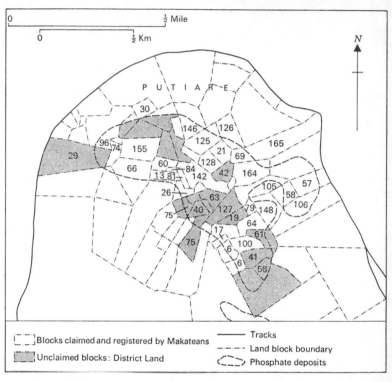

FIG. 7.2. Claimed and unclaimed land in Putiare phosphate area. After L. Lippert. Source: A.C.O., J. 30, c. 124. See appendix for extended key.

section of the map of northern Makatea, it will be seen how the remaining claims were scattered and interspersed with 'district' land over the Putiare phosphate area (see Fig. 7.2).

A further complication lay in the fact that many of the claimants among interrelated families had small lots in different parts of the island. Altogether in the 1890–1 register, 158 males and 59 females are listed as co-owners. The distribution of their claims is given in Table 7.2. Some 66 per cent of the claimants had their names inscribed for more than one block or group of blocks. A few made eight, two made ten, and one made eleven claims to co-ownership.

TABLE 7.2. *Makatea Land Claims*

No. of Blocks	1	2	3	4	5	6	7	8	9	10	11
No. of Claimants	121	39	21	15	7	4	1	6	0	2	1

SOURCE: A.C.O., J. 32, c. 124.

Even if it had been possible to arrange for compensation to be paid to groups of co-owners, the legal situation was easily exploited by Jean Delpit who requested the Papeete Court in 1910 to order a new survey, before recognizing any of the Company's contracts. The court and the administration shrank from such an unpopular measure. Delpit then attacked the Bonhoure–Touze contract for district domain phosphates, taking up the cases of forty-six proprietors who claimed to have been deprived of part of their blocks. The test case of Hiti a Hiti against the C.F.P.O. was lost before the Papeete High Court in March 1911. Delpit went on to plead other causes on behalf of those who had failed to register their blocks. But he never won a case; and if he was backed by German money (as was suspected) it was money wasted. The last hearing dragged on till 1920, when a petition from Hiti a Hiti was dismissed by the Council of State.

Other voices were raised in France expressing doubts about the validity of the original contracts made by Goupil and the administration's concession of phosphates on district domain. The French Deputy, Maurice Violette, placed the whole question of Makatea before the Colonial Budget Commission in 1912.[1] Governor Bonhoure wrote a long and able reply, arguing that only the administration and not the district councils had the power to transfer unregistered property to Europeans (A.C.O., J. 32, c. 124. Bonhoure to Ministry of Colonies, 16 Mar. 1912). He also contended, more doubtfully, that all payments to proprietors were held by the administration in the *Caisse des dépôts et consignations*, Papeete, till their rights had been decided. In Paris, however, the Inspector-General of Colonies

---

[1] And for his attacks on Vermeersch accusing him of partiality in the registration of land titles, see *Annales coloniales*, 19 Aug. 1916.

was still not satisfied that proper measures had been taken to find out what these rights were. Nor was he clear how a ton of phosphates lifted from private or from district land was to be distinguished for the purpose of paying royalties, given the lack of boundary lines (A.C.O., J. 30, c. 134. 'Note', 10 Apr. 1911). These and other points produced some worried memoranda in the Colonial Ministry.[1] Officials came to the conclusion that little could be done to sort out the tangle of claims in terms of area. While they considered, the Company went ahead and opened up its first block in northern Makatea at the beginning of 1911. Bonhoure posted a special agent to the island with orders to look after the rights of the administration.[2] His instructions reveal how little thought had been given to the problems of supervising the exploitation of phosphates. The boundaries of land blocks were to be determined with the help of Polynesian proprietors and another interested party—the Company surveyor. There was no provision for a land court. In short, the determination of the area of district domain was left to an unskilled official at the mercy of the Company itself. Bonhoure thought disputes with co-owners unlikely. If any arose, they were to be settled by the Administrator at Fakarava. The special agent was further instructed to count truck loads and compare his count of tonnage with Company estimates of phosphate exported. The Company, concluded Bonhoure, had decided to begin with the Umara block—'appartenant au district comme n'ayant pas été revendiquée'. This was untrue. The Umara block had been claimed and registered in 1891 and the claim published uncontested.[3]

By 1913 the export of phosphates had reached the figure of 82,000 tons. Polynesian proprietors, where their claims were recognized, had been paid about 200,000 fr. (£8,000) in compensation and royalties. The administration had received 150,000 fr. for district domain, in addition to registration fees and import duties. Supervision by the special agent was fairly

---

[1] A.C.O., J. 32, c. 124. 'Note sur la situation de la propriété dans les É.F.O.', 19 July 1911; 'Note sur le régime des terres dans les Établissements français de l'Océanie' (n.d.).

[2] A.C.O., J. 30, c. 124. Bonhoure to Buchin (special agent, Makatea), 31 Jan. 1911, encl. in Bonhoure to Ministry of Colonies, 16 Mar. 1912.

[3] A.C.O., J. 32, c. 124. 'Île et district de Makatea' (claims register), no. 61 in *Journal officiel*, no. 14, 734. This block was claimed by Metua a Teata, Tauura a Teata, and Tepure a Manua and had a superficial area of about 600 sq. metres.

perfunctory, reported a colonial inspector in 1914 (A.C.O.,
E. 62, c. 122. Revel to Ministry of Colonies, 30 May 1914).
There was no check on the total tonnage lifted from district
domain. Interference on behalf of Polynesian proprietors made
Administrator Marcadé the enemy of the Company, which
tried to have him removed from the Tuamotu. The time had
come, concluded Inspector Revel, to introduce new mining
legislation.

It was not till 1916 that the Colonial Ministry asked the
governor whether there was still any outstanding land case
which might prejudice legislation. After receiving Governor
Jullien's assurances on this point, the Ministry prepared a decree
for formal ratification in October 1917. Its clauses made mineral
concessions to private companies legal in French Polynesia.
Such concessions were not to exceed 2,000 hectares in the case
of phosphates and could be revoked at any time by the administration. Article 61 of the decree stipulated that an indemnity
was to be paid for the occupation of other lands near the mines.
If such land was the subject of multiple claims, an agreement
could be concluded with one proprietor only. In a case where
all proprietors refused to sell or lease land, the area could be
expropriated by the governor. Nothing was said of previous
contracts or the royalties promised to Polynesians and the
administration.

The Company at last had its way. In June 1918 Étienne
Touze requested a concession on Makatea in an area of 2,000
hectares (the northern two-thirds of the island). Governor
Jullien's decision to grant this request, without conditions, was
published in the *Journal officiel de la République*, 2 May 1919.

It would be easy enough to blame the administration for the
long delay in providing a firm basis for the exploitation of the
colony's only mineral asset. Certainly the rather rigid terms of
the 1887 land decree and the way in which it was applied made
it impossible to set much store by any contracts made with local
'proprietors'. The problem of communal tenure was much
bigger than Makatea and probably beyond solution with the
slender means available to the administration at the end of the
last century. But it should not have been difficult to step in and
prevent the Goupil family or Queen Marau from speculating
profitably once the existence of phosphates was known. Here (as

often before and since) the colony's officials, and in particular Vermeersch, were manipulated by the leading figures of the European and *demi* population who ran Papeete's politics. Once two companies had been allowed to negotiate through these intermediaries, it was difficult to resist the argument that private capital should not be frightened away. Senior officials, moreover, could hardly oppose operations that had been permitted to go so far by the Colonial Ministry. Charles Marcadé, as Administrator of the Tuamotu, did his best to secure compensation for Makatea proprietors, but left the colony in 1914. When the decree of 1917 made a legal concession possible, compensation was a matter of company charity not written contract.

Both the Ministry and the colonial government at Papeete hoped for some financial support for the local budget from the operations of the C.F.P.O. After a legal battle in 1913 when the Company was awarded a rebate on customs duties, a decision of the Council of State in 1917 reversed the tendency towards free imports and secured the payment of duties incurred since 1909. On the other hand, the colony did not make much out of duties on the export of phosphates. The Company had to compete with its parent organization which paid no duties on imports at Ocean Island and paid only 6*d.* on every ton of phosphate exported. Consequently, governors at Tahiti kept the local export duty down to the same level, despite the demand of the Administrative Council for a higher tariff. Before 1914 revenue from this source amounted to only 1 per cent of general revenues and the total amount was less than export duties from pearl shell. But a beginning had been made; and new taxes followed as the Company prospered after 1918. In 1961, the Company paid some £184,500 in export duties on 369,000 tons of phosphate worth about £1,800,000 (*Statistiques* . . . 1962: 23). In addition, there were import duties, *octroi de mer* taxes, and the stimulus to local trade given by nearly 2,000 employees who made their purchases from Papeete.

The second contribution of the Company to economic and social change in the colony has been through the employment of wage labour. On the whole, the labour problem was solved in the way foreseen by Rozan. Up till the date of the concession, the Company employed about 50 to 150 Tahitians and Leeward

Islanders every year for 50 fr. (£2) a month, food, and housing. The supply of unskilled men had to be constantly renewed. In November 1909, the Company proposed to bring in Japanese contract labour on a longer-term basis. Both the Administrative Council and the governor's Privy Council opposed the suggestion. Governor François and the Colonial Minister, Trouillot, were in favour, but they cautioned the Company to keep quiet about the number to be introduced and avoid alarming the European population at Tahiti which was nervous about Asian settlers (A.C.O., J. 29, c. 123. François to Ministry of Colonies, 26 Mar. 1910). Twenty-one Japanese were employed in 1910, and 250 were brought in the following year. After 1926, Indochinese, Chinese, Japanese, and Polynesians made up a labour force of 600 or 700 which declined sharply in the 1930s and was largely replaced by Cook Islanders after the Second World War. These, in turn, were not recruited after 1955 when labour was provided mainly by 500 or so French Polynesians.

Finally, it should be noted that the Makatea inhabitants— some 160–200 in all—were almost forgotten in the manœuvres between rival companies. The extent of their agriculture on the plateau before 1907 is very uncertain, though it was not unimportant. Rozan, in his survey of 1908, estimated that compensation for destruction of crops would average 875 fr. per hectare, at the rate of 25 fr. for a coconut tree, 40 fr. for a breadfruit tree, and 10 fr. for an orange tree. This suggests that such trees were fairly thinly scattered; and secondly, that intensive cultivation was not practised away from the narrow strip of fertile littoral near the two coastal villages. It was claimed in 1911 that the Umara block in the northern sector of the island contained fifty coconut trees and one breadfruit. But, by then, the administration had adopted the policy of holding any compensation for proprietors at Papeete in the *Caisse des dépôts et consignations*, until the difficult question of 'ownership' of phosphate areas was decided. As it never was, very little of this compensation may have been handed out, though royalties for phosphate lifted from district lands were paid to the district council and divided among the island families until 1909 or 1910.

Another serious loss of livelihood for Makateans must have been at Moumu village where the shore line was taken over by the Company for its installations and loading wharf. Together with a similar concession at Temao beach, the occupied area amounted to some two and a half kilometres in length with a depth of 200 metres from the shore-line to the base of the plateau. In effect, the principal village of the island was submerged in the port of Vaitepaua Settlement. Much of the male population was engaged initially as labour and figures among the large number of 'Polynesians' in the Company's first records of recruitment. Other families gradually drifted to the neighbouring Tuamotu or further afield to Tahiti. The phosphate workers numbered as many as 500 to 600 by the 1930s. And none of these, except for a few Chinese, was engaged in agriculture on an island whose economy was revolutionized by the discovery of the most profitable 'cash crop' in French Polynesia and the mainstay of a faltering economy for fifty years.[1]

APPENDIX

NORTHERN MAKATEA PHOSPHATE CLAIMS: SAMPLE

Map reference No. (Fig. 7.2)	Name of block	Register of claims		
		Name of block subdivisions	Claim no.	Claimants (co-owners)
6	Apoo	Apoo	109	Tataratoa a Taiahaa
17	Faataipahe	Faataipahe	109	Nuihau a Vairau
				Teapoo a Faatoro
				Puupaiterai a Maui
				Hautepo a Taaroa
41	Manutiahitau			(Unclaimed)
56	Paafatitiri			(Unclaimed)
61	Parofai			(Unclaimed)
100	Teiriiri	Teiriiri	27	Tauhuhu a Vairau
		Part of Faataipahe	27	Teopa a Vairau
				Huti a Hio
64	Pehunia	Part of Pehunia	58	Paraoa a Tematuanui
				Tohitia a Hiti
19	Faifai			(Unclaimed)
127	Tiori			(Unclaimed)
75	Raaira			(Unclaimed)
148	Vaiapunua	Part of Vaiapunua		Maro a Roo
58	Papaa	Papaa		Teriri a Maomao
79	Rora	Rora		Taura a Tiihiva
				Aveia a Taurua
				Urarii a Takehu
				Terouru a Roo
				Teroao a Terai
106	Teofai	Part of Teofai	3	Hiti a Hiti
58	Papaa	Papaa		Moe a Tauura
				Nauatu a Maoake
				Heiura a Vairaaroa

[1] For a discussion of the problems posed by the withdrawal of the Company, see Anglade (1966) and Doumenge (1963: 41–67).

57	Paiava	Part of Paiava	119	Metua a Teata
				Raiura a Tapu
105	Teniumaa			(Unclaimed)
164	Vaituaropaa	Part of Vaituoropaa	8	Nauatua a Maoake
165		Vaitemahane	8	Tetauhiti a Maomao
				Tatehau a Tuao
				Mana a Tapu
				Maro a Tapu
				Tuhoa a Tapu
				Torohia a Hina
				Ruarai a Tehono
30	Hoaua	Hoaua	39	Tevivi a Maomao
				Tumau a Tinai
				Mauara a Tinai
				Hina a Mahono
69	Puatia	Puatia	17	Hiti a Hiti
125	Tiafai	Tiafai	17	Haoatua a Vairaaroa
21	Fareara	Fareara	17	Faava a Vairaaroa
126	Tiomaoma	Tiomaoma	17	Tuaha a Metua
128	Tipapa	Tipapa	17	Tevivi a Maomao
?	Tehapare	Tehapare	17	Heiura a Vairaaroa
				Aio a Vairaaroa
				Mataua a Tapu
				Taahiti a Maomao
				Hoaia a Maui
				Tepare a Hiti
				Roiti a Nuuhau
42	Maraeiaro			(Unclaimed)
63	Pehau			(Unclaimed)
81	Rutu	Part of Rutu	55	Teahu a Tahua
84	Taharoapuno	Taharoapuno	110	Faratoa a Matuanu i
13	Aufaroa	Aufaroa	110	Terii a Haoa
66	Piroeapapaepera	Piroeapapaepera	110	Temana a Tehaurai
60	Pareohira	Pareohira	110	Tetavira a Matuanui
				Moerai a Hurumoa
				Vaikava a Matuanui
				Oriori a Matuanui
				Poraoa a Matuanui
				Teare a Matuanui
				Tane a Matuanui
74	Puutiare	Part of Puutiare	10	Haupapauri a Maua
155	Vaiohua	Vaiohua	10	Teopa a Vairau
96	Teavaro	Teavaro	10	Maoae a Teata
				Rua a Taaroa
				Tarau a Tuamea
				Teotahi a Aora
29	Hivava			(Unclaimed)
146	Vaiapaia	Vaiapaia	115	Maio a Hiti
142	Umara	Umara	61	Metua a Teata
				Tauura a Teata
				Tepure a Manua
26	Fareumu	Fareumu		Raiura a Tapu
				Teotahi a Aoro
				Peritua a Tiki
				Terega a Fauora
				Terai a Manua

BIBLIOGRAPHY

A.C.O. Archives des Colonies (Rue Oudinot, Paris), série Océanie.

Agassiz, A. 1903. *Reports on the Scientific Results of the Expedition to the Tropical Pacific, in the charge of Alexander Agassiz, by the U.S. Fish Commission Steamer*

'*Albatross*', *from August 1899 to March 1900, Commander F. Moser, U.S.N.*, commanding, vol. IV, *The Coral Reefs of the Tropical Pacific*, Cambridge, Mass.

Anglade, M. 1966. 'Makatéa L'Île des Phosphates à la veille de la fin', *La Dépêche de Tahiti*, 4 and 5 Mar. 1966.

Annales coloniales. 1916. Paris.

Anon. 1959. 'Makatéa: Bilan social-économique d'un demi-siècle d'expérience', *Journal de la Société des Océanistes*, vol. 15, 1959, p. 202.

Belshaw, C. S. 1950. *Island Administration in the South West Pacific*, London.

Compagnie . . . 1908. *Compagnie Française des Phosphates de l'Océanie* . . . *Statuts*, Paris.

Danks, K. H. 1956. *Industrial Activity in Selected Areas of the South Pacific*, South Pacific Commission Technical Paper, no. 90, Noumea.

Doumenge, F. 1963. 'L'Île de Makatéa et ses problèmes', *Cahiers du Pacifique*, no. 5, Dec. 1963, pp. 41–67.

Ellis, A. F. 1935. *Ocean Island and Nauru*, Sydney.

Friederici, G. 1911. *Ein Beitrag zur Kenntnis der Tuamotu-Inseln*, Leipzig.

Journal . . . 1902. *Journal officiel des Établissements français de l'Océanie*.

Morrell, W. P. 1960. *Britain in the Pacific Islands*, Oxford.

O'Reilly, P. 1952. 'Étienne Touze (1871–1951) et l'origine de la Société des Phosphates de Makatea', *Journal de la Société des Océanistes*, vol. 8, 1952, pp. 277–81.

Pope, H. B. 1921. *Nauru and Ocean Island*, Sydney.

Simons, R. T. 1908. *Mining Journal*, 2 May 1908.

Statistiques . . . 1962. *Statistiques du commerce extérieur des territories d'outre-mer en 1961*, Ministère des Finances et des Affaires Économiques, Paris.

Statuts . . . 1909. *Statuts de la Compagnie Française des Phosphates du Pacifique*, Paris.

8

POPULATION GROWTH IN THE PACIFIC ISLANDS

The Example of Western Samoa

PETER PIRIE[1]

NATURAL increase of sizeable human populations at rates which double numbers within a generation is a twentieth-century phenomenon. Among the earliest populations to experience this development were some in the South Pacific islands. Rates in excess of 3 per cent annually were being observed, in Western Samoa for instance, in the 1920s.[2] Since this time natural rates of this magnitude have occurred in several other parts of the world, notably Latin America, South-east Asia, and, less certainly, in some countries of South-west Asia and Africa. In the Pacific Islands these rates have continued both to increase and be distributed more widely.

Natural rates in excess of 3 per cent now occur in most Polynesian populations and several in Micronesia. At the same time some of the lowest rates, still associated with high mortality and lowered fertility, continue to occur in some islands. In Melanesia, only the Fijians at present exceed a 3 per cent

---

[1] Dr. Pirie is Associate Professor of Geography, University of Hawaii, and Research Associate, East–West Population Institute, East–West Center, Honolulu.

[2] This occurred in 1920 and thereafter in 1924, 1925, 1926, 1938, and regularly after 1947. These rates are based on registered births and registered deaths. Both these rates are subject to irregular registration but the official rate of increase for the 'Samoan' population was 3·3 per cent between the census enumerations of 1926 and 1936. Although this figure too may be questioned (Pirie, 1960: 72; Pirie 1964: 96), there is no doubt that the Samoan population expanded at an un-precedented rate between 1920 and 1930, assisted to some extent by the population structure having been biased toward youth by the effects of the 1918 influenza epidemic. Additional corroborative evidence may be found in Keys (1927: 5–21). Note, however, that as Golson points out in Chapter 1, a very high rate of natural increase may have occurred on many islands in the decades immediately following initial settlement.

increase while other populations, particularly in New Guinea, the Solomons, and the New Hebrides, show a range extending in some local cases into persisting natural decline. But even here, among the Tolai of New Britain for instance, there is promise of future rates no less spectacular than those in other Pacific islands (Epstein and Epstein, 1962: 70–82). In the last decade, change has been swift and accelerating. The first census in the New Hebrides for instance indicated an annual growth rate of about 2·5 per cent (1967).

The factors contributing to this regional characteristic of steeply rising population growth curves deserve some examination. That the Pacific Islands exhibit this characteristic to such a marked degree requires an explanation. Some comparisons are also needed with other areas of rapid population growth to discover what factors they have in common. The trend in the Pacific is the more peculiar as it follows hard upon the earlier tendency towards depopulation. In the nineteenth century the ultimate extinction of several Pacific populations was forecast by many observers and declining numbers were a widespread characteristic.

The evidence of depopulation appeared soon after the arrival of vessels from Atlantic countries into the Pacific. Carried with them were contagious diseases from which the oceanic peoples of the Pacific had been isolated. Records of single epidemics taking substantial proportions of island populations begin in the latter decades of the eighteenth century, and continue well into the twentieth. The culmination for several island groups was the influenza pandemic of 1918. While these effects of disease were observed and recorded only in the late eighteenth century, their introduction may have begun much earlier. We know that Magellan in 1521, and later Schouten and Le Maire, Mendaña, Quiros, Tasman, Dampier, Roggeveen, Wallis, Carteret, and Bougainville all had ships and crews in the Pacific preceding Cook. It is very possible that they intro-' duced epidemic pestilences at their various points of contact, and sailed on oblivious of the disaster left behind. We need not consider the question of accidental infections by contact from Asia about which nothing is yet known, although the possibility need not be dismissed on this account.

In addition to sporadic epidemics, the general incidence of

disease appears to have been raised in most areas so that several introduced diseases became endemic. Combined, the two types of disease affected the balance between fertility and mortality to produce depopulation.

After an initial period of occasional contact between islanders and foreign voyagers, permanent settlement occurred in most of the more significant groups. Runaway sailors, other assorted adventurers, and traders were usually the first to take up residence. They were followed by missionaries, consuls representing foreign governments, planters, and, later, by administrators. By the beginning of this century, most Pacific Island groups had been in contact with the rest of the world with such a frequency and to such an extent that the risk of accidental disease introduction was limited to instances of world-wide pandemic. But even today some very isolated communities, particularly on atolls, continue to be vulnerable to disease introduced by occasional contacts.

The history of disease introductions into the Pacific is not unique; the American Indians suffered similarly and several other isolated populations, on Greenland for instance, can be cited (e.g. Borah, 1951; Christiansen et al., 1952). But the physical form and scattered distribution of the Pacific Islands create a diverse forum in which detailed differences in form and history can be seen to affect the demographic outcomes in measurable ways. Most of the disease-causing organisms were prevented from spreading freely out into the Pacific by the magnitude of the trans-oceanic distances. The spread of many diseases of biological origin was limited during the prehistoric period and such diseases were progressively fewer in number as the distance and oceanic separation from Pacific rim areas increased.

In the more remote islands, particularly in Polynesia, the list of diseases introduced by alien contact after the seventeenth century is so comprehensive that one is left to wonder what causes of mortality, beyond errors of hygiene associated with child-rearing and the usual degenerative diseases, were left to many island peoples. This mystery is not dispersed by readings from the earliest explorers of Polynesia who, while they often refer to disease, most frequently identifiable as yaws and filariasis, go on to stress the robust health and profusion of the newly discovered peoples. This question is not so interesting in the Melanesian areas, where endemic diseases were more widespread and alien contact often more recent and more controlled.

When diseases were introduced, island by island, sometimes valley by valley, the lack of immunity conferred on the peoples by their long isolation caused the effect of the diseases, often insignificant in other parts of the world, to be greatly magnified. Once the introduction occurred, the peripatetic islanders greatly assisted foreign seamen, missionaries, and others in the subsequent dispersal. While some diseases, notably measles, influenza, and smallpox, caused abrupt and spectacularly fatal epidemics, others, particularly tuberculosis, gonorrhoea, and dysentery, worked more relentlessly and continuously to increase mortality or lower fertility.

Secondary causes of a raised level of mortality may lie in social, political, economic, and psychological disruption caused directly and indirectly by alien interference in the traditional systems of the islanders. To balance these, however, are the humanitarian works and medical assistance rendered by missionaries and other early visitors.

As the physical separation, small area, and fragmentation of the Pacific Islands at first protected their populations from spreading pestilence and, after their introduction, caused their effect to be the more dreadful, so in the recent period these conditions have contributed to the efficiency of mortality control. Where size, inaccessibility, or physical obstacles have been associated with an island group, so dispersal of modern medical applications has been hindered, but where the islands occur in manageable sizes and small numbers, and have attractive physical conditions, so have their health programmes thrived. The belated improvements only now taking place in New Guinea and several other Melanesian groups illustrate this theory. But medical care has been virtually identical with public health in most island groups, and as such has also been associated very closely with the spread, effectiveness, and quality of total administration. In general, public health problems have been among the first to receive the attention of island administrators. Since the whole area has been essentially colonial, financial and technical aid came in from the administering powers with varying, but usually reasonably liberal, generosity once an administrative structure was put together. Public health under these circumstances has a very positive attraction for administrators; small programmes, involving minor amounts of money and administrative effort, will speedily produce spectacular results which may be easily measured and displayed. Economy, paternalism, and administrative efficiency may be served at one and the same time in a way not found in other areas of government.

This is not to dismiss the devoted work of administrators, doctors, and other medical workers in many Pacific groups. Sometimes expectation of life, infant mortality, and general levels of physical well-being have been abruptly improved by the medical talent or administrative enthusiasm of one man working in an island micro-system. But development has been very uneven, as the population-resource problems now developing in several groups will show.

The emergence of the Pacific Islands as a region in which extremely rapid population growth is occurring, or may be anticipated in the near future, is due to several local causes. The favourable physical environments, the good accessibility by sea and, recently, by air, the selective amenability of the island peoples to foreign influence, administrative and advisory, are contributory causes. But possibly more important than any of these are the ready-made administrative divisions of easily manageable size consequent upon the small areas and dispersal of the islands themselves. Local health problems of small scale and relative isolation lend themselves to enthusiastic medical administration of a relatively uncomplicated but effective nature; they may be perceived as problems to which solutions are possible. The demographic similarities of the Pacific Islands with other tropical areas of small unit size are too obvious to ignore: Costa Rica, Singapore, Ceylon, Taiwan, Mauritius, and several islands in the Caribbean are cases in point.

The Course of Population Change

The course of population change in the Pacific Islands after significant numerical information became available is illustrated by four contrasting examples shown in Fig. 8.1. Common features are depopulation in the early stages of continuous contact (often beginning well before adequate documentary accounts, which usually depended upon the missionaries, were written) followed by a period of stability and, eventually, increasingly rapid recovery. The timing of each stage reflects a variety of different forces working on each population; the

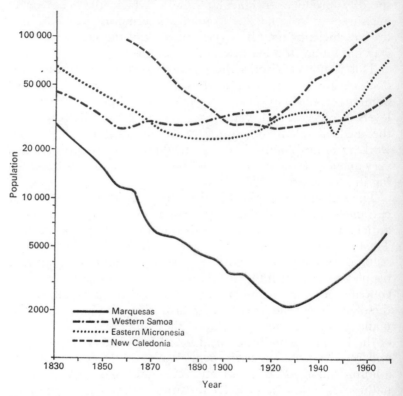

FIG. 8.1. Population trends in Marquesas, Western Samoa, Eastern Micronesia, and New Caledonia, 1830–1966. Sources: see Table 8.3; McArthur, 1956[?], part 1 and 1967; Department of the Interior, 1952–69; Richard, 1957; South Seas Bureau, 1919–32; Le Borgne, 1964; Malignac, 1957.

most important are intensity of contact, stability of the indigenous society, and the benevolence and efficiency of the later administrations. A fifth type, characteristic of Western Melanesia, cannot be included for lack of data but would presumably show a long-term slow decline reversed to a gradual increase only in the last two decades.

Western Samoa is representative of Western Polynesia and

shows a moderate decline, and an early recovery about 1860, followed by rapidly accelerating subsequent growth. By contrast, the eastern Polynesian type represented by the extreme Marquesan example demonstrates the most damaging and prolonged effect of foreign contact. Population decline began about 1790, or possibly before, and continued until about 1929. There were several causes of this excessive mortality and the variety of introduced infections was obviously a major one. Smallpox and tuberculosis were particularly destructive. Some traditional institutions, including infanticide, cannibalism, and institutionalized warfare, continued to contribute to mortality well into the historical period. The social organization of the Marquesas disintegrated more rapidly and more completely than was common in other groups, and with it political leadership and the customary economic organization. Psychological malaise, widespread alcoholism, and opium addiction may have assisted the decline. However, even increased mortality is scarcely likely to have been the sole cause of depopulation. The rate demonstrated would require lowered fertility as well (McArthur, 1967: 292–5). While neither grief, nor ill health, physical or mental, are conducive to mating or fertility, it is likely that the introduction of venereal diseases was the major cause of lowered fertility here as in other Pacific islands, even until the present era.

The example of Eastern Micronesia (included are the present districts of Truk, Ponape, and the Marshalls) has been used to show a Micronesian type which is initially similar to Western Samoa, with a relatively short depopulation period with the beginnings of recovery obvious about 1900. Their troubled political history then presented conditions which did not favour population growth, and sustained recovery began only after American administration assumed control following the Second World War.

The Melanesian population of New Caledonia has been in constant and close contact with a foreign administration for over a century and yet population growth remains slow, and even this situation has existed only since about 1925 when population decline levelled off. Except for the longer period of their colonial administration, and the degree of dispossession imposed upon their lands and culture, the history of the New

Caledonia-Melanesian population decline and growth is not dissimilar to that of other Melanesian populations further west—merely somewhat better documented. Of all the examples, only Western Samoa has regained the numbers claimed for it in the 1830s.

The size of the Samoan population in the proto-historic period, at the beginning of continuous alien contact, can never be known exactly, and the best estimates will probably be derived eventually from a combination of archaeologically examined settlement patterns and an ecological assessment of the degree of prehistoric utilization of natural resources.

Preliminary work by several archaeologists, notably Janet Davidson and Roger Green, suggests that proto-historic settlement patterns in Samoa were more diverse than has previously been suspected. Rather than the predominance of nucleated coastal villages first noted by the early missionaries, it was more frequent for pre-contact settlement to be dispersed over a much greater proportion of the *nu'u*[1] land. The description of the Falefa valley, Upolu, by La Pérouse as 'perhaps the largest village in the South Seas or rather . . . a very extensive inclined plain covered with houses from the summit of the mountains to the water-side' (La Pérouse, 1807: 96) thus becomes more credible. Settlement remains, distributed in the relatively undisturbed commercial copra plantations at Mulifanua, Falcata, and Vailele, conform to this dispersed pattern, extending two or three miles inland from the coast. La Pérouse's description of Fagasa on Tutuila indicates that the coastal nucleated type was concurrent and occurred at least where physical or political conditions tended to favour it; settlements associated with persons of high rank and political power were often nucleated. The movement away from the interior must have begun well before the arrival of missionaries in Samoa, although they documented the final stages of the trend (Pirie,

---

[1] The *nu'u* is essentially the village, the village community, and the land it uses or claims.

1964: 37–8 and 40–1). For instance, the abandonment of the politically important village of Vaigafa on the southern slopes of Upolu behind Lotofaga has been confirmed historically and archaeologically as occurring some time before 1830. There are several other examples of a similar movement.

There is a possibility that this trend was merely a redistribution, and did not entail a significant decrease in population. The density of population implied by La Pérouse's description, however, did not persist into the historical period, when in 1858 only 1,750 persons were counted in the villages of the Falefa valley (Murray, 1858). The causes for the drift seem to be related to early European, but pre-missionary, contact. What these extraneous forces could have been is not certain. The possibilities include an awakened desire for trade goods to be had from the occasional visiting ships, and depopulation caused by newly introduced disease. Likely reasons would also include a new dimension in warfare, caused by the introduction of firearms. One of the major functions of the castaway Europeans, first known to have been in Samoa about 1800, and to have reached a significant number by 1830, was instruction of their patron chiefs in the European skills of musketry, war, and political integration. The availability of firearms need not have been very great to have accomplished a change in the perception Samoan chiefs had of the art and use of war. It is possible that the disposition and utilization of population under the control of major chiefs changed as a result. The wars known to have characterized the period 1802–30, culminating in the sacking of A'ana district and the permanent depopulation of inland settlements in the area, seem not to have been typical of Samoan customary wars, but a modified and more dreadful form. They were perhaps sparked off by motives similar to those which had earlier promoted the violent emergence of dynastic forms of monarchy in Hawaii, Tahiti, and Tonga.

It is most likely that several diseases, including at least tuberculosis, dysentery, gonorrhoea, and possibly some epidemic diseases as well, were introduced prior to the establishment of the missions. There is as yet little or no documentation of this process although a tradition of an epidemic answering to the description of cholera which 'raged with fearful violence many years ago' was recorded at an early stage by one missionary (Turner, 1861: 222). Williams declared Samoa free of venereal disease in 1832, but it does not seem likely that he was in a very good position to judge, and he may have been thinking of syphilis, rather than the less obvious, but demographically more important gonorrhoea (Williams, 1832). The prevalence of yaws as an endemic disease in Samoa before contact would have immunized most of the population against syphilis, but infections, repeated and untreated, of gonorrhoea may cause physiological infertility.

From the mid 1830s contact between Europeans and Samoans became massive as missionaries became established, and whalers, numerically much more important, began using Samoa as a port of supply and refreshment. By the 1850s Samoa had a European population of over 100 persons and during the whaling heyday, until the mid-1850s, many hundreds of Europeans, visiting for short periods, must have passed through each year. Traders and visiting trade vessels became more numerous as the visits of whalers declined.

This type of contact had a much lighter effect in Samoa (and in Tonga and Fiji) than did similar activities in Eastern Polynesia. The exact reason for this is not known, but some possibilities come to mind. Western Polynesia is likely to have been less isolated biologically than was Eastern Polynesia, so that the introductions did not have as great an impact. Another is that the contact with Europeans may have been more formal, regulated and ordered by chiefly or family authority. The possibilities for the transmission of certain types of disease, notably venereal, may then have been much less than in the Eastern Polynesian groups where the contacts were marked by greater promiscuity. This view is not always upheld by the descriptions of these contacts in Samoa given by the missionaries or the visitors themselves. However, as in fishing, accounts of sexual activities often owe more to exaggeration and a colourful imagination than to truth. It is possible too that yaws were less prevalent in Eastern Polynesia than in the west so that syphilis when introduced could have had a much greater effect there. Yaws is a disease with specific ecological requirements and is confined to areas of continuously high temperature and humidity. It is possible that the drier and more drought-prone islands of Eastern Polynesia did not continuously provide optimum conditions for its spread and persistence.

The problem of the relatively small recorded effect of alien contact on the Samoan population raises the question why, if the population was so sturdy, it had not grown larger. Samoa is now believed to have been inhabited for several centuries before the birth of Christ by peoples from whom the present Polynesians are descended. Carbon dates now available take the period back into the first century B.C. but the wide distribution implied for the occurrence of such dates, associated with somewhat remote inland as well as coastal settlement (Davidson, 1967; Green, 1967), implies an earlier origin. Dates have been derived from Tonga back to 400 B.C. From the evidence of pottery layers, Tonga appears to have shared with Samoa a similar culture although Samoa apparently lacks the earliest phase (Green, 1968). This implies a later settlement, probably from Tonga. An initial group of demographically minimum size, say 400 persons, over a 2,000-year history of settlement in a favourable natural environment, of an area sufficient to provide easy subsistence living for up to 350,000 persons, cut off from many biological sources of disease and with relatively few cultural restraints, may be expected to produce a population of high density using the cultivable area intensively. In Hawaii, for instance, a population of some 300,000 persons developed under similar conditions in a period half as long.

There are few indications that this occurred: Samoan subsistence agriculture appears to have been of low intensity, and resource utilization shows little evidence of having been any more than casual. But there is much evidence that agriculture was much more widespread than it had become when first described by the missionaries. Remains, including house sites and walls, are to be found in many inland situations far removed from present-day settlement or agriculture, sometimes on soils which are not suitable for sustained agriculture. Wright has noted that the forest cover of Samoa has a 'peculiar pattern of local dominants, with large unexplained changes in forest composition and . . . [a] widespread persistence of species properly belonging to second-growth seral communities', and that this is 'convincing evidence of the former existence of extensive inland villages' (Wright, 1963: 91). This does not necessarily

O

imply population pressure, or the prior occupation of all more favoured sites. The land-holding, producing, and consuming unit was the *nu'u*, and over the lands attached to it settlement may have been distributed for a variety of reasons, political, strategic, or social, as well as economic.

The population sagged to 34,000 by 1853, but with apparently little social disruption or expressed resentment towards the noxious presence of foreigners, notably missionaries, such as occurred in several other Pacific islands. Up to the 1780s, by which time the Samoans had apparently been little affected by outside contacts, the population change cannot have been very great. Between 1830 and 1855 the population appears to have declined on the average about 1·25 per cent annually. Assuming this was its maximum rate, the population is unlikely to have been much above 100,000 persons at the time of La Pérouse's description. Conversely, it is difficult to imagine reasons why it should have been appreciably less. Over 2,000 years this represents only 0·4 per cent annually; a modest rate, containing provision for a high mortality, and considerable emigration (since it seems that Samoa provided the nucleus for population dispersals into the rest of Polynesia) to match the characteristic high fertility assumed to be in the vicinity of 3·5–4·0 per cent.

There is little certain evidence in Samoa of contagions of the type which swept other Pacific islands, or very reliable evidence of catastrophic population decline. It seems that the population fell gradually, as the result of a generally raised mortality caused by the more insidious type of disease, tuberculosis, and dysentery, for example, or a frequent series of small epidemics such as those recorded in 1830 and 1839 (influenza) and 1848 (whooping cough). Pratt, one of the missionaries particularly interested in population, stated that in northern Savai'i 'there has been a great deal of sickness and a large number of deaths; in fact the people are visibly melting away and they acknowledge it themselves; whole families die off, their houses fall into decay, and their lands are overgrown with bush' (Pratt, 1849).

Several diseases, notably smallpox, appear never to have arrived in Samoa. Tuberculosis although a frequent cause of death does not appear to have been the scourge it was in the Marquesas and among the Maoris of New Zealand. Venereal diseases do not appear to have had the effect in Samoa which many observers noted so ruefully in Tahiti.

The earliest counts of the Western Samoan population contained in the initial writings of the missionaries, consuls, and a few naval visitors, are necessarily vague, generalized, and sometimes conflicting. The Revd. John Williams, who established the London Mission in 1830, thought that the population was between 40,000 and 50,000, but his opportunity for observation was limited. Wilkes, commanding the U.S. Exploring Expedition in 1839, received an estimate from the missionaries of the London Missionary Society which seems to summarize the perception of the missionaries at that time. The figure for Apolima is too high, but elsewhere in the same document it is given as seventy-five persons living in twenty houses (Wilkes, 1845: 108). A British naval officer, Sir Edward Home, received a similar figure from L.M.S. sources in 1844.

TABLE 8.1. *Population Estimates, 1839 and 1844*

1839		1844	
Upolu	25,000	Upolu	25,000 (with 5,000 'heathens')
Savai'i	20,000	Savai'i	16,000 (with 600 'heathens')
Manono	1,100	Manono and	
Apolima	500	Apolima	1,400 (all Christian)
Total	46,600	Total	42,400

SOURCE: Wilkes, 1845: 130 and L.M.S. sources (see Pirie, 1964: 43).

The first L.M.S. census was taken in 1845 and although the document itself has never been found, references to it, and many of the district totals which were used in its compilation, have survived. Stair reported that the total 'population at that time [1845] was about 40,000; an underestimate probably but it certainly did not exceed 45,000' (Stair, 1897: 58). The total included Tutuila and Manu'a so that the western isles would have had a population of about 35,000. This figure is substantiated by a reconstruction of detailed district and village distribution which indicated a population of between 20,000 and 21,000 for Upolu including Manono and Apolima and 14,000–15,000 for Savai'i (Pirie, 1964: 44 and Fig. 4). The next L.M.S. census occurred in 1853 and it seems to be the most reliable count made in the nineteenth century giving not only island-by-island totals but also some data on age and sex.

TABLE 8.2. *Population, 1853*

Upolu	15,587
Savai'i	12,444
Manono	1,015
Apolima	191
Total	29,237

The structure of the population showed that 36 per cent of the population was about 14 years or under while the masculinity ratio was high (116:100) although not particularly so for younger people (*Samoan Reporter*, 1854). Counts later in the century, several by the L.M.S., confirm that the size of the population in Western Samoa was of this order. It remained virtually static, between 29,000 and 30,000 persons, until the 1870s with a tendency to rise in some years, alternating with small decreases associated with epidemics or other disruption.

The first official census taken after German annexation showed a population of 32,815 Samoans, in addition to about 2,000 other residents. That the Samoan population was tending to rise must have become obvious about 1880 and it continued to increase erratically, interrupted by decreases in epidemic years, notably from measles in 1893, and dysentery, whooping cough, and reintroduced measles during the German period, until 1918 when the influenza pandemic struck Western Samoa. This epidemic is by far the best documented in Samoa and, although some doubt exists as to the actual number of deaths, it demonstrated all too vividly the possibilities of drastic decline due to introduced epidemics. Nearly 30 per cent of all adult males died, 22 per cent of all adult females, and 10 per cent of all children. The total loss was about one-fifth of the population. Some groups registered more extreme losses. Among Samoan *matai*[1] the loss was about 45 per cent while among Samoan churchmen the losses were even higher, 47 per cent among the L.M.S. pastors, 65 per cent among Roman Catholic catechists, and 97 per cent of the L.M.S. Council of Elders. It was observed

---

[1] A *matai* is the head or titled member of an *aiga*. The *aiga* is the extended family group of blood relatives and others included by marriage or adoption.

at the time that middle-aged Samoan males with a tendency towards obesity were particularly vulnerable. Not only were the survivors bereft of relatives, friends, and leaders, but to some extent they lost faith in their church, and in the goodwill of the governing authority—since 1914, the New Zealand military.

After 1921, the administration of Western Samoa was properly assumed by New Zealand under mandate from the League of Nations. The epidemic disaster of 1918, the fact that American Samoa had been successfully quarantined against the pandemic, and had been built up as a model of public health under tropical conditions by the U.S. Navy, made the New Zealand authorities particularly sensitive to the issue of public health. The results were not long in showing; the Health Department was completely reorganized, utilizing modern medical procedures rare until that time in the tropics, and operated mainly by trained 'native' personnel which was even rarer.

The women of each village were organized into 'Women's Committees' to supervise care of mothers and children, sanitation, and water supplies. The results were spectacular; the incidence of environmental diseases such as dysentery, gastro-enteritis, and typhoid fever fell with gratifying speed. Tuberculosis and yaws were attacked vigorously. Infant mortality dropped from over 200 per 1,000 live births to less than 80 during the first years of the New Zealand administration. The rate of natural population growth exceeded 3 per cent in each year between 1924 and 1927, a rate unparalleled in those times. While the effect of the 1918 epidemic on the age and sex structure contributed, the acceleration was undoubtedly due largely to a reduction in mortality.

How fragile such improvement may be was demonstrated after 1927 when the Mau movement of civil disobedience to the New Zealand administration disrupted the work of the Health Department in most rural areas. Because registration fell away to useless levels the effect of the Mau on mortality cannot be measured but by the 1931–3 period infant mortality, for instance, is estimated to have almost doubled from the level achieved in 1926–8. Political conditions gradually mended, and in 1936, after full reconciliation was achieved, a census was taken. Whatever the effect of increased mortality, the rate of increase revealed for Samoans was rapid enough—3·1 per cent annually during the period.

Since this time, the rate of natural increase has risen with minor fluctuations to 3·8 per cent annually between 1961 and 1966. But actual rates of growth have been much lower (2·7

TABLE 8.3. *Population of Western Samoa, by Islands, 1839–1966*

Year	Source	Population			Annual av. diff. (per cent)
		Savai'i	Upolu	Total	
1839	Cmdr. Wilkes[a]	20,000	26,600	46,600	..
1845	Pirie (reconstruction)[b]	15,000	21,000	36,000	..
1848	Capt. Maxwell[c]	15,000	18,000	33,000	−2·6
1853	LMS Census[d]	12,444	16,793	29,237	−2·1
1863	LMS Census[e]	12,670	17,556	30,226	+0·3
1874	LMS Census[f]	12,530	16,568	29,098	−0·6
1879	Swanston[g]	12,500	16,500	29,000	0·0
1887	Plessen[h]	13,000	16,950	29,950	+0·4
1900	Census	14,022	18,793	32,815	+0·7
1906	Census	12,816	20,662	33,478	+0·3
1911	Census	12,372	21,182	33,554	+0·0
1921	Census	11,976*	20,625*	36,422	+0·9
1926	Census	12,636*	24,052*	40,231	+2·1
1936	Census	16,575*	35,657*	55,946	+3·1
1945	Census	19,103	49,184	68,197	+2·3
1951	Census	23,561	61,348	84,909	+3·7
1956	Census	26,898	70,429	97,327	+2·8†
1961	Census	31,948	82,479	114,427	+3·3†
1966	Census	36,161	95,218	131,379	+2·7†

* 'Samoans' only—excludes those with 'European' status who are included in the total.

† These rates are significantly below the natural rates of growth owing to emigration of Western Samoans to other countries.

SOURCES:

[a] Wilkes, 1845: 130.
[b] Pirie, 1964: 44 and Fig. 4.
[c] Maxwell, 1848.
[d] *Samoan Reporter*, 1854.
[e] Whitmee, 1875 (reference in Foster, 1875).
[f] Whitmee, 1875.
[g] Swanston, 1879.
[h] Plessen, 1887.

After 1900, all figures are derived from official census reports. An additional source is U.N., 1948.

per cent between 1961 and 1966) because emigration has assumed great importance. Since 1951 Western Samoa has shown a net emigration of 13,500 persons. Their main destinations are New Zealand, American Samoa, Hawaii, and the United States mainland.

Population growth is now significantly affected by the magnitude of the outward flow as well as the balance between fertility and mortality. Should the flow be interrupted actual rates of population growth could resume the natural level of about 3·8 per cent annually.

Mortality

The high rate of natural increase may be attributed to a general decline in mortality at all ages, and a consequent tendency for the population to have an increasing proportion of persons in the younger age groups. This in turn has produced a population in which a relatively small proportion has a high risk of death once the critical first months of life are past. This is undoubtedly due to improvements in the efficiency and areal distribution of services in the Health Department, better administration of the rural village population, and the achievement of a good level of education in hygiene and sanitation utilizing the long-standing high levels of literacy and the prevailing interest in general education.

The structure and cost of public health in Western Samoa is summarized in Table 8.4.

The cost per head has remained virtually static since 1956, while the proportion of government expenditure invested in health has fallen from 17 per cent in 1956 to 10 per cent in 1966. There is a general hospital in Apia, which can provide most basic services required of a modern hospital, and fifteen district hospitals, distributed in rural village centres, which can handle routine needs. The expenditure in relation to the results achieved is extremely low and is related to the heavy reliance put on locally trained personnel.

The health service may be characterized as one which provides a reasonable level of control of common, infectious, and environmentally related illness, but which cannot provide a high standard of service for the more uncommon or complex ailment. It remains true that undue suffering and preventable mortality is still related to lack of expert care and inaccessibility of facilities as well as ignorance and fear on the part of patients and their families. The most frequent infectious

TABLE 8.4. *Some Indices of Public Health Organization in Western Samoa, 1966*

	Total	Rate *per capita*	Rate per 100,000 persons
Cost in $ Samoan*	584,150	4·4	..
No. of fully qualified medical practitioners	7	..	5
No. of medical practitioners trained in Fiji (S.M.P.)	43	..	33
No. of other medically related professionals (including registered nursing sisters)	37	..	28
No. of nurses	243	..	185
No. of hospital beds	533	..	400

* Since 1967 Samoan currency has been quoted in *Tala* ($) worth about 57½p sterling.
SOURCE: Health Department, Western Samoa.

diseases are: influenza, infant and other diarrhoeas, measles, gonorrhoea, typhoid fever, dysentery, and infective hepatitis. Filariasis, tuberculosis, and meningitis are still not infrequent diseases, but yaws, previously a major problem, is now well controlled. The incidence of tuberculosis and filariasis has also been greatly reduced as a result of eradication and control campaigns. Deaths have never been well reported in Western Samoa. Until 1965 the Health Department kept its own record of deaths which usually differed quite widely from the official registrations.

TABLE 8.5. *Total Number of Deaths Recorded in Western Samoa, 1962–6*

	Registrar	Health Dept.	Diff.
1962	571	818	+247
1963	428	808	+380
1964	739	659	−80
1965	702	726	+24
1966	844	..	..

SOURCE: Health Department, Western Samoa.

In 1966 registrations were reorganized and the two methods merged. While the proportion registered is now higher than previously, it remains true that a varying proportion of all deaths, but at least 10 per cent in any one year, go unregistered. The official crude death-rate in 1966 was 6·4 per 1,000, but it is likely that the actual rate is at least 7·5 per 1,000. Under such circumstances, the reporting of cause of death will be even worse. Nevertheless, in recent years, the Health Department has begun to record these data. They are summarized in the following table:

TABLE 8.6. *Causes of Death, 1962–5 (Selected Causes as a Proportion of All Deaths)*

	Proportion (per cent)
Degenerative diseases (including heart disease, cancer, and 'senility')	37
Infectious and environmentally related diseases	27
Accidental	6
Tuberculosis	4
Gastro-intestinal infections	5
Gastro-intestinal ulcers	2

SOURCE: Health Department, Western Samoa.

Infant mortality is relatively low, but its magnitude is difficult to determine because of under-registration. Registration of deaths is inferior to that of births so that the official infant mortality rates are lower than actual levels. The most recent official rate is 43 deaths per 1,000 live births (1966); the actual rate will be significantly higher, and indirect evidence suggests that it is in the vicinity of 60 per 1,000 live births. The downward trend of four decades appears to have levelled off, and has possibly been reversed.

The quality of recent statistics on mortality makes it impracticable to use age-specific mortality rates derived from registration of deaths. Wander (1970), using the Coale–Demeny model stable population method, estimated expectation of life at birth in 1966 at 60·8 years for males and 65·2 years for females. These figures are close to those calculated for 1956, 62·3 years for males and 65·5 years for females (Pirie, 1964: 95), and for 1951 when they were 59·2 years for males and 62·3 years for females (McArthur, 1956: 175–6).

Western Samoa may be classed as one of those countries in which relatively simple measures, an effective but relatively unsophisticated public health organization, stable and orderly administration, widespread literacy, and community interest in

TABLE 8.7. *Children 'Ever Born' and 'Still Living' of Women in Age Groups 15–19 and 20–4 Years in Western Samoa in 1956, 1961, and 1966**

Years	No. of children per woman, 15–19 years		Total number of children of women, 15–19 years		Difference between no. of children 'ever born' and 'still living'	Proportion of difference to no. 'ever born'
	Ever born	Still living	Ever born	Still living		
1956	0·14	0·12	667	596	71	10·6% loss
1961	0·12	0·11	664	617	47	7·1% loss
1966	0·10	0·10	689	638	51	7·4% loss

Years	No. of children per woman 20–4 years		Total number of children of women, 20–4 years			
1956	1·33	1·18	5,092	4,540	552	10·8% loss
1961	1·33	1·21	6,010	5,475	535	8·9% loss
1966	1·41	1·28	6,191	5,621	570	9·2% loss

* This table has been constructed on the following assumptions:

That the difference between the numbers 'ever born' and 'still living' reported by mothers in the two youngest age groups 15–19 and 20–4 years will include a high proportion of infant deaths although deaths of children of older age (i.e. over 1 year) will also be included.

That the trend exhibited by the proportion of loss will parallel that of infant deaths, although the proportion will be larger. It is estimated, very roughly, that about two-thirds of the loss relating to children of women of 20–4 and about 85 per cent of the loss for women of 15–19 years will be infant deaths, so that for 1966 infant mortality is estimated at approximately 60 per 1,000.

The table also suggests that mortality at young age declined significantly between 1956 and 1961, but that since 1961 there has been no change, or possibly a very slight increase. There is also an indication that the fertility of females 15–19 declined in the 1956–66 decade (probably due to the tendency to postpone or avoid pregnancy at this age) while fertility among women of older ages has increased.

education, all fostered by the persistence of cohesive social and political groupings based on the village, have combined to reduce mortality to a relatively low level. Since independence, however, the easy and popular emphasis put upon Public Health by the Trusteeship administration has been quietly downgraded as the more urgent problems of development and political survival have supervened. As yet, although progress has been stalled, there is little evidence of significant retrogression.

Fertility

While some hard decisions have been made regarding the role of public health and mortality control within the national priorities, the harder decisions relating to fertility have only recently reached the stage of discussion. There is no official policy on limitation of family size, and there is considerable opposition to the idea from all religious groups in Western Samoa, on the grounds that it is against Samoan custom.

Meanwhile, the trend toward monetization of the village economy, an increasing dependence on paid employment and remittances from relatives overseas, and a widespread desire for urban or overseas migration have done little so far to induce Samoan women to limit the size of their families. The average size of the completed family in 1966 was 7·6 children (based upon number of children born to women of recently completed fertility, i.e. 45–9 years). The equivalent figures were 7·0 in 1961 and 7·2 in 1956. Only about 6 per cent of Western Samoan women pass out of reproductive age without having children, an extremely low level which must be little above naturally occurring infertility. About 35 per cent of all women of recently completed fertility in 1966 produced 10 or more children; the maximum number claimed by any one mother was 24 children.

The levels of fertility to be observed in Western Samoa are rare in the world. They are due to the retention of traditional attitudes toward the bearing of children, as an activity doing honour to oneself, to one's husband, and to the *aiga*; to the continued absence of any real economic penalty to village-dwelling women in the maintenance of a large family; and to a somewhat casual attitude to marriage, divorce, and mating in general, all of which appear to be frequent. Contributing also is a marked improvement in the general level of health so that mating and fertility are promoted. Samoan fertility seems always to have been high but modern conditions have permitted its potential to be more fully realized.

The fertility rate in 1966 was about 245 children born per 1,000 women of reproductive age (15–44 years). It is impossible to be certain of this rate since it must be estimated. As both births and infant deaths are seriously under-registered, this figure is a composite one based on adjusted births, and estimated infant deaths. The rate had increased significantly since 1956 when, using the same methods, the rate was calculated to be about 220. It was also up slightly on 1961, when the rate was about 240 children per 1,000 women.

A somewhat better guide to the replacement potential of the population is the child–woman ratio, which may be calculated without recourse to estimate, being derived only from data observed in the census. It includes, however, some survival at young age in addition to fertility.

TABLE 8.8. *Child–Woman Ratios*

(Number of children 0–4 years per 1,000 women 15–44 years)

		Ratio per 1,000	Standard error	Change (per cent)
Western Samoa				
Total	1966	1,086	6	+2
	1961	1,064	7	+10
	1956	969	7	+14
	1951	852	7	..
Rural only	1966	1,167	7	+13
	1956	1,035	8	..
Urban only	1966	806	14	+9
	1956	737	16	..
American Samoa	1966	743	14	−18
	1956	909	16	..

These ratios indicate that in Western Samoa the proportion of young children to females in the reproductive age range (i.e. 15–44 years) has risen at each census since 1951 when data of this type first became available. But the rate of increase has decelerated on each occasion, declining from 14 per cent between 1951 and 1956 through 10 per cent to 1961, to only 2 per cent to 1966. It seems likely, from these figures, that the next census could show that the apparent rise in fertility has peaked, but unless an extremely effective family limitation programme is begun in the meantime, the prospect is for the fertility level to continue at an extremely high plateau. Although there is some indication that fertility is affected by a dependence on paid employment, and by urban living, the ratio increased for the urban population by 9 per cent in the decade 1956–66. While this increase is slower than that for the whole population, 12 per cent, the implication that urban fertility is rising at all is unwelcome. Replacement in American Samoa by contrast is now well below that in Western Samoa, a reflection, no doubt, of monetization of the American Samoan economy which is now far ahead.

Employment

In the absence of any official interest in reducing fertility, it is worth examining some of the institutions which may be operating to cause a spontaneous reduction. Of these, the most powerful is likely to be paid employment, as opposed to a continued dependence upon customary village agriculture. The necessity of providing for the needs of a large family out of money incomes, likely to be small in Western Samoa, may act as a discernible deterrent to high fertility. The number of persons in paid employment in 1966 was 11,266 on whom a further 26,414 persons were dependent. Together these indicate that 29 per cent of the total population is dependent upon paid employment rather than on the traditional village system. While the number of persons showed an increase on the numbers recorded in 1956 and 1961, the proportion of persons in paid employment in the total population fell slightly, from 8·9 per cent at the two former census years to 8·6 per cent in 1966. The indication is that not only is the proportion in paid employment not increasing as it should do if internal economic development were progressing at an acceptable rate, but that it is even falling behind. Only about 225 new paying jobs each year are being created in Western Samoa, an increase of only 2·1 per cent annually. The opportunity to migrate overseas to areas where paid employment is available is obviously relieving many Samoans of the problem of finding paid employment in a sluggish domestic economy.

The proportion in customary village agriculture, 15·2 per cent, remained static over the 1961–6 period, employing 19,900 persons, while the proportion 'not economically active' including children, village-dwelling women, and others not contributing directly to the economy increased to 76·2 per cent.

This proportion has been increasing slowly, from 75·5 per cent in 1956 when data of this kind first became available.

It is therefore unlikely that fertility is being much affected by an increase in the dependence upon paid employment. The sluggishness in this sector is reflected in the slowness of urban growth. Apia, the only town, had a population of 25,480 persons in 1966, an increase of 3·2 per cent over 1961. The proportion of the total population living in Apia was 19·3 per cent, a rise of only 0·6 per cent in ten years. The population is subject to considerable outward migration as persons accustom themselves to urban living and perhaps paid employment before moving overseas. Inward movement from the villages is considerable although much of it is floating or cyclic, close ties with the home village being maintained by a high proportion of the inhabitants. The low proportion of Western Samoans living in Apia is a deceptive guide to the degree of urbanization affecting the population as a whole. Since most emigrants take up urban residence overseas, the degree of urban experience of the whole population is considerably greater; approximately 25 per cent of all Western Samoans are at present living in urban areas.

Again, it is evident that emigration is serving as an outlet for forces which, were they contained in Western Samoa, would cause excessive pressure on existing facilities and organization. The outflow obviously has some advantages for Western Samoa, temporarily easing the strain of excessive population growth, particularly since recent economic difficulties have been greatly aggravated by mischance, in the form of crop diseases and hurricane damage. But the quality of the outflow is as important as its size and the indications are that this is high to a degree which is detrimental to economic progress at home. Emigration is being used as a substitute for the vigorous investment needed to expand employment and urban facilities. A continued high rate of emigration is needed but this should be accompanied by a greatly accelerated rate of job creation and urban growth within Samoa, which would slow the exit of the better qualified persons. To permit already advanced nations, such as New Zealand, to benefit from Samoan capital and skills, painfully accumulated, at the expense of development at home is to reduce Western Samoa to a hinterland community. This is not in accord with the ambitions of the Samoan people expressed when they elected to become an independent nation.

While the growth of economic alternatives has been slow in the last decade, the development of customary village agriculture has scarcely kept pace with population growth. Of the total area of 702,000 acres, about half, 350,000 acres, is cultivable. Of this area, 171,500 acres, or 49 per cent, are already in use, supporting crops, mainly coconut, cacao, banana, and taro, all of which are used partly for subsistence and partly for export. Hence all are vulnerable to increasing domestic consumption at the expense of an export surplus. They have also proved vulnerable to pests, storm damage, and price fluctuation.

The unutilized area, still in forest, is the poorer half in terms of soil fertility. Some areas of best quality soil still remain uncleared, while elsewhere plantings have extended into areas not recommended for permanent use (Wright, 1963: 96; Pirie, 1964: 106–10). But it is generally true, particularly on Upolu, that the remaining forested areas suitable for agricultural development are on cooler, wetter inland slopes and that the soils are more acid, leached, and initially more fragile than those already utilized. The cooler, moister areas will not support either coconut palms or cacao. They are, however, well suited to banana and subsistence root crops in terms of climate, but the low nutrient status of most of these soils means that under the present system they must be fallowed. The growing of commercial export crops in this way is grossly uneconomic both in terms of labour and in the destruction of natural resources. The development of non-rotational, large-scale, technologically sophisticated systems, which will allow disease to be properly controlled, is very necessary. This is presently being attempted for bananas in Western Samoa, but the results are not encouraging to date.

The rate of areal expansion in response to population increase is difficult to establish as land-use data are fragmentary. A comprehensive survey, based on recent air-photos, was made in 1956 and established the agriculturally used area as 132,000 acres of which 103,000 was in customary village agriculture. Estimates made in 1926 give 50,400 acres as the area in customary agriculture, then coconut palms and subsistence crops only.

This indicates a rate of expansion of 2·4 per cent annually between 1926 and 1956. The rate is likely to have been much higher than this in the post-war years of expansion in the production of cacao and bananas. Bryant (1967: 152–5), in a detailed survey of western Upolu, using air-photos taken in 1942, gives data from which a rate of 5 per cent annually can be derived. Since 1956 the rate for all lands has returned to about 2·4 per cent annually. Population density on village land was 1·6 acres per person in 1926, 1·7 acres in 1956, and 1·4 in 1966.

While the over-all pressure of population on space may be summarized by the use of these measures of density, the quality and degree of utilization of the area must also be considered. The intensity of use is not high in Western Samoa as can be shown by low productivity per acre: $WS 45 for copra and $WS 130 for cacao based on 1966 prices. Per acre returns from bananas can be much higher and where intensively planted (i.e. 400 trees per acre) may rise to nearly $WS 650 per acre. In most Samoan plantings, the intensity is lower and the returns over several years are reduced by the necessity of fallowing, since fertilizer continues to be sparingly used.

The rate of land development is obviously lagging behind the rate of population growth. Even with urbanization, diversification of employment, and emigration, the work force engaged in customary village agriculture increased at 2·7 per cent annually between 1961 and 1966.

Although the rate of agricultural expansion is modest, it will, if continued, cause all the land suitable for clearing and development to be fully utilized within thirty years. An increase in the actual rate of population growth, caused by a decline in emigration for any reason, could put increasing pressure on existing agricultural resources, and cause a more rapid expansion of the agriculturally used area. A successful campaign to increase agricultural production using existing rather than more intensive methods could have a similar effect. When this stage is reached, further population expansion can be absorbed only by increasingly intensive use of developed land, with increasing habitation densities. The rural population of Western Samoa, even allowing for some improvement in agricultural techniques, would seem to have an upper limit of about 350,000 persons, if present living standards are to be preserved. This figure is likely to be achieved in little more than thirty years, even at present rates.

Conclusion

Some small consolation for Samoa may lie in the probability that ominous as these projections are, those for some other areas such as Tonga and the Gilbert and Ellice Islands are more alarming; Western Samoa may well benefit from observing the methods used by these governments in dealing with similar problems in more limited environments and at an earlier time.

Another consolation may lie in the demonstrated tendency for projections made in the past for Western Samoa to be proved wrong. The 'conservative' projections made on the basis of the 1956 census (Jupp, 1961: 403–5; McArthur, 1961: 395; Pirie, 1960: 73) have proved too generous in each case, as emigration assumed an importance not anticipated in the late 1950s.

This account of the vagaries of population change in Western Samoa has shown that since the 1780s external factors, of differing kinds, applied at varying intensities, have greatly affected the rates of change. The major problem for whoever has been administering the country has always been the need to counteract these trends where they are excessive or destructive, and to accommodate the change and the domestic problems which follow in their train. Western Samoa has provided an advance model of population development in the Pacific Islands which we may anticipate will be followed, with local variations, by most other island groups. Some groups, Tonga and the Gilbert and Ellice Islands being the extreme examples, have already reached more critical densities in relation to local resources without achieving the fertility and lowered mortality levels current in Western Samoa. Others, American Samoa, the Cook Islands, and Tahiti, have progressed further with the possible solutions: greater urbanization, more diversified economies, programmes of family limitation, and higher rates of emigration. But in all these cases, the trends have been initiated externally and are dominated by alien interests.

Since the initial decline in population was halted, about 1860, the population in the western islands of Samoa has shown most clearly, and usually at an earlier time, those trends in population growth, common to other Pacific island populations, which are induced or affected by external forces. Meanwhile, although greatly changed, a distinctive and viable Samoan culture has survived the onslaught of Western civilization. The acceptance or rejection of those institutions with which population change has been associated has always been largely by Samoan decision. Now, more than ever, this is again true.

The measures to be adopted to cope with impending population problems will be those decided upon by Samoans working through their own government. For this reason the Samoan case deserves close scrutiny by those island peoples who must attack and solve their own population problems, within the confines of their own territory. There must be a way which suits local conditions in the Pacific Islands and the people of Western Samoa must be among those who find it first.

BIBLIOGRAPHY

Borah, W. 1951. 'New Spain's Century of Depression', *Ibero-Americana*, no. 35, Berkeley and Los Angeles.

Bryant, N. A. 1967. 'Change in the Agricultural Land Use in West Upolu, Western Samoa', unpublished Master's thesis, Department of Geography, University of Hawaii, Honolulu.

Buxton, P. A. 1926. 'The Depopulation of the New Hebrides and other Parts of Melanesia', *Trans. Roy. Soc. of Medicine and Hygiene*, vol. 19, pp. 420–58.

Christiansen, P. E., Schmidt, H., Jensen, O., Bang, H. O., Andersen, V., Jordal, B. 1952. 'An Epidemic of Measles in Southern Greenland' and 'Measles in Virgin Soil'. Papers 1 and 2, *Acta Medica Scandinavica*, vol. 144, fasc. 4, pp. 313–22 and 430–9.

Davidson, J. M. 1965. 'Archaeology in Samoa and Tonga', *N.Z. Archaeological Assoc. Newsletter*, no. 8, pp. 59–71.

——— et al. 1967. 'Additional Radio-carbon dates for Western Polynesia', *Journ. Poly. Soc.*, vol. 76, June 1967, pp. 225–7.

Department of the Interior. 1952–69. *Annual Report of the Administration of the Trust Territory of the Pacific Islands*, Washington.

Epstein, A. L., and Epstein, T. S. 1962. 'A Note on Population in Two Tolai Settlements', *Journ. Poly. Soc.*, vol. 71, pp. 70–82.

Foster, S. S. 1875. U.S. Consular Despatch, Apia, *Despatches to State Department*, vol. 3, no. 28, 8 Feb.

Green, R. C. 1967. 'Settlement Patterns: Four Case Studies from Polynesia', in W. G. Solheim II (ed.), *Archaeology at the Eleventh Pacific Science Congress*, Social Science Research Institute, University of Hawaii, Honolulu, pp. 101–32.

—— 1968. 'West Polynesian Prehistory', in Yawata, I., and Sinoto, Y. H. (eds.), *Prehistoric Culture in Oceania*, Honolulu.

Hamlin, H. 1931. 'The Problem of Depopulation in Melanesia', *Yale Jour. of Biology and Medicine*, vol. 4, pp. 301–21.

Jupp, K. M. 1961. 'Population Expansion in Western Samoa', *Jour. Poly. Soc.*, vol. 70, pp. 401–9.

Keys, R. F. 1927. 'Medical Work in the Apia-Falefa District', *Appendices to the Jour. of the House of Representatives*, New Zealand, Paper A-4a.

Lambert, S. M. 1934. 'The Depopulation of Pacific Races', *B.P. Bishop Museum Special Publication*, no. 23, Honolulu.

La Pérouse, J. F. G. de. 1807. *A Voyage round the World* (1785–8), 3 vols., London.

Le Borgne, J. 1964. *Géographie de la Nouvelle Calédonie, et des Iles Loyaute*, Noumea.

Malignac, G. 1957. *Rapport démographique sur la Nouvelle Calédonie*, Paris.

Maxwell, Captain. 1848. British Consulate in Samoa, No. 4, 18 Mar., Foreign Office Records 58/63.

McArthur, N. 1956[?]. *The Populations of the Pacific Islands*, mimeo, 6 vols., Department of Demography, The Australian National University, Canberra.

—— 1961. *Introducing Population Statistics*, Melbourne.

—— 1967. *Island Populations of the Pacific*, Canberra.

Murray, A. 1858. Letter dated Apia, 27 June, South Sea Letters, Box 27, London Missionary Society.

Pirie, P. N. D. 1960. *The Population of Western Samoa: a Preliminary Report based upon the 1956 Census*, Department of Geography, Australian National University, Canberra.

—— 1964. 'The Geography of Population in Western Samoa', unpublished Ph.D. thesis, Australian National University, Canberra.

Pitt-Rivers, G. H. L. 1927. *The Clash of Culture and the Contact of Races*, London.

Plessen, L. 1887. Memorandum to Foreign Office, 3 Mar. 1887, in 'Correspondence respecting the Navigators' Islands', 5532.

Pratt, G. 1849. Letter dated Matautu, Savaii, 1 Nov. South Seas Letters, Box 22, London Missionary Society.

Richard, D. 1957. *United States Naval Administration in the Trust Territory of the Pacific Islands*, 3 vols. Washington.

Samoan Reporter. 1854. no. 15, Jan. 1854.

Scragg, R. F. R. 1957. *Depopulation in New Ireland*, Administration of Papua and New Guinea, Sydney.

South Seas Bureau. 1919–32. *Annual Report to the League of Nations*, Tokyo.

Stair, J. B. 1897. *Old Samoa*, London.

Steinberger, A. B. 1876. *U.S. Congressional Papers*, no. 161, p. 32.

Swanston, R. 1879. *Despatch to Foreign Office from British Consulate Samoa*, 4 June 1879.

United Nations. 1948. 'The Population of Western Samoa', *Reports on the Populations of Trust Territories*, no. 1, New York.

Wander, H. 1970. 'Fertility and Mortality in Western Samoa, 1961/66', *Report of the Statistical Office, Treasury Department*, mimeo, Apia.

Wilkes, C. 1852. *Narrative of the United States Exploring Expedition* (1838–42), 2 vols., London.

Williams, J. 1832. 'Narrative of a Voyage performed in the Missionary Schooner "Olive Branch"', unpublished manuscript, London Missionary Society Library, London.

Wright, A. C. S. 1963. *Soils and Land Use of Western Samoa*, N.Z. Soil Bureau, Bulletin no. 22, Wellington.

9

LAND TENURE IN THE SOUTH PACIFIC

R. G. CROCOMBE[1]

WITHIN the Pacific area people often emphasize the great diversity of tenure systems: those where even forest rights were held by individuals and those where even garden plots were held by social groups; those in which inheritance was predominantly matrilineal and those where it was patrilineal; those found on atolls and those at 8,000 feet on mountainous slopes. But in world perspective, all the tenure systems in the Pacific had much in common, both in the environment and in the cultures of the peoples, and these factors set the boundaries within which each tenure system evolved and operated.

All fell within the humid tropics. There was no use of metals and tools were of stone, wood, and bone. There was no writing and therefore no permanent record of land rights. Large concentrations of population were rare, with most hamlets or villages containing less than 100 people and only rare examples of villages of up to 2,000 people under extraordinary circumstances. There were no towns or cities and no nation-states with stable centralized governments. Economic specialization was limited and the vast majority of people grew the bulk of the food they consumed. All the societies depended partly on horticulture and partly on hunting (and/or fishing) and gathering. Many people shifted their homes periodically within a given area but there were no true nomads. There were no cereals (the staple vegetable foods being tubers or tree crops) and techniques for food storage were very limited. There was no grazing or herding, animal husbandry being limited to very small numbers of pigs, chickens, and dogs in some areas. Even the techniques of cultivation followed a single, broad South-east Asian tradition which was markedly different, for example,

[1] Dr. Crocombe is Professor of Pacific Studies, University of the South Pacific, Fiji.

from the way similar crops were cultivated in South America. These factors limited the range of tenure arrangements found in the Pacific at the time of European contact.

THE NATURE OF LAND RIGHTS

Before examining the broad patterns of tenure that emerged within the above framework, a brief digression on the nature of land tenure is desirable. It is not, perhaps, sufficiently recognized that human beings do not own land: what they own is rights to land, that is, rights *vis-à-vis* other human beings. The notion of tenure, then, is a notion of exclusion. If we say that this man has the sole right to plant vegetables here, or that that clan has the right to hunt there, we mean that all persons other than the rightholder(s) are excluded from doing these things unless additional arrangements are made to transfer, share, delegate, or abrogate those rights.

Attempts to classify tenure systems as 'individual' or 'communal' are as misleading for the Pacific as elsewhere. They obscure the fact that in all tenure systems some rights in most lands are held by individuals (whether acquired by inheritance, purchase, or group membership, or by virtue of a particular status such as mother's brother, mortgagee, chief, etc.). Some rights are held by groups (lineages, county councils, or communes) and others by the community as a whole.

Almost invariably there are many different rights in any one parcel of land and they are often held by different parties. One man or group may have a right to plant tubers, another the right to harvest coconuts, another the right to hunt birds and another the right to tribute, all on the same area of land. This is not as confusing as many Westerners believe, for in Western countries also a multiplicity of different rights to any piece of land is usually held by the holders of titles, easements, and mortgages as well as by local bodies, governments, and others. Land rights also vary in relation to the type of terrain, the process of acquisition, and the status of the right-holder. Thus rights to forest land may differ significantly from rights to house-sites, rights to land acquired by conquest often differ from those acquired by adoption, and the rights of chiefs often differ from those of commoners.

LAND RIGHTS IN THE PACIFIC

The degree to which rights were defined and subdivided in the Pacific Islands was related to the value of the land to the people concerned, and to the amount of effort invested on it. Land which was of little use was generally held by groups and not subdivided in detail. Land which was highly productive, but of commodities of which there was a considerable surplus, was also held by large groups. Rights of individuals and small groups came to be associated only with those products for which labour had been invested. Thus, for example, rights to many sago swamps in coastal New Guinea were held by large groups, and small group rights were exercised only over such trees as individuals or families planted, tended, or cut and processed. The same principle applied in many places to materials for housebuilding, plants with medicinal properties, and stones for walls, borders, and pathways, even when these commodities were located in gardens which were the property of individuals.

Maximum delineation of rights, on the other hand, occurred when the commodities wanted were in short supply or required a high input of labour. Such delineation was sometimes by subdivision of area into small individual or family plots, sometimes by restriction of time so that persons had equal periods of access to the limited resources available, and sometimes by restrictions on the quantity of the commodity that any one person could take.

The nature of pre-contact land rights in the Pacific will be analysed briefly in terms of the major use to which the land was put by the people concerned. This approach has been used, rather than an analysis in terms of rightholding units (tribes, clans, lineages, etc.), because the nature of the social units varied such a great deal and a single word is thus used to describe a range of different phenomena. For example the word 'tribe' is used by Williams (1940: 26) to describe a Papuan group which was without unified leadership and whose identity was based largely on linguistic affinity and common territory. This is a very different group from that which Hiroa (1934: 102) called a tribe in Mangaia, Cook Islands, and which was typified by a hierarchy of leaders and processes of tribal government. Words used to describe the rightholding units are too imprecise to permit of accurate analysis on that basis.

Residential Land

Residence patterns in the Pacific were characterized by hamlets or villages. Almost nowhere did nuclear families each occupy a single house in isolation from others. Where residence was in isolated houses, they usually contained a wider range of persons than a nuclear family. More frequently houses were built in clusters of three to thirty with occasional examples of several hundred houses in the one place. The housing units were of three main types—those containing one nuclear or extended family; those containing a number of families; and those in which different categories of persons occupied different buildings.

Units usually containing one nuclear or extended family included the Motu people of the south coast of New Guinea who lived in houses over the water. The principal rights to a residential locality lay with the village section, but to a particular house and house-site lay with the adult male householder (Groves 1963: 19). Large houses accommodating many families include those of Truk in the Caroline Islands which ideally housed a group of women belonging to the same lineage, plus their husbands and young children (Goodenough, 1961: 124).

The majority of the Pacific peoples, however, lived in housing complexes in which different categories of persons occupied different buildings. Among the Enga of the New Guinea highlands the men lived, five or so to a house, in houses which were the property of the occupying sub-clan. Each married woman had a separate house which she shared with her unmarried daughters and her young sons (Meggitt, 1965: 19–24). In Samoa the chief occupied one house with his wife and young children, the widows and single women another, the widowers and single men another, the untitled men and their families others again. There were separate houses for cooking, for guests, and for meetings. Proprietary rights to the whole housing complex were held by the descent group and rights of use of particular buildings were exercised according to one's status in the rightholding group.

Sacred and Ceremonial Land

Lands set aside for sacred and ceremonial purposes tended to be small in area and the rights to them held by corporate groups.

These must be treated separately from lands believed to be sacred but not actively used. Such lands were sometimes extensive but of little value to the people concerned because of relative infertility and inaccessibility (as the interior of Futuna, French Polynesia—Panoff, 1964: 111) or fear of sickness associated with them (as in certain localities in Chimbu, New Guinea highlands—Brookfield and Brown, 1963: 42).

Land for Cultivation

In most of the South Pacific, rights to subsistence gardens were held by individuals, but they were subject to the rights of the wider group to which they belonged. What appeared to early observers as large communal gardens were often no more than a number of contiguous individual gardens, usually on land associated with a particular descent group. Co-operation between neighbouring gardeners (under the leadership of a garden specialist) was common, but was limited to particular tasks at certain stages in the agricultural cycle.

The rights to cultivation land of individuals were usually scattered. This was often related to topographical and ecological variations within the territory to which the person held rights, and was a means of ensuring access to each resource zone. But the scattering of an individual's gardens cannot be explained solely by the distribution of varied terrain types. The extent to which persons cultivate on land other than that to which they held proprietary rights is a striking feature of Pacific tenure systems. Among the Orokaiva of coastal Papua, Rimoldi (1966: 70) found that only fifteen gardens in a sample of thirty-four were on land which belonged to the lineage of the cultivator. Of the remainder, five were on land of another lineage within the same clan, ten on land of another clan within the same village, one on land of a branch of the same clan in another village, and three on land of a different clan in a different village. In such cases, there was a clear distinction made between the permanent right of the landholder or landholding group, and the temporary use right of the borrower. The right of the latter usually ends with the completion of the cultivation cycle.

Such spatial diversification of holdings may often be determined more by social and political factors, than by economic necessity. On Pacific atolls, which are characterized by extreme topographical uniformity, we still find that each individual or small group held plots scattered widely over the component islets—and often on more than one atoll. This resulted from the need to maintain multiple links of mutual obligation with many different people. The acquisition of land entailed obligations, often complex in nature and extending over a long period, to the person or group from whom it was obtained, and the exercise of land rights was usually a function of one's status in relation to particular individuals and social groups.

Planted food trees (as distinct from wild trees which are dealt with under foraging) were usually the property of individuals or of siblings. In many instances rights to the trees could be held by parties other than those holding rights to the land they grew on (e.g. Bena Bena—see Howlett, 1962: 68). Throughout Polynesia, Micronesia, and much of Melanesia any bona fide traveller could take coconuts to slake his thirst, or ripe fruit to satisfy his hunger, from almost any tree. In many societies specific kin and affines could take produce on certain occasions. Sometimes it could be taken without asking, sometimes a request was necessary but approval of it obligatory.

Hunting and Gathering Rights

In Polynesia and Micronesia hunting was marginal at best, being confined to birds, rats, lizards, and the occasional wild pig. Hunting was much more important in Melanesia where the larger, more varied land masses harboured a wide range of edible birds, mammals, marsupials, and reptiles which included cassowaries, wild pigs, wallabies, bandicoots, crocodiles, and snakes. But hunting was everywhere only a supplementary source of food, though its contribution of protein was often dietarily significant for inland peoples who had little access to sea foods.

Rights to hunt were usually held by relatively large groups, and though it was usually said that the game caught belonged to the successful hunter, he was usually obliged to share his prize with specific kin, and often with particular kin of his wife.

Foraging was also of less importance in Polynesia and Micronesia than in Melanesia where in some cases it was a major source of food and raw materials. This was usually in swampy areas where stands of wild sago provided a vast reservoir of starchy food. In some instances any member of the tribe could cut and use sago from any part of the tribal territory (e.g. Tor—see Oosterval, 1961: 87–8), but in other cases such reserves of wild sago were exploited only in times of shortage, the normal supply being obtained from more productive, well-tended groves owned by families (e.g. Waropen—see Held, 1957: 348). In Marshall Lagoon on the south coast of Papua, the fruits of wild mangroves are an important seasonal food, but they are abundant and require no husbandry and may be gathered by any member of the community at any time.

Unique resources led to unique tenure provisions. The megapode bird on Savo Island in the British Solomon Islands lays its eggs deep in beach sand where they are incubated by sun heat. The laying fields are divided into plots averaging ten yards square, each of which produces several hundreds of eggs per week. Each plot is the property of an individual, though subject to certain limitations (Allan, 1957: 159–62). Only Savoese can acquire these rights, and originally only members of certain Savoese lineages could hold them. Likewise the salt springs of highlands New Guinea were too few for each descent group to have its own. Rights were therefore sometimes shared in such a way that one group used them at one time and another group at another (Meggitt, 1958: 309–13).

Water Rights

The degree to which rights to areas of water are subdivided among individuals and small groups is related to the difficulty of marking boundaries as well as to the value and relative scarcity of the benefits accruing to the rightholders. The people of Frederick Hendrick Island (Irian Barat) were skilled in exploiting their swamps and waterways for food and raw materials, and demarcated the rights of groups and individuals with considerable precision (Serpenti, 1965: 111). In much of the Pacific shallow lagoons were divided among small descent groups using reef passage, coral heads, and platforms that were exposed at high tide as boundary markers. Larger lakes and lagoons were harder to divide and they often gave a relative abundance of the commodities obtained from water—both factors leading to less subdivision and to exploitation in common by large groups. But where there was a limited but valuable supply of a certain commodity, rights were defined more clearly and the rightholding units were smaller.

Sub-surface and Over-surface Rights

To the extent that Pacific islanders used materials under the surface of land or water, they usually belonged to those who held the surface rights.[1] Two minor exceptions lie in leaning trees and flying birds. Whereas in English law the fruits of a tree which leans over a boundary belong to the persons over whose land they hang, in the only examples noted in the Pacific they belong to the person from whose ground they spring. Likewise birds hunted from one area of land can, in some places at least, be claimed by the hunter even if they land on the ground of others. In Siane, on the other hand, game hunted on the land of other tribes belongs to the landowners and not to the hunters.

Rights of Access

Land access was on foot and water access by canoe or raft. In the high islands of Polynesia, land routes were of two kinds. The internal routes ran from the coast to the hilly interior within each district. The inter-district routes ran round the island near the coast and cut across districts at right angles to the internal roads. Although the paths themselves seem to have been regarded as belonging to the descent groups whose land they crossed, access to them was usually permitted to a much wider range of persons than those who had rights to plant and reside. The fullest record of access routes is that given for Hawaii by Apple, who notes (1965: 25) that certain portions of some paths were reserved to persons of high rank.

Rights to travel through reef passages were also frequently

---

[1] With the exception of rights of access which were often held by a wider group.

restricted to particular tribes or groups, and tribute was sometimes paid to the head of the group which controlled the passage. Access rights on rivers depended, in part at least, on the size of the river and the size of the political unit. In Kapauku (Irian Barat) rivers and large lakes were open to all for access and gathering, but small lakes were regarded as the property of local lineages, though they could be used by any member of the political confederacy. Streams, however, were the exclusive prerogative of those with rights to the contiguous land (Pospisil, 1965: 194–5).

Processes of Land Transfer

Throughout the Pacific, inheritance was the most important process by which individuals acquired their land rights. Inheritance was predominantly from the father's side in mainland New Guinea and in Polynesia, predominantly through the mother in Micronesia, but in Melanesia, apart from New Guinea proper, there are both matrilineal and patrilineal systems, as well as ambilineal and bilineal. But nowhere was any one principle of inheritance applied exclusively, and nowhere was inheritance the only means of transferring land rights. Such terms as patrilineal and matrilineal refer to ideal patterns which apply in the majority of instances. But a man may have no son, or he may have too many among whom to share his limited lands and principles had to be modified continually to meet particular circumstances. As Nayacakalou (1961: 125) has said, 'the people in a village cannot be bothered with neat pigeonholes . . . what they are concerned about are the exigencies of their daily lives'.

Sale of land was unheard of in Polynesia and Micronesia, and in most parts of Melanesia. But in a few areas of Melanesia land sale was practised (e.g. Gahuku-Gama—see Read, 1954: 10), though it was never the main mechanism of land transfer. Gifts of land rights to individuals were common under a variety of circumstances. Cook Islanders often gave a portion of land to a high-ranking woman when she married out (Crocombe, 1964: 54). The Gilbertese were one of many peoples who gave land in expiation of offences or for saving a life (Cartland, 1953: 1). Transfers of these kinds were seldom at the discretion of individuals. More usually a group or its leaders made such decisions, and residual rights to the land in many cases remained with the donor group unless special arrangements were made to annul the residual rights (e.g. the Garia—see Lawrence, 1967: 115–17).

Reallocation within the land-holding group was common—sometimes by formal decision of elders or the whole group, but more often by another member of the group making use of land which had not been taken up by its previous occupiers after the normal fallow. Other forms of adjusting the relation of people to the land were also practised. Adoption, abortion, and infanticide were widespread means of tailoring population to resources and the more extreme examples come, as one would expect, from the most rigorous environments. Maude (1937) shows how in the less fertile Gilbert Islands infanticide had to be practised by almost every family. These processes are selective and the choice was often made in order to avoid future tenure difficulties—either by reducing sheer numbers, or being selective of sex, or doing away with children whose existence created potential future disputes over land or leadership.

But all these processes usually accounted only for routine internal adjustments. Famine, tsunamis, and hurricanes also reduced populations periodically but nevertheless lands often became so full that tensions developed which the routine social and climatic processes could not provide for adequately, and then larger-scale techniques were resorted to: warfare and resettlement being the main two. Warfare solved problems usually by reducing the population or readjusting boundaries to better accord with needs. Resettlement was possible only to the extent that there was vacant land to resettle and as population grew over time chances for successful resettlement diminished. But attempted resettlement probably solved more land problems than actual resettlement, in the smaller islands particularly, as the standard reaction to population pressure (usually manifested in dispute) was for the minority or disfavoured group to put to sea in search of a new home. Probably most such persons perished either at sea or on arrival at another populated island at the hands of people not wanting strangers. The infertile Line Islands, Palmerston, Niihoa, and Necker, and many others, show evidence of attempted resettlements which failed, presumably for lack of water.

POST-CONTACT CHANGES

Following European contact, metal tools and weapons (axes and guns in particular) replaced less efficient equivalents and made possible the exploitation of larger land areas or a reduction of working hours to produce the same quantities as before. To acquire the products of industrial technology one had to sell land to Europeans, work for them, or produce cash crops. Whichever choice was made had significant repercussions on land tenure.

The relative values of different categories of land changed markedly. Shallow lagoons which produced *bêche-de-mer* and forests containing sandalwood were traditionally among the less valuable resource areas in the islands, but commerce gave them tremendous value (see Ward, Chapter 4). The most valuable lands of the eastern Pacific had been the artificial swamps and irrigated terraces which grew taro, the rich valley pockets which grew bananas, and the areas close to settlements which produced breadfruit. All these crops grew continuously in one place and produced a large tonnage of food per acre. But none was suited for transport or preservation under the circumstances of the nineteenth century. The providore trade wanted storable foods—sweet potatoes, arrowroot, gourds, yams (Fig. 4.2)—all of which (with the exception of yams in Tonga and Fiji) had been subsidiary foods planted in small quantities. The new trade led to arable land taking on new value, and competition for its use increased greatly, giving rise to much dispute.

The providore trade died away in the late nineteenth century and was replaced by the export trade, which was mainly in tree crops (coconuts, cocoa, coffee, rubber, citrus). With the exception of vanilla (which is grown in significant quantity only in French Polynesia) all other cash crops require a larger area to provide a living than does subsistence production. The transition from subsistence to cash cropping, then, is accompanied by a need for more land per head. The opposite trend applied with foraging land—most of the products of which were replaced by imported substitutes.

Whereas new economic plants were readily adopted, imported livestock (mainly horses, cattle, and goats) were accepted only on a small scale. This was partly because a herd of cattle requires a larger area than many of the blocks into which people divided their land, and partly because the necessity for fencing was sometimes regarded as an affront by neighbours who had rights of access and by those kinsmen who had rights of use.

In no instance was it possible for individuals in Oceania in pre-contact times to live other than by the exploitation of land and water in which they held appropriate rights. The coming of trade resulted in paid employment and the consequent possibility of living without the exercise of land rights. The proportion of people who live without the exercise of such rights is still very low, certainly less than 10 per cent of the population of the Pacific, although in some territories, such as Fiji, the proportion may exceed 25 per cent. Cash income from work is also generally low and employment often insecure, so many who do have jobs continue to use some land in order to demonstrate that they have not relinquished their rights to it.

Social and Political Changes

Mission influence from the early nineteenth century resulted in an increase in the size of the unit within which war did not take place, and in smaller islands peace was established where it had not occurred before. But the missions could not stop the emergence of larger warring units which were facilitated by the new technology.

In the latter half of the nineteenth century the Euro-American colonizing powers established even larger political units and warfare became the prerogative of the colonizing governments. Physical violence was no longer acceptable (at least officially) as a means of acquiring land rights. This was a major change in land tenure, for it seems that the indigenous tenure systems could only cope with changes of a certain magnitude. The major transfers were made by warfare or under threat of warfare. Stopping warfare, then, did away with the usual means for adjusting land rights to major changes in demographic circumstances. Missions and colonial governments were clearly aware of the disruptive effects of warfare, but being inadequately aware of its function in the distribution of land resources, they seldom made substitute provisions to meet this need.

The abolition of warfare did away with the need for 'no-man's lands' between groups, and these were usually encroached upon from both sides and eventually filled. They have been, nevertheless, a frequent cause of subsequent dispute.

The colonial powers tended to increase the rights in land held by the state and by individuals, and to decrease the rights held by intermediate persons and groups. Fiji was an exception, as there the government expanded and formalized the traditional hierarchy of social groups.

A particular land tenure problem arises in societies where inheritance is predominantly matrilineal. It soon becomes known that Europeans, who have so much property, regard themselves as patrilineal, and almost all Pacific islanders have adopted Christianity, a particularly patrilineally oriented religion. Moreover, all colonial powers in the Pacific regard matrilineal inheritance as an aberration which should, immediately or eventually, be adapted to the 'proper' patrilineal or bilineal form.

Economic forces work in the same direction. In most pre-contact matrilineal societies annual crops provided the basis of subsistence and wealth. In those cases where rights to land were inherited mainly through the mother, a man could leave some economic trees to his son. Today, however, tree-crops (coconuts, coffee, cocoa, and rubber) have increased greatly in number and importance, and extensive planting of economic trees has resulted in conflict between the rights of the men who planted them, and their sons on the one hand, and the rights of the matrilineal landholding group on the other.

Notions of land being sacred to persons of a particular lineage or other social group reduce the mobility of people to some extent, and the transferability of land very considerably. Even where economic or political pressure is intense, such as in developing towns, it is not always sufficient to overcome resistance to changes of attitude. The Motu people of Port Moresby, the Samoans of Apia, and the Rarotongans of Avarua have accepted strangers as informal tenants or squatters but have been extremely reluctant to relinquish proprietary rights to any party.

Alienation

Alienation of the best land to foreign settlers was extensive in the larger islands (see Farrell, Chapter 2). In Hawaii most of the highly productive lands were alienated by 1900. Much of the best land in Fiji was alienated before annexation by the United Kingdom in 1874. In New Caledonia the French Government took over the land, leaving only reserves for indigenous people. The Solomon Islands, New Hebrides, and New Guinea were infested with malaria which, along with the aggressiveness of the people, deterred foreign settlement until the twentieth century.

In Papua large areas were acquired by the Australian Government simply by declaring them 'waste and vacant' and offering them for lease to European settlers. The reason that more was not acquired in this way was that not enough settlers could be attracted to take up the lands and many of these lands remained waste and vacant in practice. In New Guinea the German Government acquired 700,000 acres. This was only a small percentage of the total area, but a relatively high percentage of the high quality land close to the main harbours. A new phase of alienation for foreign settlement took place in the New Guinea highlands under Australian Administration in the 1950s. This concerned mainly fertile valley floors which had been relatively lightly populated because of warfare and sickness but which, with peace and a rapidly growing population, would soon have been taken up by indigenous people.

The interest of the United States in Eastern Samoa and Guam was exclusively military, and almost all the land alienated was for military purposes. In the Mariana and Caroline Islands Japan rented the bulk of the agricultural land from the landowners and imported 70,000 Japanese and Okinawan settlers. These settlers were repatriated after the Second World War and the land reverted to the islanders. The Japanese surveyed and registered almost all land in the territory but the records were lost during the war and little has yet been done by the United States administration to re-establish them. As with her other Pacific territories, America's interests in these islands is a military one and until recently intensive concern with land matters has been confined to military requirements.

The small, isolated islands with limited resources—the Marshalls, Gilberts, Ellice, Tokelau, Cooks, and outer Society Islands—experienced very little alienation except when they contained a valuable economic resource like the phosphate on

Angaur, Nauru, Ocean, and Makatea Islands (see Newbury, Chapter 7).

Colonial Policies

Between 1843 when France annexed Tahiti, and 1901 when New Zealand annexed the Cook Islands, almost every piece of land in the Pacific Ocean came under the effective control of one or other of the colonial powers. They all attempted to introduce legal systems which would facilitate the resolution of land disputes, the increase of agricultural productivity, and in some cases the availability of land to foreign settlers.

In the French colonies, the civil law of France was introduced, with little modification to suit local needs. Particularly in French Polynesia, where patterns of inheritance differ in many respects from those of France, the imposition of the metropolitan law has led to deception, confusion, and very low rural productivity.

New Zealand created in her colonies a Land Court modelled on the New Zealand Maori Land Court which had been set up largely to facilitate transfer of land rights to European settlers. These courts were intended to determine rights in accordance with local custom, but they all seriously misunderstood the nature of customary land tenure, particularly in relation to inheritance. What had been ambilineal systems wherein one acquired specific rights from either one's father or one's mother (or some but not all rights from both) were assumed to have been bilineal systems wherein all persons acquired a share of all the rights of both the mother and the father. Thus the number of rightholders in each piece of land more than doubled in each generation.

In Papua and New Guinea, Australia left land disputes to be resolved in accordance with 'custom'. But, as in many other parts of the Pacific, warfare, sorcery, and other traditional mechanisms for the resolution of land disputes were outlawed. Disputes could be taken to a government officer, but he had neither the time nor the knowledge of local language and land tenure to allow him to base his decision on valid criteria, nor adequate machinery to enforce a binding decision. This vacuum was filled from 1964 with the creation of new legal machinery and the return of the major responsibility in land matters to the local people.

In Fiji and the Gilbert and Ellice Islands, the United Kingdom set up local lands commissions using traditional precedents and usually in the hands of indigenous leaders. Along with Tonga these were probably the most efficient tenure systems in the Pacific during the colonial era, but they are too rigid for today's conditions, and more liberal provisions for transfer in particular are widely advocated.

Post-colonial Trends

The Kingdom of Tonga is the only Pacific territory which has never been a colony. There a unique system of land tenure was introduced whereby all land was deemed to belong to the state, but was divided for purposes of administration into large estates each of which was assigned to one or other of the 33 statutory nobles. Within each estate land was divided into $8\frac{1}{4}$-acre blocks, each of which was allocated to one householder, who was also given a $\frac{1}{4}$-acre house-site in the nearest village. The Tongan system is most fully described by Maude (1965). Its main problems result from the influence of the nobility on the working of the system. Nevertheless, Tongan land tenure merits widespread study. It is of interest to note that Tonga is one of the very few Pacific territories which has been able to maintain productivity *per capita* despite a rising population.

Since independence in 1962 Western Samoa has considered a number of tenure reforms but has not yet taken any major step. The Samoan legislature is composed solely of chiefs who are reluctant to approve any move which will reduce their powers over land.

The Cook Islands became self-governing in 1965 and the premier announced his government's intention of modifying tenure legislation by introducing certain traditional precedents to overcome some colonial problems. This has not yet been undertaken.

Tenure systems modelled on those of the colonial powers have been markedly unsuccessful in facilitating increased productivity. The process of devising tenure systems suited to the present and future needs and aspirations of the various island peoples is still moving relatively slowly, and the co-ordination of land tenure reforms into comprehensive development programmes is just beginning.

ATIU ISLAND—A MICROSTUDY[1]

Atiu, although the third largest island in the Cook Group, is only ten square miles in area and has a population of about 1,500 people. The changes, and pressures towards change, that have taken place in land tenure in Atiu illustrate in microcosm many of the changes which have taken place throughout the Pacific in the past 200 years.

The island is roughly circular, and from the fringing reef rise cliffs of upraised coral which form the edge of a rocky plateau about half a mile wide. On the inner edge of the plateau is a depression which contains the island's most fertile land, some of which is permanent swamp and ideal for taro cultivation. Inland the ground rises to a system of eroded, flat-topped ridges which radiate out from the centre of the island.

At the time of first European contact the island was divided into seven wedge-shaped districts, whose boundaries ran from a high point in the centre of the island to the outer edge of the fringing reef (Fig. 9.1). Each of three of the districts was headed by one of the island's three *ariki* or high chiefs, and the other four by senior chiefs called *mataiapo*. In pre-contact times the people lived on the lower slopes just inland of their taro gardens, their house-sites being levelled by digging into the hillsides and using the soil to extend the site forward.

Tengatangi, one of the seven districts of the island, demonstrates common features of the land tenure system. As shown in Fig. 9.2, it was divided into four subdistricts which ideally ran from the central hills to the coast, although one in Tengatangi did not. The three smaller subdistricts were headed by *mataiapo* and the largest by the *ariki* (high chief) of the district. Within each sub-district were separate hamlets each headed by a lesser chief (*rangatira*). The *ariki*'s subdistrict was central. It contained most swamp for taro cultivation and most gardening land. Informants' claims that it was the most populous subdistrict are supported by the fact that it has more extensive and more numerous house platforms.[2] The large *marae*, which was

[1] Most of the field work on which this study is partly based was carried out in the 1950s.

[2] If we accept the rough estimate of 2,000 people for the whole island given by Captain Cook in 1777 (Cook, 1821, 5: 264) and again by Williams (1837: 18) in 1823, there would have been an average of a little under 300 persons in each district, about 80 per subdistrict, and 20 to 30 in each hamlet.

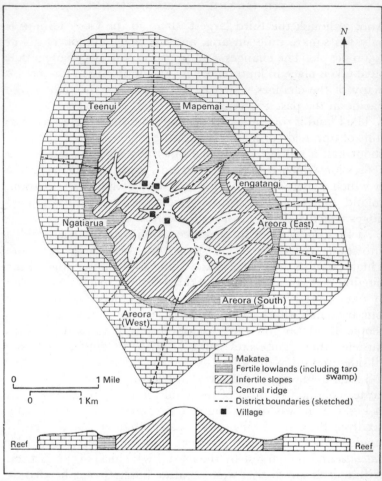

FIG. 9.1. Atiu Island. District lands and soil types. District boundaries are sketched. Soils after Grange and Fox, 1953.

the religious centre of the district, is still visible today near the high chief's former house-site.

Highly valued land was further subdivided amongst much smaller groups for exploitation. This is demonstrated by Fig. 9.3 which shows lot sizes as at 1952. The high central ridges were of little use in pre-contact times and were little divided, but since their use as villages they have been intensively

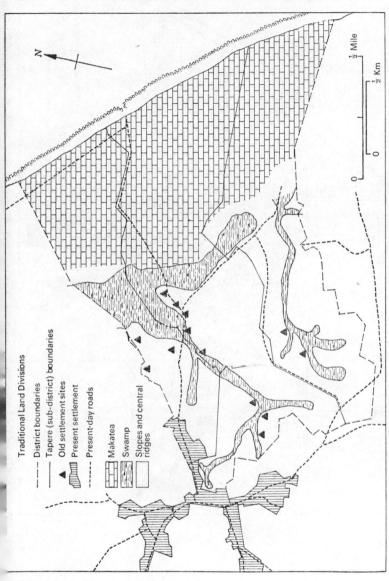

Traditional Land Divisions

--- District boundaries
—— Tapere (sub-district) boundaries
▲ Old settlement sites
▨ Present settlement
--- Present-day roads

▦ Makatea
▥ Swamp
☐ Slopes and central ridges

N

0 ½ Mile
0 ½ Km

Fig. 9.2. District of Tengatangi. Traditional land divisions with traditional and modern patterns of settlement. District and subdistrict boundaries are sketched. Source: field data.

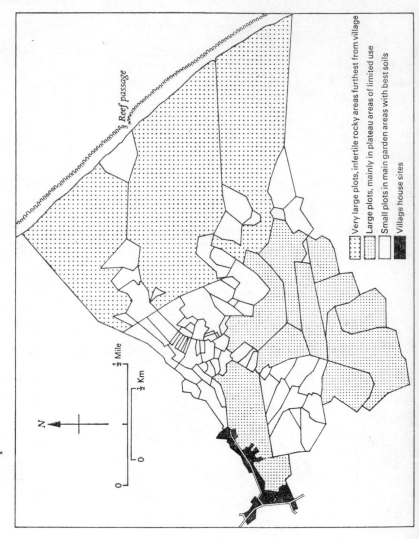

Fig. 9.8. Size of land plots in Tengatangi District, 1952. Boundaries are sketched. Source: field data.

Very large plots, infertile rocky areas furthest from village

Large plots, mainly in plateau areas of limited use

Small plots in main garden areas with best soils

Village house sites

⅓ Reef passage

N

0   ½ Mile

0   ½ Km

subdivided. Conversely, the former residential area near the gardens was presumably more closely subdivided when the hamlets were located there. On the rocky coastal plateau large groups of relatives used large tracts in common. Particular portions were in some cases cut out for use by particular families, but in general the whole of each subdistrict held its coastal plateau land in common. This is still the case today.

Scarce resources facilitate the emergence of increased power for those who control rights to them. The one reef passage in the district was spoken of in the name of the high chief, and though all men of the district could use it he was given a small part of each catch as tribute. There was also a special swamp spring containing a chemical which improved the strength and keeping qualities of fibres which were soaked in it. The spring was more than adequate for the needs of the whole island and all had access to it. No direct reciprocity was made to the landowning group for its use.

Atiuans say that from pre-contact times until relatively recent years all land on the island was associated with one rank title or another. With the exception of conquest, each lineage was autonomous in so far as the internal allocation of its lands was concerned. The only available substantiation comes from Land Court records which show that most of the lands were awarded to their respective claimants without dispute, and despite an interval of 180 years between first European contact and the Court sitting, there is a discernible correlation between original lineage affiliation and the subdistrict in which the lands were claimed. This correlation is far from exact, for in recent years the Court has granted inheritance from both parents instead of one, and marriage gifts, adoptions, and other particular arrangements have tended to blur the outlines. The general pattern is nevertheless clear.

With the exception of conquest, adoption, or asylum given to refugees, all land rights were acquired through either one's mother or one's father. Inheritance was normally from the parent in whose family and lineage one resided, rights to the land of the other parent lapsing unless that parent had been the sole heir to the lands concerned. One did not necessarily acquire rights to use all the lands of the parent from whom inheritance was claimed and, particularly with large families, planting lands were apportioned to various sections of the family.

By custom one did not acquire rights through women except in the event of uxorilocal marriage, illegitimacy, lack of male heirs, or when other abnormal circumstances arose. Such atypical situations arose in just over one-fifth of the cases studied. All claims to land in the district were traceable to a single male ancestor, with one exception. In this exceptional case, the source of the land was a female some three generations back from the claimants. She was quite possibly the sole issue of an earlier male ancestor but my information on the point is incomplete.

Informants' statements and evidence given to the Court show that the retention of land rights under custom required acts of use. There was no fixed period of non-use before rights were considered to be completely extinguished, the actual time for any particular case being determined by the exercise of rights by other rightholders, the need for land, and the status of the parties concerned.

Within the lineage group, the rights of component families and individuals were determined by discussion in the light of needs and of accepted principles and priorities. The final decision, or confirmation of agreement, was a matter for the lineage head. Meetings were held when a dying titleholder wished to settle the distribution of lands before his death, at an adoption, or when lands were to be given in marriage or to a refugee.

Post-contact Changes

Throughout the Pacific, European contact frequently resulted in change in settlement patterns, most commonly a gathering of scattered hamlets into relatively large villages, and often a shift towards the coast. In Atiu the former trend operated but not the latter. The first outsiders known to have landed on Atiu after Cook were Tahitian missionaries who arrived in 1823 and set about bringing the people together from their scattered hamlets to a single centre where they could be given religious instruction away from the environment of their heathen religious practices. All districts meet on the central ridge and each district built its new village on its own lands on one of the ridges radiating out from the central point where the church was built. The three southern districts combined to form a single village. A coastal site would have created difficulties: if a single village were formed people would have had to live on the lands of another district; if separate villages were formed, the influence of the evangelists would have been reduced. The people of each subdistrict initially occupied a particular section within the new village. The previous owners of the land on which the village was built agreed that each family be given a house site for itself and its issue for so long as they cared to remain, but that in the event of their dying out or moving away the land would revert to its original owners. No payment or compensation was made.

The new inland village was without water and was located on infertile land. The people therefore retained their houses on the planting lands. The practice then began of having one house in the village and another (a smaller simpler structure) near the gardens. This practice remains today and is widespread in the Pacific where government or mission pressures have necessitated living far from gardening lands.

With the arrival of the missionaries, acquisition of land by conquest ceased. Polygamy was stopped, and those with more than one wife were required to set the others aside. They returned, with their issue, to their natal lineages and acquired land rights there. These, too, were widespread trends in Polynesia.

In pre-contact times every family grew crops only for its own consumption or for distribution on social and ceremonial occasions. But in the first half of the nineteenth century some of the many whaling, trading, and mission ships which began to frequent the South Pacific also called at Atiu to trade. Fresh foods for the ships' stores, and arrowroot and coconut oil for resale elsewhere, were the first commodities exploited commercially. Coffee, vanilla, cotton, and oranges were later introduced and planted for export. The high chiefs established a market house to regularize trade with ships, and controlled it themselves until towards the end of the century. The chiefs at times instructed their people to plant particular crops, and monopolized their sale, but production was by small groups on family holdings. The tree crops were planted in very small quantities and not in regular rows. All of them seeded and spread. Atiu custom permitted the inheritance of economic trees and movable property to individual cognatic kin (i.e. in practice those descended from females of the owning groups, but living elsewhere). Even more widely spread were rights to take an occasional harvest of chestnuts (*mape*) and other products on occasions when ceremonies necessitated additional supplies.

There was no clear precedent for the exploitation of fruits grown for sale, and the traditional practices could be rationalized as justifying any of several approaches. No new rule seems to have been applied, and disputes over the use of cash-crop trees became a perennial problem. Atiu was no exception in this regard. All the peoples of the Pacific had to adjust their tenure systems to new economic and political circumstances. Few changes were to everyone's advantage and widespread conflict occurred in the application of old rules to new situations.

European traders, usually only two or three of them at any one time, resided on Atiu from the 1840s onwards. Every one for whom details are available lived under the protection of one or other of the three high chiefs, and was supplied with land, and usually a wife, by the patron chief. As in much of the Pacific, the missionaries who visited Atiu regularly warned the chiefs against selling land to foreigners. Europeans were few and as the chiefs allowed them to use such tribal land as they needed for their subsistence, no land sales took place in Atiu. It was protected by its lack of resources and its forbidding reef, for in islands where there were natural harbours and abundant resources, foreign interests almost invariably acquired control over significant areas of land. In Atiu the only lands alienated were small areas given to the missions for churches and residences.

As in most of Polynesia, Micronesia, and Fiji, chiefly power over land increased after European contact until one or other of the colonial powers took the islands over. Thereafter chiefly powers over land waned rapidly except in colonies of the United Kingdom and, to a lesser extent, Germany. The fact of the people being brought together in one settlement from their formerly scattered hamlets was conducive to an increase in the power of the high chiefs. This was accentuated by the high chief's role as mediator between the people on the one hand, and traders, missionaries, and warships on the other. They also represented the island on the Federal Council of the Cook Islands after its formation in 1892. The most outstanding chief, Ngamaru Ariki, bought a ship and promoted export production on a large scale, employing his tribal followers as labour.

The latter part of the nineteenth century is still referred to by the Atiuans as the time of the *mana ariki*—or power of the high chiefs. During this period, they say, the high chiefs were little influenced by their subordinates in the rank hierarchy, and freely deposed title-holders who did not obey their orders. They claim that the high chiefs usurped 'all power' over the lands, and Land Court evidence does indicate that some arbitrary allocations were in fact made. By the turn of the century, at least one title in each of the subdistricts of Tengatangi was held by a member of the high chief's extended family. When the senior branch of the family died out in 1911, there was considerable dispute as to who should take the title. One factor which helped the successful contender was his promise that he would 'give back the people's lands'. Informants said that this 'giving back' referred to the fact that during the previous generation the high chiefs had assumed control over all unoccupied lands, and had also assumed considerable authority over occupied lands. These powers, they said, were to be relaxed, and the lineages were again to resume control of their respective lands. While the power of the high chiefs did increase during the nineteenth century in respect to lands in their districts, even in pre-contact times he had rights to demand produce for district ceremonies and to prohibit the use of land or crops for certain periods in order to reserve supplies of food. Very probably he also had considerable influence in the selection of lesser chiefs.

The Colonial Period

New Zealand annexed the Cook Islands in 1901 and set up a Land Court, to facilitate increased production and to prepare the way for European settlers. The legislation forbade wills, gifts, sales, and other means of transfer among islanders which had constituted a means of adjustment of land rights to meet changing needs. Sale to the government was provided for. Though it was intended that title to all lands on the island be investigated, the Court was fully occupied on other islands until 1909 when the Resident Commissioner who established it retired. By that time it was apparent that European settlement was not going to eventuate, and it was not until 1952 that the bulk of the lands were investigated and titles issued.

In conjunction with the Court investigation in 1952, all lands in the district were surveyed, boundaries were fixed, and accurate plans were drawn. The Court was required by the legislation to determine ownership in accordance with 'ancient native custom', an almost impossible requirement when the context in which the customs operated was so altered by the introduction of commerce, the abolition of warfare, and other radical changes. Moreover, the Court had no research data on which to base its assumptions about customary practice, and could rely only on the statements of witnesses about customary principles—a very different thing.

The Court used three different principles in dealing with the three major categories of land. As there were no villages before the advent of the Europeans, the Court worked on the assumption that no ancient custom existed in relation to village lands, and generally awarded only to those persons actually resident on the particular section, irrespective of the origin or nature of their right. The descendants of the pre-contact owners of the village lands voluntarily waived their claims to either title or compensation. Taro gardens are generally very small and often intensively cultivated. Rights by blood had to be reinforced by recent usage before the Court would make an award. In all other lands the Court recognized the claims of a much wider range of people, often irrespective of use in the last two generations or more, provided a blood right could be traced to the recognized owning ancestor. Other factors were recognized in special cases.

Though the political and judicial powers of the high chiefs were considerably reduced after annexation, and their powers over land were challenged by the existence of a Court which (in the early years at least) publicly announced that chiefly powers over land were to be nullified, it was not until the Court sitting of 1952 that these powers in fact became void. Nevertheless, chiefs of the *ariki* family acquired rights in more land, and in more districts, than did commoners. The average commoner in 1959 had rights in 2·96 plots of land in his own subdistrict, 2·76 plots in the other three subdistricts in the district, and 4·8 plots in all other districts on the island. The average of the four titleholders of the *ariki* family was 5·25 plots in his own subdistrict, 11·25 plots in the other three subdistricts of the district, and 12·75 plots in all other districts on the island.[1]

The most common indigenous form of inheritance was by descent from the parent in whose lineage one resided, and only in exceptional cases did rights pass through females. But the Court included females equally with males in determining original title and, in determining succession to deceased owners, granted title to all descendants of the previous rightholder. This was not in accordance with custom, as it precluded allocations by family agreement as well as the hiving off of females who married out, of absentees, and of adoptees. As a result the number of rightholders now increases each generation in geometric progression.[2]

In Atiu the average section of planting land is six acres in area, and following the Court investigations an average of eighty persons held rights in it. Most of the rights acquired in other subdistricts and other districts were acquired by the operation of the Court, which generally gave equal rights to all descendants of the individual named as the 'source' (whether in the male or female line and whether living on the island or not).

The Court was given mutually incompatible tasks—it was supposed to adhere to custom, but the legislation permitted it to grant only one class of right—a freehold order.[3] Under Atiu

---

[1] Chiefs other than those of the *ariki* family had very little more land than commoners. This illustrates the relative decline in power of the lesser chiefs.

[2] While the Land Court previously recognized some selective criteria in granting succession, it has for the past decade been forced by a decision of the Appellate Court to ignore such criteria. Wills and gifts (which were provided for by custom) were precluded by law.

[3] The term freehold order as used by the legislation has a very different connotation from freehold in its accepted English sense, for among other things an islander with a 'freehold' title cannot sell, will, or otherwise dispose of land.

custom there were many different categories of rights depending on the nature of their origin—whether through males or females; whether varied in accordance with the nature of the right conferred; whether it was a right to plant or merely to collect wild fruits; whether a right to use or merely to participate in decisions about land; whether a right to inherit or to receive tribute from the land in question. The Court was required to determine whether or not a person had a right and if so to award that person a freehold interest. This necessitated the Court's making a value judgement to decide, among the many individuals who had rights of one form or another, which of them it would recognize. Those whose rights were recognized had them standardized by the Court into 'freehold' rights, irrespective of their nature under custom. This standardization was not without advantage, for a considerable amount of dispute had previously existed owing to the multiplicity of rights held in any portion of land.

There was no provision for awarding to lineages or other groups, though there was provision for awarding to chiefs such lands as belong to them by virtue of their office. This latter provision was applied only to the *marae* or sacred ground, and other very small areas.

An error of the Court which was not imposed on it by the legislation was its practice of awarding to persons irrespective of their lineage affiliation. Under custom, land belonged to a defined social group, with a defined leadership system, though the membership of the group was subject to variation. The Court practice has resulted in each piece of land being tied to an ever-increasing number of individuals who are not organized under any system of leadership, and without any provision for transfer or adjustment to suit particular needs. Under custom, land rights were held by members of a single social group.

Informants say that it was 'proper', in former times, for commoners to marry within their own districts, but that this custom has long since ceased to apply. It was only the holders of titles, they claim, who ideally took wives from other districts. Most men now marry women from districts other than their own. Of the thirty-five marriages in Tengatangi at the time of this study, in twenty-six cases one spouse was from another district or another island, and in the other nine cases both husband and wife were from Tengatangi.[1] If, under native custom, land rights were inherited equally from both parents, then the rights of most individuals would be spread fairly evenly throughout the island, but this is not so.

As with land ownership, so with land use, the titled families (particularly those belonging to the *ariki* family) tend to spread over a wider range of both subdistricts and districts. Of the twenty-five commoner households in Tengatangi,[2] twenty-one grew all their subsistence crops within one subdistrict; the other four used land in two. In the matter of cash crops, nineteen of the twenty-five commoner families grew all their cash crops within one subdistrict; the remaining six used two. A household, therefore, does not necessarily grow all its subsistence and cash crops within the same subdistrict, and taking all crops into account, sixteen of the twenty-five households used land in only one subdistrict while six used land in two, and three used land in three.

Of the fifteen chiefly households, nine grew all subsistence crops in one subdistrict, five in two, and one in three. Six grew all their cash crops in one subdistrict, six in two, two in three, and one in four. Taking all crops into consideration, only four of the fifteen chiefly households planted in one subdistrict, four used two, four used three, two used four, and one used five.

The defining of boundaries by the Land Court did away with one major cause of dispute, and has contributed to security of tenure. The determining of owners, in those cases where there was dispute, has likewise made for stability. But the system of awarding equally to members of a number of lineages, knowing that the number of owners and the number of lineages to which they adhere is increasing constantly, has introduced an element of rigidity which offsets the advantages of the Court system. For a person must first obtain the consent of a multitude of co-owners before making use of the land.

In so far as effects on production are concerned, the *per capita*

---

[1] Of these nine, five had partners from different subdistricts within the district, three were from the same subdistricts but from different minor lineages within it, and one was a marriage between parallel cousins (within the same lineage).

[2] Five atypical households were omitted from this analysis—they were those of the L.M.S. pastor, the Catholic caretaker, an employee of the high chief, the policeman, and a woman (with issue but no husband) who lived outside the village and did not plant.

output of export crops has shown no increase since the court awards were made. In fact the highest *per capita* exports were obtained during the period of chiefly power, when the significant factor appeared to be the existence of a functional system of leadership.

Some years ago the New Zealand Government introduced a scheme for the extension of citrus orchards, whereby long-term financial and technical help was made available. At the same time legislation was introduced requiring that this would be available only to individuals and that the one acre of land on which each orchard was to be established would have to be vested by the owning group in the particular individual concerned before assistance would be granted. This system, known as the 'occupation right' system because it gives exclusive rights of occupation to one member of the rightholding group, could be broadened to facilitate reduction of the number of owners of all lands on the island.

Self-government

The Cook Islands became internally self-governing in 1965. The next phase in Atiu's land tenure system cannot be predicted though some current tendencies may be indicative. To some extent the people have resumed their system of informal allocation within the rightholding group, but with markedly less unanimity than before, as the right of the titleholder under law is of the same order as that of all other rightholders, an increasing number of whom no longer belong to his lineage. Moreover, informal partition has no legal validity and the Court seldom permits legal partition.

In so far as the allocation of land among co-owners is concerned, the chiefly powers which were annulled by the Land Court have not been replaced by any alternative system. With such large landholding groups, some system of leadership or organization appears essential. Organization of production has been partially replaced by powers held by the Island Council and Village Committees under which they periodically order the planting of specified minimum quantities of subsistence crops.[1] In recent years it has also been replaced to some extent

[1] The *Cook Islands Review* of Jan. 1967 noted that the Atiu Village Committees

by planting agreements of the co-operative movement whereby each member is obliged to plant a stated amount of a particular crop—usually a cash crop. In work organization, there is a marked increase in the use of tractors and other mechanical equipment, and in the hiring of labour for cash. The co-operative has begun some experiments in the exchange of labour among members.

Owing to the large numbers of rightholders, almost half of whom have migrated to Rarotonga, New Zealand, and elsewhere, it is virtually impossible to negotiate a lease, which is the only legally recognized form of transfer of land rights. This leads to informal arrangements about the use of land for cash cropping which are not only short-term and insecure, but also conducive to exhaustive techniques of land use. Some efficient system of transfer of rights is essential as the rigidity of the Court system of succession has led to a situation where some very small families own large tracts of land which they cannot use, whereas some large families are hampered by an excess of rightholders on relatively small plots of land. The large number of rightholders has not infrequently led to the most forceful members of the family acquiring control of all the family lands while the others migrate to Rarotonga and elsewhere.

In 1960 only three families on the whole island lived permanently on their planting lands, away from the village. All were special cases, but they could be the forerunners of a trend to reside again on the planting lands, as has already developed on some of the neighbouring islands. This trend seemed to be at least partly due to multiple ownership, wherein actual possession is the only effective way to exclude a multitude of co-owners.

In the pre-contact era, the major stress in the system was probably instability of ownership due to a lack of a centralized authority to safeguard rights over the whole island. The mission era introduced such a centralized authority and concomitant stability, though at the cost of greatly reducing the rights of the commoner in relation to those of the high chief. The Land Court adjusted this relationship to the extent of leaving the owning groups without effective leadership and created a

had just ordered each able-bodied man to plant one taro patch, 100 sweet potato plants, 10 bananas, and 50 each of yams, arrowroot, and dry-land taro.

situation wherein a multitude of owners each holds a plethora of fragmented rights in a number of portions of land.

Changes in the tenure system itself have been made in response to pressures of external origin, but changes in the distribution of lands within the system have taken place in accordance with the power and influence of the particular component groups and individuals. The current external pressure on Atiu's land system is the recently established, autonomous Cook Islands Government. What modifications it will introduce are yet to be seen.

BIBLIOGRAPHY

Allan, C. 1957. *Customary Land Tenure in the British Solomon Islands Protectorate*, Western Pacific High Commission, Honiara.

Apple, R. A. 1965. *Trails: From Stepping Stones to Kerb Stones*, Honolulu.

Brookfield, H. C., and Brown, P. 1963. *Struggle for Land*, Melbourne.

Cartland, B. C. 1953. 'Land Tenure in the Gilbert and Ellice Islands Colony', unpublished report, Tarawa.

Cook, J. 1821. *The Three Voyages of Captain James Cook Round the World*, vol. 5, London.

Cook Islands, 1967. *Cook Islands Review*, Rarotonga.

Crocombe, R. G. 1964. *Land Tenure in the Cook Islands*, Melbourne.

Goodenough, W. H. 1961. *Property, Kin and Community on Truk*, Yale University Publication in Anthropology no. 46, New Haven.

Grange, L. I., and Fox, J. P. 1953. *Soils of the Lower Cook Group*, Soil Bureau Bull. no. 8, Wellington.

Groves, M. 1963. 'Western Motu Descent Groups', *Ethnology*, vol. 2, pp. 15–30.

Held, G. J. 1957. *The Papuas of Waropen*, The Hague.

Hiroa, Te Rangi (Buck, P.) 1934. *Mangaian Society*, Honolulu.

Howlett, D. 1962. 'A Decade of Change in the Goroka Valley, New Guinea', Ph.D. thesis, Australian National University, Canberra (mimeo).

Lawrence, P. 1967. In Hogbin, I., and Lawrence, P. (eds.), *Studies in New Guinea Land Tenure*, Sydney.

Maude, A. 1965. 'Population, Land and Livelihood in Tonga', Ph.D. thesis, Australian National University, Canberra (multilith).

Maude, H. E. 1937. *Report of Colonization of the Phoenix Islands by the Surplus Population of the Gilbert and Ellice Islands*, Government Printer, Suva.

Meggitt, M. 1958. 'Salt Manufacture and Trading in the Western Highlands of New Guinea', *The Australian Museum Journal*, vol. 12, pp. 309–13.
—— 1965. *The Lineage System of the Mae Enga*, Edinburgh.

Nayacakalou, R. R. 1961. 'The Bifurcation and Amalgamation of Fijian Lineages over a Period of Fifty Years', *The Fiji Society Transactions and Proceedings*, Suva, vol. 8, pp. 122–33.

Oosterval, G. 1961. *People of the Tor*, Assen.

Panoff, M. 1964. *Les Structures agraires en Polynésie française*, Centre Documentaire pour l'Océanie, Paris.

Pospisil, L. 1965. 'Kapauku Papuan Laws of Land Tenure', *American Anthropologist*, vol. 67, no. 4, part 2, pp. 186–214.

Read, K. 1954. 'Cultures of the Central Highlands, New Guinea', *Southwestern Journal of Anthropology*, vol. 10, pp. 1–43.

Rimoldi, M. 1966. *Land Tenure and Land Use Among the Mount Lamington Orokaiva*, New Guinea Research Bulletin no. 11.

Serpenti, L. M. 1965. *Cultivators in the Swamps*, Assen.

Williams, F. E. 1940. *Drama of Orokolo*, Oxford.

Williams, J. 1837. *A Narrative of Missionary Enterprises in the South Sea Islands*, London.

10

INDIGENOUS HORTICULTURE IN MELANESIA

Some Recent Changes in Eastern New Guinea,
the Solomon Islands, and the New Hebrides

DAVID A. M. LEA[1]

THE indigenous population of the areas under discussion is
approximately 2,500,000,[2] nearly all of whom live in villages
and derive most of their sustenance from the resources of their
own local territories (Bureau of Statistics, 1963: 1). The
indigenous economies naturally reflect a wide range of environmental conditions but most are based on horticulture, with
fishing, hunting, gathering, cash cropping, and trade[3] as subsidiary activities.

The most widespread form of horticulture is that usually
known as shifting cultivation and is practised in the lowland
tropical forests and savanna woodlands occupying the greater
part of Melanesia. A small patch of forest is cleared with axes
and fire but only the soil in the hole containing the plant is
tilled. Gardens are interplanted, with each plant being individually cultured, and after one to three years the garden is

---

[1] Dr. Lea is Professor of Geography, University of Papua and New Guinea.

[2] The Melanesian population of the various territories is as follows: Papua
631,047 (1968), the Trust Territory of New Guinea 1,677,274 (1968), the British
Solomon Islands Protectorate 147,000 (1968), and the Condominium of the New
Hebrides 63,448 (1966).

[3] Before the Europeans entered the area, sago, salt, and fish were the main food
items that stimulated active trade; the *hiri* between the Motuans of the Port
Moresby area and the Koita of the Purari delta (Williams, 1932–3) and the
exchanges between the Iatmül and the Kavleman in the Sepik District (Bateson,
1932: 290) are examples of this. Most other exchanges were in ceremonial items
such as shells, shell rings, axes, ceremonial paraphernalia, feathers, and pigs. The
exchanges of the Kula Ring are the most interesting examples of ceremonial
exchange. Many exchanges took place through a series of middlemen; shells, for
example, reached some of the most inaccessible parts of New Guinea.

abandoned to a long bush fallow of at least eight years to restore fertility to the soils and to suppress weeds and insect pests. However, almost 1,000,000 people live between 4,000 and 7,000 feet in the intermontane valleys of the central cordillera of New Guinea. Highland horticulture contrasts with lowland shifting cultivation in its dependence on the sweet potato and by having ditching, occasional mulching and planting of a tree fallow, the tillage of grassland soils, and a short fallow period followed by a long cultivation period.[1] Both highland and lowland agriculture are similar in that there are many sedentary elements in both systems. Village settlement sites are considered permanent and boundaries of village lands are usually clearly defined;[2] within village boundaries most or all land is claimed by small groups such as clans or sub-clans whose members are linked by a classificatory or biological relationship. Planted trees and palms such as coconut and betelnut palms, *Artocarpus atilis* (breadfruit), *Pommetia pinnata* ('taun'), and *Gnetum gnemon* ('tulip') in the lowlands and *Pandanus jiulianetii* and *P. brosimos* and the highland breadfruit, *Ficus dammaropsis*, in the highlands are important sources of food and other products.[3] In some areas, particularly those with a marked dry season, irrigation of taro has resulted in the cultivation of permanent gardens[4] and in swampy areas and places liable to regular inundation permanent gardens exist on levees or man-made islands (Serpenti, 1965).

The non-horticultural people are the urban dwellers (some 104,000 in New Guinea in 1966), the fishermen of some coastal villages and small islands, and some 90,000 sago-eaters who

---

[1] The best descriptions of highland agriculture are in Brookfield, 1962 and 1964, and Brookfield and Brown 1963: 43–59; the last contains a detailed account of Chimbu agriculture. See also Howlett, 1962; Reay, 1959: 10 ff.; and Meggitt, 1958.

[2] Formerly boundaries were changed only by warfare or the fear of warfare. As the various administrations gained control, boundaries were frozen and in some areas this has resulted in unequal distribution of men and land and in numerous disputes.

[3] For a more comprehensive list of food-producing trees and palms see Massal and Barrau, 1956: 27–43, and Barrau, 1958.

[4] Irrigation was, and still is, practised among a few New Guinea groups such as the Mafalu (Williamson, 1912: 33) and the Karam (Burnett, 1963). The most dramatic manifestations of irrigation are the extensive irrigated taro terraces of Pentacost and West Santo in New Hebrides, and in New Caledonia (Barrau 1956b). Extensive flights of abandoned taro terraces in the interior of Viti Levu provide evidence of a considerable population there in earlier times (Ward, 1965: 18).

live in extensive but thinly populated floodplain and swampy areas of the Sepik, Fly, and Purari rivers of New Guinea.[1] However, the sago-eaters and the fishermen usually cultivate small gardens on levees or any other raised or suitable ground,[2] and the town dwellers are often partly dependent on garden produce from their home villages or grow some of their food in small gardens in or around the towns.

Subsistence gardening has shown relatively little apparent modification from the pre-contact situation compared with social, demographic, and political changes. There has been a general decline in gardening techniques but Europeans have wisely made few deliberate changes and those that have taken place indicate, in a passive sort of way, the effects of culture contacts and general cultural decline. The most important changes were caused by the introduction of steel cutting edges[3] and non-indigenous plants, both of which arrived in some areas via well-established trade routes before the first Europeans.[4] The effects of the introduction of steel are discussed by Salisbury who found that labour-saving tools and pacification[5] resulted in a labour surplus which meant that in most areas men were underemployed.[6] Salisbury probably overstated his case, for recent studies by Crocombe and Hogbin (1963b), Rimoldi (1966), Fountain (1966), and Waddell and Krinks (1968) suggest that not a great deal of time was spent in cutting activities. So even if his time ratio of three or four to one between stone and steel implements is reasonable, and recent

[1] In the areas cited the people make use of natural stands of sago palms as well as planting some palms themselves. Sago was formerly used in Eastern Melanesia. Barrau (1956a: 183) records that according to tradition, sago flour was extracted in both Pentecost and Tanna; Guiart notes similar usage in Santo (1958: 35–6). In South Tanna one man described to me in detail the old extraction process, very similar to that now used in New Guinea.

[2] The Waropen of Irian Barat built platform gardens alongside their pile houses (Barrau, 1958: 15).

[3] Few new tools were accepted. The main exception is the spade which is widely used for tilling and ditching in the New Guinea Highlands. Even today the digging stick is the most popular agricultural tool in lowland areas.

[4] For example see Salisbury, 1962a: 118, 187. For details of introduced crops see Barrau, 1958 and 1960.

[5] Cessation of warfare helped to create a labour surplus for formerly 'a great deal of energy was devoted to warfare' (Belshaw, 1954: 4).

[6] Fisk (1962) sets up a model by which he shows that areas reaching saturation point in relation to land resources would have little surplus as a result of such a technological change.

work by Townsend (1969) suggests that it is, the time saving would not be as impressive as thought. However, steel did mean that time was saved and that men were free to work for Europeans or, if they stayed in their villages, could have more leisure or could concentrate on bigger and better ceremonies and ceremonial crops, there being little need to extend subsistence crops (Salisbury 1962a, 1962b, and 1964). Surplus labour was rarely channelled into cash cropping because the indigenes did not have any incentive (Fisk, 1964) or any worthwhile financial reward.[1]

Before pacification was imposed by the various administrations, new crops, particularly those indigenous to inter-tropical America, had been slowly disseminated, and tobacco, cucumber, pumpkin, watermelon, cassava, and maize had reached many areas. After pacification some early government patrols distributed seeds of European vegetables (Salisbury, 1962a: 42) and labourers working on European plantations or visiting other villages often returned to their own villages with new planting materials.[2] In this way many new crops were introduced and disseminated, but with the exception of cassava, *Xanthosoma*, and sweet potato (in some areas), they did not replace the staple foods. Introduced crops are still considered mainly as supplementary foods or relishes. Where the staple crop has changed, particularly where there has been excessive dependence on the easily grown cassava, some serious nutritional problems have arisen (McKee, 1957: 18), but generally this has happened in association with cash cropping, and imported foods have been able to make up for nutritional deficiencies. Barrau, for example, notes that on the west coast of New Caledonia coffee is harvested from May to August, the season when the annual work of building the yam ridges and taro terraces must be done. Taro has disappeared and yams are now planted at the end of the coffee harvest and with much less care than was given to them formerly. In this context *Xanthosoma* and bananas, which are easier to grow, have become more important and the traditional subsistence crops have lost

[1] The increase in leisure may have been one of the factors which, like disease, the freezing of village boundaries, and the cessation of fighting, often took the spice out of life and led to a general decline in cultures.

[2] Natives travelling with the author have often collected propagating material of food plants and varieties of yam, taro, and banana unknown in their own villages.

importance (Barrau, 1958: 84–5). As men become more interested in cash cropping it seems inevitable that yams will be replaced by cassava and sweet potato, and taro (*Colocasia*) will be replaced by *Xanthosoma*. These crops are less time consuming, higher yielding, and generally faster maturing.[1] It should be noted, however, that these new crops are very similar to traditional staples and it seems that in the initial stages of culture contact 'the acceptability of a new food plant is in proportion to the similarity it has to traditional subsistence crops so that it involved no change in land use technology or land holding' (Barrau, 1958: 86). Thus maize, the only cereal successfully introduced, was accepted because it resembles 'pit pit' (*Saccharum edule*) which has an edible inflorescence (Barrau, 1958:49).

New varieties of plant species already adapted in ecological and human terms were also widely disseminated in this period, often to great effect. Frazer (1964: 150) shows how new types of taro which tolerate dry conditions were introduced into Fiji and were one of the factors that led to the abandonment of the irrigated taro terraces of Viti Levu. The spread of new varieties of yam, taro, sweet potato, and bananas has, like the introduction of new plants, added variety to the diet and in a few cases diet has been definitely improved.[2] Total yields have been increased by the dissemination of varieties which are high yielding while others have allowed new environments to be cultivated. An example is the spread of yam varieties which are tolerant to wet conditions (Lea, 1966: 7).

It is, however, in the growing of cash crops that the most dramatic changes are taking place today. These are most significant in their economic context but they also have far-reaching effects in weakening traditional forms of organization and land use (Ward, 1965: 210). Every year more and more Melanesians are practising some form of cash cropping, and in New Guinea over 60 per cent of the males of employable age are engaged in the full-time or part-time production of cash crops.

The growing of cash crops is a comparatively recent develop-

---

[1] See Allen (1957: 189) who states that in the West Solomons the best species of taro have died out and sweet potato has become the staple.

[2] The Okinawa variety of sweet potato introduced into New Guinea by the Japanese during the war has a high protein content (Bailey, 1963*b*: 24).

ment in all the territories under discussion. Cheetham (1962–3), Miles (1956), Shand (1963), Crocombe (1964), and many others have dealt with attempts to encourage indigenous commercial agriculture in Papua and New Guinea before the war and they all came to the same general conclusion that these schemes, nearly all based on some form of compulsion (Miles, 1956: 324–6), foundered on problems of land tenure, work organization, motivation, and income distribution. Cheetham (1962–3: 68) rather generously estimates that from just over £1,000,000 earned from agricultural exports in Papua and New Guinea in 1938–9, no more than a quarter of total exports by value was produced by village farmers. In the late 1930s indigenous production in the New Hebrides was estimated at one-sixth of total production of cash crops while in the Solomons indigenous production was rarely more than one-seventh (N.I.D., 1945: 564, 657).

Most of the income from native crops before the Second World War was obtained from the products of the coconut tree, and plantings on a non-plantation basis involved no changes in land use or land holding. With coastal people like the Tolai of New Britain 'the arrival of European traders enabled them to cash in on an already existing but imperfectly utilized resource' (Salisbury, 1962b: 333).[1] Before 1939 there were few incentives for natives to accumulate money and their few cash needs were met by selling their labour, although there were exceptions and in some localities significant amounts of cash were obtained by selling food to urban areas (e.g. Mele village near Vila), and by the sale of handicrafts, fish, animal products, minerals, or land. Generally, commercial effort and needs ran parallel to the subsistence economy and were not integrated into the indigenous way of life. As Barrau says 'the beginning of native commercial agriculture represented a re-orientation of existing agricultural practices rather than the introduction of entirely new practices' (Barrau, 1960: 7). When cash was needed for some specific purpose, coconuts were collected and copra prepared.

[1] In Fiji there has been some commercialization of subsistence crops, particularly bananas and *yaqona*. In the areas under discussion some cash income is obtained by selling surplus garden production at local markets but the potential for replacement of imported foods is very great, especially if vegetable marketing boards were established.

Although pre-war agricultural development was concentrated on the establishment of European plantations, many Melanesian plantation labourers, who usually worked away from their villages for periods greater than two years,[1] developed new aspirations (and prejudices) and gained experience of a money economy as well as cash crops. It was also on the plantations that Melanesians first saw cattle and better breeds of indigenous animals such as dogs, fowls, ducks, and pigs. When they returned to their villages they occasionally took with them better breeds of the traditional animals, but this has not led to any great dietary change. Poultry is still rarely eaten in many areas, being kept for feathers (Conroy, 1953: 27) or for sale to Europeans, and pigs, although larger than they were, are still primarily an indication of wealth and are only occasionally eaten on ceremonial occasions. It is goats and cattle that now offer the greatest potential, in spite of problems of grazing rights, technological novelty, and danger to crops. Studies by Allen (1957: 24) in the Solomon Islands and by Anderson (1962) and Jackson (1965) in New Guinea show that there is a widespread desire among Melanesians to own cattle both for the prestige of ownership and as a source of meat and wealth.[2]

Since the war and particularly since 1956, the indigenes have been making an increasing contribution to commercial farm production (Shand, 1963; I.B.R.D., 1965: 82). Figs. 10.1, 10.2, and 10.3 show the indigenous production of copra, coffee, cocoa, and rubber by districts in the New Guinea territories

[1] In 1950 the indenture system in New Guinea was replaced by a system of labour under agreement, all penal sanctions against workers being removed.

[2] In all the island groups most of the cattle are owned by Europeans or Chinese and are primarily used to control growth of grass and regrowth and to supply meat to plantation labour. Until recently livestock rarely made any significant contribution to plantation income for markets, both local and overseas, have not been available because of a lack of freezing or canning works. Even today in Papua and New Guinea locally killed cattle supply only a fraction of requirements (imports of meat and meat preparations into Papua and New Guinea were valued at over $A8,100,000 in 1967–8). There has been a significant increase in interest in cattle in the New Hebrides since cold storage was installed in Vila and Santo and exports (mainly to French Polynesia) have risen sharply in the last few years. In 1968, the approximate number of cattle in each of the island territories was as follows (numbers owned by indigenes in brackets):

Papua and New Guinea 59,335 (4,425);
B.S.I.P.   9,969 (1,000);
New Hebrides   69,100 (5,300).

and the Solomon Islands, and Fig. 10.4 shows how indigenous production is increasing relative to plantation production in

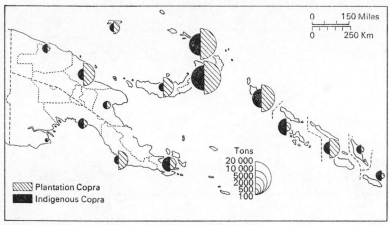

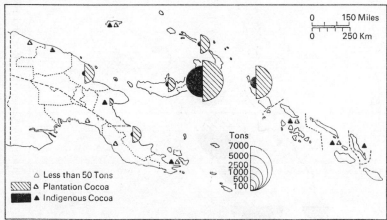

FIG. 10.1. Indigenous and expatriate copra production in Papua New Guinea and the Solomon Islands, 1968. Production for the Eastern District of the B.S.I.P. includes the Santa Cruz Islands. Sources: B.S.I.P. (Agric. Dept.), 1968; D.A.S.F.; Bureau of Statistics, Port Moresby.

FIG. 10.2. Indigenous production of cocoa, 1968. Sources: As in Fig. 10.1.

New Guinea. Similar trends are apparent in the Solomon Islands where indigenous production has increased (Tedder, 1966) and is now between 70 and 80 per cent of total production (B.S.I.P. Agric. Dept., 1968). In the New Hebrides it is widely

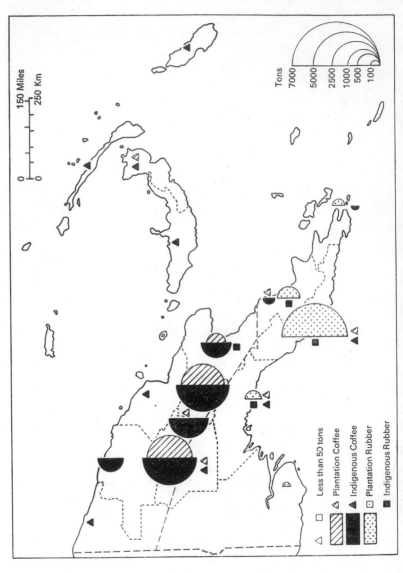

Fig. 10.3. Indigenous production of coffee and rubber, 1968. Sources: As in Fig. 10.1.

believed that the indigenous share of production is now about 60 to 65 per cent of the total and still increasing. In New Guinea there has recently been a considerable diversification of agricultural production. Fig. 10.5 and Table 10.1 show that the most important of these new crops are coffee and cocoa but

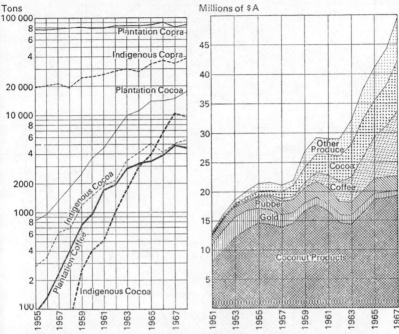

FIG. 10.4. Indigenous production and plantation production of principal commodities in Papua and New Guinea. Coconut oil was converted on the assumption that 1 ton of coconut oil = 1·6 tons of copra. Sources: The Annual Reports of T.P.N.G.; D.A.S.F. Crop Statistics 1969; Bureau of Statistics 1968.

FIG. 10.5. Value of principal commodities in the export trade of Papua and New Guinea, 1950–68, by three-year running averages. Sources: Oversea Trade Bulletin; T.P.N.G.

rice, passionfruit, pyrethrum, rubber,[1] tobacco, tea, and pea-nuts are of importance in some areas, while truck crops and fruits supply local markets. With the exception of food crops which are supplied to towns and plantations, copra remains

[1] Rubber production except for ⅓ ton produced in the Morobe District is restricted to Papua and indigenous production is only about 0·23 per cent of total production.

the only agricultural crop of any importance in both the Solomons and the New Hebrides (see Figs. 10.6 and 10.7).

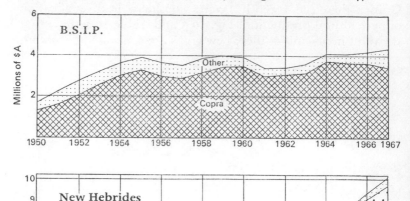

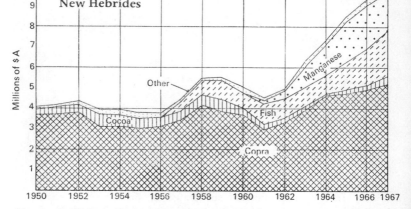

FIG. 10.6. Value of copra in the export trade of the British Solomon Islands Protectorate. Sources: **B.S.I.P.** *Biennial Reports* and Comptroller of Customs and Excise.

FIG. 10.7. Value of copra and other principal commodities in the export trade of the Condominium of the New Hebrides. Note the production of frozen fish began in 1958 and manganese in 1963. Severe hurricanes occurred in 1960 and 1964. Sources: Condominium of the New Hebrides, *Biennial Reports* and Customs Department.

Nearly all the increased production comes from smallholder gardens which are the basis of indigenous economic development. Gardens viewed in this context are an active agent of change and are a catalyst for some widespread ecological, social, political, and economic changes.

THE ABELAM: A CASE STUDY

Some of these changes and important recent developments can be illustrated by the Abelam, who are a group of some 30,000 people living around the outstation of Maprik on the southern slopes of the Prince Alexander Ranges in the Sepik District

TABLE 10.1. *Value of Principal Commodities as a Percentage of the Value of Total Export Production*

	1954	1968
PAPUA AND NEW GUINEA		
Copra and coconut oil	74·6	36·3
Gold	12·6	1·4
Rubber	5·5	3·3
Coffee	0·5	24·3
Cocoa	2·3	20·0
Timber	1·6	8·4
	97·1	93·7
BRITISH SOLOMON ISLANDS		
Copra	84·6	68·4
Timber	3·6	26·6
Shell	10·4	0·8
Scrap Metal	0·2	1·2
Cocoa	..	1·0
	98·8	98·0
NEW HEBRIDES		
Copra	78·4	53·5
Cocoa	16·3	5·2
Coffee	2·3	0·6
Frozen Fish	..	23·0
Manganese	..	14·5
	97·0	96·8

SOURCES: As for Figs. 10.5, 10.6, and 10.7.

of New Guinea. They live in about eighty villages and (if 260 square miles of unsettled and virtually unused grassland within their territory are excluded) in an area of about 290 square miles. This gives an overall population density of 110 people per square mile, but men and land are very unevenly distributed and in parts of the Wosera population densities rise to 400 people per square mile (Fig. 10.8).

Justly renowned for their 'Tambaran' houses, their art work, and the cultivation of large ceremonial yams,[1] the Abelam serve as a good example for two reasons. First, they were studied by an anthropologist, Dr. Phyllis Kaberry, in 1939–40

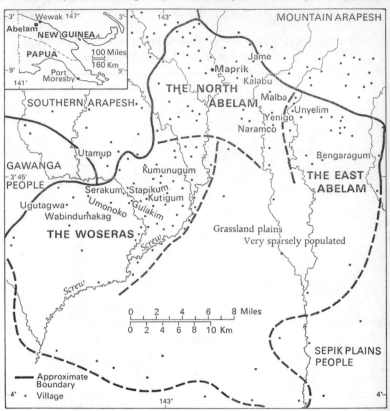

FIG. 10.8. Abelam regions and population distribution. This map was first published in *Pacific Viewpoint* (Lea, 1965) and is used here with the kind permission of the editor, *Pacific Viewpoint*.

shortly after permanent European contact was made in 1937 (see Kaberry, 1941, 1941–2, 1965–6).[2] Secondly, European

[1] These are the most obvious manifestations of the closely integrated Yam and Tambaran Cults (for details see Kaberry, 1941: 355–8) which are 'bound up with kinship obligations and co-operation, with political authority, with the economic system, and a set of values and a whole body of moral and ritual sanctions operating in widely different departments of social life' (Kaberry, 1941: 367).

[2] A patrol station was established at Maprik in 1937 and an agricultural station at Bainyik in the following year.

contact has had a markedly different impact on the relatively sparsely populated northern Abelam areas from that on the densely populated south-western part known as the Wosera. This intra-cultural comparison means that social and environmental stresses (e.g. land shortage, poor nutrition, land disputes, and deteriorating garden habitats) which are characteristic of the Wosera, can be studied as a factor inducing cultural change (Lea, 1965).

It appears that Richard Thurnwald was the first European to go through Abelam territory when, in 1914, he travelled from the Sepik River to the north coast approximately along longitude 143° E. There followed a long, poorly documented and traumatic period of culture contact with labour recruiters and alluvial gold miners.[1] In 1937 the *New Guinea Handbook* stated that much of the area was unexplored 'but consequent upon activities of prospectors . . . government influence is gradually being extended' (1937: 93). By the time permanent European contact was made the initial transition period from 'stone to steel' was over and many of the most important crop introductions had been made. Kaberry, in 1940, reported: 'European articles such as axes, knives, matches, razor blades, beads, lap-laps, belts, pipes and spoons have been adopted, and such vegetables as tomatoes, cucumbers, beans, onions and pumpkins are grown. Apart from the suppression of head hunting, fighting and burial inside dwelling houses, the administration has not interfered with native custom' (Kaberry, 1941: 236). Since then many other crops have been introduced but probably the dissemination of native varieties within the area has been of greater significance. In pre-contact times there were regional preferences for certain types of yam within the Abelam area. Today these prejudices are breaking down. The most interesting example of the dissemination of native varieties in the Abelam area has been the spread of the *asagwa* variety of yam (*Dioscorea esculenta*) which is high yielding, has a high protein content and will tolerate a wide range of environmental

[1] For an example of long contact Kaberry reports that two natives living in Kalabu village had been indentured under German rule. The traumatic aspects can be illustrated by the murder of a recruiter at Lehinga and a subsequent punitive expedition (Territory of New Guinea, *Annual Report* 1936/7: 35). In 1937 there were fifty gold miners in the area (Territory of New Guinea, *Annual Report* 1937/8: 122).

conditions including occasional flooding. In pre-contact times this variety was grown in the Wosera area only (Lea, 1966).

The Abelam are shifting cultivators growing mainly yams[1] and taro (*Colocasia esculenta*) in gardens known as *ka* gardens, which average just over half an acre in size. These gardens are very productive and despite considerable interplanting with crops such as taro (yielding approximately two tons an acre) bananas, beans, green vegetables, corn, cucumbers, tobacco, and sugar cane, yields of *D. esculenta* (*ka*) alone vary from six to nine tons per acre (Lea, 1964: 101–7). Each garden is intensively cropped once; most of the main crop of yam and taro matures within nine months of planting, but the harvesting of secondary crops such as banana, 'pit pit' (*Saccharum edule*), sugar, paw paw, and propagating material for new gardens continues until the fence collapses or garden regrowth swamps the useful plants, usually six months to a year after the main harvest. The garden remains under fallow for a period of from five years to occasionally more than twenty years depending on factors such as the availability of land, rights of access to land, and the productivity of the soil. The Abelam also obtain significant amounts of food from planted trees and palms. The flour extracted from the pith of the sago palm (*Metroxylon sagu*) is the staple food during a dietary lean period which lasts from about March to early June. During this period most of the protein in the diet is provided by green leaves, the most important by far being the leaves of the *Gnetum gnemon* (Lea, 1964: 139 ff.). Coconuts are important in the diet all the year while the breadfruit (*Artocarpus atilis*) and the 'taun' nut (*Pommetia pinnata*) are seasonal. Food items such as tinned meat and fish, salt, sugar, and rice are gradually becoming more important in the diet in all areas. Among the North Abelam in particular tinned meat and rice (grown and milled locally) are making an increasingly beneficial contribution to diet especially in the dietary lean period, and the more sophisticated items now being offered for sale in many trade stores are certainly providing a stimulus for the acquisition of money.

The principal focus of Abelam interests and values is not so much on the ordinary food crops or gardens, but on the growing

---

[1] Most of the yams are *D. esculenta* (*ka*) but a few are *D. alata* (*wapi*), *D. bulbifera* (*lipma*), *D. pentaphylla* (*yabweo*), and *D. nummularia* (*wapi*).

of long ceremonial yams up to 12 feet in length (Forge, 1962: 10) in special gardens known as *wapi* gardens which are only about one-tenth of an acre in size. These gardens are taboo to women and children and the yam growers have to observe sexual taboos during the yam growing period. Although ceremonial yams are not important in terms of diet, it is on their ability as yam growers and within the context of the yam cult that men acquire fame and positions of leadership within the village.

Until recently the agricultural cycle in both *ka* and *wapi* gardens reflected the seasonal rainfall distribution. Clearing took place towards the end of the dry season (August to September), planting of yams at the beginning of the wet (October to January) and harvesting of yams six to nine months later in the middle of the dry season (May to August). In the last twenty years however, there has been a trend among the North Abelam to plant *ka* gardens in all months of the year.[1] This is partly due to encouragement by Administration officers in an attempt to alleviate the annual lean periods with their excessive dependence on sago, but also due to the disruption of a fairly strict agricultural calendar (cf. Kaberry, 1941: 233, 346, 350) caused by absenteeism of adult males and the breakdown of the communal (and reciprocal) labour necessary in the preparation of a garden.[2] In terms of diet this tendency has had a beneficial effect for tubers are more nutritious than sago,[3] but the breakdown in the seasonal orientation of activities has meant that during the ceremonially active period (the dry season) men are faced with a choice of activities and often the ceremonial suffers (cf. Belshaw, 1954: 98).

[1] Belshaw (1954: 98) notes a similar tendency throughout Melanesia, particularly in some parts of Gela (Florida Island).

[2] It appears that in most years there is no significant difference in the yields of yams planted in the dry season or the wet season. This certainly applied to 1962 when the author carried out yield trials. In a drought, such as that of 1965, yams planted in the dry season were so small that they were not harvested when the yam vine dried out after six months and were left in the ground undisturbed and harvested a year after the initial planting.

[3] In the Wosera (where until recently the Administration has not been active and from where few men were recruited), the old agricultural calendar is still observed and Drs. Bailey (1963*a* and *b*) and McLennan (personal communication) found a significant weight fluctuation during the year. As money becomes more common there is an increasing dependence on trade store foods which often has detrimental effects on diet (McKee, 1957: 15).

The increasing dietary acceptance of the sweet potato has also resulted in the productive life of some gardens being extended, for cuttings are planted in gardens after the yams are harvested.[1] This means that gardens are producing root crops for fifteen to eighteen months instead of just nine. When rice is planted as a cash crop the gardening period may be even longer. Huge rice gardens are planted[2] and when the rice has been harvested the gardens are planted with yams in the traditional manner and then, if the fence does not collapse, they may be planted with sweet potatoes in the manner just described. Thus gardens are being cultivated for longer periods and land is used more frequently because the population is increasing[3] and some former gardening land is taken out of production for cash crops. As a result, the cultivation factor falls rapidly.[4] From a long-term point of view, without any technological change this can only result in deterioration of the garden habitats especially when the fallow period falls to less than ten years (Nye and Greenland, 1960: 130).

Within the subsistence gardens it is difficult to tell what is happening, for no quantitative studies were made of Abelam gardens before 1961. Certainly the Abelam and especially the Woseras are not showing as much pride in their gardens as they once did. Informants repeatedly asserted that the yams are not as big as they used to be[5] and that the gardens are more untidy than formerly. The *ka* gardens no longer have

---

[1] There is no evidence that sweet potato, cassava, or any other crops are as yet displacing the staple garden crops which are difficult to grow (cf. Ward, 1960: 40) although sweet potato is replacing sago in the dietary lean period. No doubt replacement will follow in a few generations as taste prejudices are broken down.

[2] These rice gardens, often four to five acres in extent, are communally cleared but are actually contiguous family gardens, each planted and harvested by the family.

[3] The overall rate of natural increase between 1956–7 and 1961–2 was 2·8 per cent p.a.

[4] The cultivation factor $= \dfrac{\text{fallow period} + \text{cultivation period}}{\text{cultivation period}}$ (Allan, 1949 and 1965).

[5] This statement was made once when I was weighing a yam of 140 lb., 8 ft. 11½ in. long. Certainly Kaberry (1965–6: 370) and bamboo measures (which show identical lengths for certain yams in many villages) demonstrate that yams were frequently over 11 feet in length. The Wosera gardens were halfheartedly weeded and tended, and indeed many gardens no longer have a pig-proof fence. As a result pigs often invade the gardens and cause considerable damage which in turn initiates numerous disputes between the gardener and the suspected pig owner.

the 'neat geometrical pattern' noted by Kaberry (1941: 239) in 1940 nor are they 'laid out in an exemplary tidy fashion', described by Thurnwald (1914: 83) who added: 'Bananas, taro, and yams are planted in straight lines and at good intervals. Rattan cords are used for laying out.' Such practices are never seen today and often even the ceremonial yams are planted in the *ka* gardens mixed with ordinary food crops. This practice is becoming more widespread so that some villages, even in the North Abelam area, have few or none of the traditional *wapi* gardens. Certainly as the geographical exclusiveness of the village continues to break down, the men in particular are spending a smaller proportion of their time in the gardens and more in visiting, employment away from the village, and cash cropping.

In relation to subsistence gardening the examination and comparison of aerial photographs taken in 1939 and 1958[1] show an intensification of land use and dispersal of settlements and gardens over a period of twenty years. Unfortunately it is impossible to map these trends owing to the poor quality of the earlier prints, and the altitude from which they were taken obscures much of the detail.

With regard to intensification it is difficult to tell whether this is solely due to increased population or whether there is more garden land being cultivated per head of population. On the whole an increasing area under crops per head of population can be assumed, for subsistence needs today are about the same as they were in the pre-contact period, while increasing areas are being planted under semi-permanent crops. The little land that has been taken out of production because some food is obtained with cash would be more than compensated for by land being planted with food for larger and better ceremonies or the keeping of more pigs.

Although grassland areas have not been extended, the bush fallow in 1958 appears to be thinner and lower than in 1939. Dispersion of gardens and settlement is partly the result of intra-village disputes in the Wosera (Lea, 1965) but in all areas there is no longer any need for group solidarity for defence or mutual protection. Also, as Salisbury noted among the Siane,

[1] Aerial photographs taken in 1939 by Adastra Airways for the Australian Petroleum Co. and in 1958 for the Division of National Mapping, Canberra.

the 'more intensive use of land near traditional enemies permits a more rational use of land based on the potentialities of the land rather than on the fear of being raided' (Salisbury, 1964: 4). Among the Abelam there is now a noticeable tendency to garden in the densely forested areas which used to separate a village from its traditional enemies.

Prior to the early 1950s surplus labour caused by labour-saving tools and the cessation of fighting (which was endemic in pre-contact times) was dispersed into some huge hostile exchanges which are recent in origin (Lea, 1964: 60, cf. Salisbury, 1962b: 329) and also into more inter-village visiting and working away from the villages.[1]

Since the Second World War and particularly since 1955-6, the most dramatic changes have centred around the widespread planting of cash crops by indigenes within the framework of traditional tenure systems where each family is encouraged to plant cash crops separately on land to which it has traditional rights.[2]

The history of cash cropping in the area, though short, has not been a happy one and many men, particularly in the North Abelam area, are suspicious of attempts by the Administration to extend planting because of past failures and falling prices. Peanuts and rice were the first cash crops introduced to the villagers. After considerable extension work by the Administration in the early 1950s there were widespread plantings of peanuts and by 1958-9 over 120 tons were grown in the sub-district. Peanuts were sold initially for $5\frac{1}{2}d$. a pound but after 1959-60 the price fell to $2d$. or $1\frac{1}{2}d$. a pound. Enthusiasm for planting dropped with the returns[3] and now peanuts are grown only for home consumption and for the local Maprik market

---

[1] Nearly all the men from the North Abelam spend an average of three years working away from their villages. Most of them worked on plantations in the Bismarck Archipelago before 1960 but in the mid-1960s 60 per cent of absentee males were in the towns.

[2] See Cheetham, 1962-3: 68. There have been no communal plantations in the Maprik area (cf. Sub-District Annual Reports, 1964-5, which report communal rice gardens). In all the villages I visited in 1965-6 the larger rice gardens were all contiguous family gardens.

[3] Cf. Anas, 1957: 81, when a drop in price from £110 to £60-70 per ton of rice resulted in loss of cultivators' enthusiasm in the Mekeo. However, money is not the only incentive. Epstein (1963: 292) recognized a decline in copra production when German regulations in 1901 forbade the use of *Tambu* (traditional shell money) in New Britain. Note that in this paper values are in £Australian or $Australian. £1A equals $2A.

which is usually glutted.[1] Production of rice has fluctuated greatly over the past few years but recently there has been some increase.[2] In the early 1960s this was due mainly to the efforts of non-Abelam people in the Dreikikir area and in the late 1960s to the desire to own motor vehicles to operate on the new Maprik–Wewak road. Rice growing provided one of the few ways of raising cash quickly. The growing of rice demands much more effort than the growing of other cash crops and it is more susceptible to the vicissitudes of weather and insect pests. As the price paid to natives for paddy is only three cents a pound many of the more sophisticated North Abelam believe that the return for growing rice is too low to warrant the effort. There is a similar tendency with coffee growing. Even when the Maprik Census District was receiving a large proportion of the coffee income in the area, most of the new planting among the Abelam was being done in the Wosera (see Table 10.2). By 1969 the North Wosera had three times as many coffee trees bearing (160,000) as the Maprik Census District.

TABLE 10.2. *Coffee Plantings by Census Districts*

	New plantings		Trees bearing	Total no. of trees	Production (lb.)
	1964	1965	1964	1964	1965
Maprik	7,113	1,150	13,216	34,796	12,105
North Wosera	23,344	7,076	6,097	54,466	1,347

SOURCE: Unpublished Maprik Subdistrict Annual Reports.

Robusta coffee (*Coffea canephora*) was first planted in the Abelam area in 1957 and is now the main cash crop. Because it has been foreshadowed for a long time that the production of New Guinea coffee will soon be in excess of the Australian and allotted overseas markets, the policy of the Department of Agriculture, Stock and Fisheries (D.A.S.F.) is neither to encourage nor discourage native plantings of coffee, but nevertheless plantings are still being made.

[1] No processing of peanuts was attempted in the area and the high freight rates to the coast are alleged to be the main cause of 'adverse marketing conditions'.

[2] Eighty-nine tons of rice were produced in the Maprik sub-district in 1960–1 giving an income of $4,682; 459 tons in 1964–5 giving an income of $25,722, and nearly 1,300 tons in 1968–9 giving an income of about $81,000.

A significant difference exists in the attitude to cash cropping between the North Abelam and the Wosera which cannot be ascribed just to suspicions or to the feeling of 'once bitten twice shy'. The North Abelam are 'remarkable for the tenacity with which they have clung to their ancestral culture' (Forge, 1962: 9), and traditional beliefs are still widely held; the introduction of new ideas or techniques is usually met with disinterested toleration or active resistance. In the Wosera, however, the characteristic features of the region are chronic land

TABLE 10.3. *Coffee in the Maprik Subdistrict*

	Mature trees (acres)	Production (lb.)	Native income ($A)
1960	n.a.	Nil	Nil
1961	n.a.	1,200	n.a.
1962	14	4,183	352
1963	58	6,615	456
1964	71	18,000*	1,500*
1965	109	54,517	6,296
1969	2,253	1,427,000*	149,500*

SOURCE: Unpublished records, D.A.S.F.
* Approximate figure only.

shortage, malnutrition, insensitive initial culture contacts by both mission and Administration and rapid increase in population; here the people depend on change and outside contacts for viability, because the subsistence economy is inadequate in the present demographic context.[1] In the northern villages where land is comparatively plentiful and fertile, traditional values are retained because the villages can remain economically autonomous (Lea, 1965: 209). The North Abelam can obtain his cash needs for clothing, trade store goods, and tax from a little cash cropping, remittances from kinsmen working away from the villages, selling native art, washing for alluvial gold, and selling garden crops in the Maprik market.[2] Until

[1] This was aggravated by the fact that until recently the Woseras were not accepted by recruiters for they had a reputation for thieving and deserting. There is no gold in the Wosera rivers, they are far from the Maprik market, and they have very few artefacts or works of art left.

[2] In 1968–9 New Guineans in the Maprik sub-district earned approximately $3,000 from the sale of artefacts, $10,300 from gold, $4,000 by selling vegetables, and $20,500 for supplying building materials and for casual labour on airstrip and

a good road to the coast was built the North Abelam had no incentive to extend plantings, and cash cropping remained a peripheral interest. In the early 1960s a little coffee was often planted, more to satisfy extension officers than in the hope of a cash return later.[1]

Throughout Melanesia field workers have noticed that the development of cash crops tends to encourage a more individualistic attitude inducing the collapse of the basic traditional system (Barrau, 1958: 9; Ward, 1965: 210–12). One way in which this can be illustrated is in a changing attitude to land tenure.

Among the Abelam the customary practice is for gardens containing annual crops to be planted on land which is the property of the gardener's group (i.e. clan or sub-clan), or he obtains usufructuary rights to the land of another group (Lea: 1969). Useful trees and palms such as coconuts, betelnut palms, and breadfruit trees are planted individually around the villages and along ridge tops without regard for land ownership, for trees planted in these positions do not prevent land being used for gardening. The trees, unlike the land, are considered to be the individual planter's property and are inherited patrilineally.[2] When land is borrowed the planter enjoys rights to the land without payment or rent to the lenders from the time when the bush is first cut until all the crops are harvested, and, if trees are planted on the upper slopes, right to the trees continues until they die.

In spite of the efforts made by extension officers to prevent it, traditional practice has been used in coffee gardens and there are several well-documented cases of men planting blocks of coffee on land to which they had only usufructuary rights (cf. Howlett, 1962: 91 ff.). It seems inevitable that as the land normally used for traditional gardens will be tied up for long periods and will provide a cash income, disputes over ownership of both land and trees will result or land rent will be demanded. In

road construction (Subdistrict Office, Maprik). This is only 73·4 per cent of the income obtained from similar sources in 1964–5.

[1] For example, in the North Abelam area many gardens have been planted with shade trees (*Leucaena glauca*) for two to four years, but little planting of coffee has followed.

[2] Sago is an exception, for blocks of palms were planted in swampy ground which is owned by clan or sub-clan.

the Wosera (renowned already for its land disputes) there is a definite tendency for groups to refuse to lend land for any purposes to men outside the land-holding group. Thus, because the man–land ratio of each land-holding group is different, the land is being very unevenly utilized. This tendency, which is happening elsewhere (Irwin, 1963: 36 and Salisbury, 1964: 8), is partly due to land shortage but also to the fact that land is valuable in terms of cash—not only for cash crops but for renting to land-hungry villages or individuals. Land in other words is acquiring a monetary as well as a subsistence value (Conroy, 1962: 23).

With perennial cash crops, therefore, three important trends may be taking place and they could account for the rise of the individual and the breakdown of traditional land tenure and patterns of work. First, land planted under perennial tree crops is associated, through the trees and long usage, with the individual rather than the group. Once cash crops are planted it is no longer 'this is our land' but rather 'this is my coffee' (cf. Townsend, 1961: 28 and Dakeyne, 1966: 51). Secondly, except for the initial clearing, all the maintenance and harvesting of cash crops can be done by individuals or by the elementary family. This is one of the factors inducing the collapse of the basic traditional system based on co-operation and reciprocity in many of the garden tasks.[1] The third major tendency is for cash cropping to act as a catalyst for social change for it heralds the rise of the individual entrepreneur who often develops into a political leader (Andrews, 1956: 28). No one of the calibre of Peta Simogun, Nimbuk, or Gulu[2] has arisen from the Abelam as yet, but power and leadership are passing from the traditional leaders, the yam growers, fighters, orators, and artists, to the new village officials such as elected councillors and 'boss boys' (cf. Epstein, 1963: 304), who are usually the most enthusiastic planters of cash crops. Those villages with the highest cash income all seem to have the most able leaders and

---

[1] This tendency is reflected in the fact that there are fewer ambitious projects being undertaken, such as the building of Tambaran houses, which require plenty of labour. Also many men said that they would rather pay higher taxes than give a day's labour every week to the council.

[2] Simogun of Dagua (Spate, 1953), Nimbuk of Erap (Crocombe and Hogbin, 1963a), and Gulu of Amele (Hancock, 1955). See also discussion of Papuan entrepreneurs in Crocombe et al., 1967 and Finney, 1968.

organizers but to date there are very few Abelam who have
any real influence outside their own villages. The two Members
in the House of Assembly who represent the Abelam both come
from non-Abelam-speaking villages to the west. Most of the
cash cropping is also being done immediately to the west of
the Abelam in the Albiges and Bumbita–Muhiang areas where
there are several progressive leaders.

CONCLUSION

From this example of the particular, generalizations can be
made about how change and culture contacts are affecting
man–land relations in Melanesia. Within the subsistence
gardens the most notable changes are an increasing diversity
of crops with often a change in the staple crop, an intensification
of land use leading to deterioration of the land in some densely
populated areas and a retrogression in traditional horticultural methods. Allied with these factors, and often contributing
to them, cash cropping is accompanied by a very gradual rise
in individualism, a change in attitudes to land ownership and
leadership, and an increasing need for, and dependence on,
money. It seems that any interest in cash cropping depends on
six factors: the absence of any overt clash with indigenous land
tenure systems, a good indigenous leader, worthwhile recom-
pense for the efforts of the people (particularly in the early
stages of any venture), help and inspiration from the Government, an incentive to obtain money, and finally some cultural
and ecological stresses. The intensification of agriculture brings
a whole host of economic and sociological changes in its train
and stresses acting on traditional systems cause a breakdown in
ethnocentrism and indigenes are unable to accept their way of
doing things as natural and best (Boserup, 1965). As the last
three of these conditions are being met in most of the areas
under discussion, it is inevitable that there should be a gradual
but growing trend away from traditional village agriculture.
If the opportunities are provided the people will become more
and more involved in commercial activities both in villages and
by migrating to the towns. In the attempt to make economic
and social progress through cash cropping much will depend
on local leadership, and on the crops grown. If the latter,

particularly copra, cocoa, and coffee, do not provide a stable and worthwhile return there will be increasing frustration and resentment among the people who will inevitably compare their own cargoless lot with that of the expatriates in their midst.

BIBLIOGRAPHY

Allan, W. 1949. *Studies in African Land Use in Northern Rhodesia*, Rhodes–Livingstone Papers 15.

—— 1965. *The African Husbandman*, Edinburgh.

Allen, C. H. 1957. *Customary Land Tenure in the British Solomon Islands Protectorate*, Honiara.

Anas, M. 1957. 'Indigenous Economic Development in the Central District of Papua', *Australian Geographer*, vol. 7, pp. 79–84.

Anderson, J. L. 1962. 'The Development of a Cattle Industry in the Territory of Papua and New Guinea', *Papua & New Guinea Agricultural Journal*, vol. 14, pp. 133–40.

Andrews, J. 1956. 'Commercial Agriculture and the Papua–New Guinea Economy', *Australian Geographer*, vol. 6, pp. 21–8.

Bailey, K. V. 1963a. 'Nutritional Status of some East New Guinean Populations', *Tropical & Geographical Medicine*, vol. 15, pp. 389–402.

—— 1963b. 'Nutrition in New Guinea', *Food and Nutrition Notes and Reviews*, Commonwealth Department of Health, Canberra, vol. 20, pp. 3–11.

Barrau, J. 1956a. 'L'Agriculture vivrière indigène aux Nouvelles-Hébrides', *Journal de la Société des Océanistes*, vol. 12, pp. 181–215.

—— 1956b. *L'Agriculture vivrière autochtone de la Nouvelle-Calédonie*, South Pacific Commission Technical Paper 87.

—— 1958. *Subsistence Agriculture in Melanesia*, B.P. Bishop Museum Monograph no. 219, Honolulu.

—— 1960. 'Plant Introduction in the Tropical Pacific', *Pacific Viewpoint*, vol. 1, pp. 1–10.

Bateson, G. 1932. 'Social Structure of the Iatmül People,' *Oceania*, vol. 2, pp. 245–91, 401–53.

Belshaw, C. S. 1954. *Changing Melanesia*, Sydney.

Boserup, E. 1965. *The Conditions of Agricultural Growth*, London.

B.S.I.P. 1965. British Solomon Islands Protectorate, Department of Agriculture, *The Coconut Industry*.

—— Various dates. *Biennial Report*, London.

—— Agriculture Dept. Various dates. *Annual Report*, Honiara.

Brookfield, H. C. 1962. 'Local Study and Comparative Method: an

Example from Central New Guinea', *Annals of the Association of American Geographers*, vol. 52, pp. 242–54.

Brookfield, H. C. 1964. 'The Ecology of Highland Settlement: some Suggestions', *American Anthropologist*, vol. 66, pp. 20–38.

—— and Brown, P. 1963. *Struggle for Land*, Melbourne.

Bureau of Statistics, 1963. *Survey of Indigenous Horticulture*, 1961–2, Konedobu, Papua.

—— 1968. *Rural Industries*, Bulletin no. 9, Konedobu.

—— Various dates. *Oversea Trade Bulletin*, Konedobu.

Burnett, R. M. 1963. 'Some Cultural Practices in the Simbai Administrative Area, Madang District', *Papua–New Guinea Agricultural Journal*, vol. 16, pp. 79–84.

Cheetham, R. J. 1962–3. 'The Development of Indigenous Agriculture, Land Settlement and Rural Credit Facilities in Papua and New Guinea', *Papua–New Guinea Agricultural Journal*, vol. 15, pp. 67–78.

Condominium of the New Hebrides. Various dates. *Biennial Report*, London.

Conroy, W. L. 1953. 'Notes on Some Land Use Problems in Papua and New Guinea', *Australian Geographer*, vol. 6, pp. 25–30.

—— 1962. 'Tradition and Trends in Agriculture', *Australian Territories*, vol. 2, pp. 21–7.

Crocombe, R. G., and Hogbin, G. R. 1963a. *The Erap Mechanical Farming Project*, New Guinea Research Unit Bulletin no. 1, Canberra.

—— —— 1963b. *Land, Work and Productivity at Inonda*, New Guinea Research Unit Bulletin no. 2, Canberra.

—— 1964. *Communal Cash Cropping Among the Orokaiva*, New Guinea Research Unit Bulletin no. 4, Canberra.

—— (ed.) 1967. *Papuan Entrepreneurs*, New Guinea Research Unit Bulletin no. 16, Canberra.

Dakeyne, R. B. 1966. *Changes in Land Use and Settlement among the Yega*, New Guinea Research Unit Bulletin no. 13, Canberra.

D.A.S.F., Papua. Various dates. Department of Agriculture, Stock and Fisheries, *Annual Reports*, Konedobu.

—— 1969. *Crop Statistics, No. 2, 1967–68*, Konedobu.

Epstein, T. S. 1963. 'European Contact and Tolai Economic Development: A Schema of Economic Growth', *Economic Development and Cultural Change*, vol. 11, pp. 289–307.

Finney, B. R. 1968. 'Bigfellow Man Belong Business in New Guinea', *Ethnology*, vol. 7, pp. 394–410.

Fisk, E. K. 1962. 'Planning in a Primitive Economy', *Economic Record*, vol. 38, pp. 462–78.

—— 1964. 'From Pure Subsistence to a Market Surplus', *Economic Record*, vol. 40, pp. 156–74.

Forge, J. A. W. 1962. 'Paint—A Magical Substance', *Palette*, Basle, no. 9, pp. 9–16.

Fountain, O. C. 1966. 'Wulukum: Land, Livelihood and Change in a New Guinea Village', unpublished M.A. thesis, Victoria University of Wellington, Wellington.

Frazer, R. M. 1964. 'Changing Fijian Agriculture', *Australian Geographer*, vol. 9, pp. 148–55.

Guiart, J. 1958. *Espiritu Santo*, Paris.

Hancock, R. N. 1955. 'Road, Rice and Rural Progress', *South Pacific*, vol. 8, pp. 46–52.

Howlett, D. R. 1962. 'A Decade of Change in the Goroka Valley, New Guinea: Land use and development in the 1950s', unpublished Ph.D. thesis, Australian National University, Canberra.

I.B.R.D. 1965. International Bank for Reconstruction and Development, *The Economic Development of Papua and New Guinea*, Baltimore.

Irwin, P. G. 1963. 'European Influence in the Blanche Bay District of New Guinea', *Australian Geographer*, vol. 9, pp. 34–42.

Jackson, G. 1965. *Cattle, Coffee and Land among the Wain*, New Guinea Research Unit Bulletin no. 8, Canberra.

Kaberry, P. M. 1941. 'The Abelam Tribe, Sepik District, New Guinea. A Preliminary Report', *Oceania*, vol. 11, pp. 233–58, 345–67.

—— 1941–2. 'Law and Political Organisation in the Abelam tribe, New Guinea', *Oceania*, vol. 12, pp. 79–95, 209–25, 331–63.

—— 1965–6. 'Political Organisation among the Northern Abelam', *Anthropological Forum*, vol. 1, pp. 334–72.

Lea, D. A. M. 1964. 'Abelam Land and Sustenance', unpublished Ph.D. thesis, Australian National University, Canberra.

—— 1965. 'The Abelam: A Study in Local Differentiation', *Pacific Viewpoint*, vol. 6, pp. 191–214.

—— 1966. 'Yam Growing in the Maprik Area', *Papua–New Guinea Agricultural Journal*, vol. 18, pp. 5–16.

—— 1969. 'Access to Land among Swidden Cultivators: An Example from New Guinea', *Australian Geographical Studies*, vol. 7, pp. 137–52.

McKee, H. S. 1957. *Some Food Problems in the Pacific Islands*, South Pacific Commission Technical Paper no. 106, Noumea.

Massal, E., and Barrau, J. 1956. *Food Plants of the South Sea Islands*, South Pacific Commission Technical Paper no. 94, Noumea.

Meggitt, M. J. 1958. 'The Enga of the New Guinea Highlands: Some Preliminary Observations', *Oceania*, vol. 28, pp. 253–330.

Miles, J. 1956. 'Native Commercial Agriculture in Papua', *South Pacific*, vol. 9, pp. 318–27.

New Guinea Handbook. 1937. Canberra.

N.I.D. 1945. Naval Intelligence Division, *The Pacific Islands*, vol. 4, London.

Nye, P. H., and Greenland, D. J. 1960. *The Soil under Shifting Cultivation*, Harpenden.

Reay, M. 1959. *The Kuma*, Melbourne.

Rimoldi, M. 1966. *Land Tenure and Land Use among the Mount Lamington Orokaiva*, New Guinea Research Unit Bulletin no. 11, Canberra.

Salisbury, R. H. 1962a. *From Stone to Steel*, Melbourne.

—— 1962b. 'Early Stages of Economic Development in New Guinea', *Journ. Poly. Soc.*, vol. 71, pp. 328–39.

—— 1964. 'Changes in Land Use and Tenure among the Siane of the New Guinea Highlands', *Pacific Viewpoint*, vol. 5, pp. 1–10.

Serpenti, L. M. 1965. *Cultivators in the Swamps*, Assen.

Shand, R. T. 1963. 'The Development of Cash Cropping in Papua and New Guinea', *Australian Journal of Agricultural Economics*, vol. 7, pp. 42–54.

Spate, O. H. K. 1953. 'Changing Native Agriculture in New Guinea', *Geographical Review*, vol. 43, pp. 151–72.

Tedder, J. L. O. 1966. 'The Solomon Islands, an Emerging Cash Economy', *Australian Geographical Studies*, vol. 4, pp. 49–59.

Territory of New Guinea. Various dates. *Annual Report*.

Territory of Papua. Various dates. *Annual Report*.

Thurnwald, R. 1914. 'Vom mittleren Sepik zur Nordwestküste von Kaiser-Wilhelmsland', *Mitt. aus den Deutschen Schutzgebieten*, vol. 27, pp. 81–4.

Townsend, M. M. 1961. 'Problems of Land Tenure on Malaita', *Atoll Research Bulletin*, no. 85, pp. 27–32.

Townsend, W. H. 1969. 'Stone and Steel Use in a New Guinea Society', *Ethnology*, vol. 8, pp. 199–205.

Waddell, E. W., and Krinks, P. A. 1968. *The Organisation of Production and Distribution among the Orokaiva*, New Guinea Research Unit Bulletin no. 24, Canberra.

Ward, R. G. 1960. 'Village Agriculture in Viti Levu, Fiji', *New Zealand Geographer*, vol. 16, pp. 33–56.

—— 1965. *Land Use and Population in Fiji*, London.

Williams, F. E. 1932–3. 'Trading Voyages from the Gulf of Papua', *Oceania*, vol. 3, pp. 139–66.

Williamson, R. W. 1912. *The Mafulu: Mountain People of British New Guinea*, London.

11

URBANIZATION
IN THE SOUTH PACIFIC
AND THE CASE OF NOUMÉA

W. D. MCTAGGART[1]

GEOGRAPHICAL conditions in general have not favoured urban development in the South Pacific, and although there exist today a number of towns of considerable local importance, they are all fairly small. The various territories in the South Pacific consist of scattered groups of islands, dispersed across a wide expanse of ocean, and fragmented politically into small units. Papua and New Guinea, with a population of over 2,000,000, is the largest unit in the region, but neither economically nor socially is it sufficiently well developed to be capable of supporting any high degree of urbanization; apart from this territory, and Fiji, whose population is in excess of 400,000, none of the Pacific territories has a population greater than 150,000. The Pacific peoples themselves, with their traditional economies, or as producers of raw materials, have had little stimulus to become urban dwellers.

None the less, a number of urban centres do exist, wholly or in part the creations of outsiders. They were founded for the most part during the second half of the nineteenth century— the main period of colonization and annexation in the South Pacific—in order to serve as ports and administrative centres for the colonial powers. In many cases these towns remained distinct from the rest of the territory in which they were situated, and impinged directly on the experience of only a small percentage of the indigenous population. Substantial proportions of their populations were of foreign extraction, and came initially from overseas, either from Europe or from Asia. But

[1] Dr. McTaggart is Associate Professor of Geography, Arizona State University.

with the passage of time these towns have come to constitute poles of attraction for indigenous migrants, and urban populations have begun to expand with great rapidity. Within the scope offered for urban development by a geographically and politically fragmented environment, urbanization has come to assume fundamental importance, and the problems this poses for the respective administrations have become grave.

The chief urban centres in the South Pacific are listed in Table 11.1, along with their population figures, the percentage this constitutes of the total population of the territory, and the percentage of the town's population accounted for by indigenous peoples.

TABLE 11.1. *Population of Main Towns**

Town	Territory	Population	Date	Percentage of territory population	Percentage indigenous in town's population
Nouméa	New Caledonia	34,990	1963	40	15
Papeete	French Polynesia	22,000	1960	26	62
Nuku'alofa	Tonga	16,000	1964	23	93
Apia	Western Samoa	21,699	1961	19	84 (1956)
Suva†	Fiji	54,150	1966	11	30
Port Moresby	Papua New Guinea	41,848	1966	2	77
Lae	Papua New Guinea	16,546	1966	0·8	81

* Includes all centres with population of over 15,000.

† Suva City. The 'Suva Urban Area' had a population of 80,248, or 17 per cent of the colony's total.

SOURCES: All figures from censuses except Papeete (estimate from Société d'Équipement de Tahiti et des Îles) and Nuku'alofa (Walsh, 1964).

Of all the territories listed, New Caledonia is the most highly urbanized. Some 40 per cent of its population reside in Nouméa, which with its nickel smelting works is the most important industrial centre in the South Pacific. The degree of concentration in Nouméa is highest for the European section of the population—a very important element of the New Caledonian population, accounting for 39 per cent of the total—since almost two-thirds are to be found in Nouméa, and many of the others live in about two dozen smaller urban centres in the interior, ranging in size up to about 1,000 inhabitants (Curson, 1965). Papeete, the capital of French Polynesia, is one of the oldest urban settlements in the region, having been founded in 1843. In 1960 it accounted for about one-quarter of the population of the territory, and over two-fifths of the population of the main island, Tahiti. Nuku'alofa, despite its considerable size, and its relative importance as a centre of population, is scarcely like a town at all. Although nearly a quarter of the population of the territory resides there, it has been described as 'an agglomeration of three agricultural villages which . . . became at once the capital, the centre of Wesleyan missionary activity, and the first port for overseas trade' (Walsh, 1964: 45). Apia, although it does have an 'urban' core, and is somewhat larger than Nuku'alofa, likewise consists largely of a series of villages. Its share of the total territorial population is slightly less than is the case in Tonga. Suva is the largest of the South Pacific towns, although the percentage of the total population resident there is decidedly smaller than in some other territories. Suva is not the only urban centre in Fiji, and in 1966 over 19 per cent of the population lived in the two chief towns— Suva and Lautoka—and the twelve other townships. None the less Fiji, where more than half the population are Indians (mostly rural dwellers engaged in the growing of sugar cane), is one of the less urbanized territories in the area.

Port Moresby, headquarters of the Papua administration since 1884 and of the combined Papua and New Guinea administration since 1945, has sometimes been referred to as a distant suburb of the Australian cities. This is due in part to the transient nature of its European population, most of whom are in the territory only for a limited period of time. Although the bulk of its inhabitants are indigenous, only a very small fraction of the territory's population resides there. It is the only substantial town in the Papuan part of the territory.

As well as these capital towns, there are a number of others which have attained considerable local importance, particularly as trading centres. In New Guinea, for example, Lae, with a population of 16,546, is the main outlet for produce from the economically important Markham Valley and parts of the highlands (Marsh, 1964), and Rabaul, with a population of 10,561, is the main centre of a copra and cocoa producing region. In the Solomons, Honiara has grown since the end of the Second World War to reach a population of about 4,500 in 1964 (Tedder, 1966: 37), and is the capital of the Protectorate. In the New Hebrides the towns are smaller, Port Vila and Luganville (or Santo) having populations of 3,072 and 2,564 respectively (McArthur and Yaxley, 1968: 29); although Santo is the smaller, it plays a very important role in the commerce of the area (Bennett, 1957). In other parts of the Pacific, such towns as do exist are little more than administrative centres, with very little active life apart from their governmental functions, or are mining camps, some of which may be only temporary settlements. But some migration does tend to take place, even to these small administrative centres, as has been the case in Rarotonga, in American Samoa, and in the Gilbert and Ellice Islands. In Guam some stimulus to migration has come from the presence of large American bases, but in the Trust Territory urban development has been very limited. From Wallis, Futuna, and the Cook Islands migration seems to take place to urban centres outside the territory itself—from Wallis and Futuna to the New Hebrides and to New Caledonia, and from the Cook Islands to various centres in New Zealand (Doumenge, 1961; Hooper, 1961). As for the mining centres, there are examples such as Vatukoula in Fiji, with a total population of 4,993 in 1966 (Zwart, 1968: Appendix p. 3) and a mining labour force in 1963 of 1,684 (Whitelaw, 1967: 7); or Makatea, where prior to the recent ending of phosphate mining, many of the population of 3,000 were immigrants from other parts of French Polynesia and the Cook Islands (Doumenge: 1963); or Thio, a nickel mining township in New Caledonia with a population of over 1,000, many of whom are Europeans.

The demographic composition of the main South Pacific towns varies considerably, and some indication of this is given in the final column of Table 11.1; the figures show that the percentage of each town's population made up of indigenous people ranges from a low of 15 per cent for Nouméa to 93 per cent for Nuku'alofa. In Nouméa in 1963, 61 per cent of the town's population were Europeans or part-Europeans, 12 per cent Asians, and 11 per cent islanders from other parts of the Pacific. In Suva in 1966, Indians constituted 51 per cent of the population, while Europeans, Chinese, and other islanders made up 19 per cent. In Papeete, 10 per cent of the population in 1956 were Europeans, and 19 per cent Asians, chiefly Chinese. The non-indigenous populations of Nuku'alofa, Apia, and Port Moresby are mainly Europeans or part-Europeans.

The variations in the indigenous content of the populations of Pacific towns are of primary importance—so much so that this may be used as a criterion for classification. There are basic differences in the historical experience, and the economic and social functions, between the 'less indigenous' towns such as Nouméa and Suva, and the 'more indigenous' ones such as Apia, Port Moresby, and Nuku'alofa; Papeete is an intermediate case. These differences are reflected in much that has to be discussed in terms of the appearance, form, and structure of the towns, as well as the roles they play within their respective territories or assume in the context of international trade and commerce.

This may be illustrated with reference to commercial or trading activities. Some idea of the varying importance of these towns as centres for trade may be gained from the figures shown in Table 11.2, which give *per capita* exports for the year 1963.[1]

TABLE 11.2. Per Capita *Exports, Selected South Pacific Territories, 1963*

Territory	Capital town	Per capita exports, 1963 (U.S. dollars)
New Caledonia	Nouméa	518
Fiji	Suva	129
French Polynesia	Papeete	123
Western Samoa	Apia	64
Tonga	Nuku'alofa	31
Papua New Guinea	Port Moresby	19

SOURCE: *Pacific Islands Monthly*, November 1965.

New Caledonia, with much the highest figure, is the most highly developed territory in the South Pacific, but is heavily dependent on the highly capitalized mining and metallurgical industry.[2] Nouméa, the least indigenous of all Pacific towns, is therefore a controlling centre in a highly monetized economy, closely integrated with markets in Europe, America, and Asia. Fiji, where the main immigrant population is Indian rather

---

[1] Imports might normally be expected to provide a better figure. But several territories have extremely high invisible exports under the headings of defence facilities and tourism, whilst others are recipients under aid schemes. French Polynesia, for example, reported imports for 1964 at more than six times the value of exports.

[2] Products of mining and metallurgy accounted for 98·1 per cent of exports by value in 1963.

than European, is an important producer of sugar cane; the sugar export industry is relatively labour-intensive, certainly by comparison with New Caledonian nickel, and the figure for *per capita* exports is decidedly lower. Suva is again a commercial town, with Indians contributing over half its population. The *per capita* export figure for French Polynesia, though lower than that for Fiji, is none the less quite high. French Polynesia has a quite well-developed external commerce in vanilla, copra, and a number of other items, and much of the trade in this is controlled through Papeete by the Tahitian Chinese. The three territories with low *per capita* export figures are those in which the main towns are predominantly indigenous in terms of demographic composition. There are both plantations and native producers in Western Samoa and exports include copra, cocoa, and bananas; there does exist some export trade from Tonga mainly in copra; in Papua and New Guinea efforts have been made to promote the growth of a number of export industries, often with the assistance of foreign (Australian) capital and management. But in all cases the impact is fairly limited, and the territories concerned have economies which are dominated by their traditional sectors.

THE FORM AND STRUCTURE OF PACIFIC TOWNS

Although all the main towns exhibit certain similarities in terms of their form and structure, some of their most important differences reflect the demographic and economic factors already referred to.

Suitability as a port was one of the main criteria guiding the choice of sites by Europeans in the South Pacific, and even in pre-European times some of the larger agglomerations of population tended to be close to the sea. Papeete has a good harbour, lies on the largest island in French Polynesia and is within easy reach of the second largest. Nouméa is located near an important gap in the off-shore reef, and its harbour offered a safe anchorage for shipping. In Suva the guiding factors were the apparent suitability for shipping, combined with ample scope for development of the town over the moderate relief of the peninsula.[1] But reclamation and site development, sometimes

[1] Suva was not in fact the first site chosen for development as the capital of Fiji;

on a huge scale, were required in most cases; in Nouméa and Suva extensive works were needed at an early stage to provide reclaimed land; parts of Apia and Nuku'alofa were also very swampy and remain so today. And in recent years important additions of land have taken place in connection with industrial development as a result of reclamation in several towns, including Nouméa, Suva, and Papeete.

One of the most striking features of all these towns is their low residential density. Suva City has a density of about 8·8 persons per acre, and the figure for the whole urban area is only 4·7. Nouméa, in the early 1950s, was reckoned to have a density of about 8 per acre, Apia had around 6·1 in 1956, and Nuku'alofa 12 in 1963. Papeete, at 30 persons per acre, has the highest over-all density of all the main towns in the region. Different factors have contributed to this low density depending on circumstances, but it is perhaps significant that in no case were there high-density urban settlements prior to the development of these sites as European administrative centres, and urban development on a large scale only began at a time when modern forms of transport were becoming available. More particular reasons apply in individual cases; in Nouméa the broken nature of the site, and the slowness with which reclaimed land became available in the town centre, drove the inhabitants to seek land in the suburbs, so causing a scattering of the built-up area at an early stage in development. In Suva a contributory factor was the history of land tenure in and around the urban area; at the time when the site was selected for development as the capital of Fiji, the land was owned by a company which had been formed with a view to selling lots to settlers for the cultivation of sugar cane. The company re-ceded to the government not the totality of the land, but only alternate blocks, and this early fragmentation of ownership has contributed to the dispersal of the town. In Port Moresby the adminis-

the original one was at Levuka, where there was already a nucleus of European settlement prior to annexation in 1874. But subsequent difficulties in developing the area led to the transfer of the capital in 1882 to its present position. The experience of Rabaul is not dissimilar, since the original administrative centre for the Bismarcks was Kokopo, where it remained until transfer to Rabaul in 1910. In the Solomon Islands the headquarters of the Protectorate government was on the island of Tulagi until the Second World War, after which reconstruction took place at Honiara on Guadalcanal, where the main American camp had been located.

tration left alienation of land by natives on a voluntary basis, and hence development has been very patchy with pockets of built-over land surrounded by undeveloped native-owned land. In the more 'indigenous' towns, notably Apia and Nuku'alofa, low residential density arises in part from the fact that many of the inhabitants of the towns are, or were until recently, agriculturists, dependent on agricultural activities for at least part of their livelihood.[1]

The 'less indigenous' towns differ quite markedly from the 'more indigenous' in their appearance. In Nouméa and Suva a bustling business centre, with office blocks and shops of all sizes, is surrounded by suburbs with apartments and bungalows, schools and shops—all the characteristics of modern suburbia. In towns like Apia or Nuku'alofa on the other hand, this degree of concentrated high-value development at the centre is missing, and buildings are fewer in number and more widely spaced. In place of suburban development in the peripheral sections of the town there are modified traditional villages, with a few selected areas of high quality residence for overseas administrators and commercial employees.

These urban or 'peri-urban' villages exist as characteristic social as well as spatial units, and their relative infrequence in Nouméa and Suva is as much a sociological as a structural fact. There are none in Nouméa itself, although several of the Melanesian communities that lie some miles to the north have pre-eminently this peri-urban character; the adults may find more or less regular employment in the town, and commute in and out, whilst their families in the village carry on some agricultural activities. There are some such villages in and around Suva (Nayacakalou, 1963; Whitelaw, 1964), especially along the fringes of the built-up area. Nuku'alofa on the other hand, which grew from three such traditional villages (Kennedy, 1959), consists almost entirely of this form of development, as does much of Apia, where there are about fifty villages (Kearns, 1964). To the west and east of Port Moresby lie the Motu and Koita villages of Hanuabada and its neighbours, where about 20 per cent of the Papuans in the town reside (Oram, 1964: 40).

In several of the main centres the problem of squatter housing

---

[1] Amongst the smaller towns the same factors apply. At Santo and Honiara low residential densities reflect the evolution from sites of war-time military camps.

has been kept under fairly firm control. This is due in part to the provision of housing by government and other employers; in Port Moresby, for example, almost all the Europeans receive some form of housing, and Oram estimates (1964:40) that 29 per cent of the Papuans were housed by the administration or by other employers, and a further 24 per cent were housed in domestic servants' quarters. In Nouméa a survey in 1961 reported 15 per cent of the sampled European households and 26 per cent of the non-European households resident in quarters provided by employers (McTaggart, 1962). It is also due in part, and especially in the more indigenous towns, to the flexibility of some of the forms of indigenous land tenure, which have permitted substantial numbers of in-migrants to establish themselves within the structure of one of the peri-urban villages. In Nouméa and Suva most land is held under freehold forms of tenure, but in Nuku'alofa and Apia only very small amounts have been made available in this way. In Tonga every adult male is entitled to claim a lifelong lease of land, including an urban section; and although in Nuku'alofa this system has been under such severe strain that it has almost collapsed, it still does exist (Walsh, 1964). In Port Moresby, on the other hand, the land tenure system has been less flexible, and despite some voluntary alienation by land-owning indigenous groups, despite the importance of employer-owned accommodation, and despite a government-sponsored programme to return unemployed migrants to their native villages, a squatter problem has developed.[1]

Both from the standpoint of urban planning and social structure the peri-urban villages are problem areas in all the main towns where they exist. Consisting as they do of essentially rural forms of settlement, they have none the less steadily increased their residential densities as their populations have expanded, giving rise to problems of water supply, health, and sanitation. It is reported that in Apia in 1956, although most of the villages had densities of less than ten persons per acre, some went as high as twenty-three, and it may be that locally the figure should be higher (Pirie, 1960: 47). Nuku'alofa has

[1] It was estimated in 1965 that 15 per cent of the Papuan population lived in some twenty squatter settlements around the fringes of the town (*P.I.M.*, Nov. 1965: 67).

no municipal government, and no organized systems of water or drainage, and in addition it occupies a site most of which lies very close to sea level; although the density may not be high, it is undoubtedly too high for this form of living.

Although these villages do conserve something of the appearance of traditional forms of settlement, the social structure and the pattern of economic activities have generally experienced rapid evolution over the past decades. In Apia one writer has remarked that although many of the outward ceremonial forms have been retained within the community represented by a peri-urban village, economic forms have changed, owing to the proximity of Apia and opportunities for wage earning (Hirsch, 1958). In Port Moresby the decadence of traditional economic structures among the Motu in Hanuabada has been well documented (Belshaw, 1957), in a fashion which underlines the precarious situation of indigenous communities who become totally dependent, families included, on the earning power of unskilled labour in an underdeveloped economy. On the other hand, in the case of Rabaul, it seems that some of the peri-urban villages have managed to conserve a certain amount of vitality; many of the inhabitants of Matupit, an island close to Rabaul, work in the town, but social structures and community life remain largely unimpaired (Epstein, 1963).

Although peri-urban villages, with at least the vestiges of some community structure and control, may be preferable to squatter settlements, they are frequently held to impede progress towards better urban conditions. They are not easily susceptible to processes of urban planning and redevelopment—in Port Moresby the town planning ordinance does not even apply to 'indigenous' land—and they can lead to anomalous situations in patterns of rating and land valuation, as well as giving rise to the unhealthy living conditions already referred to.

ECONOMIC FUNCTIONS

All the major urban centres in the Pacific are ports, and they thus form an essential link between the territorial economy and the world of international trade. Most are administrative centres, either of autonomous states or dependent colonies. Certain towns in the area, especially some of the smaller ones, are indeed very little more than ports and administrative centres, and reveal a very high degree of dependence on these activities. A large percentage of the European population of Port Moresby consists of public servants, and it is only their presence that enables other commercial and trading activities to be carried on. In Nuku'alofa it has been estimated that between 25 and 30 per cent of the active population is dependent one way or another on the administration for a livelihood (Walsh, 1964: 49). But whilst these two activities are rarely absent, a number of others are added to them in varying proportions, depending on the economic situation of the respective territories. Practically every Pacific town has some form of tourist industry, and most are endeavouring to expand this activity by the construction of new hotels, and the improvement of transport facilities; Fiji, for example, hoped to increase the number of tourists visiting the territory annually from 30,000 in the early 1960s to something like 90,000 by 1970, and in 1969 85,163 tourists visited the country (Fiji, 1969: 132). Certain centres also have important military functions, which generate a considerable quantity of subsidiary employment; Nouméa has both an army and a naval base, and Papeete has been greatly affected by the establishment of a nuclear testing zone in French Polynesia. Industrial activities are very limited, except perhaps in Nouméa where there is a nickel smelting works, and to some extent in Fiji, where there are sugar mills in a number of centres and a range of manufacturing in Suva: none the less, most of the larger towns have food processing industries, breweries, soft drink factories, and other similar establishments (Danks, 1956).

Commercial or trading activities exist in all centres, but their significance varies considerably from place to place. As a rule trading activities, especially the more specialized activities, tend to be concentrated in the town, and only the most basic form of activity is represented in the rural areas. In French Polynesia, for example, where 26 per cent of the population resides in Papeete, 40 per cent of the business licences issued in 1960 were in respect of businesses in the urban area; and furthermore, these paid 75 per cent of the total fees collected, the fees being based partly on turnover. Naturally the degree of concentration in Papeete varied according to the type of business; whilst 32 per cent of the general merchants were to be found in Papeete, the figure for artisans was as high as 80 per cent (Bach, 1961).

There are some significant differences between the economic functions and employment structure of the 'less indigenous' and the 'more indigenous' towns. Commercial turnover in Nouméa, Suva, and Papeete is higher than in Port Moresby, Apia, or Nuku'alofa; whilst 20 per cent of the active population in Nouméa in 1963 were reckoned to be engaged in commercial activities, the comparable figure for Nuku'alofa in 1956 was only 5·2 per cent (Walsh, 1964: 49). Nouméa also has a high industrial component—23 per cent—and this compares with a figure of less than 7 per cent for Nuku'alofa; nearly half the adult male population in Nuku'alofa was engaged in agricultural pursuits, and this is a feature of some of the 'more indigenous' towns. In Nouméa the comparable figure in 1963 was only about 2 per cent.

The functions of these towns draw them into certain forms of relationship with their respective hinterlands. They are administrative, educational, and commercial centres for their territories, exhibiting in some instances a notably high degree of centralization. But two particular forms of the relationship with hinterlands are worth noting, the one because of the relative insignificance of its impact, the other for its importance.

Relatively insignificant is the impact of urban growth as such on the general level of economic development in the rest of the territory. It is perhaps as a result of the generally rudimentary level of industrial development that this appears to be the case, since there is little to stimulate the production of raw materials locally to serve as a basis for urban industry. There has apparently been limited stimulus for the development of market gardening to supply the urban centres with sufficient fresh fruit and vegetables. In New Caledonia, where labour has been in very short supply for several years now, and where earnings in the mining and metallurgical industries are high, the returns from agriculture are relatively poor, and the perpetual state of agricultural crisis and high levels of food imports from Australia and New Zealand are therefore to some extent comprehensible (Angleviel, 1961). But even in those territories where unemployment is much higher than in New

Caledonia, and where it might be thought the existence of a considerable urban market would stimulate production, this has not necessarily been the case. Papeete depends heavily on all manner of imported foodstuffs (Cunningham, 1961), and the situation as regards Port Moresby has been described as follows:

Port Moresby contrasts strongly with Rabaul in many . . . features. In each stage of its growth can be traced a tendency to destroy the life of its hinterland rather than to develop it. For example, the Hanuabadans (living in a peri-urban village) long ago gave up gardening and came to depend on imported food and wage work. As the roads reach out from Port Moresby more villages are similarly affected. . . . There are great fluctuations in vegetable prices in the town, but market gardening is said not to be properly rewarding (Wilson, 1963: 215–16).

There are, on the other hand, many examples of successful development of cash cropping for supply to local urban markets (see, for example, Crocombe and Hogbin, 1963; Belshaw, 1964); but these seem to indicate that particular factors of personal initiative and enterprise are necessary, and that the mere existence of a good urban market is not enough to encourage a sufficient expansion of the supply. A similar situation appears to prevail as far as fishing is concerned. Only recently has the fishing industry in Nouméa been put on a rational basis (Cassier, 1962), and in other parts of the Pacific development of commercial fishing has often been the result of the investment of Japanese capital, intent on supplying the Japanese market.

If the economic impact of urban development has apparently been limited, the demographic impact has been considerable. Although several of the towns in the South Pacific are dominated by populations of foreign origin, in-migration has led over the past few years to a rapidly increasing urban component amongst the indigenous peoples. Growth rates in most of the main centres have been higher than growth rates for the territories as a whole. Nouméa grew 57 per cent between 1956 and 1963, whereas the total population of the territory increased by just over 26 per cent; the Melanesian population of Nouméa increased by 117 per cent. Nuku'alofa, amongst the 'more indigenous' towns, grew by 63 per cent in the same period, compared with a 27 per cent increase in the total population of Tonga. Between 1956 and 1961 Apia's population increased by

19·5 per cent, compared with 17·6 per cent for Western Samoa as a whole. In Fiji the population of Suva increased by 45 per cent between 1956 and 1966 as against an increase of 38 per cent for the colony.

As is only to be expected, migration tends to be selective. Since migrants are in search of employment, they are likely to include large proportions of males of working ages. In Suva, for example, it has been noted that in 1956 39·3 per cent of the Fijian males and 35·7 per cent of the Fijian females were between the ages of 15 and 29 inclusive, compared with figures of 26·2 per cent and 27·5 per cent respectively for the Fijian population as a whole; and in these same age groups there were 134 males for every 100 females (Ward, 1961: 264). Similar trends have been reported for Papeete (Kay, 1963a), and in Nouméa the preponderance of males in 1963 is indicated by a sex ratio for the Melanesians of 114.

But although there is an imbalance between the sexes, it is not nearly so great as that which often existed amongst indentured populations: and even the degree of imbalance that exists at the moment is less than it used to be. It is quite evident that amongst the indigenous populations there are considerable segments made up of families—husbands, wives, and their children—long established as residents in the towns. In Suva it is not at all hard to find urban Fijians of the second and even the third generation; and figures quoted for length of residence in Suva showed that over half the household heads had lived there for at least ten years, and 78 per cent for five years or more (Ward, 1961: 265). Even as early as 1950 the same feature was noted in Nouméa, and employers seemed to appreciate the value of their long-service Melanesian employees (Feugnet, 1951: 88; McTaggart, 1963: 130).

It is perhaps significant that stability in residence and employment in the town is a characteristic of heads of households. It appears that the high level of migration in recent years, whilst it has certainly brought a very large number of new residents to the towns, has been at least in part the result of the growth of short-term migration, especially amongst the younger people. Even in the case of persons not intending to remain very long in town, a certain period of residence there seems to be considered desirable—and may even be socially necessary—in order to gain some experience of modern living. Hence a certain dichotomy has been observed in the indigenous populations of several of the major towns, where it is possible to distinguish between the permanent and settled elements on the one hand, and a temporary element on the other, consisting of persons who may be spending only a matter of a few weeks in town before returning to their villages (Howard, 1961; McTaggart, 1962; Kay, 1963*b*). Such temporary residents often utilize the homes of their already established relatives or friends; in a survey in Suva in 1959 it was found that 77 per cent of the Fijian households had relatives staying with them (Nayacakalou, 1963: 35), a percentage that was slightly higher than that in the rural areas, despite the very different conditions prevailing in the town.

The generally short distances between the towns and their indigenous migration hinterlands have permitted contacts to be readily maintained between urban and rural relatives, and a number of authors have commented on the extent to which certain aspects of traditional social norms and practices as distinct from economic structures have been conserved (Bellam, 1964; Hirsch, 1958). Although some communities—Wallis and Futuna by migration to the New Hebrides and New Caledonia, the island of Ouvea in the Loyalty Islands by migration to Nouméa—have lost substantial percentages of their populations by migration, few have seen their indigenous social systems completely destroyed as a result.

There appears no definite pattern in location of areas from which the majority of migrants are drawn. Sometimes the migrants come in greatest numbers not from the districts which are nearest to the town, but from others much further away. Loyalty Islanders form the majority of the Melanesians in Nouméa, even though for them a journey to Nouméa usually entails a trip by air. In Suva likewise many of the migrants come from smaller islands of the provinces of Kandavu, Lau, and Lomaiviti, and comparatively few come from Ra, one of the most populous areas of the main island (Ward, 1961). In Nuku'alofa, on the other hand, the majority of the people come from Tongatapu, the island on which the town stands.

Through the complexity of the present-day urban situation in the South Pacific, one or two features stand out. Although all the important centres are of European creation, a distinction may be drawn between those in which the population of overseas origin predominates (Suva and Nouméa) and those in which the indigenous population predominates (Port Moresby, Apia, and Nuku'alofa especially). This variable—the degree of predominance of one or other of these broad population groups —should not be regarded as an independent one, since it is closely connected with, and largely reflects other factors in the political and economic history of the territories concerned. This distinction coincides, however, with differing levels of economic advancement and participation in the international economy, and differing levels of 'urbanization' reflect this. In Suva and Nouméa the completeness of the break with agricultural and other rural pursuits is much more clearly marked than in Apia or Nuku'alofa; not in the sense that ties between town and village are weaker, but that the different functions performed by these towns have given rise to a much larger 'urban', as opposed to 'semi-urban', population. Between the more extreme types one finds the intermediate case of Papeete.

But although the apparent degree of 'urbanization' varies considerably, independently of the magnitude of the population, the effects of urban development (even in territories such as Tonga and Papua and New Guinea) should in no sense be underestimated. It is in these urban centres that innovations are being introduced which, by the very nature of the urban society existing there, may make rapid progress in acceptance, even in rural areas. The towns remain prime points of contact with the outside world, and important mechanisms in the process of development of their respective territories.

NOUMÉA: A CASE STUDY

Although Nouméa, with its high standards of living, and its substantial European population, is unique among South Pacific towns, it is nevertheless a good example to illustrate some of the processes characteristic of the region as a whole. Its growth rate in recent years has been high, as various streams of migration, both internal and international, have added to its population, and many of the problems associated with rapid growth—housing shortages, haphazard and inefficient development, speculation, slums, and so on—have been felt very acutely. Its population is very heterogeneous, being composed of Europeans, Melanesians, Asians, and Polynesians, many of whom are only very recent arrivals in town. But where Nouméa is perhaps unique among South Pacific towns is in being better equipped to deal with the problems created by its own expansion. Its fully settled European population ensures the provision of a generally high standard of education throughout a substantial sector of the population. Although many of the most responsible posts in the business, industrial, and administrative hierarchies have always been filled by persons from overseas, these functions have been able to count on an adequate reservoir of local ability at other levels. In the same manner, the wealth of the territory and the fact that its economy is one of the most highly developed in the whole Pacific region, have ensured that sufficient financial resources have been available to implement at least some of the policies adopted. Not everything has been done in Nouméa that ought to have been done; nor has everything been an unqualified success. But it is true that the economic and social standards prevalent in Nouméa are those to which other, less fortunate territories aspire, and therein lies much of the interest of Nouméa as a case study.

The origins and development of Nouméa

The decision by the French Government in 1853 to annex the island of New Caledonia was taken on the recommendation of a committee appointed to investigate the possibilities of developing penal colonies in various parts of the world; New Caledonia had been noted as one suitable locality, and its annexation was suggested in order to maintain it in reserve, pending a final decision (Person, 1953). The site of Nouméa was selected in 1854 by Tardy de Montravel, one of the captains instructed to annex the island, as fulfilling what appeared to him to be the main needs for the capital of a penal colony. The anchorage was sound, and access to the open sea through a nearby gap in the reef was good; around the site were a number of smaller islands which could be used for penal institutions, thus effecting some separation between these and the more normal functions of the proposed town.

Settlement began almost immediately. The military authorities erected a number of buildings along the crest of a small peninsula that curled out from the mainland just opposite the Île Nou (formerly the site of a trading post belonging to an English trader called Paddon) (Fig. 11.1). As soon as the news of the annexation spread, a number of civilians arrived, chiefly from Australia, and they too took up what land they could find

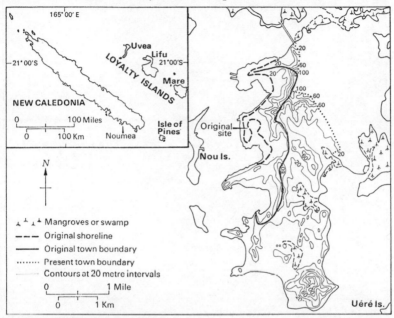

FIG. 11.1. Location and site of Nouméa. Source: McTaggart, 1963.

in the vicinity. Within a few years it was evident that the original site was much too cramped, and did not offer enough level land to meet the requirements of the immediate, let alone the distant future. A major development plan was therefore drawn up in 1860, which envisaged land reclamation on a large scale in the central parts of the town, as well as in the Quartier Latin to the immediate south. The promontory as well as certain other features were to be levelled to provide the necessary material. Upon the level land a rectangular street plan was to be laid out, covering the whole of the town centre, and extending up into the Quartier Latin (Fig. 11.2).

With the help of convict labour, which began to be available in the middle of the 1860s, this project was largely completed by 1877. But long before this it was evident that the town could not be contained within its proposed boundaries. Settlers continued to arrive, and finding no room in the central parts of the town, were obliged to settle further out, utilizing the valleys which spread out to the east and south. By 1880 there

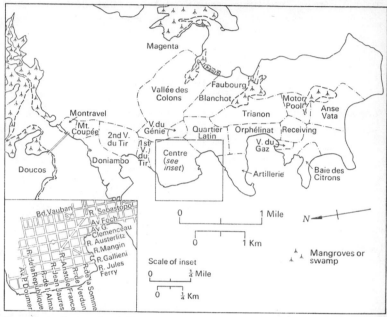

FIG. 11.2. Street plan of central Nouméa and sections of the town. Source: McTaggart, 1963.

was extensive settlement in Vallée des Colons, Faubourg Blanchot, and Orphélinat (Fig. 11.2), this rapid development reflecting the level of economic activity in the territory, which depended largely on the penitentiary as its main industry.

The decision to discontinue the transportation of convicts to New Caledonia as from 1898, and to allow the penal establishments in the territory to run down over a period of years, brought the expansion of Nouméa to a halt. Two of the island's other main activities were also threatened—the pastoral industry, which had found the penitentiary to be its main client, and the incipient mining industry, which had come to depend on supplies of convict labour. Nouméa was threatened with the departure without replacement of a substantial number of its inhabitants—the military and administrative personnel attached to the penal institutions. In point of fact the European population of Nouméa declined from 5,755 in 1906 to 5,504 in 1911, exclusive of the penal element.

The resurgence of the town had to await the maturing of the mining and metallurgical industries. Although nickel had been mined in substantial quantities since about 1880, New Caledonia being at the time one of the world's main producers, the industry was subject to major fluctuations; nickel was an unfamiliar commodity, whose usefulness was still to be generally appreciated. Market conditions stabilized somewhat in the early years of the twentieth century as total world output of nickel rose, and a more rational organization in New Caledonia became feasible. Smelting operations commenced in 1911 at Doniambo, just to the north of Nouméa, and from that time on the town was a significant industrial centre. Initially, however, the effect of this development on the urban landscape was small. The factory was outside the town, and was fairly small to start with. It depended on indentured Asian labour—mainly Vietnamese and Indonesians—nearly all of whom were housed in labour lines close to the factory itself.

After its years of rapid growth in the nineteenth century Nouméa expanded fairly slowly until the Second World War. Economic conditions were favourable during much of the 1920s, but the effects of the depression in the 1930s were severe. The mining and metallurgical industries were badly affected, and the labour force—still mainly Asian—dwindled. Many of the European settlers in the interior were reduced almost to subsistence farming in order to keep alive. In Nouméa an ambitious programme of redevelopment initiated in the 1920s had to be abandoned with only a few items completed—including, fortunately, a new water supply for the town. Some idea of the growth of the town during these decades may be gained from the population figures quoted in Table 11.3. Between 1911 and 1936, the European population increased slowly from 5,504 to 8,215, probably mainly by natural increase; the percentage of locally born amongst the French (non-penal) population of Nouméa was 60 per cent in 1911 and 80 per cent in 1936, and Nouméa's share of the French population of New Caledonia as a whole remained fairly constant—47 per cent in 1911 and 50 per cent in 1936. The penal or convict element in the population declined steadily, and by 1936 was down to only 224. All the three significant non-European elements likewise experienced growth in numbers during this period, followed by a period of decline. The numbers of Melanesians—who required special permission to reside in Nouméa, and in general were there only as labourers in the docks or in commercial establishments—reached a peak in 1921 and declined thereafter. For the Asians the peak year appears to have been 1931,[1] following several years of investment and development in the 1920s. The numbers of other Pacific islanders, Wallisians and New Hebrideans, were small.

TABLE 11.3. *The Population of Nouméa, 1911 to 1963*

Ethnic group	1911	1921	1926	1931	1936	1946	1951	1956	1963
Europeans and 'assimilés'	5,504	6,502	6,555	7,297	8,215	10,462	11,450	15,188	21,342
Melanesians	1,233	1,299	894	727	869	NI	NI	2,432	5,274
Indonesians	287	705	1,066	1,856	1,493	NI	NI	1,306	1,991
Vietnamese	88	168	817	1,559	616	NI	NI	2,258	2,417
Tahitians	..	..	..	..	..	NI	NI	465	1,959
Wallisians/ Hebrideans	362	240	169	95	106	NI	NI	586	1,976
Indians	62	50	14	33	5	NI	NI	..	..
Penal element	2,581	1,090	524	379	224	..	..	..	..
No information	..	..	..	..	..	..	..	..	31
Total	10,117	10,054	10,039	11,946	11,304	NI	NI	22,235	34,900

NI = no information.   SOURCE: Census returns.

Whilst the years prior to 1940 witnessed at best only slow rates of growth, the war years marked a turning-point. Almost every aspect of New Caledonian life was affected, and many of the changes initiated in these years are continuing. One of the first aspects to be affected was mining and metallurgy. In the immediate pre-war years sales of nickel—a strategic metal—had been on the increase, particularly in Japan, and such sales continued until after 1939. The fall of France complicated dealings in nickel, since much of New Caledonia's output was sold there, but when finally other arrangements were completed

[1] There is some evidence to suggest that the peak year was earlier, and that the Asians were already declining in number before 1931 (see *Bulletin du Commerce*, 5 June 1929).

with Australia and the United States, there was no difficulty in disposing of all that could be produced. Labour was ensured by retaining all contract labourers in their positions for the duration of hostilities.

The outbreak of hostilities with Japan had further effects; the Japanese in the territory (there were 1,430 Japanese in New Caledonia in 1936, of whom some 350 were resident in Nouméa) were interned, and finally removed from the territory altogether. Their departure left a gap in the retailing trades and in market gardening in Nouméa, later to be filled by Vietnamese as they came to be released from the mines.

The town of Nouméa was also profoundly affected by the presence of some 80,000 American troops in the vicinity between 1942 and 1946. Such large numbers posed serious problems of health control, water supply, and sanitation, as well as presupposing considerable development of transport and port facilities. Whole new areas around the town were opened up, and covered with buildings some of which, though only intended to be temporary, were still in use twenty years after the cessation of hostilities.

It was perhaps the social and economic life of the territory which was most completely transformed. The American presence stimulated all kinds of economic activities, and all the main ethnic groups in New Caledonia were affected in one way or another. Large numbers of Europeans were able, as a result of the wider opportunities, to extricate themselves from the indebtedness into which they had fallen during the depression and some made small fortunes; those who had remained in the interior as peasant farmers were often tempted away from their properties by the lure of high wages in Nouméa. But not even the considerable movement of Europeans to Nouméa was sufficient to satisfy the needs of war-time labour, and Melanesians had to be brought in as well. In 1946 all Asians were liberated from their contracts, and Melanesians were granted freedom to reside where they chose.

Some of these developments continued, and can be traced in the population figures for Nouméa in the post-war period. The European population of the town expanded during the war, but even more rapidly afterwards; it more than doubled between 1946 and 1963, and by this latter date had come to contain 64 per cent of all the Europeans in New Caledonia. The numbers of Melanesians in town rose steeply, and doubled between 1956 and 1963. The period also witnessed rapid growth of the Tahitian and Wallisian sections of the town's population, especially after 1953. Repatriation of Indonesians was commenced after the war, but some chose to remain, forming the nucleus of a population that appears to be more or less permanently established. The Vietnamese, whose numbers had risen considerably during the war years as a result of natural increase, posed a more difficult problem since civil war had broken out in Indochina, but by 1964 the repatriation of the bulk of them had been arranged.

In the past few years Nouméa has therefore been faced with the problem of coping with a rapidly growing population, containing a number of different ethnic elements, whose needs and expectations are not necessarily the same. The different population groups do not all exhibit the same intentions as regards permanent residence, or preferences for certain types of employment or living conditions. Comparatively little is known about their aspirations, and little has been done to plan for their incorporation in one urban community. The following sections will discuss first some of the factors which have guided planning in Nouméa, and secondly, some of the factors in a diverse ethnic and social situation which should in reality have commanded more attention than they have.

Urban Space Management

As was the case for most of the colonial towns laid out by Europeans in the course of the nineteenth century, Nouméa was subjected initially to processes of planning and design. As a deliberate and conscious foundation, it did not at first grow indiscriminately, since immediate decisions were required with regard to street plans, communications, and land available for alienation. This aspect was even more important to Nouméa than elsewhere, in view of the unsatisfactory site, which required immediate and substantial modification.

But the 1860 plan, to which reference has already been made, was the only deliberate large-scale effort on the part of the administration in the nineteenth century to guide the development of the town. In laying out the street plan, in conceiving and executing the works programme necessary to carry it out, the administration considered it had done what was expected of it, and that afterwards it was necessary only to allow individuals to carry out their own projects. Despite the fact that the area designated by the administration was soon found to be inadequate for the town that was growing up, and that its limits were largely ignored by private developers, no further positive policy of urban planning was adopted until after the Second World War was over.

Intervention by the administration in other aspects of urban development was not, of course, totally lacking. Rating policy was observed to be having adverse effects on urban growth by encouraging building at considerable distances from the centre, even when land nearer in was not fully utilized, and extensive changes were effected in the rating system in 1875, intended not only to counteract this trend, but also to encourage construction (for fuller discussion see McTaggart, 1966a). Fire and health hazards in the town were acute, and this prompted administrative action on several occasions; timber housing was repeatedly proscribed—with little apparent effect, since by the turn of the century the great bulk of the buildings in the town were of timber. Regulations first promulgated in 1876 sought to control the uses to which premises might be put, with a view to excluding dangerous and obnoxious activities from residential areas. And in 1907 appeared the first of a series of regulations in the interests of health and hygiene, governing in detail the type of construction that was to be authorized in the town. These have since been extended to govern the conditions in which a wide variety of commercial enterprises may be carried out.

Other forms of administrative intervention included the development of services and facilities normally considered to be public responsibilities. Since the establishment of municipal government in Nouméa in 1879, the municipality had taken responsibility for communications, for water supplies, and for a number of other aspects affecting the health and welfare of the inhabitants. Negotiations were undertaken with a private company for the provision of electricity in the town, which was finally achieved in 1930. But it was not considered necessary or justifiable to assume a wider measure of direction of urban development, and the town was left to shape itself according to the needs of the moment and the desires of its citizens.

A revision of the role of the administration in urban development followed as a result of the Second World War. The presence of large numbers of American troops in the town for a number of years had necessitated the setting up of a number of specialized services to ensure the efficient functioning of water supplies, health measures, fire control, traffic control, and so on; rents in the town had to be brought under control in view of the inflated demand. And with the adoption in France at the end of the war of programmes of planned reconstruction, similar administrative initiative was recommended for the overseas territories. Legislation requiring all such territories to provide themselves with town plans for their major urban centres was enacted in 1945 and 1946. New Caledonia was slow to act on this, partly as a result of the difficulty of recruiting qualified planners, and partly through difficulty in reaching a consensus of opinion in Nouméa as to the desirability of the proposals put forward by the planners. Finally, in 1964, a town plan, coupled with a set of building regulations, was adopted by the territorial assembly.

The central part of the town (Fig. 11.2), the original site of Nouméa, is designated as a zone of commercial buildings and apartments. The great majority of the town's retail outlets are to be found there, as well as a considerable percentage of the commercial and administrative office space. Residence is permitted either in the form of detached houses or apartments, and buildings may be constructed right up to the limits of the designated carriageway. Similar provisions apply to parts of the main roads leading out from the centre of the town towards the suburbs, and to certain of the already established shopping areas outside the town centre, as for example at Vallée du Tir, and Faubourg Blanchot; the Quartier Latin, long considered almost as part of the town centre, is almost entirely covered by these provisions.

Along the dockside in the centre of the town a port zone has been demarcated. As well as dockside facilities and warehouses, this section has always contained a number of industrial establishments, and several blocks of lower-grade accommodation used by the larger firms for lodging their non-European employees. The new regulations require the removal of all residences from this area, except those needed for the efficient functioning of permitted activities.

Around the old town centre and the Quartier Latin lies a band of older suburbs, developed for the most part during the first phase of Nouméa's expansion in the years before the turn of the century; the housing in these suburbs is characteristically of timber, although a number of new masonry houses are appearing in between the older wooden ones. These areas, along with the newer suburbs further out, and thus comprising most of Vallée du Tir, Vallée des Colons, Faubourg Blanchot, Trianon, Orphélinat, and Vallon du Gaz, are residential zones, with restrictions imposed on the nature of industrial activities that may be carried out there, and limits to the percentage of each plot which may be covered by buildings. Similar provisions, but of a more exacting nature, apply to the newer suburbs in the southern part of the peninsula, in particular at Anse Vata and Baie des Citrons, which are considered 'tourist' zones, and in which a high standard of residential construction is demanded.

Industrial zones are limited to two areas, Doniambo, where the nickel works are at present, and the Ducos peninsula which lies further to the north-west, and which is developing residential areas as well. It is hoped that eventually 'Motor Pool' and 'Receiving', two sections of the town that retain many buildings put up by the Americans during the war, will become residential suburbs. Within the urban area there are no Melanesian 'peri-urban' villages as such, although some of the nearby Melanesian communities at Pont des Français and St. Louis, a few miles north of Nouméa, do have this character. Nor is the squatter problem serious; only on Ducos peninsula are there substantial areas of low-quality housing erected by in-migrants themselves; but their legal status is not that of squatters, since they usually pay a ground rental for the land occupied.

The limited role which the administration has elected to play in governing the development of Nouméa is due to two factors. First, it has accepted that only a certain number of problems fall within its jurisdiction. It considers that it has a duty to ensure that all buildings put up conform to certain standards of safety and aesthetics, and that the general lay-out and growth of the town, resulting from the multiplicity of private individual efforts, should not be such as to cause unnecessary difficulties in communications or services. Zoning is being employed to 'harmonize' the functions of each area, and the Public Works Department and the Municipality share the responsibility for seeing that all new proposals for subdivision and construction conform to regulations. Secondly, even if it had a positive programme of redevelopment, the administration at present has no financial means for carrying it out. Its approach hitherto has been based on the assumption that its duty is confined to directing the efforts of others, rather than assuming responsibility itself.

It is perhaps hardly surprising that some friction should have developed between the administration, with its concern for a compact and well-ordered town, and other organizations whose functions require them to adopt a wider view of the town's problems. One such organization is the 'Société Immobilière et du Crédit de la Nouvelle-Calédonie', a part-private part-public organization, founded in 1956 to lend money to persons wishing to build houses, or to develop small-scale businesses. One of its first and most obvious concerns was the acute housing shortage in and around Nouméa. Between 1936 and 1956 the town's population increased by nearly 11,000, from 11,304 to 22,235, but the total number of new constructions authorized for this period was just over 1,300, or an annual average of only sixty-seven. Many of the houses in Nouméa were in need of replacement, being of timber construction and by then over fifty years old. It is scarcely to be wondered at that overcrowding had become widespread, and that a large percentage of the available housing was seriously substandard. At the end of the war the Municipality had taken over about 140 corrugated iron huts left by the Americans at Receiving, and used them for housing as a 'temporary' measure (some were still in use in 1966). However, the 'Crédit de la Nouvelle-Calédonie' had, by the end of 1964, granted loans on well over 800 private houses in Nouméa, financed over 200 individual houses under HLM and HBM[1] schemes and in another smaller co-operative scheme on Ducos peninsula, and

---

[1] HLM (habitation loyer modéré) and HBM (habitation bon marché) schemes are low-cost housing projects.

was reported to be starting in 1964 on another collective housing project some seven or eight kilometres to the north of the town (*Bulletin du Commerce*, 29 Jan. 1964). It is not entirely true that the administration has played no part in developments promoted by the 'Crédit'. In some instances the government has provided the land, and assisted actively with the laying out of the sites, and with the provision of roads and other services. But the concern of the 'Crédit' has been to raise the general standards of housing as quickly as possible, and its policies have contributed materially to the continued spread of dispersed development around the fringes of the town. The 'Crédit' insists on prior ownership of the land to be used for building in the case of most of its private loans, and since the demand created by the availability of housing loans has given rise to an intense wave of land speculation, prices have risen enormously in and around the town; clients of modest means are therefore obliged to select distant plots, whose prices they can afford. During the years 1960 to 1965 it was seldom possible to find a plot of land within the municipal boundary for sale at less than 5,000 Pacific francs per are.[1] At Magenta, some miles further out, land could be obtained at half this price. This effect is sufficiently strong to be noticeable in the figures for population growth in certain of the 'circonscriptions' close to Nouméa. Whilst the population of New Caledonia as a whole grew by 26·3 per cent between 1956 and 1963 and that of Nouméa by 57·4 per cent; the populations of Dumbea and Mont Dore, the districts adjacent to Nouméa, grew by 63·0 per cent and 105·0 per cent respectively. The town planner reported in 1954 that Nouméa had on average only twenty persons per hectare, or eight to the acre, and there has been no increase in density since then.[2]

Demographic and Economic Structure

If the administration has been mainly concerned with urban convenience, and the 'Crédit' with raising housing standards, both have none the less been working within the framework of a plural society, and they have to some extent been made aware

---

[1] This is equivalent to about $US 725 per are, or $2,900 for a quarter acre plot.
[2] For some of the effects of land speculation on the development of Nouméa see McTaggart, 1966b.

of the peculiar kinds of problem posed by these circumstances. But the administration, whether in the course of town planning or in its other activities, does not normally make a practice of discriminating either against or in favour of any one of the ethnic groups in the population, not at any rate as a matter of policy. The 'Crédit' has been bound more by rules governing prudent lending policy than anything else, although it has on occasion sought to introduce elements of differentiation in its treatment of some lending to Melanesians, in view of their land tenure system. But a closer analysis of the demographic and economic structure of the town reveals that although the notion of ethnic group means comparatively little at the legal level, it has, in the prevailing circumstances, become a variable of some significance as far as economic and social characteristics are concerned. The ethnic groups may characteristically have different intentions as regards residence and employment in the urban areas, different educational backgrounds; and perhaps different needs *vis-à-vis* the administration and other services.

However, an adequate analysis of the town's demographic and economic structure is difficult in view of the unsatisfactory data available from census and other sources: certain types of data are given only for the population of New Caledonia as a whole, and not broken down by ethnic groups or urban areas. The analysis which follows will therefore draw on several sources, not all of which are totally satisfactory, and not all of which use identical definitions in the classification of material.

Table 11.4 shows the general demographic situation in the town at the two most recent censuses, and gives some indication of the changes that took place in the intercensal period. The European population, although it remains the dominant element as far as numbers are concerned, fell from 68 per cent of the town's population in 1956 to 61 per cent in 1963, despite a 41 per cent increase in number. The Melanesians increased substantially both absolutely and relatively. The evolution of the Asian population is complicated by the movement of Vietnamese in connection with their proposed repatriation, but the Indonesians, the more stable element of the two, more or less held their position within the general increase. The Polynesian and Wallisian elements increased very markedly indeed, and by 1963 had come to constitute a significant section of the population. All groups showed increasing concentration in Nouméa during the intercensal period, although the figures are extremely variable from one group to another.

The over-all structure of the work-force in Nouméa in 1963 can be seen from the figures in Table 11.5. These show the industry classifications for the town, along with those for the two adjacent 'circonscriptions', and those for New Caledonia as

TABLE 11.4. *The Population of Nouméa, 1956 and 1963*

	1956				1963		
	Number	Percent. of Nouméa's population	Percent. of group's population	Percent. increase 1956–63	Number	Percent. of Nouméa's population	Percent. of group's population
Europeans and 'assimilés'	15,188	68	60	41	21,342	61	65
Melanesians	2,432	11	7	112	5,274	15	13
Indonesians	1,306	6	45	52	1,991	6	56
Vietnamese	2,258	10	66	7	2,417	7	86
Polynesians	465	2	59	321	1,959	6	77
Wallisians	586	3	48	237	1,976	6	65
Total	22,235	100	33	57	34,959*	100	40

* Does not include thirty-one persons whose ethnic group was undeclared.
Source: Census reports 1956 and 1963.

a whole. The figures as a whole reveal that despite the immense importance in the economy of nickel mining and metallurgy, only a comparatively small percentage of the work-force is engaged in these industries. Only 3·9 per cent are engaged in extractive industries (mining) and 12·2 per cent in manufacturing, which includes metallurgy.[1] In Nouméa and the immediate vicinity, with the exception of Mont Dore which has some mines, the percentages in mining are lower than the national average, and the percentages in manufacture tend to be higher. Nearly 84 per cent of those engaged in manufacturing lived in Nouméa itself. Yet the town is obviously dependent to a great extent on the administrative and commercial functions it performs, since in Nouméa these two categories between them accounted for almost half the work-force.

The 1963 census, unfortunately, does not give the ethnic

[1] Some of those included under 'transport' are in fact engaged full-time in the mining industry, in haulage of ore from mines to the coast.

TABLE 11.5. *Percentage of Active Population (15 Years of age and over) in the Nouméa Region, by Industry Classification, 1963*

	Nouméa	Dumbea	Mont Dore	Total New Caledonia	Percentage of total in industry group to be found in Nouméa
Number of active persons	13,296	143	821	30,471	43·7
Percentage engaged in:					
Agriculture, fisheries, forestry	2·2	27·2	21·3	38·0	2·5
Extractive industries	1·1	1·4	6·1	3·9	12·7
Construction, public works	13·7	7·0	17·9	9·3	63·8
Water, electricity, etc.	1·1	0·7	0·9	0·7	70·8
Manufacturing	23·4	22·4	19·1	12·2	83·8
Transport, communications	8·1	9·8	5·4	5·1	69·3
Commerce, business	19·8	14·0	7·3	11·2	76·8
Administration	28·7	17·5	20·4	18·5	68·9
No information	1·9	0·0	1·6	1·1	

SOURCE: Census of 1963.

breakdown of these figures, and other sources are needed to estimate the dependence of the various groups on different industries. Closer analysis does in fact reveal that each group, according to its circumstances, is characterized by its own particular demographic history and structure, and this is reflected in its occupational structure as well.

Europeans and 'Assimilés'

The existence of a large European population permanently resident in Nouméa is a feature that distinguishes the town from other urban centres in the South Pacific. As Table 11.4 indicates, the Europeans constitute nearly two-thirds of the population of the town. As well as being large, the European population is also very diverse, and in no sense does it constitute an élite group, as it sometimes does elsewhere; socially and economically it extends across the full range of strata, and every level of occupation and living is represented.

The growth of the European population in Nouméa has resulted from three processes, from natural increase, from in-migration of Europeans formerly resident in the interior of New Caledonia, and from immigration from overseas, mainly France. But it is very difficult to determine the relative importance of these elements in contributing to the increase in numbers. In 1963 a total of 739 births were recorded in Nouméa amongst the European population, and 173 deaths: these figures would suggest crude birth- and death-rates of 35 per 1,000 and 8 per 1,000 respectively, with a rate of natural increase of 27 per 1,000. But it is not certain that all these births (or deaths) should be properly attributed to the European population of Nouméa, since it is not known with what rigour place of residence is recorded.[1] Continuing in-migration from the interior is attested by place-of-birth statistics in the census. In 1963 the percentage of the Europeans in New Caledonia resident in Nouméa was 65 per cent as opposed to only 48 per cent in 1936. And of the Europeans in Nouméa in 1963 who had been born in New Caledonia, 28 per cent had been born outside the

---

[1] Crude birth-rates for some of the other groups, accepting the figures as quoted (*Bulletin du Commerce*, 5 Feb. 1964), would be Vietnamese 38 per 1,000, Indonesians 45, Polynesians 61, and Wallisians 98.

town.[1] As for immigration from overseas, Europeans born overseas numbered 5,180 in Nouméa in 1956, and 8,618 in 1963, an increase of 66 per cent. It is perhaps significant that immigrant Europeans are almost all to be found in Nouméa, and not in the interior, the percentage in 1963 being 94 per cent. This section of the population includes some permanent immigrants whose intention it is to remain indefinitely in the territory, and others, employed in government, industry, commerce, or mining, whose presence is only temporary.

Taken as a whole, the European work-force in New Caledonia differs in a number of respects from the other ethnic groups. The percentage of the European population recorded as active is slightly higher at 36·7 per cent than the figure for the other groups with the exception of the Indonesians; and the percentage of European females economically active—20·7 per cent—is definitely higher than most of the others; but it is difficult to define 'economically active', and this factor may not be very important. What is quite clear is the virtual monopoly of superior positions held by Europeans in New Caledonia, a feature which must be as characteristic of the town as it is of the whole territory. The Europeans, who constitute 38·5 per cent of the total population, and 40 per cent of the active population, accounted for 98 per cent of those in the liberal professions, 97 per cent of high-ranking commercial employees, 92 per cent of the high- and medium-ranking civil servants, and 88 per cent of the employers (entrepreneurs) in industry and commerce: by contrast they accounted for only 18 per cent of labourers and apprentices, and 12 per cent of all persons engaged in agriculture and fishing. Europeans are not concentrated in a few activities; they make up 49 per cent of those in extractive industries, 59 per cent of those in metallurgy, and 67 per cent of those in administration. But they hold a very clear monopoly of positions of high responsibility, and even at lower levels of management their hold is strong.

Several of these trends, observable in 1963 from the census figures for the whole territory, may be substantiated for Nouméa itself in an earlier period. Some figures are available concerning

[1] The movement is, of course, two-way, but Nouméa shows net gain. In 1963 the census recorded 4,056 persons resident in Nouméa, but born in other parts of New Caledonia, and 2,797 resident elsewhere but born in Nouméa.

European and Melanesian occupations in Nouméa in 1956[1] (Census Report, 1956), and information referring to all ethnic communities may be gathered from the results of a sample social survey carried out in the town in 1961 (McTaggart, 1962).

The figures from the 1956 census are shown in Table 11.6 below, both for Europeans and Melanesians. The percentages of total populations gainfully employed are fairly similar, although the Melanesian figure is slightly higher; neither gives any hint of under-employment or unemployment. There appears to be a greater tendency for Melanesian females to be occupied than European. But there are striking differences observable in the proportions employed in the different groups, and this bears out what has been said previously. The high-status occupations —the professions, educational and scientific professions, and the higher-level white-collar occupations in both the administrative and private sectors—clearly represent areas of European dominance, as do sectors such as 'technicians and artisans', and 'industrial and commercial entrepreneurs'. Even in the lower grades of clerical employment, Europeans are predominant. The 'other employee' sector, covering a wide range of types of manual work, although of considerable significance in the occupational structure of the European population, was of less relative importance than its counterpart amongst the Melanesians.

From the 1961 social survey some further impressions may be gained as to the structure of the European work-force in Nouméa. Of the gainfully occupied Europeans interviewed, 41 per cent were classed as 'white collar' salaried workers—a rather higher figure than might be suggested by the 1956 figures quoted in Table 11.6; amongst the non-Europeans the comparable figure was only 2 per cent. 'Labouring' grades accounted for only 22 per cent of the Europeans interviewed— perhaps a slightly lower figure than is given for 1956—whereas amongst the non-Europeans the figure was 77 per cent.

---

[1] Unfortunately the information is of limited value, since it attempts to show employment structure of Europeans and Melanesians only, broken down by 'socio-professional' categories. The categories adopted are a confused mixture of industry categories ('agricultural operators', 'liberal professions', 'teachers') and status categories ('lower-grade office workers', both administrative and private, 'labourers').

TABLE 11.6. *Socio-Professional Structure of the Work-Force, Europeans and 'Assimilés' and Melanesians, Nouméa, 1956*

Categories	Europeans and 'Assimilés'				Melanesians			
	Males	Females	Total	Per cent	Males	Females	Total	Per cent
Primary industry	129	11	140	2·3	26	3	29	2·9
Professional	70	47	117	1·9	3	1	4	0·4
Educational, scientific	73	107	180	3·0	3	3	6	0·6
Technicians, artisans	480	77	557	9·2	6	2	8	0·8
Industrial and commercial entrepreneurs	316	98	414	6·8	5	2	7	0·7
White collar, upper grade	192	12	204	3·4	0	1	1	0·1
White collar, lower grade	895	770	1,665	27·5	83	25	108	10·7
Other employees	1,798	246	2,044	33·7	485	94	579	57·4
Domestic employees	11	90	101	1·7	9	153	162	16·1
Military, police	580	2	582	9·6	103	0	103	10·2
Miscellaneous family help	9	45	54	0·9	0	2	2	0·2
	4,553	1,505	6,058	100·0	723	286	1,009	100·0
Percentage of total population occupied	58·01	20·50	39·87		53·28	26·60	41·49	

SOURCE: Census Report 1956.

Table 11.7 shows the industry classifications of persons interviewed in the survey. These figures suggest that in terms of the industries upon which the Europeans and non-Europeans depend, there are a number of quite significant differences. The European work-force, as well as containing a wide range of status groups under the heading of socio-professional categories, likewise indicates a wide range of industry groups; there is no single sector of the work-force in which the European population is not represented. But dependence on administration, commercial activities, professions and armed services seem to have been much greater than amongst the non-Europeans. In industry (including the nickel works) and building trades their contribution to the labour force is, on the other hand, somewhat less.

TABLE 11.7. *Industry Classification of Active Persons in Households Studied in the 1961 Survey, Nouméa*

	Europeans		Non-Europeans	
	Number	Per cent	Number	Per cent
Administration	57	16·2	18	10·3
Armed services	24	6·8	2	1·1
Professions	17	4·8	..	..
Commerce	132	37·5	37	21·1
Industry	75	21·3	69	39·5
Trades and building	34	9·7	35	20·0
Horticulture and fishing	4	1·1	9	5·1
Domestic service	9	2·6	5	2·9
Total	352	100·0	175	100·0
Unspecified	15		14	

SOURCE: McTaggart, 1962: 28 and 43.

Of the 367 occupied Europeans in the sample, 104, or 28 per cent, were from households described as 'immigrant'. These included some only temporarily in New Caledonia who were almost totally accounted for by employment in administration, or in large-scale industrial and commercial firms, and others intending to remain permanently; these exhibited an occupational structure more like that of the locally born Europeans, although it was significant that they seemed to have a generally higher level of training.

Melanesians

Up until the end of the Second World War, the position of the Melanesians in Nouméa was similar, qualitatively speaking, to that of the indentured Asians. They were required to remain in their reserves, unless given permission to leave, and in principle the administration permitted departure only in the cases of persons whose services had been requested. Those who resided in Nouméa were the responsibility of their employers and lodgings had to be provided for them. In their demographic structure the Melanesians also revealed features similar to those of the indentured populations. In 1921, for example, the sex ratio (males per 100 females) in Nouméa was 538, falling to 258 in 1936. By 1956, after a decade of free migration, the sex ratio had fallen to 126, and by 1963 to 114.

Table 11.8 shows the origins of the Melanesian population of Nouméa in 1963, distinguishing between those born in Nouméa itself, those born in the New Caledonian mainland or in the Îles Belep, and those born in the Île des Pins or in the Loyalty Islands.

TABLE 11.8. *The Melanesian Population of Nouméa by Place of Birth, 1963*

Place of birth	Number	Percentage of Nouméa's Melanesian population	Percentage of total Melanesians reported born in each area
Nouméa	1,101	21	54
New Caledonian mainland and Îles Belep	1,284	25	5
Loyalty Islands and Île des Pins	2,815	54	19
Total	5,200	100	13
No information	74		

SOURCE: Census report, 1963.

Melanesians from the Loyalty Islands and the Île des Pins make up the majority of the Melanesian population of Nouméa; 54 per cent of the 1963 population had been born in the Loyalty Islands and in addition to these a substantial proportion of those born in Nouméa, being children of Loyalty Islanders, would consider themselves as such. Not only is the actual contribution from the Loyalty Islands greater than that from the rest of the territory; so also is the proportion of people absent from home. The final column in Table 11.8 shows the Nouméa Melanesians as a percentage of the total Melanesians reported as born in the areas designated. Whilst the percentage of mainland Melanesians in Nouméa is only 5 per cent, the percentage of absentees in the Loyalty Islands rises to 19, and in the case of Ouvea (the most crowded of the Loyalty Islands) to 26 per cent.[1]

The survey in 1961 suggested that it was possible to distinguish temporary and permanent elements in the Nouméa Melanesian population (McTaggart, 1962: 10–12). Whilst some families are clearly settled in the town, holding steady jobs and only returning to their villages during their annual leave, others oscillate back and forward, spending limited periods in town, for purposes of work, recreation, schooling, or medical treatment, and frequently using the homes of their settled urban relatives as a base. Of the thirty-six Melanesian householders visited in the survey, thirty declared that they intended to remain indefinitely in the town: twelve had relatives staying with them as temporary residents at the time.

The existence of this temporary element in the Melanesian population of the town generates a considerable amount of travel between the villages and Nouméa. Between the Loyalty Islands and Nouméa the great majority—90 per cent in 1961— travel by air rather than by sea: examination of the passenger figures for the years 1953–61 showed that there was some seasonal fluctuation, with a tendency for Melanesians to return to their villages during the months of July, August, and September, when demands for labour in village agriculture were high. A sample period of fourteen months covering travel to and from

[1] On the mainland equally high figures are attained, but only locally: by 'circonscription' the percentage of the Melanesian population absent from home and resident in Nouméa varied from 3 per cent to 31 per cent. See Guiart, 1960.

Lifou by air was used to examine the nature of passenger movements. Forty-nine per cent of the trips by adults were made by Melanesian males, and 29 per cent by Melanesian females. Altogether 54 per cent of the trips were made by persons who travelled three times or more during the fourteen-month period, indicating a considerable amount of repeated journeying by certain individuals (McTaggart, 1963: 115–16).

Data on occupational patterns amongst the Nouméa Melanesians are not very satisfactory. In general it seems that hitherto the Melanesians have tended not to work in mining or metallurgy. In 1963, for the whole of New Caledonia, only 11·5 per cent of the male Melanesian work-force outside agriculture was employed in mining and metallurgy; it was more usual to find them in administration, building, transport, and commercial activities, but almost invariably at an un-skilled level.

The 1956 census figures for Nouméa (Table 11.6) do show the extent to which the Melanesians depend on jobs in the lower skilled categories. Over 50 per cent are manual workers of one kind or another, and they seem to reach only posts of minor responsibility in the various clerical grades open to them. The proportion in the 'entrepreneur' category is negligible. Similar findings arise from the 1961 survey; of the fifty-eight occupied Melanesians covered, none were entrepreneurs, and fifty-four were classed as labourers; twenty were employed in industry, but this figure included a whole household of tempo-rary workers who had come to spend several weeks at the nickel works, in order to buy cement and corrugated iron for a building in their home village. Commerce accounted for eleven and administration for ten. There is no evidence to suggest that even among the Melanesians who have remained many years in Nouméa there has been any real progress towards posts of higher responsibility and remuneration.

Asians

The Asians in New Caledonia owe their presence to the indentured labour system which operated in one form or another until the end of the Second World War. Until then, strict control over residence and employment of Asians in New Caledonia was maintained, and it is therefore, as in the case of the Melanesians, only over the last twenty years that the Asians have been free to establish their own ecological and economic patterns. The circumstances of indenture, and the events connected with repatriation exercised a profound influence on all aspects of the lives of the Asians in Nouméa. The original population consisted largely of adult males, constantly depleted by repatriation and renewed by fresh import. When the Second World War prevented any further repatriation or replacement, the Asian populations began to increase through excess of births over deaths. But the older section of the population has remained very unbalanced in terms of sex ratio. The sex ratio (males per 100 females) of the adult Asians in New Caledonia were 246 and 446 for the Indonesians and Vietnamese respectively in 1936: in 1956 the sex ratios for the Asians over 35 years of age were 272 for the Indonesians and 299 for the Vietnamese, and in 1963 for the Asians over 40 years of age, 234 for the Indonesians and 256 for the Vietnamese. In 1956, on the other hand, the sex ratios amongst the Asians less than 35 years old were 108 and 95 respectively, for those under 40 years of age in 1963, 104 and 100. A corollary of this is the increase in the percentages of the Asians born in New Caledonia, rising for the Indonesians from 49 to 57 per cent between 1956 and 1963, and from 59 to 65 per cent for the Vietnamese.

Before the Second World War, despite the existence of the nickel works at Nouméa and its heavy demand for indentured labourers, only a comparatively small percentage of the Asians resided there—33 per cent of the Indonesians and 26 per cent of the Vietnamese in 1936. However, as Asians were liberated from the mines during the war, and more especially during the immediate post-war years, they moved to Nouméa in substantial numbers. As can be seen from Table 11.4, 56 per cent of the Indonesians and 86 per cent of the Vietnamese lived in Nouméa in 1963.[1]

[1] A substantial number of Indonesians have remained in parts of the interior, especially in the north-east, engaged in agricultural occupations. The 1963 census was taken at a time when many Vietnamese were living in Nouméa in anticipation of their repatriation. In 1964, after the completion of the repatriation operation, it was reported that a total of 3,535 Vietnamese had been repatriated (*Bulletin du Commerce*, 5 Feb. 1964), and that 972 Vietnamese remained in New Caledonia: these were largely concentrated in Nouméa, where they numbered 837 (*P.I.M.*, May 1965).

What evidence there is seems to suggest that both Asian groups partly deserted the mining and metallurgical industries when they were free to do so. Some remained, and benefited from the rapid rise in earnings characteristic of that industry in the post-war period. In 1956, 29 per cent of the active male Indonesians and 42 per cent of the active male Vietnamese in New Caledonia were in either extractive or metal-working industries; but many others, especially Vietnamese, were involved as contract hauliers, carrying ore from the mines to the coast. In Nouméa the 1961 survey indicated that a larger proportion of the Vietnamese were entrepreneurs (13 out of the 48 occupied persons in the Vietnamese section of the sample) than Indonesians (4 out of 44), and 21 Vietnamese as opposed to only 5 Indonesians were engaged in building, construction, and other similar trades (McTaggart, 1962: 27–8). The number of persons employed in the nickel works was greater for the Indonesians than for the Vietnamese (12 as opposed to 9), but the proportions did not differ significantly. Entrepreneurs in retailing and vegetable gardening were quite significant amongst the Vietnamese, there being eleven as opposed to three Indonesians, and it appears that a number of Vietnamese who had succeeded in building up substantial businesses are among those who have elected to remain in New Caledonia, and not be repatriated.

Polynesians and Wallisians

Although migration of other Pacific islanders to New Caledonia is of long standing, it is only recently that the movement has assumed real importance, and this is reflected in the population figures for Nouméa given in Table 11.3. Whilst before the Second World War the numbers of other Pacific islanders in Nouméa never exceeded 400, they began to rise rapidly in the early 1950s, and there were just over 1,000 in 1956. Since then they have risen spectacularly, and they accounted for 12 per cent of Nouméa's population by 1963. Shortages of labour had been experienced in the mines since the end of the Second World War, despite mechanization. Wallisians, some of whom had come to know of New Caledonia through military service, were brought over to work on the hydro-electric project at Yaté in the early 1950s, and after the completion of this work many sought work in the mines, or in the new sections of the nickel works then being built at Nouméa. Once the news spread a more or less spontaneous migratory movement started, and has continued since, with fluctuations which reflect the outlook in the nickel industry as a whole.

The migration involves young male workers for the most part, but since many are married, and do bring over their wives and families as soon as they can, the sex ratios in the Wallisian and Tahitian populations are not abnormal: the figures were 112 and 109 respectively in 1963. But the age structure does reveal a marked absence of teenagers and older persons. Only 26·7 per cent of the Wallisians and 17·8 per cent of the Tahitians in 1963 had been born in New Caledonia. The 1961 survey indicated that Wallisians appeared to be more settled in New Caledonia than the Tahitians: more of the latter expressed the intention of returning to their homes after having worked for a number of years in New Caledonia. Between 1956 and 1963 the percentage of Wallisians and Tahitians resident in Nouméa increased, as can be seen from Table 11.4. This is due in part to the completion of work at Yaté, where there were 332 Wallisians and Polynesians in 1956 and only eight in 1963. At the same time the number of Wallisian and Polynesian males employed in building and public works declined from 252 in 1956 to 208 in 1963.

The Wallisians and Polynesians depend heavily on the nickel industry for employment. This was evident in the 1961 survey of Nouméa, which found that seven out of the fourteen active Wallisians covered were employed at the nickel works, and

TABLE 11.9. *Numbers of Male Wallisians and Polynesians Employed in Metallurgy, 1956 and 1963*

	1956		1963	
	Number	Per cent of male work-force	Number	Per cent of male work-force
Wallisians	43	8	210	30
Polynesians	93	28	396	56

SOURCE: Census Reports, 1956; 1963.

nineteen out of the twenty-three Tahitians. The numbers recorded at the censuses as employed in metallurgy (and therefore working in Nouméa) show a sharp increase, as can be seen from Table 11.9. But the level of skill attained, whilst sometimes higher than for the Melanesians, is seldom very great: in the 1961 survey all fourteen occupied Wallisians covered were classed as 'labourers', and twenty out of the twenty-three Tahitians.

Distribution of Population in Nouméa

Not since 1936 have figures been published showing the distribution of population in the town either as a whole or by ethnic groups.[1] Estimates based on a number of sources indicating the approximate distribution of households in 1961 have been used to prepare Fig. 11.3, which shows the density of households in each section of the town. The numbers of households have been related to the area of land in each suburb owned privately, and subdivided, thus ensuring that densities are not affected by tracts of empty hill slopes and other vacant land in the area. The highest densities occur in the older, central areas, despite the fact that many commercial and industrial enterprises are also concentrated there. In what used to be the outer suburbs, where suburban development began in the later years of the nineteenth century, such as Faubourg Blanchot, Vallée des Colons, and Trianon, the densities are somewhat less. This is partly due to the fact that the initial subdivision was not very intense, and the configuration of lots hindered subsequent intensification (McTaggart, 1966b). More recent subdivisions have been more intense, in view of the rapid rise in land prices, and hence one finds that in the more distant areas, such as Montagne Coupée, Anse Vata, and Baie des Citrons, densities rise.

There have been some factors in the history of Nouméa's development which have tended to produce *de facto* segregated areas of some significance. Before the Second World War, all non-Europeans in the town were subject to residential restrictions. Employers of non-European labour normally concentrated their workers together in a place which was convenient: there were large numbers of Vietnamese and Indonesians lodged close

[1] See McTaggart (1963: 147) for a summary of these figures.

to the nickel works; other commercial firms had blocks of accommodation in several parts of the town centre, and some even in certain parts of the suburbs. Practically all of these enclaves of non-European settlement from pre-war days have been retained in use, and still house non-European labourers; these labourers, though critical of the standards, and free to

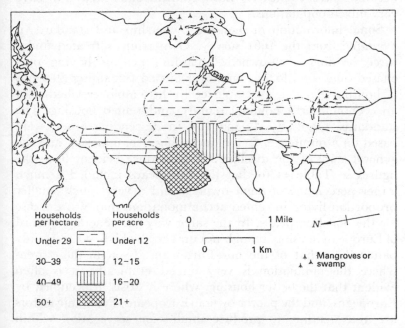

Households
per hectare

Households
per acre

Under 29   Under 12

30–39   12–15

40–49   16–20

50+   21+

0   1 Mile

0   1 Km

N

Mangroves or
swamp

FIG. 11.3. Household densities within Nouméa. Source: McTaggart, 1963.

lodge elsewhere if they so choose, are frequently unable to afford to dispense with whatever accommodation the employer can provide.

The rapid growth of the population of Nouméa since 1945, both European and non-European, has put tremendous pressure on housing resources, and some degree of segregation has appeared as a result of the boom in new house construction. One low-cost housing scheme at Montravel was limited exclusively to Melanesians, but this has produced only a small segregated community. The great majority of new private building in the developing suburbs has been by and for Europeans.

Whilst European households formerly resident in the older parts of the town centre have moved out to take up new housing in the suburbs, non-Europeans have frequently taken over the old houses thus vacated and frequently divided them up so that several households live where formerly there was only one. In this way, whilst many of the newer suburbs have become almost exclusively European, the older areas now have very mixed populations.

Some information on housing ownership and standards is available from the 1961 survey. Ownership is treated under three headings—self-owned (including persons having purchased houses on loans), employer-owned (including all forms of housing given to an employee by his employer whether at an economic or a nominal rental), and rented housing. The standards, grades I, II, and III, in descending order, were based on a number of factors including size, material, and the general state of the dwelling. It is at once evident from the figures in Table 11.10 that the Europeans included a much larger percentage of home-owners, and a very much smaller proportion living in rented accommodations than was the case for the non-Europeans. In the same way the general standard of European housing, though not universally high, was certainly better than that of the non-Europeans. Even in those areas where the population is very mixed ethnically, it is often evident that the better housing, where it exists, is occupied by Europeans, and the poorer by non-Europeans. Economic factors are thus tending to produce small-scale segregation within certain sections of the town at the same time as they are favouring a somewhat segregated redistribution of the population as a whole.

Conclusions

The picture that emerges of Nouméa is a complex one. It is much more complex than the vision either of the town planner or of the more socially conscious credit organizations. The fact of migration is one of its essential elements; post-war migrants have had to establish themselves in the town on their own responsibility, in jobs and in housing, in competition with the already established European population, and they have attempted to solve their problems in a variety of ways. There are Melanesians who virtually commute between their villages and their relatives in town; there are Vietnamese who have crowded their large families into tiny shacks in the midst of their vegetable gardens, or who live in their tiny shops in the town centre; there are Wallisians and Tahitians who, if they choose to bring their families, have to crowd them into one-room apartments intended by their employers to house bachelor

TABLE 11.10. *European and Non-European Housing, Nouméa Survey, 1961*

	Europeans		Non-Europeans	
	No.	Percentage	No.	Percentage
Ownership				
Self-owned	126	40	9	7
Employer-owned	40	15	32	26
Rented	99	37	80	66
	265	100	121	100
Standard				
Grade I	148	56	15	12
Grade II	63	24	26	22
Grade III	54	20	80	66
	265	100	121	100

SOURCE: McTaggart, 1962: 35, 47.

workers. Even amongst the Europeans some of the migrants have been forced to adopt similar solutions, and some, especially in-migrants from other parts of New Caledonia, still live in accommodation of a very low standard.

But the great majority of the Europeans are much better off than the migrant non-Europeans can hope to be in the foreseeable future. Their problems in employment and housing have been real, but of a totally different order—problems of rising land and building costs, problems of transportation to work, to shops and to schools, problems of provision of water and electricity supplies. Nouméa is a European town—growing characteristically in the manner of a European town, with new suburbs round the fringes and poorer in-migrants crowding to the centre—but it is also a plural society, in which the effect of economic and ecological factors is, at present, to accentuate rather than diminish some of the differences in standards between the various ethnic components that make it up.

BIBLIOGRAPHY

Angleviel, J. 1961. 'Problèmes de maraîchage en Nouvelle Calédonie', *Revue du Centre de Productivité et des Études Économiques*, no. 1, pp. 10–21.

Bach, C. H. 1961. *Polynésie française: Rapport preliminaire d'enquête d'urbanisme sur Papeete et sa banlieue*, Papeete.

Bellam, M. 1964. *The Melanesian in Town: A Preliminary Study of Urbanization of Adult Male Melanesians in Honiara*, multilithed M.A. thesis, Victoria University of Wellington.

Belshaw, C. S. 1957. *The Great Village: Economic and Social Welfare of Hanuabada, an Urban Community in Papua*, London.

—— 1964. *Under the Ivi Tree: Society and Economic Growth in Rural Fiji*, London.

Bennett, J. 1957. 'Vila and Santo, New Hebridean Towns, 1957', *Geographical Studies*, vol. 4, pp. 116–28.

Bulletin . . . *Bulletin du Commerce*, Nouméa.

Cassier, R. 1962. 'Thriving Fishermen's Cooperative in Nouméa', *South Pacific Bulletin*, vol. 12, pp. 29, 56.

Census Report. 1956. *Recensement général de la population de la Nouvelle Calédonie*, Institut National de la Statistique et des Études Économiques, Paris.

—— 1963. *Résultats statistiques du recensement de la population de la Nouvelle Calédonie*, Institut National de la Statistique et des Études Économiques, Paris.

Census Reports. Reports for other years held in administration files, Nouméa.

Colonial Office. 1964. *British Solomon Islands Protectorate Report, 1963–1964*, London.

Crocombe, R. G., and Hogbin, G. R. 1963. *The Erap Mechanical Farming Project*, New Guinea Research Unit Bulletin no. 1.

Cunningham, G. 1961. 'Food for Tahiti', *Economic Geography*, vol. 37, pp. 347–52.

Curson, P. H. 1965. 'The Small Urban Settlement in New Caledonia', *South Pacific Bulletin*, vol. 15, pp. 22–4.

Danks, K. H. 1956. *Industrial Activity in Selected Areas of the South Pacific*, South Pacific Commission Technical Paper, no. 90, Nouméa.

Doumenge, F. 1961. 'Les Îles dépendantes de la Nouvelle Calédonie et leurs problèmes', *Les Cahiers d'Outre Mer*, vol. 14, pp. 393–430.

Doumenge, F. 1963. 'L'Île de Makatea et ses problèmes', *Cahiers du Pacifique*, no. 5, pp. 41–67.

Epstein, A. L. 1963. 'The Economy of Modern Matupit', *Oceania*, vol. 33, pp. 182–215.

Feugnet, M. 1951. 'Enquête sur la situation sociale des indigènes à Nouméa', *Études Mélanésiennes*, no. 5, pp. 82–116.

Fiji. 1969. *Annual Report*, London.

Gauger, R. 1965. 'The Urban Zone of Santo on the Island of Espiritu Santo', *South Pacific Bulletin*, vol. 15, pp. 25–7.

Guiart, J. 1960. *Les Données de l'économie agraire mélanésienne dans le centre nord de la Nouvelle Calédonie*, roneo, Paris.

Hirsch, S. 1958. 'The Social Organization of an Urban Village in Samoa', *Journ. Poly. Soc.*, vol. 67, pp. 266–303.

Hooper, A. 1961. 'The Migration of Cook Islanders to New Zealand', *Journ. Poly. Soc.*, vol. 70, pp. 11–17.

Howard, A. 1961. 'Rotuma as a Hinterland Community', *Journ. Poly. Soc.*, vol. 70, pp. 272–99.

Irwin, P. G. 1962. 'External Influences on the Geography of the Blanche Bay District of Northern New Britain', unpublished paper presented at ANZAAS Congress, Sydney, 1962.

Jullien, M. 1963. 'Aspects de la configuration ethnique et socio-économique de Papeete', in Spoehr, 1963: 47–62.

Jupp, K. M. 1958. *Report on the Population Census, 1956*, Territory of Western Samoa, Apia.

Kay, P. 1963a. 'Urbanization in the Tahitian Household', in Spoehr, 1963: 63–73.

—— 1963b. 'Aspects of Social Structure in a Tahitian Urban Neighbourhood', *Journ. Poly. Soc.*, vol. 72, pp. 325–71.

Kearns, F. J. 1964. *Special Characteristics of the Apia Urban Area*, mimeo, working paper for South Pacific Commission technical meeting on urban local government, Aug., 1964.

—— 1965. 'The Urban Centre of Apia', *South Pacific Bulletin*, vol. 15, pp. 31–3, 46.

Kennedy, R., and Dart, J. R. 1964. *Report to the South Pacific Commission on a visit to Vila, Efate, New Hebrides, January 1964*, Department of Town Planning, University of Auckland.

Kennedy, T. F. 1959. *Geography of Tonga*, Nuku'alofa.

Marsh, D. R. M. 1964. *Special Characteristics of Towns in Papua and New Guinea*, mimeo, working paper for South Pacific Commission technical meeting on urban local government, Aug. 1964.

McArthur, N., and Yaxley, J. F. 1968. *A Report on the First Census of the Population, 1967*, Honiara.

McTaggart, W. D. 1962. *A Social Survey of Nouméa, New Caledonia*, Department of Geography, Australian National University, Canberra.

McTaggart, W. D. 1963. *Nouméa: A Study in Social Geography*, multilithed Ph.D. thesis, Australian National University, Canberra.

—— 1966a. 'Nouméa, New Caledonia: Factors Influencing the Development of a Colonial Town', *The Town Planning Review*, vol. 37, pp. 55–67.

—— 1966b. 'Private Land Ownership in a Colonial Town: The Case of Nouméa, New Caledonia', *Economic Geography*, vol. 42, pp. 189–204.

Nayacakalou, R. R. 1963. 'The Urban Fijians of Suva', in Spoehr, 1963: 33–41.

Oram, N. D. 1964. 'Urbanization, Port Moresby', *South Pacific Bulletin*, vol. 14, pp. 37–43.

Person, Y. 1953. *La Nouvelle Caledonie et l'Europe, 1774–1854*, Paris.

P.I.M. Pacific Islands Monthly, Sydney.

Pirie, P. 1960. *The Population of Western Samoa*, Department of Geography, Australian National University, Canberra.

Spoehr, A. (ed.) 1963. *Pacific Port Towns and Cities*, Honolulu.

Tedder, J. L. O. 1966. 'Honiara', *South Pacific Bulletin*, vol. 16, pp. 36–42.

Walsh, A. C. 1964. 'Urbanization in Nuku'alofa, Tonga', *South Pacific Bulletin*, vol. 14, pp. 45–50.

Ward, R. G. 1961. 'Internal Migration in Fiji', *Journ. Poly. Soc.*, vol. 70, pp. 257–71.

Western Samoa, 1962. *Population Census, 1961*, Apia.

Whitelaw, J. S. 1963. 'Suva, Capital of Fiji', *South Pacific Bulletin*, vol. 14, pp. 33–7.

—— 1967. 'Gold Production and the Mining Community in Fiji', *New Zealand Geographer*, vol. 23, pp. 1–15.

Wilson, R. K. 1963. 'Aspects of Industrialization in Papua-New Guinea', *Aust. Econ. Papers*, vol. 2, pp. 199–221.

Wong, J. A. 1963. 'Distribution and Role of the Chinese in Fiji', unpublished M.A. thesis, University of Sydney.

Zwart, F. H. A. G. 1968. *Report on the Census of the Population 1966* [Fiji], Legislative Council Paper no. 9 of 1968, Suva.

INDEX